KAY HINTON

JOSEPH CRESPINO

STROM THURMOND'S AMERICA

Joseph Crespino is a professor of history at Emory University. He is the author of *In Search of Another Country: Mississippi and the Conservative Counterrevolution* and the co-editor of *The Myth of Southern Exceptionalism*. He lives in Atlanta, Georgia.

STROM THURMOND'S AMERICA

STROM THURMOND'S
★ AMERICA ★

JOSEPH CRESPINO

★ ★ ★ ★ ★ ★ ★ ★ ★ ★ ★ ★ ★ ★ ★ ★ ★ ★ ★ ★

★ ★ ★ ★ ★ ★ ★ ★ ★ ★ ★ ★ ★ ★ ★ ★ ★ ★ ★

HILL and WANG

A DIVISION OF FARRAR, STRAUS AND GIROUX   NEW YORK

Hill and Wang
A division of Farrar, Straus and Giroux
18 West 18th Street, New York 10011

Copyright © 2012 by Joseph Crespino
All rights reserved
Printed in the United States of America
Published in 2012 by Hill and Wang
First paperback edition, 2013

The Library of Congress has cataloged the hardcover edition as follows:
Crespino, Joseph.
    Strom Thurmond's America / Joseph Crespino. — 1st ed.
        p.   cm.
    Includes bibliographical references and index.
    ISBN 978-0-8090-9480-6 (alk. paper)
    1. Thurmond, Strom, 1902–2003.   2. Legislators—United States—Biography.
3. United States. Congress. Senate—Biography.   4. South Carolina—Politics
and government—1865–1950.   5. South Carolina—Politics and government—1951–
6. Southern States—Politics and government—1865–1950.   7. Southern States—
Politics and government—1951–   8. Southern States—Race relations.
9. Civil rights movements—Southern States—History—20th century.
10. Politicians—South Carolina—Biography.   I. Title.

E748.T58 C74 2012
328.73'092—dc23
[B]

                                                                        2011048025

Paperback ISBN: 978-0-8090-8434-0

Designed by Abby Kagan

www.fsgbooks.com
www.twitter.com/fsgbooks • www.facebook.com/fsgbooks

1   3   5   7   9   10   8   6   4   2

TO CAROLINE

CONTENTS

PART FOUR: MYTHS, MEMORIES, AND LEGACIES

AUTHOR'S NOTE

I met Strom Thurmond once. It was in the Charlotte airport in early August 1992. We had been on the same flight from Washington, and I didn't spot him until I was gathering my belongings at the end of the flight. I had interned on Capitol Hill that summer and had heard reports from friends about Thurmond's unusual appearance. Several rows ahead of me, I saw an elderly man with hair so brightly colored it looked almost orange. Not being very quick on the uptake, I thought, That must be what Strom Thurmond looks like. Only when nearby passengers reached over to shake his hand did I realize it was the senator.

I wanted to shake his hand too. Being in Washington and meeting politicians that I had seen on television had been a thrill. But when I got through the jetway, Thurmond was standing over to the side and a line of people had already formed to meet him. I almost joined it, but didn't. I wasn't a constituent, and I felt self-conscious standing around, waiting to greet a man best known for his old segregationist harangues. It seemed enough to say that I had seen him. But I was conflicted, and after walking down the concourse about a hundred yards, I looked back. The line was gone now. There was just the eighty-nine-year old Thurmond by himself, shuffling slowly through the crowd, a briefcase in one hand, a travel bag in the other, and a package under one arm.

Without thinking, I went back and introduced myself. I told him I'd be happy to help him get to his next flight. He asked if I was certain

I had enough time; he didn't want to delay me in my own travels. I had plenty of time, I assured him, and picked up his bag. We walked together for about ten minutes. We talked about the congressmen and senators from my home state of Mississippi, and he said kind things about each of them. I said that I was on my way to visit my girlfriend, who was from Florence, South Carolina, and I made some silly comment about South Carolina girls—I guess because it seemed like the kind of small talk one made with Strom Thurmond. I got him to his flight and shook his hand again, and he thanked me. And that was it.

In writing this book, I've wondered at times if some of this is not another effort on my part to carry Thurmond's baggage. More often, though, I have found myself fighting the urge to walk away, to not stand in line and meet the man face-to-face.

There is no simple or straightforward way to write about a figure as controversial as Strom Thurmond. I cannot stand outside history and reflect neutrally on his life and legacy, because my story intersects with his. That was literally true in the Charlotte airport, but it is figuratively true as well, for I grew up in a South and live in a country today that has been shaped by the man's actions.

My hope is that a critical, dispassionate history of Strom Thurmond's America can help illuminate some of the forces that have shaped politics in the twentieth-century United States, and that continue to influence each of our own Americas today. My greater hope is that doing so might provide a measure of thoughtfulness, openness, and reason to the discussion of larger issues about which so many of us today seem only to scream and shout.

STROM THURMOND'S AMERICA

INTRODUCTION

Strom Thurmond is remembered today as one of the great American hypocrites: the firebrand segregationist who had a black daughter. He was the presidential candidate of the "Dixiecrat" party in 1948 and the lead author of the 1956 Southern Manifesto, a denunciation of the Supreme Court's decision in *Brown v. Board of Education*. He remains the holder of the Senate mark for the longest one-man filibuster, a record he garnered in opposing the 1957 Civil Rights Act.

Thurmond is also known as the avatar of the Republican Party's "southern strategy." He quit the Democratic Party at the high-water mark of the civil rights revolution, helped Barry Goldwater win five Deep South states in 1964, and led a historic shift of white southerners into the GOP. Four years later, Thurmond rallied southerners to save Nixon's nomination and, in the general election, pried votes away from the third-party candidate George Wallace. In return, Nixon slowed down school desegregation and tried to nominate two southerners to the Supreme Court. These signal events of the 1960s helped precipitate the conservative takeover of the GOP, one consolidated by Ronald Reagan and maintained in part through subtle but consistent racial appeals.

This history, recounted in several Thurmond biographies and invoked in countless books on modern American politics, tells the story of how Strom Thurmond's South transformed the nation. It has provided a powerful explanation for the continuing significance of racism in American politics, despite the vast changes that have taken place in

4 ★ STROM THURMOND'S AMERICA

the South since the 1960s. Yet the story of the southern strategy has become so familiar as to dilute its power either to enlighten or to shame. Americans on the left invoke it as a way of reducing the origins of modern conservatism to mere racism. Americans on the right ignore it as liberal cant, explaining away Strom Thurmond and his ilk as marginal figures in the history of their movement.

A reexamination of Thurmond's life and career holds important insights for Americans across the political spectrum. This book uncovers forgotten or unknown stories about Thurmond that when placed alongside the better-known accounts of his racial politics help trace the contours of what might be called Strom Thurmond's America, a time and a place that are critical for properly understanding not only Thurmond's legacy but also key aspects of American politics in the second half of the twentieth century.

Consider a story about Thurmond and right-wing Americanism in the midst of the Cold War. In November 1961 he was in Los Angeles and surrounding suburbs for a five-day speaking tour after drawing headlines that fall for spurring a Senate investigation into the Kennedy administration's alleged "muzzling" of military leaders.[1] Thousands of Americans were joining right-wing organizations and attending anti-Communist seminars. Just ten days earlier, President Kennedy had given a speech in Los Angeles in which he warned about "the discordant voices of extremism."[2] One of the president's aides had drafted the language to counter the "mugwump, Know-Nothing pocket of resistance on the right" and "strengthen . . . the Administration in the forthcoming Thurmond hearings."[3]

Before California, Thurmond had been in San Antonio, suburban Chicago, Dallas, Memphis, Little Rock, and Flint, Michigan.[4] At this last meeting, a local Democrat who had come to spy on the proceedings was astounded "to hear an audience in this modern industrial city cheer a Southern segregationist Senator with wild enthusiasm."[5] Other people were surprised as well. Loyalists back home hailed Thurmond's campaign as a "story of major importance," one that was helping "bring South Carolina back into the mainstream of American political affairs."[6] Reporters in Los Angeles speculated about Thurmond harnessing the energy of the radical Right to lead a third-party run in 1964, just as he had done in 1948, this time heading not a regional racial movement but a national right-wing crusade.[7] A more likely scenario had Thurmond bringing southern conservative Democrats into Barry Goldwater's camp should the Arizonan win the GOP nomination in 1964.[8] Here were commentators noting the potential of a "Sunbelt coalition" linking southern and western conservatism several years before the term had been coined.

Or reconsider one of the most familiar stories about Thurmond, his record-breaking filibuster against the 1957 Civil Rights Act. Thurmond's stonewalling had almost no political impact, at least not beyond protecting his segregationist image in South Carolina. The civil rights bill passed almost as soon as Thurmond ended his twenty-four-hour and eighteen-minute speech. Yet Thurmond helped lead another filibuster of much more abiding significance in shaping the political culture of postwar America. It involved a campaign by labor groups to remove section 14(b) of the Taft-Hartley Act, the provision that allowed states to pass right-to-work laws. Southern and southwestern states had led the way in passing such laws, which were critical in their industrial recruitment efforts. In 1965, repealing section 14(b) was labor's number one goal, and all indications were that they would reach it, but Thurmond led a coalition of southern Democrats and conservative Republicans with extensive backing from business groups that preserved 14(b).[9] Taft-Hartley's defenders were so well organized that the longest speech Thurmond had to muster was a mere five hours and fifty-three minutes.[10] The 1965 fight was a critical victory for business groups and would be one of labor's last hopes of recovering the organizing rights it had enjoyed under the 1935 Wagner Act.

Added to these stories about anticommunism and pro-business politics are accounts of Thurmond's role in forging a coalition of conservative Christian activists decades before journalists started talking about the Christian Right. Thurmond joined the board of Bob Jones University in the early 1950s, and it was in his Governor's Mansion in 1950 that the influential publisher Henry Luce first met Billy Graham. Thurmond, a Southern Baptist, was a powerful ally for evangelical and fundamentalist leaders, many of them migrating westward in the postwar period to pursue popular ministries, intent on advancing Christian values in an era when the United States battled an atheistic Communist enemy.[11]

These events and others like them suggest an unappreciated aspect of Thurmond's career. To be clear, Thurmond was a thoroughgoing racist who, despite some relatively progressive positions early in his career, stoked white reaction and submitted to the new politics of race only when the political consequences of doing otherwise had become obvious. He was, in short, one of the last of the Jim Crow demagogues. But he was also one of the first of the post–World War II Sunbelt conservatives, a fact often eclipsed by his racial politics. He did not start out as one and slowly morph into the other as he shed his racist heritage. From the late 1940s through the early 1970s, he was both at the same time. It would seem impossible given what we know about southern demagogues and Sunbelt conservatives, yet understanding this paradox yields a number of insights into the origins of the modern American Right.

One of the most important involves the role of race in conservative politics. The southern strategy narrative is not wrong. Conservative Republicans did pursue disaffected southern Democrats who represented a mother lode of votes that they had to tap in order to win influence in the GOP and compete on the national level. Yet by isolating white southerners as carriers of the racist gene in the modern GOP, the southern strategy narrative actually understates the role of racial reaction on the right. It is not as though conservative Republican Party builders held their noses or ignored their better angels while recruiting white southerners. Most of them were as convinced as were their recruits about the presence of Communists inside the civil rights movement. They were also certain that liberal opponents were merely using civil rights to push what they saw as a broader socialist agenda of labor and economic rights that threatened business interests. Their embrace of someone like Strom Thurmond grew naturally out of their larger political worldview, one that consistently ignored or dismissed the moral imperative of the modern civil rights struggle. In addition, these conservative Republicans pursued not just white southerners but also disaffected Democrats in the North and the West—many of whom were in revolt against the New Deal coalition over how liberal social reforms were transforming the racial composition of their neighborhoods, workplaces, and schools.[12]

When this history is viewed through Strom Thurmond's eyes, the importance of white southerners' *northern strategy* becomes clear. Thurmond was convinced that plenty of whites in the North and the West would feel the same way that white southerners did about racial issues if presented with similar circumstances. During his Dixiecrat presidential campaign, he warned northerners how Truman's civil rights proposals would break down segregated neighborhoods such as Harlem, the South Side of Chicago, and Chinatown in San Francisco. White southerners relied on conservative Republicans with strong ties to northern businessmen to defeat fair employment legislation. In the 1950s, Thurmond explained rising crime rates and white flight in Washington, D.C., and other northern cities as the inevitable result of racial desegregation, a view with which many white homeowners in Detroit and other northern cities readily agreed. By the late 1960s, as a seeming epidemic of lawlessness and street protest spread throughout the country, Thurmond read the politics of law and order—and the growing consensus from the Carolinas to California that supported freedom of choice and an end to busing—as confirmation of long-held positions.[13]

In addition, too often the story of Thurmond and the southern strategy becomes shorthand for a political realignment that was propelled as much by a broad and complex series of social and economic developments.[14] The migration in the postwar period of capital, population, and political power from the Northeast and the Midwest to the southern and southwestern states—the Sunbelt, as it was dubbed by the Nixon campaign strategist Kevin Phillips—covers many of these changes. Cold War military spending directed by powerful southern congressmen funded new defense and defense-related industries that brought white-collar professionals to the Sunbelt. The migrants who moved southward and westward arrived there on interstate highways and bought homes in new suburban developments subsidized by the federal government. At the same time, a large segment of the southern population that was disproportionately poor and black was migrating out of the region. Southern and southwestern civic boosters created a healthy "business climate" in their areas, keeping taxes low and unions out. Sunbelt legislatures helped subsidize capital flight from the declining Rust Belt. At the same time, the mechanization of farming led to a massive flight of jobs away from the low-paying agricultural sector.

Thurmond shaped and was shaped by these developments. When he became the Dixiecrat presidential candidate in 1948, he broke sharply with his labor-friendly past and aligned himself with the most conservative economic forces in the South and the Southwest. As governor, he was among the first of the postwar southerners who recruited industry to the South, helping to transform the political economy of the region. In the Senate he joined Barry Goldwater on the Labor and Public Welfare Committee and became one of that body's two most outspoken promoters of "free enterprise" and among the staunchest critics of organized labor. He was also one of the Senate's most devoted anti-Communists, as his muzzling campaign exemplified. His support for every weapon that military contractors could dream up made him one of the best friends of the Pentagon in Congress, an eager contributor in building the Cold War military-industrial complex that helped create the Sunbelt.

Recasting Thurmond as a Sunbelt politician necessitates new ways of thinking about the history of the Sunbelt. Too often that history is told as a story about political economy, and southern history as a story about race. Scholars argue whether it was economic change or racism that created the modern Republican South, and a both/and issue gets framed as an either/or debate.[15] In the process, they make facile distinctions between Sunbelt conservatives, who are figured as modern, principled, and broadly ideological, and southern conservatives, who are figured chiefly as backward and racist. A leading study of Sunbelt conservatism in Orange County, California, for example, argues, "Racial issues were far more central to the texture and fabric of southern politics and to that region's conservatism." In Orange County, racism "was only one of a host of issues in a broader conservative package."[16] Even if one admits the unusually powerful role of race in southern politics, the formulation assumes that in the South racism was not merely "one of a host of issues" but the *only* issue. Conservative white southerners' Cold War anticommunism, antilabor politics, conservative religious beliefs and opposition to liberal church groups, criticism of judicial activism, and hyper-militarism—all of this becomes merely a function of their desire to maintain white supremacy. Such a view not only provides a flattened portrait of a southern conservative like Thurmond but also presents Sunbelt conservatives as racially innocent, free from any taint of racial politics.[17]

Thurmond is left out of not only Sunbelt history but also the history of conservatism more generally. The foundational figures were Goldwater and Reagan, as everyone knows. Yet in 1948, when Goldwater was still a year away from running for the Phoenix city council and Reagan was still an actor, Thurmond was a presidential candidate denouncing federal meddling in private business, the growing socialist impulse in American politics, and the dangers of statism, themes that would dominate the postwar conservative movement. Even Thurmond's fellow southerner Jesse Helms is more closely associated with modern conservatism. This is not how Thurmond saw himself. At the opening ceremony of the Strom Thurmond Institute at Clemson University in 1982, Thurmond argued that his States' Rights campaign had made possible the "milestone" of Goldwater's 1964 effort.[18] An aide recalled how the initial proposal for the Clemson institute was for the "Strom Thurmond Center for the Study of Southern Politics." Thurmond turned his nose up at the title. "He didn't see himself as a southern political leader," the aide recalled. "He viewed himself as a national—if not international—figure."[19]

Strom Thurmond's America was filled with Strom Thurmond Americans. They are most commonly referred to as Dixiecrats, the nearly 1.2 million Americans who voted for Thurmond in 1948. Yet that label, and the relatively poor showing he made in that impetuous campaign, tends to trivialize Thurmond's place in the history of right-wing populism. Thurmond became a national figure at a time when "conservatism" was still a dirty word in American politics and anathema in his native South. He could never have used the term in 1948 and survived politically. Conservatives were "economic royalists," the greedy Wall Street Republicans who had plunged the country into the Depression. They were utility executives and lawyers who had tried to stop Franklin Roosevelt from bringing the South cheap electricity, or industrialists who had mistreated the honest laboring people of the South and looked upon the region as the North's own colonial enterprise. To call himself a conservative was to play into the hands of southern Democrats who said that Thurmond's group was a Trojan horse used by oil and gas interests and their wealthy banking and in-dustrial friends to keep the government out of their businesses.

Thurmond predated the founding generation of what is com-monly understood as the modern conservative movement. He was a closer friend to William F. Buckley Sr. than to William F. Buckley Jr., the founding editor of *National Review* and one of the central figures of modern conservatism. Buckley senior, who restored an antebellum es-tate in Camden, South Carolina, and became a friend and regular cor-respondent with the then governor Thurmond, would have had no problem identifying as a Strom Thurmond American. "I don't know of any other man in public life whose views I entirely approve of," he wrote to Thurmond in 1956. His son had just started a new magazine, and Buckley sent Thurmond a year's subscription. He told Thurmond that his son was "a very fine public speaker" and "very sound," adding, "He is for segregation and backs it in every issue."[20]

One of the most notorious editorials Buckley junior published in *National Review*'s early years came during a signature battle in Thur-mond's career, the fight against the 1957 civil rights bill. "Why the South Must Prevail" appeared four days before Thurmond's historic filibuster: "The central question that emerges . . . is whether the White community in the South is entitled to take such measures as are neces-sary to prevail, politically and culturally, in areas in which it does not predominate numerically? The sobering answer is *Yes*—the White community is so entitled because, for the time being, it is the advanced race."[21] Buckley junior and Thurmond would seem to occupy separate poles in conservative politics; their accents alone marked their different backgrounds and experiences. It is easy to forget that Buckley was once a fledgling writer and publisher trying to insinuate himself into a world of politics and letters, the son of a nouveau riche oil baron, and that Thurmond was a priceless contact for father and son both. Later, after the sea change inaugurated by the civil rights movement, Thurmond would not be the only conservative leader with a segregationist record in need of scrubbing. The mid-twentieth-century American Right was a smaller, more interconnected world than we often remember.

Thurmond's life is interesting because it can be used to challenge conventional narratives in southern and American history, yet it is also interesting simply as a life—an extraordinarily vigorous and long one, full of emotional and psychological complexity, unexpected turns, and unanticipated consequences. It contains an epic quality. He was the son of a talented but stunted politician, a man whose crime of passion earlier in life limited his career, though it did not staunch his ambition. Avenging the frustrations of the father became the motivation of the son, even as the son's youthful act of passion threatened to upend his own ambitions and, with them, the hopes of father and son alike. His career was linked both to battles that remade his native South and to political evolutions that transformed post–World War II America. The revelations after his death of Essie Mae Washington-Williams, Thurmond's biracial daughter, provided a reflection on the legacy of slavery and segregation, a twenty-first-century parallel to Thomas Jefferson's relationship with his slave mistress, Sally Hemings.

As galling as Thurmond's hypocrisy was, the disclosure that he fathered a black child has made it all the easier to relegate him to a distant past that is no more. There he remains as a caricature of an older, unambiguously racist South, not a flesh-and-blood person who helped create the America we live in today. It is easier that way. By categorically condemning Thurmond, we reaffirm our own morality. Liberals can remember him as the simpleminded dinosaur evoked in the southern strategy narrative, a villain whose party switch and kingmaking explain all one needs to know about the rise of the Republican Right. Conservatives can dismiss him as an anachronism, a colorful but ultimately irrelevant figure in the origins of *real* conservatism. In truth, Thurmond was neither. He remains today one of the great American hypocrites, yet there is more than just hypocrisy to his story. And the hypocrisies that exist were not just his or the white South's alone; they were also America's. Staring these facts in the face is uncomfortable, yet it is what makes our looking all the more essential.

★ ★

PART ONE

UP FROM EDGEFIELD

★ ★

1

EDGEFIELD, U.S.A.
(1902–1932)

On December 5, 1902, John William Thurmond and his wife, Eleanor Gertrude, of Edgefield, South Carolina, welcomed the arrival of James Strom Thurmond, their second son. The child was born and raised a son of Edgefield. At the turn of the twentieth century, that accident of birth was sufficient to provide a politically minded white boy with a sense of heritage and calling.

Edgefield County was the home of ten governors and lieutenant governors of South Carolina. It has also bequeathed some of the more legendary figures in southern history. Preston Brooks, the South Carolina representative who in 1856 viciously assaulted the antislavery advocate Charles Sumner on the floor of the Senate, was a native. So was the U.S. senator Andrew Butler, Brooks's relative, whom Sumner had allegedly insulted in a speech several days earlier, which had prompted Brooks's attack. Two leaders of the Texans at the Alamo, James Bonham and William Barret Travis, were from Edgefield, as was "Pitchfork" Ben Tillman, one of the most infamous demagogues of the Jim Crow South.

In a state known for producing passionate, quick-tempered leaders of lost causes, Edgefield stands out. William Watts Ball, the longtime editor of Charleston's *News and Courier,* immortalized Edgefield as a quintessential southern locale. "Their virtues were shining, their vices flamed," Ball wrote. "They were not careful reckoners of the future, sometimes they spoke too quickly, and so acted, yet in crises an audacity that might have been called imprudence by milder men made them indispensable to the state." Another encomium from Ball so succinctly summarized the mythology of Edgefield that the town elders had it painted on the side of a store facing the village square: "It has had more dashing, brilliant, romantic figures, statesmen, orators, soldiers, adventurers, daredevils, than any county of South Carolina, if not of any rural county of America."[1]

Established in 1785, Edgefield County has always bridged the up-country and low country, the most salient division in South Carolina politics dating from the American Revolution to the demise of the white primary in the mid-twentieth century. The low country experienced its heyday in the eighteenth and nineteenth centuries, dominated by trade in Charleston and large-scale rice, sugar, and indigo plantations. In the late nineteenth century, the up-country became one of the first southern areas to embrace industrialization, primarily cotton mills, though more diverse industries followed after World War II.

Renowned for its record of political leadership, Edgefield has also been notorious for its violence. In its earliest days as a frontier society, brutal confrontations between white settlers and Native Americans were a way of life in sparsely settled areas of western Carolina. In the antebellum period, law officers were few, and vigilantism was commonplace. So too was dueling. Yet a new chapter was written in Edgefield's bloody history during Reconstruction.

The county was a hotbed of violence in 1876, the year that Wade Hampton and the "Red Shirts" overthrew the Republicans, restoring Democratic rule and white supremacy. The violence began in Edgefield County on July 4, 1876, the hundredth anniversary of American independence. A confrontation between African American militiamen and several local white rifle clubs led by the former Confederate general Matthew Butler turned bloody. When the black men took refuge in their "armory," a room above a Hamburg storefront, white men massed in the street below. Shots were fired back and forth. After one white man was killed, the mob opened fire with artillery and drove the militiamen from their stronghold. About thirty black militiamen were captured. Five were executed on the spot. The rest were eventually turned loose and fired upon as they fled; at least two more were killed.[2]

Wade Hampton, the Democratic candidate for governor, maintained an aura of racial benevolence, promising to serve as "the Governor of the whole people."[3] Yet it was the Red Shirts' coordinated campaign of terror that was the key to Democratic success. Matthew Butler joined with Martin Gary, a fellow Confederate hero who had moved to Edgefield to practice law, to mimic the reign of violence and intimidation that had allowed white Mississippians to restore white supremacy in that state the previous year. On Election Day, Martin Gary delivered a rousing speech to some fifteen hundred Red Shirts who had gathered at Oakley Park, the stately antebellum mansion he owned in Edgefield—just 150 yards from where Strom Thurmond would be born, twenty-six years later.

White vigilantism against African Americans continued unabated in the decades that followed Hampton's campaign. It became an integral part of the crusade to disenfranchise black voters, an effort that reached its apotheosis in the new constitution of 1895. By the time Strom Thurmond was born, violence at the polls had become relatively rare only because white political power had become so firmly established. White vigilantism against blacks, however, continued well into the twentieth century. In roughly the first two decades of Thurmond's life—from 1904 to 1918—a lynching took place in South Carolina, on average, every four months. This, of course, accounted only for murders that were actually reported. Many were never discovered, and white men regularly killed blacks with impunity. When local prosecutors went to the trouble of filing charges, whites easily won acquittal from juries of their peers.[4]

Benjamin Tillman, the man who more than any other embodied the racist violence of the era, was a close family friend of the Thurmonds'. Tillman was born near Trenton, just south of the town of Edgefield. He rose to prominence in state politics and was elected governor in 1890 as the defender of the small farmer. Though a stalwart agrarian reformer, he was careful to appropriate populism for South Carolina Democrats, avoiding the biracial coalitions that characterized populist movements in some southern states. In 1894, he replaced Matthew Butler in the U.S. Senate, where he served until his death in 1918. He was an influential advocate of the 1895 constitution, which replaced the Reconstruction-era document and helped secure the disenfranchisement of African

Americans. Nationally, he became well-known as a regular source of intemperate racist outbursts.[5]

Ben Tillman was disreputable in his own day, but to later generations he would become one of the most villainous figures from a disgraceful era in the nation's past. To the young Strom Thurmond he was a towering, irascible figure, the biggest, most important man he had ever met. Strom recalled as a boy his father loading up the family in a wagon to travel the six miles to Senator Tillman's place near Trenton. His father told him to walk up to the "stern" Tillman, offer his hand, and introduce himself. "What do you want?" Tillman asked. "I want to shake hands with you," the boy answered, refusing to be intimidated. "Well, why in the hell don't you shake then?" Strom took his hand and gave it as manly a shake as he could.[6]

Thurmond loved to tell this story of his first political handshake, but by far the most important influence on the boy came not from the man whose hand he shook but from the man who stood nearby, his father, John William Thurmond, known locally as Will. Thurmond's mother was a beloved and revered figure, the daughter of a prominent family in Edgefield, and as an adult Strom would regularly write affectionate letters to her. Yet Will Thurmond was the dominant figure in the lives of his children.

Strom was the second oldest of six, three boys and three girls. It was from Will that Thurmond developed his obsession with good health. The family grew its own grain, which Will would have delivered to a local mill to be ground into whole wheat flour. Strom continued the practice into his seventies, buying bran directly from a mill. While his brothers would both become doctors in Augusta, Strom inherited his father's love of politics. Will Thurmond regularly brought home for lunch or dinner politicians traveling through Edgefield, and Strom would accompany his father on work trips to Columbia. He recalled watching the general assembly from the gallery and meeting the members of the South Carolina Supreme Court, a body with which Will sometimes sat as a special judge. "He was my idol," Thurmond said of his father. "I tried to imitate him as much as I could."[7] Strom hung an enlarged photograph of Will in his Senate office and made copies of a letter his father had written to him in 1923, when he graduated from college. Titled "Advice," the letter listed rules to live by:

Remember your God.

Take good care of your body and tax your nervous system as little possible.

Obey the laws of the land.

Be strictly honest.

Associate only with the best people, morally and intellectually.

Think three times before you act once and if you are in doubt, don't act at all.

Be prompt on your job to the minute.

Read at every spare chance and think over and try to remember what you have read.

Do not forget that "skill and integrity" are the keys to success.

> *Affectionately.*
> *Dad*[8]

Visitors to his Senate office received a copy as tokens from Thurmond, along with pens, buttons, and other political knickknacks.[9]

Born in Edgefield County in 1862, Will Thurmond was the son of Mary Jane Felter Thurmond, originally of New Orleans, and George Washington Thurmond. A veteran of three wars—the Indian Wars, the Mexican War, and the Civil War, in which he served as a corporal in the Confederate army—G. W. Thurmond was present at Appomattox when Lee surrendered to Grant. Strom's grandmother, however, was the source of Will's "ambition and his ideals" and was responsible for the bulk of his education.

By his late twenties and early thirties Will Thurmond was one of the most promising young men in Edgefield. He had attended the University of South Carolina for one year before studying law in the office of John C. Sheppard, one of the ten South Carolina governors to have hailed from Edgefield. Passing the bar in 1888 with distinction, Thurmond was immediately elected county attorney. In 1894 and 1895 he represented Edgefield in the general assembly and in 1896, with the backing of the U.S. senator Ben Tillman, who recognized the young Thurmond as a political comer, he won election as solicitor of the Fifth Judicial Circuit, which included Columbia. Thurmond would later serve as Tillman's personal lawyer, and the two men remained close political allies. During Woodrow Wilson's administration, Tillman used the full measure of his guile to have Thurmond appointed U.S. attorney for one of two federal districts in the state. Tillman's biographer baroquely described the appointment as a "petal" on Tillman's "odious rose of spoliation." Indeed, Will Thurmond was no easy man to have had appointed. His bright early prospects had been diminished by an incident in 1897, an encounter that forever altered his life's trajectory and would have a profound influence on his son's life as well.[10]

In the late afternoon of Wednesday, March 24, 1897, the thirty-four-year-old Thurmond shot and killed a man named Willie Harris just off the main square in Edgefield. The two men had gotten into an argument over a political appointment that Harris's father had not received, and Harris blamed Thurmond for the slight. A newspaper account noted Harris's "very hot language," though one onlooker described the exchange as innocuous and another as "friendly . . . I saw nothing to get mad about."[11] No one disputed, however, that Willie Harris had drunk too much whiskey.

There were conflicting reports of the shooting, one by Thurmond himself and the other by the lone eyewitness, a Captain Dubose, the owner of the hotel where Harris was staying, who was walking with the victim at the time of his death. In his deposition, Will Thurmond provided lurid details of Harris's profanity-laced invective and threatening gestures, including waving a large knife, in the Lynch drugstore. Thurmond testified that Harris declared "I have a damn good knife and a Colt's pistol in my pocket" before walking out of the store. He returned shortly thereafter to wave the knife in front of Thurmond's face.[12]

According to Thurmond, Harris later walked by his office and continued the harassment. Thurmond claimed that during the exchange Harris sprang as if to rush the door and assault him. Thurmond kicked Harris backward. When Harris threw his right hand under his coat, Thurmond fired, killing him with a shot to the sternum.[13]

Captain Dubose's account was less elaborate. He had walked a few steps ahead of Harris but had stopped to listen to Harris's heated denunciation of Thurmond. Dubose's recollection of the conversation accorded generally with Thurmond's, but the testimonies diverged as to Harris's actions. Harris never sprang on Thurmond, according to Dubose, nor did Thurmond kick him backward. Harris simply yelled at

Thurmond, "You are a low, dirty scoundrel," after which Thurmond pulled his pistol and fired.[14]

Reports that Solicitor Thurmond, one of South Carolina's chief law-enforcement officials, had committed murder caused a scandal. "How can we hope that the people will respect the laws and human life," editorialized the *Baptist Courier*, "when our officers, sworn to execute and enforce the laws, put such a low estimate upon human life?"[15] "The pity of it!" declared the *Carolina Spartan*. "Solicitor Thurmond stands no more chance of conviction for killing Harris than the average Edgefield man who shoots a negro."[16] Speculation turned to whether Thurmond would show up for the next term of court in Columbia to fulfill his duties as solicitor.[17]

An interim official was appointed until Will Thurmond's murder trial in August in the Edgefield Courthouse, only yards away from the scene of the murder. It was a small-town spectacle. The attorney general of South Carolina appeared in person to lead the prosecution. Joining him at the behest of the Harris family was the hero of Hamburg, General Matthew Butler. Defending Thurmond was the ex-governor John C. Sheppard, in whose office Thurmond had sat for the bar, along with J. H. Tillman, Pitchfork Ben's nephew, who five years later would be tried and acquitted himself for the murder of the Columbia *State* newspaper editor N. G. Gonzales.[18]

Despite the luminaries on hand, the trial itself was uneventful. The jury took a mere thirty minutes to determine that Thurmond had acted in self-defense. The verdict, as reported by the *Edgefield Advertiser*, was "according to general expectation."[19] An account in *The State*, however, mocked the proceedings: "Poor Will Harris, like many another murdered man, sleeps unavenged under the sod of Edgefield. Solicitor Thurmond can now return to his official duties in the prosecution of murderers with a spirit purified for the task and a reputation so enhanced by his experience as to make doubly effective his appeals to juries to vindicate the law against murder."[20]

The murder of Will Harris did not diminish Will Thurmond's standing among his fellow townspeople, yet it stunted his career in state politics. The election returns of 1902 left no doubt. Thurmond was one of three candidates in the Democratic primary for a seat in the U.S. House of Representatives from South Carolina's Second District.

Despite a strong showing in Edgefield and Saluda counties, Will did not even make the runoff election.[21] It would have been a humiliating experience for someone for whom expectations had been so high just a few years earlier. Will Thurmond would never run for elective office again. His only consolation was the birth in December of his second son, James Strom, a child that his wife, Eleanor Gertrude, had carried through the sweltering summer months of Will's political evisceration.

Strom Thurmond came of age at a time when the heroic memory of the Red Shirt campaign of 1876 was a totem for white South Carolinians, one invoked for political effect by Ben Tillman's generation. When opponents would try to tweak Tillman by questioning his lack of service in the Civil War, Tillman responded, "I have a little record of 1876 . . . and have had a little to do with managing elections."[22]

Will Thurmond took part in such rituals as well, recounting his own record of 1876, when the state had been saved from Republican rule. At age fourteen he had helped guard the poll at the Shaw and McKie's Mill precinct in Edgefield County during the presidential election. "There were six or seven negroes to one white man," he recalled. "I had been taught to handle a long pistol for the occasion, and the boys of my age and all white men of the neighborhood, young and old, were at that precinct determined to carry the election for white supremacy." Thurmond added: "I believe that the Negroes should be fairly and justly treated, but the Caucasian race discovered, conquered and brought civilization to this country, and I don't think any other race should be permitted to participate in the politics of this country."[23]

This was the unapologetic public testimony of the man who had the strongest influence on Strom Thurmond's life and career. These kinds of memories passed on from his father, along with the lessons learned from his Edgefield heritage, prepared Thurmond for a long discipleship in the cult of the Lost Cause. Yet in the years that Strom Thurmond came of age, one need not have been a son of Will Thurmond's or a resident of Edgefield to be instructed in the folly of Reconstruction and racial equality. In early-twentieth-century America, the mythology of the Lost Cause had transmogrified into a national conventional wisdom. The memory of the iniquitous postwar period made possible the reconciliation of North and South.

White Americans in both regions could agree on a simple formula: the South had lost the war, but the North had lost the peace. Slavery had been a mistake, defeated southerners could admit, but gracious northerners conceded the sin of trying to foist social equality on the prostrate South. In the violent restoration of white rule, southerners had simply acted as any brave, self-respecting people would. It was the consensus confirmed by distinguished professors at the nation's leading universities. They wrote the definitive histories of the period and sent out waves of graduate students to record in detail the alleged graft, greed, and incompetence of the coalition of carpetbaggers, scalawags, and coloreds. At the reunions held at the grand old sites of the unfortunate conflict, aged veterans shook hands across old battle lines. The errors had evened out. All was forgiven.[24]

In 1915, this national mythology received its most audacious rendering—replete with engaging romantic subplots, a traveling orchestra, and a state-of-the-art publicity campaign—with the release of D. W. Griffith's *Birth of a Nation*, the grandest cinematic creation of its era. Based on the novel *The Clansman* by the North Carolina native Thomas Dixon Jr., the film was set in a fictional South Carolina up-country town called Piedmont. Recounting in lurid detail the tragedy of the war and the evils of "Radical Reconstruction," it told of heroic southern white men who did not cower at the sight of the oppressor but defended their womenfolk, their homeland, and their way of life. Yet the white men of Piedmont did not merely restore sanity to a region turned upside down. They gave birth to a nation, one symbolized in the film's final scene by the double marriage of the sons and daughters of two families, one northern, one southern.[25]

The film played to packed audiences in Columbia in the fall of 1915 and again in the winter of 1916 in both Columbia and Augusta. Whether Strom Thurmond ever saw the film as a teenager is unknown.[26] His family certainly had the means to attend. Advertisements in *The State* where nationally known ministers stressed how "a boy can learn more true history" from watching the film were sure to have appealed to Will Thurmond, who was always mindful of his children's education and advancement.[27] Yet regardless of whether young Strom ever saw the film, he knew the story because it was the valorous tale in which he had been instructed since birth, the story of what *The State* described as white South Carolinians' "heroisms, the triumphs of their own families, their own forebears."[28]

However tempting it is to look back on Thurmond's childhood in Edgefield as an education into a regional heritage distinct from a national one, a tutelage into a world of heroes and traditions set apart from the cultural and political touchstones of America, that was simply not the case. The actual experience as the young Thurmond would have lived it was never so subversive of the national narrative. The history he learned was of a place and a people that had grown up together with the nation itself.

He would have been told that Edgefield and surrounding areas experienced savage battle during the Revolutionary War and that the town and the county were founded in 1785, only two years after the war itself ended.[29] As a young man, he walked among the Confederate graves in Willowbrook Cemetery, directly behind the Baptist church that his family attended, reading the names of soldiers who had died defending their home in the War Between the States. And he learned too about the tragedy of what came after that war, the folly of Reconstruction and the glory of Redemption that had set the nation on solid footing once again. In this way, the history that young Strom Thurmond learned about his people and his place in the world was never simply a part of the South's history. It was for him always a part of American history.

Strom Thurmond's earliest and most enduring memory of politics dated back to 1912, when he was a nine-year-old boy attending a political debate with his father. It would become Thurmond's political just-so story.[30] The race was between the incumbent governor, Cole Blease, and Ira B. Jones, a former Speaker of the South Carolina House of Representatives and the chief justice of the South Carolina Supreme Court. A picture of Ira Jones and Will Thurmond is preserved in Strom's personal papers at Clemson. Attached is a typewritten caption: "J.S.T. decided on this day to some day run for Gov. of S.C."[31]

To a reporter who inquired about the event in 1961, Thurmond told how "the best man, so I thought, was unable to protect himself in a debate." He elaborated on the scene in subsequent years, providing the most detailed account during an interview in 1980:

> They put up a platform for them to speak on and brought a big pitcher of water. Jones, he made a good talk, a literary talk. But he just didn't stir the people. Well, Cole Blease was a fiery kind of fellow and a great orator. You could see people who were not really the thinking people who were carried away by the speech. I could see then the influence that he was going to have over the state for being such a good speaker . . . After hearing him speak, I knew that I was going to run for governor. And I was going to learn to speak, and I would never let a man do me like Blease did Jones that day.[32]

Will Thurmond and Jones were longtime friends who had served together in the general assembly, and in 1912 Thurmond worked for Jones as his campaign manager. Jones was the figurehead and Thurmond one of the leading figures in a coalition of middle-class business and professional interests, the "town folk," which included newspaper editors, ministers, other middle-class reformers, and, by 1912, a relatively mellowed Ben Tillman and much of South Carolina's political establishment.[33]

What united them all was their opposition to Bleasism, an eponym that covered an array of alleged ignorance, illegality, and anarchism. Blease's opponents derided him as an embarrassment to the state. Blease scoffed at progressive programs in education and health, recklessly replaced experienced state officials with incompetent friends, stoked the impudence of unschooled laborers against established local and state leaders, and made indiscriminate use of the governor's pardoning power. He also openly advocated lynching as a means of solving South Carolina's racial problems. Thurmond's cohorts were no less committed to white supremacy, but they chafed at such brazenness, which they believed tarred the state in the eyes of powerful outside interests.[34]

The larger forces that gave rise to Bleasism were rooted in an economic transformation that was remaking society and politics in South Carolina. Independent yeoman farmers who a generation earlier had worked the land were increasingly drawn into the newly expanding cotton mill industry in the Piedmont. In 1880 there were only a dozen mills in South Carolina. Twenty years later there were 115; by 1920 there were 184.[35] The earlier generation of poor white farmers had made up the bedrock support of Pitchfork Ben, who had denounced the monopolistic interests that kept down the price of cotton and had reassured their sense of dignity as proud, free white men. What Tillman had done for the yeomen, Blease did for the mill hands, the "lintheads," the unpropertied who moved with their families by the thousands into mill villages dotting the Carolina up-country. Town leaders worried over the influence of these uneducated masses and the power of their "bloc vote" in swinging elections.[36] The term would become synonymous with the "black vote" in the civil rights era—and it was the bane of Strom Thurmond's political existence—but in this earlier period the dangerous foreign element in South Carolina politics was working-class white laborers.

These tensions came to a head in Blease's reelection campaign in 1912, one of the stormiest and most bitterly contested campaigns in a state famous for them. The heyday of Blease's influence in state politics—from his election as governor in 1910 through World War I—witnessed a notable rise in voter participation rates, but none surpassed the 1912 election, when 80.2 percent of the registered electorate went to the polls.[37] Despite having the support of the state's most influential citizens, Jones's attack on Blease's "anarchy" could not match the withering derision of his opponent. Presenting Jones as a tool of elite financial interests, Blease excoriated him above all for failing to defend white womanhood. He charged Jones with having endeavored "to force social equality among the white ladies and children of this country, with the negro men." He berated Jones for voting against a separate railroad carriage law for whites and blacks, a vote that Blease charged was due to Jones's being in thrall to greedy railroad interests. Blease titillated the crowd with stories of "white ladies, your wives, your mothers, your daughters and your sweethearts," being forced to ride in coaches "right next to and sometimes jammed up against a big black Negro wench, or a stinking Negro buck."[38]

Blease's scorn was not limited to Jones. As Jones's campaign manager, Will Thurmond himself came under fire. Blease nicknamed

Thurmond "Pussyfoot Bill," a reference to his alleged behind-the-scenes political manipulation, an insult that suggested he did not come out in the open and address his enemies like a man. He accused Thurmond of funneling corporate cash into Jones's campaign, evidence that Blease used to affirm his status as the candidate of "the people," and he pointed to Thurmond's trial on murder charges years earlier to undercut Jones's criticisms of his pardon record.[39]

The candidates did not meet in Edgefield that year, so the meeting in Saluda, about twenty miles from Edgefield where Will Thurmond kept a branch law office, is likely the one that Strom attended.[40] Twenty-five hundred people were on hand. So many of them were pro-Blease that Jones accused his opponent of packing the crowd with "Blease howlers." One of Strom Thurmond's fellow townsmen shot back, "Yes, there's a hundred from Edgefield here." Watching Jones stumble along, unable to rouse his own supporters, must have been a painful experience. The judge's halting, ineffective speechmaking only fed Blease's mockery of his opponent. "What is his claim to be governor?" Blease asked the crowd. "He hasn't presented a single reason for his election. He can't even make a speech."[41]

Jones was "absolutely a child in Blease's hands," lamented Ben Tillman in a letter to Will Thurmond late in the campaign.[42] The situation became so dire that an aged Tillman, who had resisted endorsing Jones out of fear of losing Blease supporters in his own Senate reelection campaign, issued a last-minute endorsement, once it was clear his own race was not in jeopardy.[43] But it was too late for Jones, who made a decent showing but could not unseat Blease.

Strom Thurmond recalled the debate between Blease and Jones as his first lesson in political self-defense, in the importance of being skilled in the verbal warfare of the stump. Yet Jones's humiliation was always matched in Thurmond's memory by Blease's mastery and the power it gave him with the masses. In 1912, at age nine, Thurmond encountered up close at an impressionable age the power of the demagogue, an experience both fearsome and alluring.

Thurmond himself drew on this background thirty-six years later, when as a presidential candidate he stoked the racist resentments of the States' Rights Democrats. It was in Birmingham in July 1948 that Thurmond offered his own form of Bleasism, swearing that there were not enough "troops in the army" to force southerners to admit the "nigger race" into their theaters, swimming pools, and churches.[44] It was Bleasism that he drew upon during the twenty-four hours and eighteen minutes he spent denouncing the civil rights bill of 1957, as well as in other firebrand orations he gave in the massive resistance era, such as a 1958 speech declaring "total and unremitting war on the Supreme Court's unconstitutional usurpations and unlawful arroga-tions of power."[45]

Yet Thurmond also remembered the disdain of his father and other townsfolk for Blease, how Blease mocked the attitudes and opinions of the "thinking people." It was one reason perhaps why later in his career Thurmond would embrace a kind of magical thinking about his ad-ventures in demagoguery, denying them outright or attempting to rationalize them into something other than mere Bleasism.

For the rest of his career the poles between which Strom Thur-mond's political ambitions would swing were established in that 1912 race. The intelligent, honorable Jones was also hamstrung and tooth-less. Blease, despicable as he was to Thurmond's father and his circle of "respectable" leaders, was stylish, clever, and formidable. It would seem that the fair-minded and the principled became vaguely commingled in Thurmond's mind with political weakness, and perhaps too with his father's failed ambitions, while what others decried as illicit and dema-gogic, Thurmond knew to be something else as well—a key to men's fears and passions, a path to the influence and renown that his father always longed for but never achieved.

Family lore records the tale of an obstinate young Strom who climbed out on the roof to avoid a whipping from his mother, yet other stories testify to his maturity and work ethic. When a neighboring farmer was called away to World War I, the fourteen-year-old Thurmond bought his crop and farmed it for him. Rather than completing another grade of high school to be added the following year, Thurmond headed off to college at the age of sixteen.[46]

He attended Clemson, which had been founded in 1889 to educate the state's rising generation in the ways of progressive agriculture and the mechanical sciences. The brainchild of Ben Tillman, the school's founding was part of an assault on the state's "aristocratic oligarchy" that Tillman believed was incubated in the classical liberal arts education offered at the state university in Columbia.[47] Thurmond studied agriculture, participated in the military training required of all students, and ran cross-country. He was one of several track team members who completed the twenty-mile run to the nearby town of Anderson. Late in his career, a journalist would pick up on the image of Thurmond as the long-distance runner as a metaphor for his political persona. Slow and plodding, Thurmond wore down opponents not by skill or intelligence but by doggedness and determination.[48]

After college, Thurmond returned to Edgefield, where he taught high school for several years before running for county superintendent of education. He was twenty-five years old when he was elected in September 1928. As a college graduate and the son of the county's wealthiest and most respected attorney, Thurmond was part of what amounted to the aristocracy in a poor rural county. There was officially no urban population in Edgefield because no town included more than twenty-five hundred residents, the census-defined threshold for urban areas. The total population was just under twenty thousand residents. Two-thirds of that was African American, and the vast majority of them lived out in the county and worked as tenant farmers or sharecroppers. Across the South, the average tenant family received an annual income of only $73 per person. Sharecroppers earned about ten cents per day.[49]

It was a sign of Thurmond's initiative and broad-mindedness that his signature effort as superintendent was to start a county-wide literacy campaign. The 1920 census had revealed that Edgefield had an illiterate population of 140 whites and some 3,000 blacks. Thurmond instituted literacy classes for whites and blacks both, but there were far more black students. By the winter of 1930, he had organized forty night classes for black Edgefieldians who could not get away from work during the day, each class with about twenty students. There was not enough money in the budget to pay for an organizer, so Thurmond did the work himself.[50]

Deeply as he believed in the value of self-improvement, Thurmond never intended to make a career as an educator. In his first year on the job he moved his office as superintendent next door to Will Thurmond's law office, where he began an informal course of study. Renowned for his legal abilities, Will Thurmond would later author *Thurmond's Key Cases*, a casebook of state law that became standard reading for law students in South Carolina. Many aspiring lawyers would have leapt at the opportunity to study under Will Thurmond, yet Strom came along at a time when the modern practice of attending three years of law school was increasingly standard. The fact that Thurmond stayed in Edgefield to study with his father rather than attend the law school in Columbia showed his unusual ambition. As he would explain years later, the advantage of studying at home was that he could continue his work as school superintendent and pack what normally would have been three years of study into one.[51]

There were disadvantages as well. It was a pragmatist's training in the law, as well as a nepotistic introduction into the clubby world of the South Carolina bar. Thurmond's legal education was completely lacking, however, in broader philosophical training. For at least one political rival, the lacuna showed up in Thurmond's later tenure as a judge. "I thought Strom was the weakest circuit judge we had since Reconstruction," recalled Thomas Pope, a lawyer and former Speaker of the South Carolina House of Representatives.[52]

Pope pointed to Thurmond's lack of formal education, yet he did not call him a dullard. Thurmond was adept at finding narrow grounds on which to argue a case, which served him well in his law practice both in the 1930s and in the early 1950s in the interim between his governorship and his Senate career. But the facility did not translate well to either the bench or the Senate hearing room. In this latter forum, Thurmond could often be found doggedly following limited, technical lines of questioning, sometimes to the frustration of witnesses and colleagues alike.

If Thurmond had any self-doubts about his training or abilities, he kept them well hidden. Only those closest to him sensed his insecurity. In the mid-1960s, Thurmond began employing a Ph.D. on his Senate staff. Two former staffers who held doctoral degrees recall how Thurmond would grandly introduce them to his fellow senators, emphasizing the honorific, often to the staffer's embarrassment.[53] For a man whose office walls bore no sheepskins testifying to his professional training or accomplishments, the titles seem to have mattered.

Another prominent son of Edgefield came to know Strom Thurmond from his earliest days and chronicled his ascent. Francis Butler Simkins, who would become a distinguished southern historian and the author of the definitive biography of Benjamin Tillman, was just five years older than Strom. For several years the Simkinses and the Thurmonds were next-door neighbors on Columbia Road. Will Thurmond and McGowan Simkins, Francis Butler's father, were both lawyers and something of political rivals. In 1912, when Will Thurmond managed Ira Jones's campaign, McGowan Simkins was Edgefield's most prominent Blease supporter.[54]

Sometime in the late 1940s or early 1950s, Francis Butler Simkins sat down to write a gossipy, thinly fictionalized memoir about growing up in Edgefield, or "Litchwood" as it appears in his text. It was never published and is preserved today only in Simkins's personal papers at Longwood University in Farmville, Virginia, where he taught for most of his career. The untitled manuscript is fascinating for the light it sheds on Simkins's onetime neighbors, who appear with the pseudonyms Hog Stoopes and his son Stone. These "fictional" characters follow so exactly the real-life accomplishments of Will and Strom Thurmond as to make the pseudonyms superfluous; at one point Simkins even slips and refers to Hog Stoopes as Will Stoopes. Despite some minor errors in facts—Simkins writes, for example, that Stone Stoopes joined the bench in 1939, when actually Thurmond joined it in 1938—the manuscript provides an intimate perspective on Will and Strom Thurmond and Edgefield.[55]

Simkins's treatment of Hog Stoopes was relatively generous. Describing Hog as "cold-blooded" in his law practice, "learned in the technicalities of the law without the remotest interest in justice or in polite culture," Simkins also pronounced him deserving of the honorary degree awarded him by the University of South Carolina. Hog was "Litchwood's man of moderation and charity" who "refused to speak unkindly of anyone," the town's "most popular citizen for forty years."

Yet the distinctive quality that emerges from Simkins's portrait of Hog Stoopes was that of a remarkably adroit fixer. Stoopes "ruled

Litchwood County through machinations so secret that one for decades could live under his authority without being aware of its existence." It was the quality that had led Blease to deride him as a
"pussyfoot." Simkins wrote of a man whose candidacy for prosecuting
attorney was bloodlessly cut short by Stoopes, as well as of a school-
master whose dismissal Stoopes quietly engineered, despite visiting the
man before he left town to tell him how grieved he was to see him go.[56]

Stone Stoopes, however, was of a slightly different breed. While
possessing his father's "sobriety, pleasing manners, industry and will-
ingness to scheme to accomplish personal ambition," he was only half
Stoopes. The other was Stone, and it was from his mother's side of the
family that he was said to have inherited a penchant for "acts of wild
folly." He had an uncle on his mother's side who "was possessed of an
energy so maniacal that he dissipated a fortune in numerous foolish
enterprises." Stone lacked Hog's "good sense and deceptiveness," Simkins wrote. What his father achieved by indirection, Stone pursued
openly and, in the process, attracted enemies.[57]

Characteristics of Hog and Stone Stoopes in Simkins's memoir provide context for a defining event in the lives of Will and Strom Thurmond. In the mid-1920s, when Strom was living at home in Edgefield
and teaching at the local high school, a situation developed inside Will's
household owing to one of Strom's acts of "folly." Among the servants
employed at Thurmond's large home on Penn Street was a sixteen-
year-old African American girl named Carrie Butler. In October 1925,
Butler gave birth to a daughter, whom she named Essie Mae. Six months
later Butler's sister took Essie Mae with her to Pennsylvania, where she
was moving with her husband. She passed the child to another sister,
Mary Washington, who raised Essie Mae as her own. Not until she was
thirteen years old did Essie Mae learn the identity of her actual mother.
Three years later she met her father, Strom Thurmond, in his law office
just off the town square in Edgefield.[58]

Essie Mae's birth in October coincided with an abrupt occupational
change for Thurmond. In the summer of 1925 he had attended summer school at Clemson for additional training in his job as an instruc-
tor of agriculture at Edgefield High School, a position to which he had
been appointed the previous year.[59] Yet a society notice in the Augusta
paper published on October 12, the very day of Essie Mae's birth, noted

that Thurmond had resigned his teaching position and accepted a job with the Hollywood Company of Florida, a real estate firm, which was expecting to base him in Richmond, Virginia.[60] If the abrupt resignation of a teacher in the middle of the school year raised any suspicions, the article did not mention them. A similar society item the following March noted his continued employment with the company.[61] By June 1926, however, Strom was back at Clemson at the annual conference of state agricultural teachers. A notice in the fall of 1926 described him as a member of the Agricultural Department of Ridge Spring High School, in a nearby community.[62] By 1927, he was back on the faculty at Edgefield.[63]

Thurmond departed from Edgefield the same month of Essie Mae's birth and returned a few months after the child had been moved to Pennsylvania. We do not know whether Will Thurmond played any role in Strom's temporary career change, or in Essie Mae's being sent to Pennsylvania. It is hard to imagine, however, that a man so careful with appearances, so mindful of his reputation in Edgefield and throughout South Carolina, and so hopeful about his son's ambitions would not have had some hand in making sure that the young man's indiscretions did not imperil his future prospects. Will Thurmond knew by hard experience how a youthful mistake could forever alter a political career. Perhaps he had used legal and financial contacts to help get Strom out of town for a while. Perhaps he handed over money to ensure the baby was transported out of the state. If that had been his desire, a quiet conversation with some of Carrie Butler's relatives was all that would have been required. Later the Thurmonds would regularly pass money to Essie Mae's caregivers and, when she came of age, to Essie Mae herself.[64]

If Francis Butler Simkins is to be believed, there may have been a difference between father and son, a sense of judgment or discretion that did not make it from one generation to the next. Yet there remains an awesome fact that testifies to the son's abilities as a fixer: the details of his act of miscegenation—a secret that likely would have ended his career had it been revealed at practically any point in his nearly three-quarters century of public service—he took with him to his grave.

2

BECOMING GOVERNOR THURMOND
(1932–1947)

In 1932, twenty-nine-year-old Strom Thurmond won election to the South Carolina Senate. He defeated the son of Pitchfork Ben, B. R. Tillman, who had spent most of his career in the Navy Department in Washington, a position that his father had secured for him. By the time he returned to Edgefield, Tillman was a dissipated man, and his last name notwithstanding, he presented little challenge to Thurmond. Indeed, speculation around Edgefield was that Will Thurmond had made a secret deal with Tillman to join the race, knowing that his presence would scare off other challengers.[1]

When Thurmond entered the state senate in January 1933, the Great Depression had been going on for almost four years. Among the rural farm families of Edgefield County, neglect and want had been the norm for much longer. The price of cotton had been in decline since World War I. Farmers' traditional woes such as the scarcity of credit and overworked fields had been exacerbated by the plague of boll weevils migrating eastward from Texas. The desperate times elicited calls for desperate measures. In 1931, Will Thurmond, the county's best legal mind, endorsed the cotton holiday proposed by Louisiana's Huey Long.[2] It was a risky scheme—a pledge by southern farmers not to plant cotton in 1932 as a way of raising prices and starving the boll weevil—yet Edgefield farmers had few other options. A letter Will wrote to President Herbert Hoover the previous year urging federal price supports for farmers—the kind of program that Franklin Roosevelt would institute within the first hundred days of his administration—captured the sense of anguish. "Of course, I am against communism, or anything tainted with red," Thurmond wrote, "but many people in this Country are getting desperate, and unless some way is furnished whereby the unemployed can get work and people can buy what they need to eat and wear, I fear our Government will soon witness a complete change of views on government, and we will have the same menace that Russia has."[3]

Will's fear of communism taking hold in the cotton fields sounds fanciful in retrospect, a clue perhaps to his son's penchant for Communist conspiracy theories. Yet the vagaries of capitalist markets were no abstraction for southern cotton farmers. Few Americans experienced more directly the pain of economic volatility. Each year southern farmers were held hostage by the complex of factors that determined the price their crop would bring. The fluctuations from year to year could be severe. In 1929 southern farmers got sixteen cents a pound for their crop. Two years earlier it had been twenty cents; four years later it would be six. Only once during the decade from 1928 to 1938 did the price of cotton change less than 10 percent between pickings. In one five-year stretch it moved over 40 percent three times—twice down, only once up.[4]

Given the economic circumstances, it is no surprise that Strom Thurmond was a devoted admirer of Franklin Roosevelt. Almost everybody else in South Carolina was. In 1932, Roosevelt carried the state with 98 percent of the vote. During his one full term in the South Carolina State Senate, Thurmond was an ardent New Dealer. The youngest member of the state senate, he was one of the earliest and most enthusiastic supporters of the Clarks Hill Dam project, a regional-planning effort for the nearby Savannah River. He was also a fervent advocate of public schooling, not surprising given his background as a superintendent. He proposed an increase in teacher salaries and an extension of the school term, measures to be paid for by diverting beer tax revenue to the state school fund.[5]

Thurmond was particularly concerned about matters of dollars and cents. He was punctilious about his personal finances, lest any home folks get the idea that he was using public office to enrich himself. He introduced a bill to cut the salaries of state officials, tried to reduce fees for hunting and automobile licenses, cut interest rates, and extended time for paying taxes.[6]

In Jim Crow South Carolina, issues of finance were never divorced from those of race. Thurmond favored a bill to exempt Ku Klux Klan property from taxation. He also authored a continuing resolution to "use only white people" as attachés, helpers, porters, and servants at the state capitol and other state buildings. This was not about limiting contact between the races—Thurmond personally employed African American domestics and chauffeurs for decades—but rather about ensuring that state funds benefited the white unemployed first.[7]

His position on the use of federal funds was similar. Thurmond backed federal relief programs, yet his support stopped at the color line. In an open letter to the "Young Men of Edgefield County," Thurmond publicized free training offered at the National Youth Administration (NYA) Vocational Camp near Columbia for "any young white men of good character."[8] He also fought to have a proposed Negro-designated Civilian Conservation Corps camp slated for Edgefield County reclassified for white men, an effort motivated by both racial and local economic concerns.[9]

None of these positions are surprising given the racial politics of the South in the 1930s. Southern congressmen were among the most devoted supporters of New Deal largesse, yet they never failed to safeguard the prerogatives of Jim Crow. Categories of work in which African Americans were heavily represented, notably farmworkers and maids, were excluded in the 1930s from laws that created modern unions, set minimum wages and maximum work hours, and instituted Social Security. Southern congressmen ensured that local officials administered New Deal programs, and they defeated efforts to include antidiscrimination provisions in New Deal legislation.

Strom Thurmond was among the state officials who ensured that whites got the lion's share of New Deal benefits. Later, as a senator, he would denounce federal welfare spending as politically motivated profligacy, the institutionalization of a federal dole that reeked of socialism, undermined personal initiative, and created unproductive wards of the state. Absent from his later harangues, however, was any mention of how federal benefits had been racially skewed toward whites in the 1930s and '40s. Back then, when the beneficiaries of federal dollars were, as Thurmond wrote in his NYA advertisement, "young white men of good character," federal welfare went unquestioned.

Over the course of the 1930s, race was increasingly becoming a point of contention between white southerners and national Democratic leaders. As a candidate and during his first term in office, Franklin Roosevelt was careful not to offend powerful white southerners. As his reelection campaign approached, however, he took steps that moderated the role of the South in party affairs and opened the door to greater black participation.

Both moves could be seen at the 1936 Democratic National Convention in Philadelphia, which Strom Thurmond attended as a delegate and member of the credentials committee.[10] Northern and western delegates succeeded in rescinding the rule requiring presidential and vice-presidential nominees to receive a two-thirds vote of delegates, which for the past half century had given the "Solid South" virtual veto power over the Democratic presidential nomination.[11] The Dixiecrat leader Charles Wallace Collins would recall that the loss of the two-thirds rule, in combination with the rising strength of African Americans and labor groups within Democratic Party circles, made 1936 "a black year for southern politics."[12]

The 1936 convention witnessed the first of many party showdowns on racial matters, and the South Carolina delegation played a starring role. The state's senior senator, Ellison "Cotton Ed" Smith, walked out of the convention after an African American pastor opened an afternoon session with prayer. Coaxed into returning, Smith walked out a second time when the African American congressman Arthur W. Mitchell of Chicago, the first black Democrat elected to Congress, addressed the convention. Only two other South Carolina delegates accompanied Smith, but the rest of the delegation, including Thurmond, joined in a resolution protesting the presence of Negroes on the convention program.[13]

Smith's walkout foreshadowed a more serious confrontation two years later. Described as "the Senate's No. 1 mossback," "the last of the spittoon Senators," and a "conscientious objector to the twentieth century," Smith was among the southern conservatives who had joined

Republicans in frustrating many New Deal priorities.[14] In the 1938 midterm elections, President Roosevelt used his considerable popularity in the South to try to unseat both Smith and Senator Walter George of Georgia. In South Carolina, Roosevelt backed Governor Olin Johnston, the hero of the state's up-country mill workers and a devoted follower of the president's "humanitarian" policies. Johnston was invited to the White House to announce his candidacy. In August 1938, on his way back to Washington from his summer vacation in Warm Springs, Georgia, Roosevelt's train stopped in Greenville, where the president's brief remarks included an oblique swipe at Smith. Late in the race, the president issued a supportive statement from Hyde Park, New York, but it would not be enough for Johnston. Cotton Ed Smith won reelection, as did Walter George in Georgia.

The reelection of the two anti–New Deal southerners was a blow to Roosevelt's prestige. It was also an ominous sign of the reservoir of resentment that could be tapped when white southerners sensed that northern outsiders—even the beloved Roosevelt—were meddling in their affairs. Smith celebrated his victory with a group of red-shirt-clad supporters at the foot of the Wade Hampton statue on the state capitol grounds.[15]

Strom Thurmond voted for Cotton Ed Smith, though he was fortunate that he was not expected to endorse a candidate. Earlier that year he had begun his new post as judge of the Eleventh Judicial Circuit. The position had opened up the previous year when Judge C. J. Ramage passed away unexpectedly. Thurmond's move to the bench surprised many people. Political observers had pegged him as an aspirant for the Governor's Mansion, not the court.[16]

On the face of things, Thurmond's move looked ill-advised. The chairman of the state highway commission, George Bell Timmerman, was expected to pursue Ramage's seat. In South Carolina, the legislature elected circuit judges, and few officials had more sway among that group than the highway commissioner, who had discretion to place lucrative projects in legislators' home districts. The power that Timmerman wielded was arguably greater than that of the governor.[17] Yet

Thurmond was so tireless in lining up support that in the end Timmerman decided not to make the race.

Where others saw isolation and uncertainty, Thurmond spied opportunity. Years later he would explain his pursuit of the bench as part of the groundwork he laid for his eventual gubernatorial run. Circuit judges rotated among various districts, he explained, allowing him to spend weeks at a time in county seats across South Carolina. Local newspapers covered his speeches opening and closing court sessions. During recesses he dined with important contacts and acquaintances, winning friends among the network of local politicians who populated county courthouses. Robert Figg, a Charleston lawyer who would become one of Thurmond's closest political advisers, recalled how during lunch breaks Thurmond would go to the YMCA to shake hands with groups of future voters. "I'm Strom Thurmond," he told them. "I'm the Judge holding Court down there . . . Someday I want you to remember, I'm going to be running for Governor."[18]

If Francis Butler Simkins is to be believed, however, Thurmond had another reason to seek the judgeship. Simkins's unpublished memoir recorded that Stone Stoopes had relinquished his senate seat because of fading popularity back home. He had interfered with the distribution of federal allotments for needy veterans of World War I and had appointed too many of his kin to patronage positions. There were more intimate mistakes as well. "Instead of drinking liquor and visiting the whore house of Augusta with other young men," Simkins wrote, "[Stone] went about trying to be familiar with some of the best girls of the community." Also, as superintendent of education, Stone had "aroused the blood of self-respecting elements" when he appointed as teacher the unqualified "Linda Long," a woman who, it was said, could barely read.[19]

Linda Long was another of Simkins's pseudonyms. Her real name was Sue Logue, and she was one of the most scandalous figures from Thurmond's past. In January 1943, Logue became the first woman ever to be executed by electric chair in the state of South Carolina. She was convicted of having contracted the murder of Davis W. Timmerman, an Edgefield neighbor who had killed her husband, Wallace Logue, but was acquitted on grounds of self-defense. The feud between the Logues and the Timmermans, two old and well-established Edgefield families, would eventually claim nine lives.[20]

Sue's loathing of Timmerman had begun years before, when she lost her job as a teacher at the local school. Strom Thurmond's appointment of Logue several years earlier had sharply divided the community. Logue had only a sixth-grade education. A schoolteacher's job in a rural county like Edgefield in the midst of the Depression was a coveted position. While some people liked Sue, others found her incompetent, "secretive," and "conniving." It was said that she ran around too much with her brother-in-law George. The handsome young superintendent Thurmond was also noted as a frequent companion.[21]

Illicit affections were the subtext of an incident that when told straight—without the wink or knowing smile with which some folks in Edgefield recounted it—became part of the lore of the noble and daring Citizen Thurmond. On a Sunday morning in November 1941, word got around of a grisly showdown at the Logue farm. The Edgefield County sheriff, himself a cousin of the Logues', went unarmed to arrest Sue, her brother-in-law George, and a devoted sharecropper, Fred Dorn, for conspiring in the murder of Davis Timmerman. He and a deputy were admitted into the house only to be ambushed. The sheriff was killed on the spot. The deputy, despite wounds that shortly claimed his life, returned fire, wounding George Logue and killing Dorn.[22]

Judge Thurmond immediately drove to the Logue farm, where a large and unruly crowd had gathered outside the house. Ambulances had carted off the wounded, but Sue Logue remained inside. The crowd outside grew restless over the murder of the popular Edgefield sheriff. Thurmond sensed the tension and the potential for further violence. As he approached the house, a man's voice inside yelled, "Don't come in, Strom, or we'll have to kill you." Thurmond turned out his pockets and opened his vest to show that he was not carrying a weapon. Insisting on speaking to Sue, Thurmond was finally told to come around the back, where an unidentified "cross-eyed fellow" carrying a shotgun met him. Thurmond forcefully told the man to put down the gun and to tell Sue that he wanted to see her immediately. Permitted entrance, Thurmond eventually convinced Sue to turn herself over to the police. An onlooker noticed how the judge grasped Sue's hand as he talked with her. A photographer from *The Augusta Herald* captured Thurmond leading Sue Logue out of the house, flanked by a law officer on either side.[23]

For Thurmond's first biographer, the incident was the metaphorical origin point for a lifetime of valor: "The hero of that hour, Strom Thurmond, has been walking into one 'no man's land' or another ever since."[24] Later biographers, however, noted the gossip about Thurmond and Sue Logue that followed him the rest of his career. The whispered talk about Sue Logue and others helps to sketch the young Thurmond as a small-town Lothario not particularly mindful of women other than to fulfill his basic sexual appetite. He pursued their affections with the same bluntness, determination, and self-interestedness with which he went after votes from fellow legislators. During his time in the state senate, he was said to have a "shady reputation" among the ladies of Columbia. A political aide who double-dated with Thurmond remembered him as "persistent" with women; another recalled that he always had to drive because "Strom needed both hands in the back seat."[25]

To an oral history interviewer in the 1970s, Thurmond explained his prolonged bachelorhood in practical terms. "I could go and come," he said. "I wouldn't be tied down, because I felt sooner or later I'd go into politics . . . I could make more contacts—if I'd had a wife it'd hold you back."[26] He pointed out that he had a mother and sister both at home in Edgefield who fed him and looked after his clothes and other domestic needs. Whatever other necessities Thurmond had at this point in his life, he met elsewhere.

Four days after the Japanese attack on Pearl Harbor on December 7, 1941, Judge Thurmond took a leave of absence from the court to enlist in the U.S. Army. He performed various tasks stateside until October 1943, when he was assigned to the Civil Affairs Division of the headquarters, First Army. His unit was made up of a number of accomplished professionals all similar in age. They worked with civilian populations in establishing local government and resettling displaced populations in the wake of Allied troop advances. Thurmond was distinguished among them for his particular loathing of "desk work." When the unit needed three volunteers to join lead troops in the long-planned invasion of the French mainland, Thurmond was the first to raise his hand.

He and two other Civil Affairs volunteers were assigned to glider units attached to the Eighty-Second Airborne Division. Little more than steel frames covered with canvas, the gliders were towed by C-47s and packed with men, antitank guns, artillery, medical supplies, and a trailer or a jeep. The crafts were morbidly referred to as "flying coffins" by the men assigned to them, and for good reason. A demonstration flight at a St. Louis airfield had ended with a wing falling off, sending the glider into a nosedive that killed the executives and dignitaries onboard, including the St. Louis mayor. Adding to the danger were the anticipated landing zones in Normandy, small fields divided by dense hedgerows that proved doubly hazardous as obstacles to be avoided in the crash landing and as enemy cover. German troops had spiked many of the fields with tree stumps and steel bars, some of them rigged to mines and other explosives. Invasion planners estimated that glider casualties could be as high as 70 percent.[27]

On the night of D-day, June 6, 1944, Thurmond was in a column of gliders that passed over Utah Beach at roughly 2100 hours. About twenty minutes later, after the column experienced heavy anti-aircraft fire, the gliders were released from their tows. Thurmond's glider broke up during the landing, but all the men survived. Despite a severely bruised knee and several cuts, Thurmond helped release a jeep that was onboard and met up with several men from gliders that had landed nearby. He led a reconnaissance party of other nearby gliders. Under constant fire for the next twenty-four hours, the men finally managed to break through to division headquarters. Later, Thurmond helped provide reconnaissance on the nearby town of Cherbourg. During that mission, he and another officer captured four German paratroopers.[28]

Thurmond's unit subsequently accompanied combat troops at the Battle of the Bulge. On V-E day he was near Leipzig, Germany, close to the Buchenwald concentration camp. Years later he remembered entering the camp and seeing "men stacked up like cordwood, ten or twelve feet high. You couldn't tell whether they were living or dead."[29] After a leave back home in South Carolina, he was transferred to the Pacific theater. News of the Japanese surrender came down only a few days after he had reached his new assignment on the island of Luzon. He stayed on in Manila for several more weeks, only to be back in Edgefield before the end of the fall. For his service, he was awarded five battle stars and eighteen decorations, medals, and awards, including the Legion of Merit, the Bronze Star, the Purple Heart, and the French Croix de Guerre.[30]

It was a valiant record of service in a war that would define America's sense of moral purpose in the world for decades to come. The war also had implications for life at home. For some Americans, the fight against fascist totalitarianism in Europe and Asia carried out with an American military that conformed to Jim Crow standards created a new sense of urgency in resolving the "American dilemma" of racial inequality. Thurmond was not among them, nor were the vast majority of white southerners.

World War II sparked political activism among African Americans, yet with it came white backlash. Black soldiers chafed under the indignities suffered in training bases across the South. In 1943 racial violence between black and white soldiers broke out at three southern camps. Black leaders campaigned for a double victory, against fascism abroad and racism at home. A breakthrough came with the executive order that President Roosevelt signed in 1941 instituting the Fair Employment Practices Committee. Though weak in regulatory powers, it set in motion a battle over racial equality in the workplace that would be a defining issue in the civil rights movement. Yet even the mildest efforts to win jobs for blacks sparked reprisals from white workers.

A million and a half southern blacks left the region for war-industry jobs throughout the country, making the racial tensions national in scope. White-dominated unions shut out black workers, and white workers led hate strikes against plants that hired blacks. On the West Coast, whites agitated for the internment of Japanese Americans and assaulted black and Latino men during the Zoot Suit Riots in the summer of 1943. The worst violence took place that same summer in Detroit, when an argument at a crowded amusement park boiled over into a race war that left thirty-four people dead and hundreds injured.[31]

Like most Americans, Strom Thurmond took away from World War II lessons about the dangers of totalitarianism and the need for vigilance against threats abroad. These were his twin themes at an Armistice Day address in North Augusta in November 1945.[32] And as was the case for many Americans, his belief in the necessity of maintaining racial segregation survived the war intact.

In South Carolina, the war sparked renewed determination to preserve white supremacy. The Supreme Court's 1944 decision in the case of *Smith v. Allwright* ruled that a Texas law barring blacks from participating in Democratic Party primary elections violated the Constitution.[33] The decision jeopardized white primary laws throughout the region, and South Carolina was one of the first states to take action. To an emergency session of the state assembly Governor Olin Johnston declared, "We will maintain white supremacy, let the chips fall where they may."[34]

Thurmond had hardly been discharged from the army in October 1945 before he started running for governor. Catching a ride home from Fort Bragg, North Carolina, with a fellow GI, he had the man stop at two or three places along the way so that he could shake hands.[35] He resumed his work on the bench, but rallies and memorials honoring returning veterans provided opportunities for informal campaigning.[36] When not in court, he traveled the state to meet local politicos and line up support.[37] By the time he officially announced his candidacy in May 1946, ten other candidates had joined the race for the Democratic nomination, the only election that mattered.

Thurmond had been waiting to run for governor since he was nine years old, when he had witnessed Cole Blease decimate Ira Jones. His campaign drew stylistic elements from Blease and Jones alike. Jones's legacy showed in the candidate's idealistic talk of economic development and governmental reform. The first speech of his campaign harked back to the "business progressivism" of earlier decades, yet it also captured the buoyant postwar mood.[38] Thurmond vowed to take advantage of the state's natural resources, attract new industries, build new highways, increase trade nationally and internationally, and raise the standard of living.[39] He and his adviser Robert Figg talked about how to develop the state "in a business and industrial way" so as not to lose the most ambitious of the twenty thousand veterans returning to South Carolina.[40]

Figg and Thurmond complemented each other well. They had met in Columbia in 1934 when Thurmond was in the senate and Figg served a term in the statehouse. Figg was renowned as perhaps the best young lawyer in the state, and as a judge Thurmond had frequently sought his advice in difficult cases.[41] Figg had served as solicitor of the Ninth Judicial District of South Carolina, but his claim to fame came defending the all-white school board in Clarendon County. The case would eventually wind up before the U.S. Supreme Court, where Figg defended the South's segregated school system in a series of school cases that would become immortalized as *Brown v. Board of Education*.

Despite his progressive economic platform, Thurmond's harangues over the "Barnwell Ring" reeked of Bleasism. The two most powerful figures in South Carolina politics, Senator Edgar Brown, chairman of the senate finance committee, and Solomon Blatt, Speaker of the House, both hailed from tiny Barnwell County, roughly fifty miles south of Edgefield. Thurmond turned them into the central villains in his purported drive to restore government to the people. At the first joint campaign appearance of all eleven candidates, Thurmond opened with an attack on "ring rule" and the "small group of scheming politicians" who allegedly ran the state for their own aggrandizement.

Like all forms of Bleasism, it was as savvy as it was unsavory. It gave Thurmond a rhetorical issue with which to distinguish himself in an overcrowded field. Brown and Blatt had never been charged with wrongdoing, and Thurmond never provided any examples. But given their power and long tenure in office, the pair had created numerous enemies. The effort corresponded with Thurmond's reform themes by appealing to the advocates of a more modern state government. In South Carolina, the governor held little power in comparison to the legislature; there was scant authority over appointments and even less control over state finances. Thurmond's call for a more powerful executive that could defend the people's interests against entrenched powers also exerted collateral damage on one of Thurmond's chief rivals, the current governor, Ransome J. Williams, who had inherited the office as lieutenant governor a year earlier, when Olin Johnston took a seat in the U.S. Senate.[42]

Talk of governmental reform dovetailed with "G.I. rebellions" taking place across the South. Relatively young, energetic war veterans won several high-profile contests over the entrenched power of older men. Alabamans elected the thirty-seven-year-old "Big Jim" Folsom, who instituted a progressive program of old-age pensions, road development, and legislative reapportionment. In neighboring Georgia, James V. Carmichael, the candidate endorsed by the reformist governor Ellis Arnall, won a plurality of the popular vote but narrowly lost the election to the reactionary Eugene Talmadge.[43]

Viewed decades later, the Barnwell Ring tactic would seem like an ingenious and relatively harmless bit of sloganeering. Yet it was also an early indication of Thurmond's ruthlessness. The evidence suggests that Thurmond had sought the two men's endorsement and, failing to get it, decided to make them the object of attack.[44] Invoking his war record, Thurmond compared the Barnwell crowd to the "gangs" of "scheming, conniving, selfish men" who had gained power in Germany and Italy. "I was willing to risk my life to stamp out such gangs in Europe," Thurmond said. "I intend to devote my future to wiping out the stench and stain with which the Barnwell ring has smeared the government of South Carolina."[45] The Nazi analogy was tasteless, not least of all because Blatt was one of only a handful of Jews who had found success in southern politics. Here, in his first major political campaign, Thurmond followed a pattern pioneered by demagogues past that he would use again: he identified an enemy against which he could pose as the defender of "the people," and he vilified it with vague and hyperbolic charges.

Thurmond finished first in the eleven-man race and faced a runoff election against James McLeod, a doctor from Florence and president of the South Carolina Medical Association.[46] This campaign proved to be the only time in his career that Thurmond was the more liberal candidate in the race. He labeled McLeod a "mossback conservative," a charge stemming from McLeod's participation in the effort at the 1944 Democratic National Convention to remove Roosevelt from the Democratic ticket.[47] McLeod responded by linking Thurmond with dangerous leftists.

He received a windfall in this regard about a week before the election. The United Press ran a brief item noting that the local Congress of Industrial Organizations (CIO) textile union in Columbia endorsed Thurmond. The state headquarters of the CIO made no formal endorsement, but the Columbia office said that most of the locals had given unofficial indications that their members would vote for Thurmond.[48]

Thurmond had a progressive labor record from his days in the South Carolina Senate, yet labor groups' active support of him developed almost accidentally. Several years earlier he had been asked to sit with the South Carolina Supreme Court in hearing a case involving the Textile Workers Union of America (TWUA) and the right of workers to ask employers to deduct union dues from their paychecks. It was a high-profile case, and Thurmond, always on the lookout for ways to impress, wanted to take the initiative in drafting a decision and circulating it among the justices in hopes of becoming the lead author. As he frequently did in important cases, Thurmond turned to Robert Figg, who wrote a decision under Thurmond's name that sided with the TWUA. A majority of the justices eventually signed on to a rival decision, however, making Thurmond's brief the dissenting opinion. During the runoff election, the McLeod campaign made an issue of Thurmond's dissent, presenting him as an enemy to business interests, which only further endeared him to labor.[49]

The CIO endorsement was potentially devastating. By far the most controversial union operating in the South, the organization was in the midst of implementing a region-wide unionization drive, Operation Dixie, that met with vicious repression by business interests and local law enforcement. They tarred the CIO as socialists and integrationists, raising the specter of white women being forced to work in crowded mills alongside black men.[50]

Thurmond stayed mum about the CIO news for several days. Denouncing the organization would only cost him those votes and potentially alienate other labor groups. But as the reaction among his supporters spread, Thurmond issued a statement refuting the "false, slanderous, anonymous circulars" that declared him the candidate of the CIO.[51] The Friday before the election, McLeod bought statewide radio time to express his shock that Thurmond had waited so long to distance himself from the group.[52]

In this, the most significant crisis in the biggest campaign of his life to date, Thurmond returned to his roots. The CIO controversy was just a proxy, as everyone in South Carolina knew, for the issue of white supremacy. Thurmond dismissed McLeod's speech as the eleventh-hour obfuscations of a desperate man. Rejecting the implication that as governor he would "be in sympathy with the [CIO] and Communistic policies, especially in relation to racial matters," Thurmond stood on his Edgefield heritage, reminding South Carolinians that it was the county that had bequeathed "great statesmen" such as Ben Tillman, Mart Gary, and many others. "Everyone knows how we in Edgefield stand on this question," he said.[53] The son-of-Edgefield defense, combined with his tireless efforts across the state, enabled a comfortable victory.[54]

It was a cold, clear day in January 1947 when forty-four-year-old Strom Thurmond was sworn in as governor of South Carolina. The wintry sunshine provided little relief to the crowd of three thousand gathered on the north steps of the state capitol.[55] The speech was too long and the weather too cold for Thurmond to deliver it in full, but the unabridged fifteen-thousand-word version that he submitted for the official record remains a remarkable document for the outspokenly progressive positions that he staked out on some of the most vexing issues in South Carolina politics.

In the weeks following his victory, Thurmond had asked Walter Brown, one of the most respected South Carolina political operatives of the day, to help him with his inaugural address. Brown, a confidant of the former South Carolina senator James F. Byrnes who later joined Byrnes's staff when he served as U.S. secretary of state, worked closely on the speech with Bob Figg.[56] It was the beginning of a close triangular friendship—the men would come to refer to one another as "the Three Musketeers"—that sustained Thurmond throughout his governorship and beyond.[57]

The speech Brown and Figg wrote says more about Thurmond's style and temperament than his ideology. Thurmond came into the governorship with the same energy and aggressiveness with which he had entered the state senate. He was the maverick unafraid of entrenched powers, and he had an inaugural address to prove it. Thurmond called for a laundry list of overdue reforms in state government—among them, an end to dual office holding and to the pardoning power of the governor, merit pay for state employees, and the secret ballot in general elections. The two points most often remembered from the speech were his positions on race. He urged the abolition of the poll tax and that "more attention be given" to Negro education.[58] For later profile writers, they provided an ironic detail: the Dixiecrat presidential candidate who used to be a racial liberal. Thurmond's defenders cited them as evidence of a relative racial progressiveness for which Thurmond did not get credit.[59]

In retrospect, however, given his bedrock support for business and free enterprise during the last half century of his career, the most extraordinary aspect of Thurmond's inaugural and first year as governor was his positions on labor. Thurmond called for a state minimum-wage law, elevators and air-conditioning in textile mills and other industrial plants, and a new workers' compensation law for the victims of "occupational disease."[60] His first year as governor coincided with a watershed year in the history of business-labor relations. In June, Congress overrode Harry Truman's veto of the Taft-Hartley Act, which neutered many of the labor laws passed under the New Deal. Among its provisions was a clause that allowed individual states to pass "right to work" laws, statutes that banned the union shop, the practice where employees were required to sign up with the union. South Carolina joined the trend of primarily southern and western states by passing a right-to-work law in 1954.

Balancing the support of labor with his goals for South Carolina's economic development was one of the more difficult tasks that Governor Thurmond faced. He continued to dip into the New Deal–era rhetorical handbag to defend "the people" against greedy private business interests. During the gubernatorial runoff election, he put his conservative foe on the defensive by coming out strongly against private development of the Savannah River.[61] As governor, he denounced the opponents of the nation's water development as "bulwarks of wealth and private interest."[62] And in September 1947, in a statement read by an aide at the opening of a real estate executives meeting in Myrtle Beach, Thurmond denounced "profiteering real estate owners" and pledged his support for rent controls. The president of the National Association of Real Estate Boards expressed his shock at hearing the governor of South Carolina sounding like a "communist."[63]

These rhetorical flourishes, however, belied the reality of Thurmond's and most every postwar southern governor's obsession with attracting outside industry. The late 1940s seemed like a world away from the dismal days of the Depression. In the postwar years the majority of American liberals came to stress "economic growth rather than redistribution, consensus rather than conflict between the 'economic royalists' and the working man."[64] In the South, this gave rise to "new Whig" leadership, southern politicians who pursued federal money and economic development as the region's panacea. As governor, Thurmond was one of the region's most energetic and effective advocates of industrial development, a distinction rarely remembered by his supporters or detractors.[65]

As a state senator in the 1930s, Thurmond had described himself as a "friend to capital but more of a friend to labor."[66] As governor, the roles slowly reversed. Over the course of his administration, Thurmond developed a love affair with business. Even in his earliest days in office, he listed industrial growth alongside governmental reform as his two top priorities.[67] And really the one was in service to the other: Thurmond wanted a more modern executive branch that could more efficiently direct the state's economic growth.[68]

His fixation on industrial development manifested itself in an early squabble over railroad freight rates.[69] The issue had been the bane of the white South, particularly in the years following President Roosevelt's designation of the region as the "nation's number one economic problem."[70] Southerners contended that freight rates set by the Interstate Commerce Commission (ICC) functioned essentially as a trade barrier that protected northern manufacturing and discouraged southern industrial development. The rate charged to ship high-cost finished goods from the South was 39 percent higher than the one charged to ship similar goods from the North. The South enjoyed favorable commodity rates compared with the North only on agricultural products and raw materials.[71] In 1945 the ICC agreed with southerners' complaint and ordered freight-rate equalization across regions, leading to a showdown in the Supreme Court.

"South Carolina wants to be on a parity—not getting any preferences but merely on a parity—with other states," Thurmond maintained. "The Confederate War is over and we want to be treated like the other states."[72] In a landmark decision in May 1947, the Court endorsed the South's position.[73] The freight-rate decision—in combination with right-to-work laws and, by the 1950s, Cold War military spending— was a milestone in the postwar transformation of southern industry.

Early on the morning of February 17, 1947—not a full month into Strom Thurmond's term as governor—a mob of thirty-five white men descended upon the small brick jailhouse in Pickens, South Carolina, and absconded with a black prisoner named Willie Earle. The previous day Earle had been arrested in connection with the fatal stabbing of a white taxi driver in nearby Greenville. The men brutally carved away a part of Earle's face, stabbing him numerous times in the chest before shooting him in the head three times. They dumped his body several miles outside Pickens, where it was discovered only a few hours later.[74]

Almost all of the members of the mob were associated with Greenville taxi companies. All but 5 of the roughly 150 cabdrivers in the city were white, but taxis were not segregated by law. In the weeks leading up to the murder, there had been a series of beatings and robberies of white drivers.[75] Black riders were blamed for the attacks, and the mob that kidnapped Willie Earle was determined to make him an example.

The lynching of Willie Earle and the subsequent indictment of thirty-one white men on murder charges culminated in what one source described as "the biggest lynching trial in the history of the South."[76] Reporters flocked to Greenville, including Rebecca West, who created an indelible portrait of a small southern city in crisis in her classic *New Yorker* essay "Opera in Greenville."[77] Strom Thurmond's denunciation of the lynch mob and his role in bringing the men to trial led *The Christian Science Monitor* to hail him as one of the South's "young voices crying in the cold."[78] It was a remarkable label for a man who in little over a year would become the head of the region's most reactionary political forces. The disjunction is assuaged, however, when one considers more closely the tumultuous politics of race in the post–World War II South.

The Earle lynching coincided with an alarming rise in incidents of white racial violence following the war. The Tuskegee Institute recorded six lynchings in 1946, a notable increase given the general decline in the practice since the mid-1930s. Many incidents involved returning African American servicemen such as Isaac Woodard. He was pulled off a Greyhound bus in Batesburg, South Carolina, after a verbal dispute with the driver. Local police gouged Woodard's eyes with the butt of their nightsticks, leaving him blind.[79]

The most notorious lynching of 1946—and the one most likely to have influenced Strom Thurmond's reaction in the Willie Earle case— occurred in neighboring Georgia that summer. Near the tiny town of Monroe, about forty-five miles east of Atlanta, an unmasked group of fifteen to twenty men shot and killed four African Americans, two women and two men, one of whom was a war veteran recently returned from the Pacific.[80] The Monroe murders sparked outrage across the nation and prompted reinvigorated drives for a federal antilynching law.[81] The murders played a major role in President Truman's executive order creating the Committee on Civil Rights.[82]

Harmful as the lynchings were to Georgia's image, the investigation shone a positive light on that state's chief executive, Ellis Arnall, who despite a race-baiting campaign had emerged as a relatively progressive governor. The Monroe lynching had occurred on the heels of the fierce gubernatorial primary election in which Eugene Talmadge had defeated Arnall's handpicked successor.[83] Arnall strongly condemned the murders, pledged a vigorous inquiry by the Georgia Bureau of Investigation, and raised thousands of dollars as a reward for information leading to an arrest.[84]

In the Earle case, Thurmond followed the lead of his Georgia colleague. Like Arnall, he sensed how closely the rest of the country tracked issues of southern justice. The Earle lynching was a "disgrace to the state," he declared. Thurmond vowed to exert "every ounce of my energy in apprehending those guilty of such crimes."[85] He sent the state constabulary to Greenville to work with local law enforcement and the Federal Bureau of Investigation, which Attorney General Tom Clark had sent to investigate possible civil rights violations. Ordering state officials to stay on the job until "every guilty person was arrested or every clue exhausted," he was pleased when officials announced in late February the arrest of thirty-one men in connection with the murder.[86] Thurmond named as lead prosecutor Solicitor Sam R. Watt of Spartanburg, renowned for his record the previous year of having convicted 471 of the 473 persons he had brought to trial.[87]

John Popham of *The New York Times* hailed the quick arrests and indictments of the thirty-one white men as a "red-letter day in the South Carolina courts." State officials had acted with "high-minded courage," he wrote, and no one deserved more credit than Thurmond, who had "earned the enmity of the purveyors of race hatred."[88] Indeed, Thurmond received dozens of cretinous letters from such elements. One of the most chilling was an anonymous note typed on his own gubernatorial letterhead. "It pay you to keep your D—— mouth shut," the letter read. "I shot the dam negro with over 2 barrel shot gun U deserve same thing if U go for enough don't U think U cant be got Hope your mother or your sister will be nex to be raped."[89]

Missives of this sort were outnumbered by letters of praise from civil rights leaders, labor union heads, and ministers in South Carolina. The African American civil rights leader Modjeska Simkins used her nationally syndicated column to laud Thurmond's decisive action, quoting at length his statement denouncing the lynchers.[90] Thurmond received a glowing letter from the African American newspaperman Osceola E. McKaine, and the author James McBride Dabbs, South Carolina's best-known white liberal, praised Thurmond's "statesman-like attitude."[91]

Admirable as Thurmond's actions certainly were, they were part of a calculated white southern rebuttal in a decades-long debate over southern violence and federal law. Since the 1920s, northern liberals in Congress had pushed a federal antilynching statute, which a united and powerful southern delegation had successfully thwarted.[92] Thurmond and other white southerners were well aware of the momentum the brutal acts in Monroe and Greenville gave to antilynching forces. With the arrests and indictments, Thurmond surpassed even Arnall in making good on white southerners' long-standing claim that they were capable of enforcing the law and that a federal lynch law was a dangerous affront to constitutional guarantees of state authority.

To truly make the point, however, South Carolina officials would have to win a conviction, which they were unable to do. Despite the fact that twenty-six of the men had given statements to the FBI in which they had allegedly admitted their involvement in the crime, in May a jury of twelve white men acquitted the defendants of all charges. Within the week, the South Carolina NAACP called for federal intervention in the case, and the South Carolina Progressive Democratic Party, a recently organized group that challenged Jim Crow voting laws, and the vice president of the National Lawyers Guild cited the Earle case as a prime example of why federal antilynching legislation was necessary.[93]

Thurmond's performance in the Earle case reaffirmed his image as a postwar progressive reformer. News articles noted his heroic service in World War II. His public statements read like the forward-thinking pronouncements of a man whose understanding of southern race relations had been tempered by his own wartime experiences. "We in South Carolina want the world to know that we will tolerate no mob violence," he proclaimed.[94]

That he would be concerned about South Carolina's image abroad owed not merely to his service in the war. Until recently, South Carolina's own James Byrnes, a good friend of Will Thurmond's and a mentor to Strom, had served as the U.S. secretary of state. He was America's chief advocate of democracy and self-determination abroad, and race relations in Byrnes's native South had been a subject of national and international attention. Handbills circulated in Charleston pointing out that while "Secretary of State Byrnes is trying to teach the Bulgarians democracy, only two out of ten people in his home state take part in elections."[95] During delicate negotiations over human rights and the formation of the United Nations, the prospect of the United States coming under investigation for antidemocratic practices in South Carolina or Mississippi was a legitimate concern to American policy makers.[96] When Thurmond talked about letting the world know that South Carolinians did not tolerate mob violence, it was in part because he knew how closely the world was watching.

Though the Cold War would create an important new dynamic in southern race relations, Thurmond's reaction in the Earle case was rooted most firmly in his past. Thurmond's actions were part of an implicit, long-standing argument among white southerners themselves about violence and the maintenance of white supremacy. It had been around at least as long as Thurmond's earliest political memory, the fateful election of 1912. During that campaign, Ira Jones attacked Cole Blease for his notorious declaration that in some cases he would lead a lynch mob himself. He decried the indignity of the state's chief executive endorsing lawlessness. "Don't make me your governor if that is what you expect of me," Jones declared.[97]

The echo of 1912 could be heard in the Earle case. Thurmond cracked down on a group of vigilante cabdrivers who had given a black eye to the state. Their actions mocked the claims of elite white southerners about their ability to keep law and order. The class tensions that pervaded the white community lay just below the surface of newspaper reports on the trial. After the acquittal, one account noted the "grim satisfaction" that prevailed in working-class textile communities surrounding Greenville. All the while, the city's town fathers scrambled to put a good face on matters, hailing the indictment and trial itself as notable "progress."[98]

Thurmond's noble handling of the Earle case would seem to suggest a road not taken. What if he had continued on this course of enlightened moderation rather than siding with the forces of reaction? Yet Thurmond's performance marked him not as a lost herald of the new order to come but rather as one of the more politically astute defenders of the racial status quo.

Evidence of this can be seen in the two other racially moderate positions that he had staked out in his inaugural address—his calls to dispense with the poll tax and for greater support for black education. By the time Thurmond took office, many southern states had already jettisoned the poll tax. North Carolina, Louisiana, and Florida had all repealed theirs in the 1920s and '30s.[99] Georgia, led by Governor Arnall, had done so in 1945.[100] The Tennessee legislature had tried to rescind its tax two years earlier, only to have the measure voided by the state's supreme court.[101] In each of the last three Congresses, a substantial majority in the House of Representatives had voted to outlaw the poll tax, but the measures died in the Senate.[102] The argument made by Thurmond and other opponents of the tax was that it both was ineffective and made for an easy target. A federal anti-poll-tax law would create a precedent for federal oversight that could undermine other aspects of Jim Crow voting laws.[103]

As for Thurmond's support for black education, it came from the same sense of noblesse oblige that had led him to start moonlight literacy classes for blacks back when he was Edgefield's superintendent of education. He subscribed to the nostrum of elite white southerners that racial conflict would lessen as the economic standing of whites and blacks both improved. Yet Thurmond was also among the first wave of southern leaders who recognized that if the South was going to preserve separate but equal education, then they had better provide some semblance of equality. His closest adviser, Robert Figg, would go much further on this point in subsequent years when he defended Clarendon County in the school desegregation cases.[104]

The Willie Earle case brought Thurmond unprecedented national exposure, all of it positive. He wrote to John Popham of *The New York Times* to thank him for his newspaper's evenhanded coverage. Afterward, he took stock of the political implications with Walter Brown, a good sounding board given Brown's years as a Washington journalist and his close friendship with Turner Catledge, a fellow southerner who was working his way up the editorial ranks at the *Times*. Some parts of Popham's stories "would not be too good for home consumption," Brown advised, but on the whole the coverage in the *Times* "places you in a very good light before the country."[105]

Popham's articles, however, included one howler that worried Brown. In a post-trial piece that contained the most glowing assessments of Thurmond, Popham tied the Earle trial to a lawsuit filed by black South Carolinians that would strike down the Democratic Party's white primary. The article reported black leaders' claim that if Negroes "had primary voting privileges they could easily cancel out any white 'resentment votes' as a Negro gesture of gratitude to Governor Thurmond for the position which he had taken in this case."[106] The idea shook Brown. "Popham got off base on this," Brown assured Thurmond. "Certainly, I do not go along with any idea that we are going to let negroes in our primary."[107]

Neither did Thurmond. By 1947, Jim Crow rule in South Carolina was under legal assault, and Thurmond was clearly on the side of those fighting to preserve the white primary. He had been in the army back in 1944 when Olin Johnston and the state assembly had readied the state for the legal challenges sure to flow from *Smith v. Allwright*, the Supreme Court case that outlawed the white primary in Texas. By the summer of 1947, the implications of the Texas case had become clear in South

Carolina. Two NAACP leaders, James M. Hinton and the newspaper editor John Henry McCray, organized the Progressive Democratic Party. Using *Smith v. Allwright* as precedent, the group challenged the seating of the all-white South Carolina delegation at the 1944 Democratic National Convention in Chicago. Though they failed to gain recognition, the Progressive Democrats received assurances of future help from the national party.[108]

Civil rights groups readied their case and waited for the Democratic primary in August 1946. That was the election in which Thurmond bested ten other candidates for governor. Little noticed at the time was the attempt by George Elmore, an African American merchant in Columbia, to vote in the party primary. The following February, Elmore filed suit in federal court.[109]

In the case that followed, Judge J. Waties Waring sided with Elmore, declaring, "It is time for South Carolina to rejoin the Union. It is time to fall in step with the other states and to adopt the American way of conducting elections."[110] Waring's voting rights decision initiated procedures that would eventually open the South Carolina Democratic Party to significant African American participation, a process that would dramatically affect Thurmond's political career.[111]

Thurmond kept a low profile in the voting rights developments. He was at the National Governors Conference in Salt Lake City delivering an address on defense preparedness when Waring issued his decision. He offered no fiery denunciations, as the South Carolina senator Burnet Maybank did. When he returned home from Utah, Thurmond released a low-key statement on the case, but mainly he kept quiet.[112]

Perhaps Thurmond was trying to avoid a volatile political issue, but he might also have simply been distracted. Among his retinue on the Utah trip was the twenty-one-year-old Jean Crouch, a recent graduate of Winthrop College and a newly hired stenographer in Thurmond's office. Crouch was a native of Barnwell County, and Thurmond knew her family well. The two had met several times at official functions, and Thurmond encouraged her to apply for a job in Columbia. Crouch put in an application for the governor's office. Mindful of the prohibition against intra-office relationships, Thurmond offered a post at a nearby state agency instead. When Crouch expressed her preference to work on the governor's staff, Thurmond took it as a sign of her lack of interest. But matters took a serendipitous turn in Utah, and when they got home, Thurmond started walking Crouch back to her apartment after work. They were married the following November.[113]

Years later Thurmond would recall that it was only after he won the governorship that he felt that he could "take time to get married."[114] Political motivation might have intruded as well. The protocols of his new office required him to regularly attend functions with a female companion. He attended several early events with his mother or sister, but they would not have suited the style that Thurmond hoped to culti-vate. Neither would the Columbia women whom he had cycled through as state senator. Thurmond had yet to finish a full year in the Gover-nor's Mansion before he proposed to Jean. Perhaps the telling fact about the role of romance in his life was that he proposed via inter-office memo. "Anticipating an early reply and hope that it shall be forth-coming as quickly as possible as upon your answer will depend my future happiness," it read. "Again assuring you of my deep love and ex-pressing the hope that the time is not too distant when we can be joined as one and live happily forever."

Thurmond's press secretary released a copy of the letter to *Life* magazine for a profile it was writing on Thurmond as a sign of the gov-ernor's dry humor. Given Thurmond's obsession with his work and career, however, it was hard to be too sure. This was the same magazine profile in which Thurmond would be photographed performing a headstand with his young wife looking on. For years political oppo-nents would mock him for the undignified pose. As with his marriage proposal, the photograph bore unwitting testimony to Thurmond's work habits: he wore a tennis shirt and shorts to match Jean's casual elegance but had neglected to change out of his business socks and dress shoes.[115]

The newlyweds returned from their honeymoon in Florida and Havana in November, two days before arguments began in federal ap-peals court in the South Carolina white primary case.[116] The decision affirmed Waring's ruling: "No election machinery can be upheld if its purpose or effect is to deny the Negro, on account of his race or color, an effective voice in the government of his country or the state or the community wherein he lives." Thurmond provided no comment.[117] The stage was set for one of the defining years of his career.

PART TWO

STATES' RIGHTS DEMOCRAT

3

LOST IN TRANSLATION
(1948)

The sources for white southerners' bolt from the Democratic Party were long in the making, but a critical trigger came on February 2, 1948. President Truman sent a message to Congress urging legislators to implement civil rights measures recommended in the 173-page report *To Secure These Rights*, issued by his Committee on Civil Rights.[1] Reaction in the South was fierce. Franklin Roosevelt had impinged on southern racial mores in dribs and drabs, but now Harry Truman attacked them head-on.

Thurmond responded to the president's speech immediately. Haste was necessary because southern governors were meeting in four days at Wakulla Springs, Florida, for a previously scheduled conference. Thurmond had his aides track down Walter Brown and Robert Figg. Luckily, they were together on a deer hunt in the low country. Thurmond caught them in the middle of a boisterous meal of oyster stew and whiskey, where a well-oiled group had just been discussing how the federals had fired on Fort Sumter again. Thurmond told Brown and Figg that they were needed for the trip to Florida and dispatched a patrol car to retrieve them.[2] En route, Brown devised a plan that would thrust Thurmond to the head of the southern opposition to President Truman.

The official purpose of the Wakulla Springs meeting was to discuss the creation of region-wide institutes of higher learning, but the president's address had created such a stir that the governors went into a closed session, lest it be obvious to the press how clearly politics had trumped policy discussions. Before the meeting, Governor Fielding Wright of Mississippi had been the most vocal leader, urging an immediate party bolt. Brown and Figg wrote a resolution for Thurmond proposing a committee to study the issue. Having suggested the committee, Brown hoped that Thurmond would be named its head.[3]

At 5:00 p.m., reporters and photographers were invited to crowd into a tense, smoke-filled room where they heard Thurmond announce a proposal for a forty-day cooling-off period. It passed by a unanimous voice vote. As Brown had figured, the governors named Thurmond the head of a committee to study the issue and report back its findings.[4] It was a public relations coup. Thurmond's name appeared in the lead paragraphs of the national news stories coming out of Wakulla Springs.[5] In office little over a year, he had already positioned himself as a power broker on the most explosive political issue that the South had faced in the twentieth century.

Upon his return from Florida, Thurmond invited reporters into his office to view the blank space on the wall where previously had hung an autographed picture of President Truman.[6] He drafted letters to all high-ranking public officials across the South soliciting their opinions on how to proceed in the coming election. The craftiness of the cooling-period proposal was that it established Thurmond as an arbiter of southern opinion without committing him to a position. What he quickly realized, however, was that not many white southerners were particularly interested in cooling off.

Editorial opinion and private letters that Thurmond received defended the southern position ferociously. "We have got to have a party controlled, directed, dominated by white people," one South Carolina newspaper wrote.[7] Richard Russell, the powerful Georgia senator considered one of the South's most measured defenders, sounded anything but measured. He called the proposals a "vicious and unwarranted attack" that threatened to "destroy segregation and compel intermingling and miscegenation of the races in the South."[8]

On February 23, Thurmond led a delegation of southern governors to Washington to meet with the national Democratic Party chairman, J. Howard McGrath. It was the most high-profile meeting that Thurmond had ever attended. He was so agitated that he could not bring himself to sit down. He paced the floor, firing questions at McGrath as though he were cross-examining a witness. The party chairman was polite but firm. *Newsweek* described the meeting with a Civil War analogy: McGrath, "puffing a huge Ulysses S. Grant–like cigar," said no so many times that Thurmond and his fellow petitioners "got no further than Gen. George E. Pickett did at Gettysburg."[9]

The McGrath drubbing combined with the vehement and still growing southern reaction threatened to make Thurmond's call for a cooling-off period seem timid. It was a moment of enormous political anxiety across the white South. Southern elected officials walked a narrow line between getting too far out ahead in criticizing President Truman, thus risking their standing with the national party in what was still a one-party South, and dropping too far behind the impassioned response among the electorate. One of the first public criticisms of Thurmond came two days after the McGrath meeting. Without mentioning Thurmond by name, the Birmingham syndicated columnist John Temple Graves proclaimed, "Cooling off is a fine thing but getting steamed up is equally necessary to results."[10] Graves amplified the slight the next day with a column that lavishly praised Fielding Wright, the leader of the hard-liners' alternate resolution in Wakulla Springs.[11]

Thurmond also took stock of how potential rivals in South Carolina were handling the crisis, particularly the U.S. senator Olin Johnston, who was up for reelection in 1950, the same year that Thurmond's term as governor ended. By law, South Carolina governors could not succeed themselves, and the Senate was the obvious next rung on Thurmond's ladder.[12] Years later Thurmond would deny that the States' Rights campaign had anything to do with his 1950 race against Olin Johnston, yet he surely recognized the opportunity that the crisis afforded in distinguishing himself from his up-country rival.[13] Despite being a "coon-shouting white supremacy man," Johnston was also the quintessential southern New Dealer, the best friend to the thousands of white South Carolina mill workers.[14] Leading the South's revolt against Truman and liberal national Democrats was ideal preparation to take on a strict party man like Johnston, something Johnston surely knew as well. He was rightly convinced that Thurmond would challenge him in 1950.[15]

A few weeks after Truman's civil rights address, Johnston made national news when he canceled his reservation for a table at the annual Jefferson-Jackson Day dinner at the Mayflower Hotel in Washington. The $100-a-plate Democratic fund-raiser was to be racially integrated (three African Americans sat together at a table in the rear). Mrs. Johnston, who served as vice-chairwoman of the dinner committee, was concerned "because she might be seated next to a Negro."[16] The senator milked the incident for maximum exposure, inviting reporters to his Washington home to snap photographs of him and Mrs. Johnston eating a quiet dinner alone. Governor Thurmond and his wife canceled their reservations as well, but only Johnston's slight made it into *Time* magazine.[17]

With events threatening to get away from Thurmond, he unveiled a new, more pugnacious approach at the March 1 meeting of the South Carolina Democratic Executive Committee in Columbia. All of South Carolina's major public officials were there, including Johnston. Striking a cautious note, Johnston was hopeful that party leaders "will start something (today) that will work out our problems," but he warned South Carolinians to "watch our step" and "please keep cool."[18] Thurmond spoke directly after Johnston but made no reference to the senator's remarks. He did not have to. "I see no need in holding back," Thurmond told the executive committee. "These proposals advocated by the president constitute an invasion of the right of self-government in the states—the president has gone too far. As far as I am concerned, I'm through with him."[19]

The 1950 Senate race was still two years away, but it was at the Democratic Executive Committee meeting in Columbia that Thurmond fired the first shot. Democratic insiders were already anticipating the Thurmond-Johnston showdown. The two men locked horns again two months later at the state Democratic convention, where they vied to be the keynote speaker, haggled over the South Carolina executive committeeman slot, and supported rival candidates for executive committeewoman.[20]

Thurmond solidified his position in mid-March in a speech broadcast on statewide radio in which he called President Truman "a political accident."[21] Supporters told him it was the best speech he had ever given, while the Charleston newspaper declared that the governor had "surged to the fore in the fight for Southern rights, and promises a strong finish."[22] The *News and Courier* criticized Johnston for being coy about whether the South should bolt from the Democratic Party. By contrast, "J. Strom Thurmond . . . is definite. He is explicit. He has left no guesswork for his constituents . . . He steps in front of Senator Johnston and other official leaders."[23]

Walter Brown and Robert Figg urged Thurmond to "rest on his attained laurels."[24] He had emerged as an important new voice at the regional level, had avoided getting tied up with the rabid forces out of Mississippi and Alabama, and had bested his in-state rival in criticizing the president. Then, in mid-April, "like a bolt out of the blue," Thurmond called Brown to tell him that he had agreed to deliver the keynote address at a meeting of southern Democrats in Mississippi the next month. Ten days earlier he had mentioned to Bob Figg that Governor Wright had contacted him about keynoting the conference, but Figg had dismissed the possibility. Surely Wright would find someone better suited to stir up the hard-liners than the author of the cooling-off resolution, he reasoned. Thurmond surprised Figg by accepting the offer. For his part, Brown supposed that the speech could do no harm, but he remained wary of the Mississippi crowd, which he viewed as extremist and politically naive.[25]

Why Thurmond decided to take the additional step of keynoting the Mississippi meeting is unclear. He was enamored with the regional leadership role he had attained. Perhaps he sensed that if there actually were a third-party movement, he might be able to lead it. Two weeks before the Jackson meeting, the executive committee of the Mississippi Democratic Party endorsed Thurmond for the Democratic presidential nomination. The reception of the news on Capitol Hill, however, was notably cool. Even those who backed a bolt from the party thought that Thurmond was not experienced enough to lead the fight.[26]

Or perhaps Thurmond began to see in the States' Rights effort a larger, national political movement deserving of his commitment. In late March, two prominent former New Dealers, Raymond Moley and Donald Richberg, delivered national radio addresses critical of President Truman's civil rights agenda. Thurmond saved transcripts of the speeches for his files. Moley, an original member of Roosevelt's brain trust who later broke with the president and became a Republican, called the civil rights program "an affront to the intelligent and loyal citizens of a dozen States."[27] Richberg, with an even longer résumé of New Deal accomplishments, denounced the Fair Employment Practices Commission (FEPC) in terms that Thurmond would echo in his presidential campaign: "By ignoring and deliberately violating the Constitution, Congress, in this law, would undertake to establish a national police state. No wonder this anti-discrimination law is a main plank in the communist platform."[28]

Moley and Richberg were part of a business-oriented conservative bloc in northern states that vigorously fought fair employment legislation at the state and national level. White southerners like Thurmond who actively courted northern business interests to come South easily recognized their common cause. Walter Brown would recall Moley's speech as evidence that Thurmond's move was not just about race, that northerners too were worried about, as Moley put it, "the imposition of a Federal police system penetrating into every corner of the South."[29]

It was in early May 1948 in a newsroom in Charlotte, North Carolina, that Bill Weisner, the telegraph editor of *The Charlotte News*, coined the term that would define Thurmond's presidential campaign. His paper was running another story about the States' Rights Democrats, the southern rebels threatening to abandon Harry Truman and the national party, and Weisner could not fit all the words into the headline he was writing. The name—States' Rights Democrats—was too long. He considered an abbreviation, "SRD," but decided that it might make too easy a target for the party's foes. "Standing Room for Democrats," they might say, or something similar. Then it hit him: Dixiecrats. His managing editor loved it. So did countless other journalists who quickly adopted the label for the renegade southerners.[30]

Thurmond hated the name. A decade and a half later, a reporter would recall the pained expressions on Thurmond's face whenever someone called him a Dixiecrat.[31] It was a "five-yard penalty in talking to the voters of the North, the Midwest and Far West," Thurmond said, and it obscured the fact that his group never intended to organize as a separate national party.[32] The fight, Thurmond maintained, was always about working within the party to reassert Democrats' long-standing support of states' rights principles.[33]

This was the theme of his speech in Jackson on May 10. Thurmond flew over with an entourage that included Walter Brown, and the South Carolinians drove into downtown Jackson on streets festooned with Confederate flags. Inside the auditorium, fire marshals struggled to keep the throngs packed in the entryways from crowding in. Mississippi governor Fielding Wright set the stage by recalling the treacheries of Reconstruction and the history of southern victimization. The day before, Wright had issued a crass message over statewide radio advising black Mississippians who sought civil rights to "make your home in some state other than Mississippi."[34] By the time Thurmond came to the podium, heat and hunger had diminished the initial crowd of thirty-five hundred.

"We have gathered here today because the American system of free constitutional government is in danger," he began. White southerners had been "betrayed in the house of our fathers," treated as a "door mat on which Presidential candidates may wipe their political shoes." He recounted a litany of southern contributions to the nation, along with a record of northern abuses, including familiar complaints about Reconstruction, but also the freight-rate controversy and a tariff dispute dating to Benjamin Harrison's administration. More than a few in the crowd must have wondered about the intentions of this young governor who only a year earlier had been hailed in the pages of *The New York Times*.

A hint of Thurmond's calculations could be found in a passage that discussed the "greatest offense" of national Democratic leaders. They had catered to the "professional agitators and mercenary missionaries of ill will" and had provoked base emotions that more enlightened public opinion in the South had largely stamped out in recent generations. "Those of us in the South who have worked hard in the cause of liberalism and constructive endeavor in the field of human and economic progress," a self-reference that no one would have missed, "have been forced to turn aside for a time to meet this upsurge of reactionism." In Thurmond's view, it was his very reputation as a progressive that made him so valuable to the states' rights cause. "The task of the liberal in the South today," he said in a revealing line, "is to save the hard-won ground which we have gained from destruction by ill-advised and irresponsible meddling from without." The charge of the southern liberal, as Thurmond defined it, was not liberal in any customary use of the word; it was to preserve prior victories, to *conserve* the status quo.

He denounced each of Truman's civil rights proposals in turn, lingering on the antisegregation plan. "We in the South know that the laws dealing with the separation of the races are necessary to maintain the public peace and order, where the races live side by side in large numbers," he said. They were essential for "the protection of the racial integrity and purity of the white and Negro races alike." He warned that "on the question of social intermingling of the races our people draw the line," before issuing his most memorable admonition:

No decent and self-respecting Negro would ask for a law to force people to accept him where he is not wanted. They themselves do not want social intermingling. They are entitled to equality of opportunity, and they will get it through our efforts. But all the laws of Washington, and all the bayonets of the Army, cannot force the Negro into our homes, our schools, our churches, and our places of recreation.

Thurmond surely recognized the line as the most racially inflammatory in the speech, and he followed it with a patronizing tribute to "our" colored people for ignoring the "false prophets who want to create misunderstanding in the South."[35]

The only official action taken in Jackson was a unanimous vote to reconvene if the national convention either nominated President Truman or reaffirmed his civil rights program. In July, it did both. The platform committee passed a strong civil rights plank without a single southern vote and despite objections by President Truman, who felt it would only further inflame the southerners. Later that evening, during the nomination of the presidential and vice-presidential candidates, Handy Ellis, the chairman of the Alabama delegation, announced that he and twelve other Alabama delegates were leaving the convention. The Mississippi delegation followed in its entirety.[36]

Thurmond did not walk out of the Philadelphia convention, though it would be regularly said that he did.[37] The South Carolina delegation had been divided over whether to follow the Deep South bolters. They stayed because an interracial group of liberal South Carolinians, the Progressive Democratic Party, had challenged the seating of the regulars, and they did not want the insurgents to be given their votes.[38]

Thurmond offered one of several seconding speeches on behalf of Richard Russell, who allowed his home-state delegation to put his name forward.[39] Russell received 263 votes, all from the South, but Truman took the nomination handily. It was customary in cases of a divided vote to offer a final motion to make the nomination unanimous. On this night, however, with nerves rubbed raw, no one bothered.[40]

Fielding Wright called a meeting in Birmingham of southern Democrats for the Saturday following the end of the convention.[41] Thurmond thought it was too soon. He sent telegrams warning against hasty action, and his office announced that he would be reviewing South Carolina guard units at Camp Stewart, Georgia, the day of the planned meeting.[42] Yet Thurmond eventually decided to juggle his schedule, and he made it to Birmingham late Saturday morning, in time for the afternoon session.[43]

As soon as he arrived, the former Alabama governor Frank Dixon and Fielding Wright approached him about running for president.[44] Numerous people turned down the nomination before Thurmond accepted it; Fielding Wright, Governor Ben Laney of Arkansas, Frank Dixon, and Senator James Eastland of Mississippi have all been mentioned.[45] Years later Laney told a researcher that Thurmond was initially chosen for the vice president slot but refused to go along, saying he would only run for president.[46] The divergent details are insignificant save that they show, first, that Thurmond was not the primary and likely not even the second-choice candidate of most people at the conference; and, second, the utter confusion and disorganization that characterized the seminal event in Thurmond's presidential campaign. "Political conventions normally are confused affairs," wrote a reporter with the *News and Courier*. "But the one here today . . . set some sort of new high in that department, or maybe it is a new low."[47]

Robert Figg was sitting at a ballpark in Charleston watching a baseball game when word came over the loudspeakers that Thurmond had been nominated as a candidate for president. Figg was horrified. Years later he vowed that if he had been in Birmingham, he would have done everything he could to keep Thurmond off the ticket.[48]

Had he been in Birmingham, Figg would have had his choice of object lessons as to why Thurmond should have declined to lead this bunch. One was the dearth of major elected officials. A handful of prominent politicians showed up—mostly from Mississippi—yet conspicuously absent were any leaders with broad political bases, such as Edward H. "Boss" Crump of Tennessee, Harry Byrd of Virginia, Earl Long of Louisiana, and Herman Talmadge of Georgia.[49] Of equal concern would have been the sights and sounds emanating from the meeting hall of rank white supremacy. Organizers had decorated the auditorium with red, white, and blue bunting, hoping to avoid a "sectional atmosphere," yet they could do nothing about the dozens of conference goers dressed in Confederate uniforms or the attendees who discovered a flag company down the street and bought up scores of Confederate banners.[50]

Among the roster of professional racists in attendance were the anti-Semite Gerald L. K. Smith; the mercurial seventy-eight-year-old former governor of Oklahoma "Alfalfa" Bill Murray along with Jonathan Ellsworth Perkins, author of *The Jews Have Got the Atom Bomb!*; and J. B. Stoner of Chattanooga, publisher of the racist sheet *The Thunderbolt*, who had actually been kicked out of the Ku Klux Klan for being too extremist.[51] Speaking from the rostrum, Lloyd E. Price, a state representative from Texas, blamed the country's problems on New Englanders who had first brought Africa's "howling, screaming savages" to the New World. The keynote speaker, Alabama's Frank Dixon, described how Truman's "vicious program" would inevitably "reduce us to the status of a mongrel, inferior race, mixed in blood, our Anglo-Saxon heritage a mockery."[52] By the time of the afternoon session, ABC, which along with CBS and NBC carried live radio coverage of the meeting, cut away because the rhetoric was so inflammatory.[53]

It was in this context that Thurmond gave his first speech as the Dixiecrats' recommended, though not yet officially nominated, presidential candidate. It was almost wholly improvisational. The decision to go to Birmingham had been last-minute. He knew he had not been the first choice, yet here he was, the head of the party, in need of words to inspire. As he looked out over the crowd, Thurmond might have remembered his experience as a boy, recalling how a decent but tentative man had failed to convince the unbalanced masses that he could stand up against the damnable enemies who threatened all they held dear. He would not repeat Ira Jones's mistake. There would be other moments to speak in reasonable tones about policies and principles. In Birmingham, however, Thurmond channeled Blease.

A film crew from Movietone News was covering the meeting, and four clips from Thurmond's speech are preserved in that newsreel footage. It shows Thurmond standing behind a narrow podium draped in bunting, a small table with a water pitcher and two glasses off to the side. Behind him are unidentified Dixiecrat leaders. In the first clip, he reads blandly from a scrap of paper that he then stuffs into his coat pocket. "A great beginning has been made in our fight for state sovereignty," he says. His voice is surprisingly high-pitched and nasal. In the second clip, he has greater emphasis, though he remains stilted, looking down at the sheets of paper in his hand: "Truman has forced himself on the Democratic Party, but he cannot force himself on the people of this great country." Distant, perfunctory cheers follow.

By the third clip he has found a rhythm. He looks at the audience now, no more papers in his hand. His back is arched, left hand in his coat pocket, his right hand with index finger extended, jabbing the air as he emphasizes his points. "I want to tell you that the progress of the Nigra race has not been due to these so-called e-man-ci-pa-tors," his voice dipping into guttural sarcasm as he stresses the separate syllables. "It's been due to the kindness of the good southern people."

The fourth clip captures the most infamous moment of his career. "But I want to tell you"—long pause as he searches his memory for the notable line from his Jackson speech—"ladies and gentlemen"—a filler phrase as he continues to search (the newsreel cameraman caught sight of only a handful of women present)—"that there's not enough troops in the army to force the southern people to break down segregation and admit the nigger race into our theaters, into our swimming pools, into our homes, and into our churches."[54]

For decades afterward, journalists summarizing Thurmond's significance in southern and national politics would recall the line ritualistically.[55] He did not say "Negro," though that was how national newspapers quoted it, a euphemism that biographers and historians followed unwittingly.[56] Nor did he say "Nigra," which was how "Negro" often sounded in a southern accent and was the word he had used in an earlier clip. This was the hard, blatant "nigger," a word that decent southern whites took pride in not using. Their avoidance of it helped distinguish them from those sorrier, lower-class whites whose hatred of blacks was understood to derive from their own insecure place in the pecking order and whom the better class of white folks believed, though they were loath to admit it publicly, to be one-half of the South's race problem.[57] Thurmond knew himself to be of the decent, better class of southerner. He had proved it during the Willie Earle trial. But in crowds of white men different rules applied. Almost all white southern men, regardless of class, would have used "nigger" in the private company of other men, where jokes were told and wry observations were made or when talk turned to manly matters of money, sex, or politics.[58] And there was no more manly matter in July 1948 than the fate of white Democracy. Thurmond knew that with this speech this throng of angry white men was testing him, and he was determined not to fall short.

Then, as soon as all the hand-shaking and back-patting was done and the Birmingham crowd dispersed, Thurmond began backtracking. It was evidence of both his hubris and his naïveté that he thought he could. Two days after the Birmingham speech, he issued a statement rejecting an offer of help from Gerald L. K. Smith.[59] "Smith's a race hater and reactionary," said Thurmond. "I'm not. I'm the friend of Negroes and I'm a liberal."[60] Thurmond was still convinced that he could use the favorable national image that he had generated in his first year as governor to advance the states' rights cause and put white southerners' best foot forward. On a conference call from the Governor's Mansion he said that he was "not interested one whit in the question of 'white supremacy'" and he wanted "the rest of the country [to] realize that we have some pretty good guys down here."[61]

It worked for a time. In the weeks following Birmingham, national newspapers portrayed Thurmond as one of the South's good guys. The press ran with the odd story of a progressive young governor leading the retrograde southern battle. The States' Righters had shown "political astuteness" in nominating someone who had fought lynching in his home state and advocated repeal of the poll tax, wrote *The New York Times*.[62] The response was just as Thurmond had imagined it would be in his Jackson speech. Harlan Trott of *The Christian Science Monitor* said that Thurmond's background as a reformer gave weight to his warnings that Truman's civil rights proposals "harm the efforts of the South to promote political equality by gradualism, and by [their] very abruptness provoke animosities that only set the Negro back."[63] *The Washington Post* found it encouraging that the man the Deep South chose to run for president had "turned his face against bigotry of the Bilbo-Rankin brand."[64] The paper ran a profile of Thurmond headlined: "Top Dixiecrat Has 'Southern Liberal' Views."[65]

Yet Thurmond would not be able to sustain this message, no matter how many high-minded treatises he delivered on the rights of states relative to central authority. His most incisive critics came from a vocal group of southern liberal editors and the African American press. "States' Rights is the issue only insofar as it concerns the rights of States to solve—or refuse to solve—their race problems," wrote John Ed Pearce of Louisville's *Courier-Journal*. "The real issue is one word, and that word is never spoken. It is one thought, and that thought is never expressed. The issue is Nigger."[66] *The Pittsburgh Courier* editorialized that what Thurmond himself meant by "states' rights" might be a bit obscure, but "we are sunlight clear on what your rabble mob of supporters means."[67]

Evidence of the "rabble mob" was not hard to find. In September, James Eastland said the South would be "destroyed and mongrelized" if it surrendered.[68] Charleston's *News and Courier*, Thurmond's most enthusiastic home-state backer, defended the "white man's party" and denounced the "Truman Party 'integration' of the Americans, so that there may be one race, a mixed race, in the United States."[69] Another editorial solicited contributions to the States' Rights Democrats to ensure against "scalawag, mixed white and negro government, FEPC government."[70]

Thurmond largely succeeded in avoiding the most vitriolic white supremacist rhetoric. Yet he continually spoke out against racial intermingling. "Racial integrity as well as peace and good order requires laws providing for the separation of the two races," he said.[71] In denouncing the FEPC, Thurmond brought up the specter of integrated office parties or union dances.[72] Even in the campaign stops he made in border states, his biggest applause lines came when he attacked racial integration. At an appearance in Maryland, he told the crowd, "We of the South think it is better not to admit persons of other race into churches, restaurants . . . and other public places. If Massachusetts and other Northern states want to encourage such intermingling, let them do it, but we will have none of it here." The applause lasted "for several minutes."[73]

It became a common theme for Thurmond. In a rhetorical ploy that southern segregationists used for the next two decades or more, he did not defend southern segregation so much as highlight examples of Jim Crow and racial injustice outside the region. With an FEPC, he said, "there would be no Harlem in New York, no Chinatown in San Francisco, no Southside in Chicago."[74] At a meeting of the Overseas Press Club in New York, Thurmond declared, "If we need a federal law for murder by lynchers, you need a federal law for murder by gangsters."[75] To the same audience he said, "If you people in New York want no segregation, then abolish it and do away with your Harlem. Personally, I think it would be a mistake."[76]

Thurmond officially accepted the nomination at a convention of States' Rights Democrats in Houston on August 11. He actually had two speeches he could have delivered that day. Brown and Figg had written one of them, as they had for his other major appearances that year. Now that he was the official candidate, though, Thurmond developed a wider circle of advisers. Party leaders in Houston wrote a substitute speech that would position him as a national candidate, not merely Harry Truman's southern spoiler. A surprised Walter Brown tuned in over the radio to hear Thurmond deliver an address that differed sharply in tone and emphasis from the one that he and Figg had written.[77]

Brown and Figg's speech began with a prolix tribute to Texas as a place combining the "spirit of the New South, and the traditions of the Old South."[78] Its intended audience was white southerners. The tone was one of aggrieved sectionalism. Harry Truman was the central villain. Thomas Dewey was mentioned only once, as a Yankee governor who had favored differential freight rates, and the Progressive Party's candidate, Henry Wallace, was not mentioned at all. The speech hailed the "political doctrines of Jefferson and Jackson" and compared Truman's civil rights proposals to ones backed by Thaddeus Stevens in the abominable aftermath of the "war between the states."[79]

The speech that Thurmond actually delivered began with a swift attack on the other three major candidates. He established the "communistic Progressive Party" as the standard against which his two main opponents should be judged. Truman and Dewey were merely watered-down versions of Henry Wallace, he argued. All three supported a "program of mis-named Civil Rights." All three backed "the fundamentals of a police state in this country" and were advocates of the "new Russian look."[80]

In Houston, Thurmond spoke not to the roughly nine thousand supporters gathered in the city coliseum, or even to the southern supporters listening at home.[81] His target public was the great white non-South. He tried to connect these listeners with his fellow southerners to form a coalition of what he called "States' Rights Americans," a people ready to resist the "shameful betrayal of our national charter" and stand up for "individual liberty and freedom." He claimed that every section of the nation—"your section and my section"—favored "human rights" and opposed lynching, arguing that southern states had worked hard to eradicate the practice and noting their success. He denounced the "sordid" attempts by Truman, Dewey, and Wallace to win the "bloc vote," by which he meant the black vote, in important swing districts in the North and the Midwest. To court these voters, Thurmond argued, candidates favored an expansion of the central government that threatened the Constitution and echoed the power grabs of authoritarian leaders in Europe.[82]

Robert Figg recalled it years later as a "ridiculous" speech. He speculated that States' Rights Party leaders "got ahold of the thing and put somebody writing it." Thurmond went along because "he probably fancied the idea of suddenly running for President of the United States on a national basis."[83] Brown and Figg knew that Thurmond was not going to win votes in non-southern states. His name would be on the ballot in only a handful of them.[84] Their speech spoke to the one group, white southerners, whose votes might actually swing the Electoral

College tally.[85] It was keyed to a strategy of winning enough electoral votes in the South to throw the race into the House of Representatives, where States' Righters could barter for an abandonment of civil rights efforts.

Thurmond boasted about the minority-party possibility, but if he ever truly believed in it, he would have had to follow Brown and Figg's line, appealing to familiar regional resentments in order to consolidate a unified anti-Truman vote in the South. Thurmond's choice of the more nationally oriented, broadly framed substitute speech—as well as his swift denunciations of racist extremists in his ranks—suggests that he imagined himself in grander terms, as a figure of national importance offering a principled critique of dominant and dangerous trends in American political life.

It was this ambition that drew Thurmond to antistatist and anti-Communist rhetoric. His Houston speech was an important and now forgotten moment in white southerners' attempt to link civil rights resistance to anticommunism. In the 1920s and '30s, members of the Communist Party in the United States were among the most radical and outspoken critics of southern white supremacy, and the tendency of white southerners to red-bait Jim Crow's detractors was not new in 1948. Martin Dies of Texas had been the first chairman of the House Un-American Activities Committee (HUAC) in the late 1930s, and the rabidly racist John Rankin of Mississippi was instrumental in reviving the committee in 1945.[86] Yet Thurmond's presidential campaign intersected with a popular upsurge in anti-Communist sentiment in post–World War II America, and he regularly cast aspersions on the motivations of Jim Crow opponents.

The week before Thurmond's Houston speech, Whittaker Chambers, a senior editor at *Time* magazine, offered bombshell testimony before HUAC about alleged Communist infiltration of the State and Treasury Departments during the New Deal. Among those named was the former State Department official Alger Hiss as well as several erstwhile members of the Agriculture Department during the years it was headed by Henry Wallace.[87] Thurmond put the hearings to political use, conjuring the specter of subversives using the FEPC to infiltrate key defense industries. "The FEPC was made to order for communist use in their designs upon our national security," he argued.[88]

National security threats were just one of many angles from which to attack the FEPC, by far Thurmond's most common topic of discussion during the campaign. He called the FEPC an example of "foreign doctrine" that would not work in "free America."[89] Thurmond traced the idea of a government commission to regulate racial equality in the workplace to Stalin's "All-Races Law" in Soviet Russia. The fact that his three opponents had endorsed such a proposal was evidence of "the extent to which communistic ideas and the advocates of such ideas have infiltrated into the United States."[90]

After the Houston convention, Thurmond agreed to meet reporters for a national press conference at the Mayflower Hotel in Washington. He mentioned the event in passing to Brown, who was mortified. The cynical Washington news corps, he was certain, would feast on the inexperienced candidate. "All Strom knew was the civil rights message of Truman," Figg recalled, "they were going to ask him about world affairs, national affairs—they were going to make him the biggest joke in the country." Brown and Figg boarded a train in Columbia at 9:15 p.m. headed for Washington and worked feverishly through the night to prepare answers for the range of questions reporters would ask. Fifty or sixty journalists crowded into the press conference the next day. Thurmond got through with no gaffes. The measure of Brown and Figg's secret success came the following day, when major newspapers carried no report of the press conference.[91]

Throughout the fall campaign, Thurmond portrayed the States' Rights Party as a popular uprising by white southerners over issues fundamental to American constitutional government. It was a grassroots revolt that began in the South but would quickly spread to every region because the issues at stake touched every American. White southerners loyal to the Democratic Party painted a different picture. States' rights was a bogus issue, they claimed. The party's ranks were filled by small-minded, backward-looking Negro haters. The silent power behind the movement, they argued, was the same economic conservatives in the region who had been looking for a foothold against Franklin Roosevelt and the New Deal since 1933.

In 1948 there was one issue that captured this criticism in shorthand

and became the chief weapon with which opponents bludgeoned the States' Rights campaign: tideland oil. Federal and state governments laid rival claims to control of the coastal areas lying seaward of the low-tide mark out to the limit of national sovereignty, traditionally defined as three miles. Properly speaking, this was the "marginal sea," but the common political descriptor was "tidelands."[92] Underneath many of those areas lay oil and gas deposits of inestimable wealth. California first leased oil concessions to private companies in the late 1930s and reportedly earned tens of millions of dollars. A dispute between the federal government and California emerged that culminated in a narrow Supreme Court decision in 1947 that did not conclusively settle whether the lands were under state or federal authority.[93]

On the same trip to Washington in February 1948 in which he and several southern governors met with Chairman McGrath to discuss Truman's civil rights proposals, Thurmond had joined the governors of Virginia, Florida, and California in testimony before Congress, urging lawmakers to respect the rights of the states relative to the federal government and grant state control of the tidelands.[94] A caucus of southerners at the Democratic National Convention in July passed two resolutions: the first opposed President Truman's civil rights proposals; the second favored state control of the tidelands.[95] States' Righters in Birmingham vigorously declared their support for state control. When the Birmingham leaders announced that they would field their own candidates for national office, suspicions grew that wealthy oil interests, eager to deal with more easily manipulated state legislatures, were using the party to promote their cause.[96]

When asked about rumors that oil money was behind the party, Thurmond said, "Not a dime has passed through my hands."[97] The talk was damaging enough, however, that he dashed off a letter to the sympathetic columnist John Temple Graves, who published it the next day. While the tideland oil question was like the "so-called civil rights legislation . . . to be reserved to the states," oil lobbyists, he declared, had not influenced him or the party.[98] Still the talk continued. The fact that the party held its official nominating convention in Houston, the capital of Texas oil country, did nothing to quell the speculation. The Humble Oil Company reportedly flew Thurmond to the Houston convention in a private plane, and the oil executive H. R. Cullen had purportedly contributed $100,000 to the campaign.[99]

Conspiracy theories about shadowy oil magnates bankrolling a third-party candidate in a tight election year made for a dramatic story line. Yet the party's existing financial documents show no record of oil contributions. More important, as the historian Kari Frederickson has argued, the shoestring budget for States' Rights campaign events belies the fantastic reports of an organization awash in a sea of oil riches.[100]

The tittle-tattle about the tidelands, however, should not obscure a more important fact about the States' Rights Democrats. The party represented the most significant opportunity to date for conservative economic forces in the region to consolidate an anti–New Deal constituency. Many of the same individuals who supported the party bolt in 1948 had been behind efforts to dump Roosevelt at the 1944 Democratic convention. The political scientist Alexander Heard wrote in 1952: "Corporation lawyers, wealthy businessmen, industrial captains, Black Belt planters—joined inevitably by a spate of malevolent opportunists— made up the backbone of the leadership of the bolts and revolts."[101] If it was not oil money alone that fueled the party, it was what the journalist Thomas Sancton called the "investing and managing communities"— "the oil and cattle men of Texas, the oil men and sugar planters of Louisiana, the mercantile and shipping interests of New Orleans, Houston, Memphis, and Atlanta, the steel and coal operators of Alabama, the textile manufacturers of the whole South Atlantic region"—a range of business interests that stretched from "the southern industrial metropolis to Old Man Johnson's 'furnish' store at the unnamed crossroads."[102]

Longtime anti–New Deal business leaders and lawyers who represented wealthy corporate clients honeycombed the party leadership. In Arkansas, they called Ben Laney "Business Ben," and his close associate John Daggett was the force behind the archconservative Arkansas Free Enterprise Association. Texas's Palmer Bradley and Alabama's Gessner McCorvey, both prominent Dixiecrats, were lawyers who represented Standard Oil of New Jersey. McCorvey also represented Humble Oil, Gulf Oil, Magnolia Petroleum, and Tennessee Coal and Iron. The chairperson of the Alabama Dixiecrats, Marion Rushton, represented Chase National Bank and Buckeye Cotton Oil. The North Carolina Dixiecrat David Clark published the *Southern Textile Bulletin*. Louisiana's Leander Perez, aside from his messianic advocacy of state control of the tidelands, was a longtime foe of organized labor and eventually helped establish the Louisiana Free Enterprise Association.[103] All of these men promoted the "free enterprise" politics that was critical to the rise of the Sunbelt.

Southern Democratic loyalists, like the attorney general of Alabama, accused such men of participating in a "giant conspiracy" controlled by the Republican National Committee.[104] The New Deal stalwart Claude Pepper, U.S. senator from Florida, summarized the economic case against the States' Righters the best. In a campaign speech in Montgomery in early October, Pepper reminded the audience how "corporation clients and big business support in the South" had used the "false façade of states' rights" to fight President Roosevelt's efforts to "give the public cheap public power," to "help Southern workers get fair wages," and to "protect the little investor or the farmer against northern speculators with whom they were tied in."[105]

Thurmond's alignment with such a group represented a dramatic departure for him. His opponent for governor had tried to tar him as a CIO supporter. Earlier in 1948 labor groups in South Carolina had wanted to recruit him to run for Burnet Maybank's Senate seat.[106] But the States' Rights presidential run severed those ties. During the campaign, textile unions in South Carolina asked him to clarify his position on labor, but he never did.[107] He had thrown his lot in with the conservative businessmen of the South, and he had nothing to say to laborers that would not alienate the States' Rights Party's most important backers. If the States' Rights campaign hardened Thurmond's racial politics, aligning him clearly with the forces of racist reaction, it had an equally important effect on his labor and economic politics as well.

The last month of the campaign provided Thurmond with some heady moments. On October 11, he appeared on the cover of *Time*. Two weeks later, *Newsweek* published a surprisingly sympathetic account of the States' Rights campaign written by two southern correspondents.

The article all but conceded the election to Thomas Dewey. Truman had made a sucker bet in gambling that the South would stand pat as it always had, the article argued. The only question was how badly the president would lose. If it was a blowout, the "Dixiecrats not only can avoid retaliation, they may even be able to capture Democratic state machines."[108]

Such analysis clashed with reports from the campaign trail. Harlan Trott of *The Christian Science Monitor*, who followed Thurmond around North Carolina and Virginia in early October, noted the small, unenthusiastic crowds that turned out to hear the "somewhat color-less" candidate.[109] Local States' Rights leaders, political amateurs all, played host to Thurmond, who traveled only with his young wife and several South Carolina state troopers. Trott and the two or three other reporters following Thurmond joined the governor's retinue for meals, one of them a dinner of spaghetti and meat sauce at a humble estab-lishment outside Hendersonville, North Carolina. Thurmond was no swashbuckler, with his "plain, high-pitched way of speaking," wrote Trott, but he was "extremely earnest, humorless, fearless and energetic." When he got going, there was "a kind of cold blaze in the Governor's eye."[110]

In South Carolina, speculation continued to swirl that Thurmond's race was just a warm-up for his Senate run against Olin Johnston. Thurmond fueled the talk by goading reporters into asking Johnston why he had not endorsed the States' Rights ticket. When asked about a possible Senate race, Thurmond noted that he was involved in another campaign at present, but added, "If I take a notion to run for the senate in 1950, I sure will do it."[111]

In his final campaign speech, delivered from the Governor's Man-sion and broadcast over ABC Radio, Thurmond claimed that his cam-paign had "made it unprofitable for any candidate for president to barter away liberty of the American people to win blocs of racial votes."[112] The next day Strom and Jean Thurmond drove to Edgefield to cast their ballots. A historically minded Associated Press reporter noted that Thurmond's bright red tie was reminiscent of the Red Shirts. Twenty-two-year-old Jean Thurmond had the honor of casting her first vote for president for her own husband.[113]

Election night was full of drama. Like most Americans, Thurmond expected a Republican victory. *The Augusta Chronicle* went to press that evening reporting that Thurmond had "declined to concede victory to the Republicans tonight."[114] Years later, Thurmond would recall that the race was so close that the Governor's Mansion received phone calls from Truman representatives asking Thurmond not to do anything until the two campaigns had a chance to talk.[115] As it turned out, Truman would not need the southerners. He defeated the Republican Thomas Dewey in the biggest surprise in American presidential history. Thurmond ran a very distant third, winning four states—South Carolina, Mississippi, Alabama, and Louisiana—and just 2.4 percent of the popular vote.

The results confirmed the limited appeal of Thurmond's candidacy. "States' Rights Americans" were almost wholly southern: 98.8 percent of Thurmond's support came from below the Mason-Dixon Line.[116] The four states he won were the only ones in which States' Rights supporters succeeded in having Thurmond named as the Democratic nominee on the ballot (Truman's name did not appear on the Alabama ballot at all). In two of those states—Alabama and Louisiana—there was significant opposition to the bolters based on long-standing support for New Deal policies. States' Righters were unlikely to have prevailed had Truman been listed as the regular Democratic nominee.[117]

The clearest indicator of Dixiecrat support was race. The four states that Thurmond won were also the four states with the highest percentage of black population. It was in the southern Black Belt—areas where whites lived in close proximity to a largely disenfranchised majority-black population—that racial concerns were most intense and that the States' Rights cause enjoyed greatest success. In South Carolina, for example, Thurmond fared relatively poorly in the upland areas populated by mill workers and small farmers, yet in the ten counties where the black population was over 60 percent, all low-country counties, he won 89 percent of the vote.[118]

On Inauguration Day, a well-publicized encounter between Truman and Thurmond put the governor back in the national news and inflamed passions among his southern supporters. Thurmond initially declined offers to participate in the inaugural festivities but, not wanting to appear the spoilsport, accepted the invitation at the last minute. From his reviewing stand, President Truman "displayed intense interest in everything passing in front of him." Yet as the car carrying Strom and Jean Thurmond approached, the actress Tallulah Bankhead, a guest of Truman's and a member of one of Alabama's famed Democratic families, "let out a foghorn of boos." Truman turned his back until the Thurmonds' car had passed, ignoring Thurmond as he waved.[119]

Eight years later Thurmond recounted for the Princeton historian Eric Goldman the story of Truman's slight. He said that Vice President Alben Barkley was at Truman's side and had started to raise his hand to acknowledge Thurmond when the president turned to him, whispered something, and Barkley dropped his hand. "But how could you expect anything more from a man as small as Truman?" Thurmond wrote.[120] Truman's indiscretion—and Thurmond's sense of unearned humiliation—only grew with age. Recalling this same story for his Senate colleagues decades later, Thurmond said that as Barkley began to raise his hand, Truman grabbed his arm, and "an open radio microphone caught the Chief Executive saying 'Don't you wave to the S.O.B.'"[121]

Thurmond was not the only one to embellish the past. In his memoirs, Harry Truman recorded that in 1948, Thurmond had led the "dramatic departure" from the convention floor in Philadelphia.[122] Over the years Thurmond corrected reporters with genuine annoyance. When Walter Cronkite in an otherwise nostalgic conversation at the 1984 Republican National Convention said that he had been in Philadelphia when Thurmond led the southern walkout, Thurmond's expression changed. "Walter, I never walked out of that convention. You got it wrong; and you're still gettin' it wrong!"[123] Perhaps the fact that he stayed was for Thurmond evidence that his campaign had not been about mere protest politics but was a fight within the Democratic Party to salvage the party's states' rights heritage. It gave impetus to his claim that he did not leave the party but that the party left him.

In later decades, Thurmond framed his States' Rights past in ways that spoke to the present. "If I had been elected president in 1948, history would be vastly different," he wrote in 1976. "I believe we would have stemmed the growth of Big Government, which had begun with the New Deal and culminated with the Great Society."[124] In an early-1980s retrospective, Thurmond talked about his campaign laying the foundation for Goldwater's southern success in 1964, the building block of the modern conservative GOP.[125]

Thurmond was right that 1948 was a turning point, but not because his States' Rights campaign marked any simple or inevitable step toward the modern Republican South. It was important because Thurmond was the first southerner in the postwar period to bring together on a regional scale the visceral politics of white supremacy with southern business and industrial opposition to the New Deal. Thanks to his presidential campaign, Thurmond now had filing cabinets full of speeches and press releases that blended the regional language of states' rights—the old-fashioned southern way of speaking in a dignified voice about the necessity of white supremacy—with inchoate themes of antistatism and anticommunism that would gain resonance in the postwar period, both in the South and throughout Cold War America. It was an imperfect rhetoric in 1948, and much was lost in trying to translate white supremacist rage into abstract conservative principle. Yet it would be refined and improved by Thurmond and others in the years to come.

4

PLUCK AND LUCK
(1949–1954)

After the 1948 election, Strom Thurmond slowly and carefully distanced himself from the States' Rights leadership. While he confirmed in the last month of the campaign that the movement would continue as a counter to the national party, he nevertheless skipped a December meeting in Birmingham where the party announced the formation of a nonprofit states' rights institute in Washington.[1] The columnist John Temple Graves for one was disappointed. Thurmond's campaign, Graves said, was the States' Righters' best argument that the movement was not about regional reaction but about the future of liberty and restrained government. "You stood for a liberalism and a light that set you apart from most of the leadership," he wrote.[2]

Walter Brown and Robert Figg, both of whom had had their suspicions about the party bolters, counseled Thurmond to make a clean break. The proposed states' rights institute sounded like "another Liberty League," Brown argued, and he expressed concern about the "reactionary and conservative background of those sponsoring the movement." These men, he warned Thurmond, were opposed to the "liberal philosophy of government upon which you were elected Governor and to which we are anchored as a matter of principle."[3]

The talk among Thurmond's inner circle about the need for him to reclaim his "liberal" credentials shows how elastic the term had become at this protean moment in southern politics. Brown and Graves had long thought of themselves as southern liberals. Both men had been avid supporters of Roosevelt during his first administration, when New Deal liberalism consisted of measures such as the Agricultural Adjustment Act and the Tennessee Valley Authority, federal programs that provided help for the desperately poor and economically backward South. A "liberal" in the 1930s South was someone who pursued a progressive but pragmatic approach to modernizing state and regional government. This was a position that Thurmond himself had taken both as a state legislator and as governor. Like many white southerners, however, Thurmond and his advisers pulled away from the national Democratic Party in direct proportion to its halting and intermittent support for civil rights for African Americans.

The 1948 campaign crystallized a new political moment. Truman's outright support for civil rights left unmoored Thurmond and other white southerners who had always prided themselves as southern progressives. They rejected what they saw as the leftward leanings of the national party, yet neither were they blind to the increasing difficulties in "managing" Jim Crow race relations.[4] "If we permit the reactionaries . . . to take over the States' Rights movement," Walter Brown wrote in a 1949 letter to Thurmond, "then I can tell you now the cause is lost."[5]

Thurmond and these so-called progressive southern Democrats were in a real bind. President Truman and the national Democratic Party were headed in a direction that they could not go. Thurmond wanted to distance himself from the reactionaries, but he understood before many that a more systematic break was inevitable. He also knew that he could not abandon the States' Rights crowd even if he had wanted to. It would give fodder to those who dismissed his presidential run as mere opportunism, and besides they were now his political base.[6] Thurmond might have sat out States' Rights events in 1949, but he was there in May 1950, at the third annual States' Rights convention in Jackson.[7] This was during his Senate campaign, when Thurmond needed to rally States' Rights support in South Carolina in his race against Olin Johnston, the quintessential southern New Dealer.

However uneasy Thurmond might have felt about operating outside the normal Democratic Party channels, the real problem was not the politics of the States' Rights group so much as the lack of political heavyweights among them. In 1949, Thurmond was a governor two years into his first term with a quixotic third-party presidential campaign under his belt. If he was going to continue to work outside the regular Democratic Party, he needed a more substantial southern politician with whom he could align.

It seemed as if he might find one in his father's old friend and Walter Brown's former boss, James F. Byrnes, the most influential of the New Deal southerners. Byrnes was the consummate heavyweight: one of FDR's favorite southern senators in the 1930s, a former associate justice on the Supreme Court, and the director of President Roosevelt's Economic Stabilization Office, a wartime agency with such vast powers that the press took to calling Byrnes the "assistant president." Many expected Roosevelt to tap Byrnes as his vice-presidential candidate in 1944, but northern, big-city elements in the party objected to the well-known southern segregationist. Harry Truman, whom Byrnes had helped mentor in the Senate, emerged as a compromise candidate. As president, Truman rewarded his old friend with an appointment as secretary of state, an office Byrnes held from 1945 to 1947.[8]

Out of loyalty to Truman, Byrnes had sat out the 1948 presidential race. Yet he had grown increasingly disillusioned with the president's domestic policies. In June 1949 he broke openly with Truman in a high-profile speech at Washington and Lee University. Denouncing the administration's proposals for "welfare state" legislation, which he said threatened to turn the American people into "economic slaves," Byrnes lamented that the United States was "going down the road to stateism [sic]."[9] Relations between Byrnes and Truman quickly turned sour. At the bottom of a typed letter about minor State Department press letters written since Byrnes's departure, Truman handwrote a postscript to Byrnes, "Since your Washington and Lee speech I'm sure I know how Caesar felt when he said 'Et tu, Brute.'"[10] Byrnes responded with a dispassionate letter defending the speech, but could not resist his own icy closing: "I hope you are not going to think of me as a Brutus, because I am no Brutus. I hope you are not going to think of yourself as a Caesar, because you are no Caesar."[11]

Over the course of 1949, Thurmond delivered a number of earnest speeches similar to Byrnes's Washington and Lee address. In an address before the Alabama Bar Association grandly titled "O'er the Ramparts We Watched," Thurmond decried the whittling away of local sovereignty, warning that Americans were "dangerously near to the 'welfare state,' and to socialism."[12] He had copies of the speech printed in pamphlet form for easy distribution. He gave a comparable speech in October before the South Carolina state convention of the United Daughters of the Confederacy, discussing the postwar pressures on America's free enterprise system and democratic government.[13]

Aware that his former boss was interested in running for governor in 1950, Walter Brown hoped to link Byrnes's campaign with Thurmond's bid for the Senate in a common anti-Truman effort. At Brown's urging, Thurmond issued a complimentary statement about Byrnes in October 1949, when Byrnes's campaign was still in the rumor stages. Olin Johnston forces started recruiting candidates to run against Byrnes so that he would not have extra time to work on Thurmond's behalf.[14]

The pieces seemed to fall into place in November 1949. Byrnes gave a widely covered speech before the Southern Governors' Conference in Biloxi, Mississippi. Afterward, Arthur Krock of *The New York Times* anointed him the leader of the "bi-partisan resistance movement against the political philosophy and the cost of the federal system which President Truman is advocating."[15] The next day the southern governors unanimously elected Thurmond the chair of the conference. Byrnes and Thurmond were set to make a powerful anti-Truman duo.[16]

But it was not to be. In May 1950, in the kickoff event for the gubernatorial race, Byrnes indirectly criticized Thurmond when answering a reporter's question about what he would do if elected governor. He would not spend all his time "appointing colonels and crowning queens," Byrnes said in a slap at Thurmond that played on his image as both politically conniving and unserious.[17] The comment was, as Brown would write later to Thurmond, "the kiss of death to any alliance."[18] When Strom and Jean Thurmond read the news of Byrnes's quotation, they "looked like they had been shot."[19]

Byrnes distanced himself from Thurmond out of an abundance of caution. He was the grand old man of South Carolina politics in 1950, and there was not much that could have prevented his election. Voters already knew the congruities between Byrnes's and Thurmond's positions. Thurmond's presidential run had tarred him as a party bolter, and Byrnes wanted to make clear that his objections to President Truman were not to be taken as a rejection of the regular Democratic organization in the state, which continued to wield enormous influence.[20] Walter Brown later speculated that Byrnes also weighed heavily his very public feud with Harry Truman. He had emerged as one of the president's most substantive critics, and Byrnes wanted to seal that status with an overwhelming victory in South Carolina. If he lined up closely with Thurmond, he was likely to lose some Olin Johnston supporters, and thus diminish his winning margin.[21]

Strom Thurmond's 1950 race for the U.S. Senate against Olin Johnston was the nastiest, hardest-fought campaign of his career. South Carolina Democratic Party rules at the time stipulated that candidates for statewide office make a joint campaign appearance in the same designated counties. The "Speaking Circus," as some referred to it, was the brainchild of the Democratic kingpin Benjamin Tillman, who, it was said, instigated the practice because he knew his skills on the stump were such that he could "whip any city slicker who had the temerity to oppose him."[22] By 1950 the practice had devolved into an exhausting ritual in which candidates crisscrossed the state at breakneck speeds, hitting a morning and afternoon event in out-of-the-way county seats, giving the same stump speech before sparse crowds of locals. Recruited supporters who traveled with the candidates, and had been coached on applause lines and heckling tactics, were often the most interested spectators. After a dozen or so appearances, with stale charges lobbied back and forth and reporters eager for a fresh angle on a familiar story, the candidates' nerves would begin to fray. The gloves would come off, and the brawl would begin.

This was almost literally true in 1950. In the third week of joint campaign appearances, at an event in Newberry, Thurmond claimed that after Harry Truman's order to desegregate the military, Johnston did not protest sufficiently. "You are a liar!" Johnston shouted from the audience. Thurmond answered by offering to meet Johnston "in front of the courthouse when this meeting is over." The two men did meet, though they exchanged only words, not blows.[23]

Even before the near fisticuffs, the Columbia *State* described the race as "a grim and somber affair, with neither of the contestants willing to poke a joke or two into their addresses."[24] There was too much at stake for the candidates, both of whom were in their prime political years. A loss for either one would make for a difficult path back into the political spotlight. The pace was so intense that Walter Brown and Robert Figg practically lived in the Governor's Mansion.[25]

Thurmond went on the attack immediately and never relented. In the first joint campaign appearance, he called Johnston Harry Truman's "fair-headed boy."[26] Tying Johnston to Truman's civil rights policies was Thurmond's chief tactic, and he contrasted his own history as a presidential protest candidate. "Don't forget that I stuck my neck out for you two years ago," he said. "Don't forget that I fought the fight for states' rights while my opponent ran out on the Democrats of South Carolina."[27] Reflecting on the campaign years later, Thurmond conceded that perhaps he had attacked Johnston too often and too harshly. The truth was more subtle and profound. Thurmond's attacks were necessary to clearly differentiate him from Johnston, who had vigorously criticized President Truman and Judge J. Waties Waring at the candidates' first joint campaign appearance. Thurmond's advisers were concerned that Johnston threatened to "steal all [Thurmond's] thunder."[28]

Among Thurmond's many racially charged attacks was the accusation that Johnston was the candidate of the CIO and the NAACP. One of his most frequent criticisms was of Johnston's record of pardons during his two terms as governor. In Chester, Thurmond cited the case of Dave Dunham, a black man "paroled" by Johnston due to "good behavior" who later attacked a white couple on a Chester road, killing the man, a twenty-two-year-old veteran who had fought to protect his girlfriend from the black ravisher. "Dave Dunham was the instrument of death," Thurmond said, "but in reality it was the pardon racket which ended the life of this young Chester county veteran."[29]

Johnston initially ignored Thurmond's attacks, claiming that he would run this campaign from a "Christian standpoint."[30] By the third week, however, he was returning Thurmond's barbs tit for tat. Both men ended up vying for the title of champion segregationist.[31] Johnston pilloried Thurmond for having appointed an African American doctor to the South Carolina Advisory Hospital Council the previous year; a campaign flyer declared it the first break in segregation since

Wade Hampton and the Red Shirts had overthrown Yankee rule.[32] The *Anderson Independent*, a pro-Johnston newspaper reporting on the incident, accused Thurmond of "checkerboarding hitherto all-white state agencies with Negroes so he can woo the race's votes next year."[33] In a blatantly disingenuous countercharge, Thurmond dismissed Johnston's tactics as an attempt to "stir the fires of racial prejudice."[34]

Thurmond's showdown with Olin Johnston was one of several closely watched elections across the South in 1950 in which anti-Truman candidates challenged moderate-to-liberal Democratic incumbents. In Florida, Congressman George Smathers battled the New Deal stalwart Claude Pepper, and in North Carolina Willis Smith took on the moderate Frank Porter Graham. In both races the anti-Truman candidate leveled racially charged accusations against the incumbents. Thurmond watched the contests closely for trends that might affect his own campaign. After Smathers won an easy victory in early May, Thurmond deemed it a triumph for the cause of constitutional government and states' rights.[35]

Hoping to avoid the same fate in North Carolina, the Truman White House swung its influence behind Frank Porter Graham, the former president of the University of North Carolina who had been appointed to the Senate the previous year to fill an unexpired term.[36] Graham was a beloved figure in the state, but he had a record of racial progressiveness that Willis Smith, along with his young campaign aide Jesse Helms, exploited shamelessly. Noting Graham's support for the FEPC, anti-Graham ads ran with the exclamation "White People Wake Up!" The spots warned against "Negroes working beside you, your wife and daughters in your mills and factories . . . Negroes riding beside you, your wife and your daughters in buses, cabs, and trains . . . Negroes sleeping in the same hotels and rooming houses." Other flyers and advertisements appeared around the state showing African American soldiers dancing with white women, the caption below explaining how Graham supported this behavior.[37] When Smith defeated Graham in a runoff election by some twenty thousand votes, Thurmond ran a campaign ad predicting that his defeat of Olin Johnston would be the third strike against "Truman's Force Program."[38]

In contrast to Florida and North Carolina, the African American vote in South Carolina played a significant role in determining the outcome of the election. Thanks to Judge Waring's decision opening the Democratic primary to black voters, there were an estimated seventy-three thousand African Americans registered in South Carolina by 1950. Both Thurmond's and Jimmy Byrnes's campaign staffs knew that they would get few if any of these votes, and they worried about how these voters, in combination with the labor vote, would affect their races.[39]

African Americans in South Carolina were hardly enthused by Olin Johnston, yet his grudging allegiance to the national Democratic Party made him the lesser of two evils. There also were rumors in the black community that Thurmond had played a role in a high-profile libel case against John Henry McCray—an African American leader in the Progressive Democratic Party and the editor of the *Lighthouse and Informer*, the state's leading black newspaper. McCray was indicted in January 1950 along with an Associated Press reporter for publishing articles about a twenty-five-year-old African American man accused of raping a white teenage girl in Greenwood County. The two journalists had merely reported an interview with the accused in which he admitted to having had sex with the girl but claimed that it was consensual. McCray and other African American leaders believed that Thurmond's Dixiecrat allies in Greenwood County were behind McCray's indictment.[40]

The McCray case contributed to a high-profile endorsement of Olin Johnston by the influential African American political activist Modjeska Simkins only days before the election. Simkins defended Johnston's race-baiting as a political necessity given Thurmond's constant attacks. Comparing Thurmond to Hitler, Simkins wrote, "He has keen intelligence, the potential power, and the fanatic zeal that makes him a danger in any democracy, a serious risk in Washington, and a deadly threat to our National prestige in the eyes of the world." She believed that Thurmond's defeat provided the best chance to end racist politics in South Carolina.[41] The Thurmond campaign responded immediately with telegrams to surrogates urging them to take out ads in local newspapers reading, "The orders have come down telling the bloc vote to scratch Strom Thurmond—White Democrats of South Carolina, the challenge is up to you. It is your time to stand up and be counted for South Carolina democracy."[42] Another campaign ad claimed that the "Truman-

Pendergast leadership in the National Democratic Party," a reference to the discredited Kansas City political boss who had helped launch Truman's career, was organizing the bloc vote in South Carolina.[43]

Despite a seesaw battle through much of the evening, in the end Olin Johnston prevailed by nearly thirty thousand votes. Johnston dominated in the industrial areas of the Piedmont, carrying Anderson and Spartanburg counties by nearly eight thousand votes each.[44] Thurmond excelled in the low country, though not to the degree hoped for, thanks in part to the larger-than-expected black vote. The roughly forty thousand African American voters who participated in the election made the difference.[45] Returns from predominantly black precincts in Columbia and Charleston suggested that African Americans voted overwhelmingly for Johnston.[46]

Thurmond's advisers offered an array of explanations for the defeat. Robert Figg thought that the outbreak of the Korean War in late June distracted voters and suppressed turnout. Walter Brown chalked it up to a combination of "the Democratic national committee, the federal machinery, the CIO, the NAACP and the war."[47] Figg and Brown both believed that Thurmond would have won had he not bolted the party in 1948.[48] Yet the consensus among Thurmond and his inner circle was that the black vote had done him in. "As you no doubt know, bloc voting was a decisive factor in the primary of July 12," Thurmond's press secretary, George McNabb, wrote to Figg. "The good white people of South Carolina should be made aware of this threat to their free elections."[49]

Thurmond did not brood over the setback. There is little indication in his papers that he took much time at all to weigh his mistakes or strategize with aides about his political future. Thurmond prided himself on not looking back, and in this moment his resistance to self-reflection served him well. He wrote a cheerful letter to Governor-elect Byrnes offering help in the transition period. It betrayed not a hint of irritation over what might have been if Byrnes had allowed Thurmond to align their two campaigns.

While Thurmond offered no retrospectives on the events of 1950, others did. Writing in 1952, the political scientist Samuel Lubell called Thurmond's loss an exception to what he described as the "conservative revolution" of 1950. Lubell pointed not just to the defeat of Claude

Pepper or Frank Graham but to the broader set of economic and social factors transforming the South, such as agricultural diversification beyond cotton and tobacco; the mechanization of traditional crops; urbanization; the growth of manufacturing; and the rise in personal incomes. Three factors in particular, however, stood out for Lubell: the failure of southern labor-organizing efforts; the rise of a new urban middle class; and the intensification of racist sentiment following the extension of civil and political rights for southern African Americans.[50] All of these developments extended beyond 1950 and created fertile ground in which Thurmond's antiliberal, racially divisive politics could flourish. Another scholar writing in these same years described the States' Rights movement as "the way southern conservatives are making contact with national conservatives and orienting themselves to national conservatism. In short, just as the southern liberal is becoming an integrated national liberal, so the southern conservative is becoming an integrated national conservative."[51] Thurmond was not yet an "integrated national conservative," but he was on his way.

What the broader anti-Truman effort was missing in 1950 was perhaps best summarized in a critical assessment of the States' Rights movement written by the conservative intellectual Frank Chodorov. "The vital need of the States' Rights movement, if it is to become a significant political force, is an economic base," Chodorov wrote in *Human Events* in February 1950. "It must appeal to self-interest. It must attract effective support from those who recognize the threat to their livelihood in the growing power of the Federal Government. It must show under the aegis of state governments lies the hope of Free Enterprise." Chodorov didn't have a solution, only a conviction: "Until the States' Rights movement offers a practical program of economic relief from unrestrained federalism, and thus attracts individuals and groups whose affairs would prosper by such a program, it must remain devitalized. Economics is the motor of politics."[52]

A week after this article was published, Thurmond received a letter from one of the leading industrial boosters in South Carolina that foreshadowed how he would eventually make good on Chodorov's vision. The letter was from Charles Daniel, owner of Daniel Construction of Greenville, which would become one of the largest construction companies in the world. Daniel had contracts worth over $20 million with Deering Milliken Company, a textile firm in Spartanburg whose owner, Roger Milliken, would become a key financial contributor not only to the South Carolina Republican Party but also to a host of conservative political movements in postwar American politics. Daniel was also a leader in the South Carolina Democrats for Eisenhower drives in 1952 and 1956.

Daniel and Thurmond had worked together on numerous industrial recruitment efforts, including a campaign to convince DuPont to build a fibers plant in Camden, South Carolina. Thurmond called on company executives at their headquarters in Wilmington, Delaware, the first time a sitting governor had done so. For the Republican businessmen seated around the table, Thurmond slyly invoked his presidential run as a way to build rapport. "As I look . . . into the intelligent faces here today," he said, "I believe we've got more brains around this table than Truman has in his cabinet."[53] Thurmond knew about the du Pont brothers—Irénée, Lammot, and Pierre—who had started the anti–New Deal American Liberty League back in 1934, and the Du-Pont officials knew about Thurmond's third-party challenge, which would have marked him as a savvy operator whose criticisms of liberal Democrats meshed with their own notions about how Harry Truman was running the country into the ground.[54]

In his letter, Daniel warned Thurmond that Milliken and the du Ponts were "greatly disturbed" over the failure of the South Carolina General Assembly to pass a bill allowing for the continuous operation of processing plants. Daniel believed that the bill's defeat as well as a proposal requiring air-conditioned factories, a labor union priority, would drive away other industries looking to move South. Daniel assured Thurmond that he had his support in the upcoming Senate race against Olin Johnston but warned that he and many of "your friends" thought Thurmond would struggle unless he came out strongly for a right-to-work law and "fair treatment to business as well as to labor."[55]

The letter was important enough that Thurmond sent a copy to Walter Brown and Bob Figg asking for advice on how he should respond. Brown, still thinking like an old southern New Dealer, dismissed it as "bunk."[56] Brown continued to see the key division in southern politics as one between the workingman and big business. That was the sensibility that Strom Thurmond had grown up with, but he was beginning to think about politics in a different way.

The exchange of letters offers a glimpse into the diverging political milieu that Thurmond straddled in the early postwar years. On one side were Brown and Figg, who represented his South Carolina Democratic heritage with its New Deal sympathies and Jim Crow obsessions. On the other were conservative businessmen like Daniel and Milliken with their preoccupation with antilabor, free enterprise politics. These men were emerging heavyweights not only in southern politics but also in postwar Sunbelt conservatism, a sphere into which Thurmond would be increasingly drawn.

In his return to private life, Strom Thurmond made a number of personal and professional choices that had implications for the political career he would resume a few years later. His choice of residence was the most important. Thurmond did not return to Edgefield, the venerable old town of his forefathers with its long heritage of producing exemplary South Carolinians. Instead, he and his young wife built a modern brick ranch-style home—the architectural emblem of postwar suburban America—in Aiken, just across the state line from Augusta, Georgia, a town that until 1950 was best known as a winter vacation spot for wealthy northerners. A mere twenty miles separate Aiken from Edgefield. Yet in 1950, the two towns were at the beginning of a process that would leave them worlds apart.

Aiken lay at the center of the Savannah River Site, a nuclear materials processing center established in 1950 by the Atomic Energy Commission. The federal government contracted DuPont to build and operate a plutonium production plant along the Savannah River. "It is as if Scarlett O'Hara had come home from the ball, wriggled out of her satin gown, and put on a space suit," wrote the journalist Dorothy Kilgallen, describing the transformation of the bucolic southern town into a modern Cold War production center.[57] The scale of the Savannah River project was monumental. As an industrial and engineering feat, it rivaled the construction of the Panama Canal. Its impact on the local area was equally vast. During the peak of the construction period, the project employed over thirty-eight thousand skilled and un-skilled laborers.[58]

When Thurmond took over as governor, South Carolina's indus-trial profile predominantly comprised textile mills in the Piedmont. That was beginning to change, thanks to the efforts of Thurmond and Governor James Byrnes as well as new measures taken by the general assembly in 1954, which passed a right-to-work law and created the South Carolina State Development Board. The Savannah River Site, however, is the best example of the critical role that the federal govern-ment, spurred by southern Democratic committee chairmen in Con-gress, played in transforming rural isolated areas of the South into engines of the nation's military-industrial complex.[59]

In Aiken, Thurmond became a leading booster of an expanding postwar Sunbelt community. He and his young wife built their home in a newly developed neighborhood that was quickly filling up with engineers and white-collar, college-educated employees of the "bomb plant," many of them newcomers to the South. Thurmond used his po-litical contacts to help organize a federally chartered savings and loan association in Aiken, which sold the mortgages to the new residents flooding the area. And he paid off campaign debts with profits from his booming law practice, a firm that specialized in representing local landowners forced to sell their property to the government to make way for the new hydrogen bomb facility.[60]

As a private citizen, Thurmond spent much of his spare time think-ing about and working on issues of national defense. He ordered a subscription to a right-wing publication, *National Republic*, which billed itself as the "magazine of fundamental Americanism," and he poured himself into his work as a military reserves officer. He was elected president of the South Carolina Reserve Officers Association in 1952 and won acclaim for quadrupling membership in one year.[61] He positioned himself for a run for the national organization's presidency in 1954, addressing the annual conventions of reserve officers in Ohio, Michigan, Pennsylvania, North Carolina, Florida, New York, and Massachusetts.[62] He succeeded at the annual convention in Omaha in June of that year.[63] In the absence of a press office, Thurmond sent out letters—press releases that included glossy photographs of himself—to national publications announcing his new position.[64]

Thurmond was so busy with Reserve Officers work that he seemed to have almost missed the historic developments concerning southern segregation in the summer of 1954. On May 17, the Supreme Court issued its long-awaited decision in the case of *Brown v. Board of Education*. Many South Carolinians wrote to Thurmond seeking advice from the former Dixiecrat leader about how best to defend segregated schools. Thurmond had nothing to offer, at least not in the summer of 1954. "I am giving a great deal of my time now to the Army Reserves and to the Reserve Officers Association," he wrote to one woman from Sumter County. He "presumed" that Governor Byrnes would outline a course to be followed, but the responsibility was on "those in public office," he said.[65] In less than a year, after he had rejoined the ranks of public officials, Thurmond would begin a campaign that made him one of *Brown*'s fiercest critics. Outrage over the liberal Supreme Court would become one of the most consistent themes of his political career. Yet as a private citizen, without an angry constituency that he needed to represent, the day that segregationist diehards would come to refer to as "Black Monday" passed with Thurmond seeming hardly to have noticed.

As full as Thurmond's life in Aiken was, no one assumed that his political days were behind him. Yet there were questions among South Carolina's political class about whether Thurmond could win again.[66] The assumption was that he would challenge Olin Johnston once more in 1956.[67] It would have been a difficult race, as much as if not more so than 1950. As bruising as the campaign had been to both men, Johnston's ultimate margin of victory, thirty thousand votes, was not insignificant. There was little to suggest that the electoral dynamics would be different six years later.

In the fall of 1954, however, Thurmond received a stroke of luck. Just two days before the deadline for certifying party nominees for the 1954 general election, South Carolina's senior U.S. senator, Burnet Maybank, died at his summer home in Flat Rock, North Carolina.[68] While Maybank's poor health was no secret, his death set off an unprecedented scramble in South Carolina as Democratic leaders debated whether to attempt another primary before the general election in November.

Thurmond was in New Jersey when he received the news about

Maybank. He immediately called Bob Figg to discuss his prospects. "Strom, you keep yourself out of this," Figg warned. He knew that Edgar Brown, finance chair and president pro tempore of the state senate, had already made calls lining up support. One-half of the Barnwell Ring that Thurmond had vilified in 1946, Brown wielded influence that made him a kind of prime minister of the state.[69] This was a once-in-a-lifetime opportunity for Brown. Though skilled as a political infighter, he did not have great support among rank-and-file South Carolinians. His secure seat in the state senate had been obtained by election in tiny Barnwell County, and his two previous attempts at statewide office generated only lackluster support. But now Brown had a path to the Senate that did not require a statewide election.

Yet Edgar Brown overplayed his hand at the Democratic Executive Committee in Columbia, Thurmond's second stroke of good fortune. The meeting took place the afternoon of Maybank's funeral in Charleston. Politicians and reporters eyed their watches, readying themselves for the mad dash back to the capital at the funeral's end. No one, however, was more crass about the matter than Edgar Brown—or at least that is how the story came to be told by Thurmond's supporters. Rumors circulated that Brown's car was the first to pull out of the funeral cortege for the trip back to Columbia, cutting across a cornfield to get a head start. At that afternoon's meeting, Brown's supporters were seen as equally pushy, tabling a motion to consider the feasibility of holding a primary and immediately nominating their man. The next day, the headline of *The Greenville News* read, "49 Persons Nominate Brown U.S. Senator."[70] In truth it had only been thirty-one—eighteen members had voted against Brown. Thurmond fastened on this revised number: "The issue in this campaign is whether thirty-one men shall choose the United States Senator or whether the people shall choose him."[71]

As lucky as Thurmond was, he never would have been elected in 1954 had he not also been audacious. A more prudent man would have followed Bob Figg's advice and stayed away. A write-in candidacy for the U.S. Senate was more foolhardy than his 1948 effort to throw a presidential election into the House of Representatives—at least that had been done before.

Yet Thurmond had reasons to believe that he could beat Brown. One involved the avalanche of telephone calls he received in Aiken from supporters urging him to run. South Carolina's newspapers had stirred up public resentment over Brown's rushed nomination. Brown and his supporters pointed out that they were merely following the law, which required that party candidates be certified sixty days before the general election, and that there was not enough time to hold a primary. Even so, the widespread public sentiment was that Brown's nomination was tainted. Thurmond received the endorsement of fourteen out of the state's sixteen daily papers and seventy-three out of eighty-six non-daily papers.[72]

Thurmond's other consideration involved Governor James Byrnes, one of Edgar Brown's oldest friends. Byrnes had been the best man at Brown's wedding, yet the two men had fallen out over the 1952 presidential election, when Byrnes was Eisenhower's chief supporter in South Carolina and Brown led the efforts to hold the state for Adlai Stevenson.[73] Perhaps Byrnes resented the fact that he himself had not been the committee's choice. Though seventy-two years old at the time, Byrnes had held the seat before Maybank and had given it up only after Franklin Roosevelt asked him to serve on the Supreme Court.

Whatever the cause, the animus led Byrnes to recruit opponents to challenge Brown. His first choice was Donald Russell, the recently named president of the University of South Carolina, a former law partner of Byrnes's, and the assistant secretary of state during Byrnes's years in the State Department. When Russell proved wary of making an enemy of Edgar Brown, Byrnes turned to Thurmond.[74] He issued a statement saying that the executive committee should have held a primary instead of naming its own candidate, and Thurmond announced his candidacy immediately afterward.[75] As governor, Byrnes boosted Thurmond's chances by skipping the conventional practice of appointing the Democratic nominee on an interim basis. He named instead the businessman Charles Daniel, who immediately announced that he had no intention of running himself.[76] Daniel would keep the seat warm until Thurmond took over.

Byrnes resisted a formal endorsement for several weeks. The experience of 1950, when he left Thurmond hanging, worried Thurmond's advisers. Walter Brown implored his old boss to take a stronger public stand for Thurmond.[77] Following Byrnes's instructions, he wrote a campaign statement for Thurmond that included a pledge to resign from the Senate in 1956 in order to put the race back into the Democratic primary. Brown met with Thurmond and Bob Figg at the Wade Hampton Hotel in Columbia to present the statement. "Strike it out," Thurmond said of the pledge, arguing that a write-in victory would justify a full six-year term. But once Brown made clear that Byrnes's support was contingent on the pledge, Thurmond relented.[78] Thurmond gave the statement, and Byrnes announced his endorsement a little over a week before Election Day.[79]

Even with Byrnes's support and the public resentment over the executive committee's actions, Thurmond faced an uphill battle. He met stiff opposition from the national Democratic Party. Thurmond and Byrnes were two of the Democratic South's most prominent dissenters, and Edgar Brown tried to turn the campaign around the issue of party loyalty. In what was billed as a "sharp rebuff," the Democratic National Committee pledged its full support to Brown and passed along $2,500 in campaign funds.[80] Yet a number of gaffes by national party officials undercut this help. The Democratic National Committee chairman, Stephen Mitchell, implied tactlessly that Thurmond's write-in candidacy would suffer because of the rate of illiteracy among South Carolina voters.[81] Worse still for Brown, a close friend of Harry Truman's told a Washington reporter that the former president was supporting Brown because of Thurmond's disloyalty to the party in 1948. Truman remained enormously unpopular in South Carolina because of his administration's racial stands. *Time* called it "the kiss of death."[82]

On Election Day, Thurmond's campaign dressed up little girls in red, white, and blue dresses and had them pass out pencils with his name on them, a crib sheet of sorts for anyone who needed it.[83] In some polling places, the write-in slot was high up on the voting machine, inaccessible to shorter voters. Voting booth curtains didn't reach to the floor, and newspapers ran pictures showing the feet of women voters standing on piles of bricks to reach the write-in slot.[84] Election managers accepted a broad range of misspellings—"Thurmand," "Thurmon," "Turman"—though they drew the line at such intolerable distortions as "Truman."[85] When all the votes were counted, Strom Thurmond won election to the U.S. Senate as a write-in candidate by nearly a two-to-one margin.[86]

5

MASSIVE RESISTANCES
(1955–1960)

On the afternoon of January 4, 1955, in room 201 of the Senate Office Building, Strom Thurmond attended the meeting of the Senate Democratic Conference. The Eighty-fourth Congress opened the next day, and the primary business was the reelection of the Texas senator Lyndon Johnson as majority leader. Johnson was the Democrats' indispensable man for his ability to reconcile the party's schizophrenic union of regional and ideological opposites. Despite the Democrats' eagerness to project an "aura of unity," one note of dissonance rang out. After Johnson's election there followed a motion to thank the campaign committee for its work. Strom Thurmond raised his hand. He had no quarrel with the committee, but he wanted to make clear that it deserved no credit for his election. "They spent money against me," he said. He did not want any Democrats in Washington "to think I owe 'em anything."[1]

"It's safe to say that no southern Senator has recently arrived in Washington with less of an air of supplication," one columnist wrote of Thurmond.[2] Over the course of his near half century in the Senate, he would come to cherish Senate traditions of decorum and collegiality, becoming in the last two decades of his career one of the Senate's grand men—knowledgeable, adroit, a consensus builder. But he did not start off that way. Thurmond was the "cactus of the Senate," bumptious, humorless, and prickly.[3]

The reasons were numerous. He chafed at the Senate custom of newcomers lying low. He had to run for the Senate three times in his first six years—his 1954 write-in campaign; his resignation and reelection in 1956; and his reelection campaign in 1960—which made a man who was, by nature, obsessed with his political fortunes even more so. Also, Thurmond now had as senior colleagues several men guilty of political slights from his 1948 presidential run, and his relationship with his South Carolina colleague, Olin Johnston, remained strained from their bitter 1950 race.

Beyond the personalities involved, early on Thurmond prized his independence and image too highly to muck around with the compromises and half loaves required in legislative consensus building. Independence led to isolation, and it was his sense of alienation from his fellow southerners that provides critical context for understanding his two most memorable actions from these years: his instigation and authorship of the Southern Manifesto and his record 1957 filibuster. In the national press and for the rest of his career, these actions sealed Thurmond's reputation as one of the South's last Confederates, a champion of white southerners' campaign of "massive resistance." Yet Thurmond's stature as a fiery segregationist has obscured the role he played in resisting other aspects of postwar American liberalism.

Thurmond's assault on the *Brown* decision was one part of a broader attack on the liberal jurisprudence of the Warren Court. The Court's rulings on cases involving internal security and subversion in the late 1950s were the starting point for his anti-Communist crusade that would mature several years later. Similarly, criminal law rulings planted the seeds for a campaign for law and order that sprouted in the mid-1960s and reached maturity in Richard Nixon's 1968 election campaign. Thurmond was also one of the Senate's most determined foes of labor unions and one of its greatest friends to business interests. His disdain for labor bosses became interchangeable with his loathing of civil rights leaders. Beginning in the 1950s, Thurmond joined a coalition of southern Democrats and Republicans to pursue an anti-union agenda that would become a defining element of national conservative politics. In the long run, Thurmond's and other postwar conservatives' antipathy to labor rights was one of their most enduring legacies.

To his colleagues, Thurmond was a brash freshman, equal parts obstreperous and shrewd. His first fight with Democratic leadership came six months into his term. Democrats opposed a Republican measure that would have cut funding to the marines.[4] Thurmond was undecided, and Lyndon Johnson paid him a visit before the vote. As majority leader, Johnson controlled committee assignments. Thurmond had wanted an appointment to either the Foreign Relations or the Armed Services Committee and had worked through a mutual Texas friend to lobby Johnson on the matter.[5] Johnson told Thurmond that he needed to vote correctly on the marines issue; Thurmond said that he had to vote his convictions. After Thurmond voted against the bill, the powerful, lanky Texan spotted Thurmond in a Senate hallway, grabbed him just above the elbow, and squeezed until it hurt. When he told Thurmond to do something, Johnson barked, he expected him to do it. Another three and a half years would go by before Thurmond made it onto the Armed Services Committee.[6]

Conflict between Thurmond and Johnson was inevitable. Both men teemed with ego, ambition, and testosterone. Thurmond loathed Johnson's imperiousness; he saw the Texan as power hungry and unprincipled. Thurmond was six years older than Johnson and had been a successful governor and a candidate for the presidency in 1948, the same year that Johnson won a Senate seat in what was widely considered a stolen election. Thurmond's election, by contrast, had come in a historic write-in campaign, yet Johnson treated him like an errand boy.

The more immediate problem for Thurmond was his pledge to resign in 1956 and run in the regular Democratic primary. He waited as long as possible to resign in order to preserve as much seniority as possible, stepping down on April 4, 1956, one day before the deadline to file for the June Democratic primary election.[7] Before that date, however, he made sure that his name was in the news concerning the dominant issue in South Carolina politics, one for which he had already earned a national reputation—segregation.

One of the first bills he introduced as a senator was legislation prohibiting federal courts from having jurisdiction over cases relating to public schools, a measure written by Bob Figg, who at the time was still arguing the side of Clarendon County schools in the *Brown* implementation case.[8] Throughout 1955, in his newsletter, radio addresses, and speeches before groups such as the Citizens' Council and the States' Rights League, Thurmond called the *Brown* decision illegitimate and unconstitutional.[9] He joined the advisory board of the Federation for Constitutional Government, an organization filled with former Dixiecrats.[10]

By the end of 1955, the rediscovery of an obscure, antiquated word—"interposition"—seemed to promise southern segregationists a new way forward in the fight against the Supreme Court. The doctrine sprang from James Madison's draft of the 1798 Virginia Resolution, which declared that when the federal government encroached on the sovereignty of individual states, those states had the right and duty to "interpose," or step in, and protect the "authorities, rights and liberties appertaining to them." For its adherents, the principle promised what Virginia's Harry Byrd described as "a perfectly legal means of appeal from the Supreme Court's order."[11] It carried less of a taint than another antique theory, nullification; segregationists actually debated the relative merits of the two. The chief interposition popularizer was the young editor of *The Richmond News Leader*, James J. Kilpatrick, though the idea received support in wider circles. Felix Morley, one of the founding editors of *Human Events*, made a case for Virginia's interposition resolution in a *Wall Street Journal* editorial and published an extended defense in *Nation's Business*, the magazine of the U.S. Chamber of Commerce.[12] A *National Review* editorial argued that the principle at stake in the interposition battle was "by no means capricious or sophistical."[13] By early 1956, the legislatures of five southern states, including South Carolina, were considering interposition resolutions.[14]

In January 1956, Thurmond began approaching his fellow southerners about issuing an interposition resolution in the Senate. The Southern Manifesto—officially known as the "Declaration of Constitutional Principles" and signed by nineteen senators and eighty-two congressmen—was the result. Though it never used the term "interposition," the manifesto denounced the Supreme Court for substituting "naked power for established law." It called *Brown* a "clear abuse of judicial power," recited legal arguments supporting school segregation, and blamed the Supreme Court for creating "chaos and confusion" in southern schools, thereby "destroying the amicable relations between the white and Negro races."[15]

The manifesto's origins and Thurmond's role in it have been disputed over the years.[16] The account published in *Time* was the one to which Thurmond took greatest exception. The magazine claimed that Thurmond had drafted an "arm-waving call for nullification" that was rewritten by "temperate Senators" like Richard Russell, Florida's Spessard Holland, Texas's Price Daniel, and Arkansas's J. William Fulbright. "At that point," *Time* reported, "Strom Thurmond elbowed his way back onto the scene, posed for photographers dictating the final draft—with which he had nothing to do—to his wife seated at a typewriter."[17] Thurmond fired off a letter to the editor, which he also released to the press, explaining that he had never used the word "nullification"—only "interposition"—nor had he "elbowed" his way back on the scene. He had never left it, he maintained, as seen by his work on a final drafting committee.[18]

If Thurmond seemed overeager to have his name associated with the manifesto, it's because he was. He had announced his upcoming resignation from the Senate ten days earlier and was heading into a primary race in a few months not knowing what kind of opposition he might face. Yet his contention that he was a member of a superseding committee that drafted the final version was, at best, an exaggeration and, at worst, an outright fabrication. His account is the only one that mentions such a committee.[19]

In campaigning for the manifesto among his fellow senators, Thurmond could be overbearing and obnoxious. He ambushed Tennessee's Albert Gore, who had yet to make a public statement on *Brown*. Thurmond alerted a group of southern reporters to be on hand in the gallery as he confronted Gore with the manifesto on the Senate floor. "Albert, we'd like you to sign the Southern Manifesto with the rest of us," Thurmond said, to which Gore shot back, "Hell, no." Gore's refusal to sign caused him trouble back home, as Thurmond undoubtedly knew it would.[20] Three weeks earlier, Thurmond had clipped a copy of a *New York Times* article that he sent to the Mississippi senator James Eastland reporting that Sidwell Friends, a private school in Washington where Eastland enrolled his children, had voted to integrate. Thurmond's one-line note read: "I thought you were opposed to integration."[21]

If Thurmond's history of the manifesto was self-aggrandizing, it was not wholly wrong. There had been no superseding committee as he had asserted, yet neither had he produced a firebrand draft out of step with the ultimate version.[22] In his files is a comparison of the final statement with Thurmond's original draft that notes seven points that were preserved. Both Thurmond's version and the final draft, for example, describe *Brown* as "illegal and unconstitutional," language that moderate southerners reportedly found so objectionable.[23] The main difference, the analysis noted, was that Thurmond's draft had endorsed the doctrine of interposition.[24]

Walter George read the Southern Manifesto in the Senate chamber on March 12, 1956. The southerners had given George the honor in hopes that it would bolster him in his tough reelection campaign against Herman Talmadge. Thurmond had maneuvered to speak directly after George. Afterward, Oregon's Wayne Morse offered a scathing rebuttal to the southerners. "On the basis of the arguments . . . of southern Senators," Morse said, "you would think today Calhoun was walking and speaking on the floor of the Senate."[25] When she heard this, Walter George's wife, who was sitting next to Jean Thurmond in the Senate gallery, observed that this in fact was a compliment.[26] Thurmond for one surely loved the comparison. His fondest hope was that his efforts might be traced in a line connecting back to such luminaries of the South's vaunted past. Perhaps that is why he retained the original signed copy of the Southern Manifesto for himself, preserving it in his Aiken office under lock and key.[27]

The Southern Manifesto initiated for Thurmond a war on the Warren Court that became the most consistent theme of his politics for the next decade and a half. Thurmond and fellow conservative southerners were determined to link the southern reaction against *Brown* with what they saw as a growing national reaction against the Court's judicial activism. In May 1956 an issue of *U.S. News and World Report* carried a picture of the former Supreme Court justice James F. Byrnes on its cover. "The Supreme Court Must Be Curbed," the headline read. The following month, in a speech before the Tennessee chapter of the Federation for Constitutional Government, Thurmond provided examples of how Congress might do it.[28] The reaction against the Supreme Court was not just regional, he argued, but gaining strength across the country.

Events the following year proved him correct. If 1954 produced "Black Monday," in 1957 there was "Red Monday," when the Court issued three decisions that struck down antisubversion statutes. The national reaction was analogous to white southerners' response to *Brown*. *National Review, The American Mercury,* and *U.S. News and World Report* all excoriated the Court.[29] New anti-Communist organizations sprang up—the John Birch Society most prominent among them—and a flurry of anti-Communist writings appeared, the most extremist of which denounced Earl Warren and the Supreme Court as the chief dupes of Communist subversion.[30]

Thurmond introduced a bill to nullify the Red Monday decisions. "The judiciary has broken the bounds of its constitutional limitations," he declared.[31] On the ABC television program *Open Hearing*, he called for the impeachment of the justices who had voted in the majority and called the Court a "great menace to this country."[32]

For Thurmond and other critics of the Warren Court, it was not just Communists who were being coddled but criminals as well. The Red Monday decisions coincided with a controversial ruling on criminal procedure. In a July 1, 1957, newsletter Thurmond informed his constituents of the case of Andrew Mallory, an African American man originally from Greenville, South Carolina, who had been arrested in Washington, D.C., in 1954 for choking and raping a white woman.[33] Police interrogated Mallory for seven hours, eventually extracting a confession, and he was convicted a year later. But the Supreme Court threw out the conviction, ruling that police had arrested him without probable cause. The Court determined that Mallory's prolonged interrogation without being formally charged represented an "unnecessary delay" in violation of federal rules.[34] In Thurmond's view, the Court showed "more concern for the rights of Communists and criminals, including rapists and murderers, than . . . for . . . innocent American citizens."[35]

Racial integration and crime had long been linked in the minds of many white southerners. For Thurmond, the *Brown* and *Mallory* decisions were of a piece, just as racial integration was behind a national crime wave. In 1958, Thurmond argued that the federal courts' "forced integration" of public schools in New York had led to an outbreak of crime in New York schools.[36] In September 1959 he clashed with the New York senator Jacob Javits after Thurmond entered into the *Congressional Record* a published report of crime and racial strife in northern cities that he linked to integration. Thurmond accused Javits and other civil rights supporters of trying to "export" New York City's crime and racial strife.[37] As for the "incontrovertible link" between integration and crime, he cited police experts and "notable ministers" like Billy Graham.[38] By the mid-1960s, he would expand these arguments into a broader criticism of Supreme Court liberalism and crime. In doing so, he joined a chorus of conservative law-and-order advocates who would gain political traction against liberal Democrats in midterm and presidential elections in 1966 and 1968.

For many Americans in the late 1950s, however, the most significant threat to law and order came not from the urban North but from the segregated South. Beginning with violence surrounding the integration of public schools in Little Rock, Arkansas, in 1957 and continuing through a series of high-profile school desegregation conflicts in the late 1950s, violence seemed epidemic in the southern states. Fueling the fire were southern politicians—Strom Thurmond chief among them—who preached outright defiance of the *Brown* decision.

In late September 1958, when the Supreme Court rejected a delay in the desegregation of Little Rock schools, Thurmond denounced the "anarchism of the court."[39] Over the next month, he delivered some of the most inflammatory speeches of his career. "The opinion of the Court is not the law," he said. "It is another attempt by the Court to substitute its false and vicious ideology for the Constitution in many fields, of which the school problem is only one."[40] The next day, he described the South's "brutal persecution" at the hands of forces that sought to rule the South "in a second 'Tragic Era.'"[41] And in a speech before the Citizens Committee for Constitutional Government in Augusta in early November 1958, Thurmond declared "total and unremitting war on the Supreme Court's unconstitutional usurpations and unlawful arrogations of power." He even reached back to his Dixiecrat days to evoke old campaign rhetoric: "If we stand determined and united, there is no power upon earth that can force us to mix the races in our schools. The federal government does not have enough troops to police the entire South, and even if it did, race-mixing still could not be forced upon a determined, organized and united people."[42]

Thurmond was not the only southern leader to use such fiery rhetoric, and his Augusta speech did call for "non-violent" resistance. The pyrotechnic phrases, however, easily obscured such qualifications. The recklessness and irresponsibility of his language are highlighted by what one source described as the "contagion of violence" that coincided with his segregationist tirades.[43] In October, white extremists dynamited a synagogue in Atlanta, and in Clinton, Tennessee, they bombed a public school that had recently been integrated.[44] The incidents suggested the dangerous ways in which rhetoric like Thurmond's call for "total and unremitting war" could be interpreted.

By 1957, the civil rights threat came not merely from court orders but from Congress. The 1956 election provided new impetus for civil rights support in both parties. For Republicans, their surprising success among African American voters led political experts to talk once again about the black vote being up for grabs. If Republicans could push through civil rights legislation, they might reclaim the loyalty of African Americans who had been leaking away to the Democrats for the past two decades or more. Correspondingly, northern Democrats were fresh off campaigns where they had been forced to explain why they continued to share a party label with conservative, racist southerners. Why should northern voters send Democrats to Congress to serve as the middlemen to powerful southern Democratic committee chairmen? Many northern Democrats questioned the South's value to the party. Only six southern states had gone Democratic in 1956. This advantage was offset, they argued, by heavy losses in black precincts in key northern swing states.[45]

For either group to succeed, it had to outmaneuver the Southern Caucus. Southern senators' power lay in their unity. For decades they had been able to block any vote on civil rights measures by utilizing the Senate rule that allowed for unlimited debate. In coordinated campaigns, the minority of southerners would talk an issue to death, or filibuster, running out the time or forcing opponents to move on to other issues. The Senate could break a filibuster under Rule 22, which allowed senators to invoke cloture, or end debate, by a two-thirds vote, but it was not easy. Senators prided themselves on being members of the world's greatest deliberative body, and many were loath to silence a colleague on principle. "When a Senator once takes the floor," a former Democratic floor leader, Joseph T. Robinson of Arkansas, used to say, "nobody but Almighty God can interrupt him—and the Lord never seems to take any notice of him."[46] The southerners took full advantage of this custom.

Southerners or senators sympathetic to the white South chaired ten of the Senate's fourteen standing committees. Leading them was Georgia's Richard Russell.[47] The fourth of fifteen children born to a future Georgia Supreme Court chief justice, Russell had been elected governor at age thirty-three and served two years before winning a special election to the Senate in 1932. A candidate for the Democratic nomination for president in 1952, he was unable to translate his Senate popularity into a broader campaign and became convinced that a southerner could not be elected president. But in Lyndon Johnson he found the next best thing. Russell poured his own ambitions into Johnson's career, helping the Texan win election as majority leader and positioning him for the Democratic presidential nomination.[48]

Though the civil rights legislation proposed by the Eisenhower administration would prove to be of modest consequence in African Americans' fight for the franchise, the symbolic importance of the 1957 civil rights bill was vast. In the historian C. Vann Woodward's assessment, the crisis the Democrats faced surpassed that of 1948, when the Dixiecrats bolted, or of 1896, when the Goldbugs left the party. It was comparable only to 1860. *The New York Times* called the 1957 civil rights bill "incomparably the most significant domestic action of any Congress in this century."[49]

The bill's significance lay in the political reckoning it prompted for southern Democrats. Lyndon Johnson and Richard Russell both knew how dire the southern position was.[50] The southern bloc in the Senate had been weakened by defections. Neither of Tennessee's senators— Estes Kefauver and Albert Gore—could be counted on, and in Texas, Ralph Yarborough's liberalism and Lyndon Johnson's presidential aspirations made them unreliable as well. Johnson's political position was fraught. A southern filibuster could destroy the delicate balance he had worked out between Democratic liberals and powerful southerners, an equilibrium that was critical to his presidential aspirations. The key to Johnson and Russell's efforts was to reduce the bill to a voting rights measure, and a feeble one at that.

The southerners' first victory was to strip the bill of section 3, which would have allowed the attorney general to initiate civil lawsuits against discrimination in schools, housing, and other public areas. The more difficult task was in diluting the voting rights provisions, which they did by narrowly passing an amendment that would guarantee a jury trial for anyone charged with depriving an individual of the right to vote. The jury trial amendment rendered the voting rights provisions all but meaningless, given that a southern jury would never convict a white election official on the charge of voter discrimination.

After passing the jury trial amendment in early August, Strom Thurmond celebrated along with his fellow southerners. They had pulled "the most venomous teeth from the so-called civil rights bill," Thurmond reported in his constituent newsletter.[51] He praised Richard Russell and Lyndon Johnson for "a magnificent job."[52]

Still, Thurmond closely watched developments in the House, where Republicans were intent on strengthening the jury trial amendment. The bill returned to the House Rules Committee, chaired by the archsegregationist Howard W. Smith, the seventy-four-year-old congressman from Virginia. Smith had no interest in any bill passing, jury trial amendment or no, and he refused to call a meeting of his committee to report the bill to the House. A majority vote in the committee could force Smith to convene the group, but House Speaker Sam Rayburn— who played the analogous role to his fellow Texan Johnson in shepherding the bill through the House—did not have the necessary votes. The Republican minority leader, Joseph W. Martin of Massachusetts, instructed the Republican members of the Rules Committee to hold their votes until Rayburn granted concessions on the jury trial amendment.[53]

Howard Smith's recalcitrance gave House Republicans an opening. On August 21 the Republicans laid out a compromise plan that allowed judges to try minor criminal contempt cases without a jury, but it guaranteed a new trial, by jury, if the penalty imposed was more than $300 or forty-five days in prison.[54] This was a face-saving measure by Martin and the Republicans. It was practically meaningless since few judges would hear a case without a jury when doing so would make it likely that the case would have to be tried twice.[55] It was enough, however, to bring leadership from both parties in both houses together. Thurmond denounced the compromise, calling the jury trial guarantee "a matter of principle, not a matter of degree."[56]

The Southern Caucus met the following day, Saturday, August 24, in what would be its last meeting before the final vote. Lyndon Johnson and Richard Russell had already anticipated a compromise coming out of the House and had prepared their argument. They were determined to pass the bill, with its meaningless compromise, without incident. The South, a Johnson staffer argued in a memo, stood "right on the brink of disaster." A showy display of objection at this late date and the South could lose "not only the ability to have any impact on civil rights legislation but any influence it has in Congress at all." The memo recalled the political precariousness of northern and western Democrats who had voted with the South on the jury trial amendment, mentioning by name Senators John Kennedy of Massachusetts and John Pastore of Rhode Island. "If the bill is killed now, they will feel that the South has betrayed them after they acted in good faith," it warned. "They will scramble to get aboard the most extreme anti-south position they can find and they will have considerable sympathy behind them." The repercussions for the South were dire, including the potential revival of section 3 and "every 'civil rights' scheme of the past 20 years."[57]

Moderate Democrats and Republicans had met southerners halfway, and Lyndon Johnson and Richard Russell believed that it was up to the southerners now to honor their end of the bargain. Russell laid out the case to the Southern Caucus in simple, unemotional terms.

Afterward, according to *Time*, Thurmond was "among the first to agree with the non-filibuster decision."[58] Russell Long of Louisiana remembered it that way as well. When he broached the subject of a filibuster, Long recalled, "the junior Senator from South Carolina (Thurmond) advised me, in the presence of other Senators, that that would be the worst mistake we could make."[59]

Thurmond would later maintain that the caucus had agreed merely that an "organized extended debate would not be held."[60] On Monday morning he had breakfast with Olin Johnston and the South Carolina congressman Mendel Rivers, who later that day told South Carolina reporters how he had begged the state's two senators to reconsider their decision not to filibuster the bill.[61] On Tuesday, the House passed the compromise civil rights bill, and Thurmond was the first to meet it on its return to the Senate. In a surprise attack that was not coordinated with the Southern Caucus, he moved to send the bill to the Judiciary Committee, chaired by Mississippi's James Eastland, for further consideration. His motion was easily defeated.[62]

By midday on Wednesday, August 28, telegrams and letters were pouring into Thurmond's office imploring him to do everything in his power to defeat the bill.[63] Every southern senator faced a similar barrage. Thurmond went back to Richard Russell to urge him to reconvene the southerners to discuss an organized filibuster. Russell refused. Nothing had changed since the last meeting. The previous agreement still held. If a majority of southern senators requested Russell to reconvene the group, he would do so. In lieu of that—and here was the point Thurmond emphasized later—Russell told Thurmond "each Senator would follow his own course."[64] The Senate scheduled a night session for that evening in anticipation of southerners making their final condemnation of the bill. Thurmond requested one of the last time slots.[65]

He gained the floor at 8:54 on the evening of Wednesday, August 28, and did not relinquish it until 9:12 p.m. the following day. He began by reading, in alphabetical order, the election statutes of each of the forty-eight states. About two hours in, Everett Dirksen passed the word: "Boys, it looks like an all-nighter." At 1:00 a.m., Barry Goldwater of Arizona asked Thurmond to yield for an insertion in the *Congressional Record*. Thurmond consented and stole away for his only bathroom break. In the long hours of early morning, gallery attendance dwindled to three: Jean Thurmond, Clarence Mitchell of the NAACP, and an unidentified man who snored softly. During the course of his speech Thurmond nibbled on cold ground sirloin steak that Jean had cooked at home and brought over in tinfoil with a hunk of pumpernickel bread. He drank orange juice, milk, and water, popped malted milk tablets, and sucked on throat lozenges. He read listlessly from the nation's foundational documents, including the Declaration of Independence, the Bill of Rights, and Washington's Farewell Address. By midday Thursday, his voice had become so faint that the California senator William Knowland, sitting on the other side of the chamber, asked him to speak up. Thurmond requested that the senator move closer. Knowland declined, saying he was "well satisfied" with his seat.[66]

Thurmond passed the previous record for the longest Senate speech, held by Senator Wayne Morse of Oregon, in the seven o'clock hour. He began winding down around 9:00 p.m., telling the story of a commencement speech he had given a few years earlier. Raising his voice to stir the slumbering audience in the back rows, Thurmond had reminded the crowd that he was "speaking for the future citizens of South Carolina," to which one of the roused backbenchers replied, "Well brother, if you speak much longer, they will soon be here, too." The laughter that filled the chamber invigorated Thurmond: "I feel so good that I believe I could speak quite a long time." The final laugh Thurmond drew unwittingly, when he closed by saying that he expected to vote against the bill—a point that by then was obvious to all.[67]

The speech filled ninety-six pages of the *Congressional Record* with estimated printing costs running to $7,776.[68] Thurmond's harshest critics were his fellow southerners. "Oh God, the venomous hatred of his Southern colleagues," recalled an aide to Lyndon Johnson. "I'll never forget Herman Talmadge's eyes when he walked in on the floor of the Senate that day and saw Strom carrying on that performance."[69] All of the other southern senators had received sulfurous telegrams through the night urging them to join Thurmond's fight. Before that, they had had to weather the public protestations of southern House members.[70] Caucus members were incensed that after months of coordinated effort by every southern senator, exertions that had effectively neutered the legislation, Thurmond was promoting himself as a lone warrior manning barricades that had been abandoned by his fellow southerners.

It was grandstanding of the worst sort, said Georgia's Talmadge, a distant cousin of Thurmond's who knew something about segregationist grandstanding.[71] Richard Russell denounced Thurmond in one of the most impassioned speeches of his long Senate career, calling Thurmond's performance an act of "personal political aggrandizement" and touting the caucus's success in preserving segregation. "I would gladly part with what remains of [this] life," he said, "if this would guarantee the preservation of a civilization of two races of unmixed blood in the land I love."[72]

Thurmond had a history with some of his fellow southerners that would have inured him to such criticism. If he saw the fury in Talmadge's eyes and gave it any thought, perhaps the thought was of 1948, when Talmadge had assured Thurmond that he would carry Georgia for the Dixiecrats only to send word through an intermediary, just weeks before the election, that Thurmond "would have to look after himself in Georgia." Among Thurmond's inner circle, Talmadge's last-minute switch was one of the chief betrayals of the campaign.[73] As for Richard Russell, perhaps Thurmond recalled his endorsement of Olin Johnston in 1950.[74] He had expressed guarded public disappointment in Russell's leadership of the caucus before, and he resented Russell's efforts to position Lyndon Johnson for the presidency.[75] When it came to swallowing the House compromise and facing constituents' questions over why he did not do more to resist the first civil rights bill passed since Reconstruction, Thurmond was not going to sacrifice one bit of his own political capital.

Yet he was not settling scores so much as positioning himself for future political challenges. His filibuster remained a political fillip for him for the remainder of the massive resistance era. Whenever constituents cast the slightest aspersion on his segregationist credentials, Thurmond could remind them of his 1957 stand, when the southern bloc wilted and he alone stood against the detestable civil rights forces.[76] His justification for his actions was so familiar to him that twenty-two years later Thurmond could recall to an oral history interviewer the precise figures in the House compromise for when a jury trial was mandated—a $300 fine or forty-five days in prison.[77]

Along with his 1948 third-party campaign and the Southern Manifesto, Thurmond's filibuster allowed him to present himself as the segregated South's fiercest defender. Consider the simple question of how he physically managed to pull off the marathon speech. One of the first questions that reporters asked him when he stepped off the Senate floor was how he was able to control his bladder for so long. The rumor that entered the mainstream media and became lore was that Thurmond had intentionally dehydrated himself in the Senate steam room so that when he consumed liquids his body would absorb them like a sponge.[78]

A rival account, which white journalists either ignored or were unaware of, circulated in the African American community. *The Chicago Defender* reported that Thurmond had actually been fitted "with a contraption devised for long motoring trips."[79] A memoir published by Bertie Bowman, a native South Carolinian and longtime African American employee on Capitol Hill, seems to confirm this. As one of the Senate's "downstairs" workers, Bowman recalled a Thurmond aide asking a Capitol handyman to fashion Thurmond a bag that "would prevent him from ever having to worry about heading for a urinal."[80]

These facts are of more than urological interest. The steam room explanation exaggerated Thurmond's physical prowess, and Thurmond's filibuster became a key event in his self-fashioned cult of masculinity. In profile interviews with reporters, Thurmond never failed to mention his strict physical regimen: prune juice every morning, no smoking or drinking, daily push-ups, and workouts with the barbells he kept in his Senate office. Jean Thurmond told reporters that letter writers to Thurmond's office often misspelled his name as "Strong" Thurmond and that the filibuster proved them correct. The steam room story burnished Thurmond's image of exceptional virility and masculine strength.

Thurmond's obsession with good health and exercise was genuine, yet it was also a part of a cultivated political image. Thurmond had been eyeing Wayne Morse's filibuster record for some years, waiting for the right time to try to break it, intent on making a display of his physical strength and commitment to defending segregation.[81] In doing so, he drew on deeply held racialized and gendered notions about how strong, responsible white men were supposed to behave. They were the protectors and providers of vulnerable white women, and they had to be constantly vigilant. Thurmond's filibuster tapped into visceral emotions that racist demagogues in the South had been mining for years. They were the passions that sent hundreds of white southerners to their local wire offices to dash off supportive telegrams to Thurmond through all hours of the night. Oliver B. Lee of Chester, South Carolina, was one of them: "I fell down on my knees and offered a prayer to give you power, to let the people in the north know we had a real living man to represent the people."[82]

If the filibuster burnished Thurmond's image as the white South's manliest defender, the fact that he felt it necessary to bolster this reputation can be connected to his consistent lack of support for the national party ticket. He had not voted for a Democratic presidential candidate since 1944: he ran himself in 1948; he voted for Eisenhower in 1952; and in 1956 he had refused to support the Democratic ticket despite the fact that he was the party's nominee for the U.S. Senate and a resolution at the state convention had bound all members to support the national ticket. Understanding the "embarrassing position" in which he found himself that year, Thurmond arranged to be on a Defense Department tour inspecting military bases in the Far East during the final weeks of the campaign.[83] Political enemies in South Carolina harangued him for his consistent betrayal of the Democratic presidential ticket. The most strident critic was Wilton E. Hall, publisher of the *Anderson Independent* and a close confidant of Olin Johnston's. Hall regularly referred to Thurmond as "Stand-On-Head," recalling the embarrassing *Life* magazine photograph, and he published reports of voting scorecards that showed Thurmond as the Democratic senator who voted most consistently with the Republicans.[84]

Any association with Republicans was dangerous in South Carolina, but particularly so during the 1957 civil rights debate. White southerners viewed the bill as Republican legislation. President Eisenhower and Vice President Nixon both had given it high-profile support. Hall, who with Johnston led the South Carolina faction loyal to the national Democratic Party, lambasted Thurmond's filibuster as political shenanigans. "All his 'oratory' in the Senate will not erase the fact that Thurmond helped put the present anti-South Republican Party in power," Hall wrote. "South Carolina voters will be waiting— and ready—when 'Stand-On-Head' comes up for reelection. Any good Democrat can trim him and he knows it. That's why all the smoke at the moment."[85]

Thurmond did fear that someone would trim him. So did Walter

Brown, who privately expressed his consternation at how far Eisenhower and the Republicans had gone in backing the civil rights bill. That is why Brown wrote to Thurmond in August and encouraged him to get extra copies of a recently published photograph showing Thurmond speaking against the civil rights legislation.[86]

Thurmond would do Brown one better. He could get the photograph, but his caucus loyalty would not be enough. Congress was going to pass some kind of civil rights law, and Thurmond needed to show not that he was loyal to the caucus but that he was loyal to the South. So as August wore on, the more that caucus members acted as if the deal had already gone down, the more Thurmond got worked up over the deal that the caucus had settled for. And as he did, he opened up more room for himself to counterattack Olin Johnston, Wilton Hall, and others loyal to Richard Russell. Best of all for Thurmond, Johnston skipped the final vote on the civil rights bill to attend a family wedding back home.[87] Thurmond, by contrast, spoke against the bill longer than any man ever had in the history of the Senate.

Aside from the Johnston gang, a backlog of ambitious officeholders eyed Thurmond's Senate seat. Thurmond had to stand for reelection in 1960—Johnston's seat wouldn't come up until 1962—and a potential challenger had emerged in the figure of Governor George Bell Timmerman Jr., who had made something of a name for himself leading southern Democrats at the 1956 Democratic National Convention.[88] After Thurmond's 1956 reelection to the Senate, Timmerman had challenged the Senate's authority to seat Thurmond, claiming that as governor he had the power of appointment for the remainder of the interim term. The Senate quickly passed a resolution asserting its authority, and Thurmond wisely ignored the incident, but Walter Brown read it as Timmerman "sparring to oppose Thurmond for the Senate four years from now."[89] Thurmond surely noted the press conference that Timmerman held after the civil rights compromise passed in the House. Timmerman said that South Carolina's senators must "stand and fight or step aside and let there be elected men with political courage who will."[90]

There was for Thurmond at least one more calculation. The small gossip column in *The Chicago Defender* that first reported that he wore a catheter-like device during his filibuster hinted at it. Thurmond's speech was designed to please segregationists back home, the *Defender* noted, yet the article ended on an oblique note: "Some shadowy family skeletons were weaving in the background and it has been said that the senator is not as anti-Negro in his feelings as it would appear to be."[91]

Exactly what "family skeletons" the article was referring to is unclear. Perhaps this was a reference to reports from 1948 in the *Baltimore Afro-American* that Thurmond had black cousins living in New Jersey and Augusta.[92] Yet it could have just as easily been referring to rumors that circulated widely in South Carolina's African American community about Thurmond's black daughter. It is unlikely that Thurmond read the article, but he knew the gossip. And even if by some miracle he was oblivious to the whispered talk, he himself knew what had happened and could anticipate the personal and political humiliation if others found out.

There was no direct link between the secret of Thurmond's black daughter and his historic one-man filibuster against the civil rights bill, any more than there was a link with his decision to lead the Dixiecrats in 1948 or instigate the Southern Manifesto in 1956. In each instance, more immediate political concerns would have preoccupied his thinking. Yet when accounting for his duplicity with the Southern Caucus, why he risked ostracism from his powerful colleagues, and why in this instance as well as in 1948 and 1956 he seemed so determined to distinguish himself as the South's last Confederate, one finds it impossible to separate the personal from the political. Whatever considerations might explain his actions in these instances, the one that cannot be documented, yet neither can be denied, was for Thurmond to act in a way that might best obscure in his public life the most perilous secret of his private life.

The image of Strom Thurmond as one of the Jim Crow South's greatest defenders—an image he so carefully cultivated—was crucial to solidifying his base and maintaining his electoral viability. It is also an essential part of modern political folklore. Yet it obscures other aspects of his career that are important for understanding southern and national politics. Just nine months into his Senate tenure, a scorecard issued by the liberal Americans for Democratic Action (ADA) gave a score of zero to nineteen Republicans and one Democrat, Strom Thurmond.[93] In a different accounting two years later, Thurmond led all Senate Democrats (and ranked second among all senators) in support of Eisenhower's legislative program. He voted with the Republican president 89 percent of the time.[94]

These facts cannot be explained by his racial politics. Accounting for Thurmond's voting record requires a broader examination not just of his resistance to civil rights but of his increasing alignment with a bipartisan coalition of business interests that waged their own campaign of resistance against the New Deal and its legacies. It was Thurmond's increasing skepticism toward labor politics and his defense of "free enterprise"—a phrase that gained new urgency in the Cold War era as the rallying cry of conservative political and economic actors—that explain his record of agreement with the GOP.[95] It also shows how Thurmond, several years before his party switch, was already emerging as a leading member of an economically conservative postwar coalition.

By the time he got to the Senate, Thurmond liked to tell reporters that the nation's "No. 1 economic problem"—Franklin Roosevelt's famous 1938 description of the South—now lay north of Washington, not south.[96] In this assessment, he continued in a campaign that he had first begun as governor, touting the South's unique business climate as a lure to northern industries. The northern economic "problems" that he referred to were issues such as high local and state taxes and outmoded industrial plants, but above all it was the North's labor unions. The South's historically low rate of unionization—aided by the early 1950s by a wave of right-to-work laws—was a major selling point used to woo new plants.[97]

In 1957 and 1958, Thurmond joined Arizona's Barry Goldwater as the two most conservative members of the Senate's Committee on Labor, Education, and Public Welfare.[98] He happily recalled years later that he proved such a noisome presence on the committee that the AFL-CIO chief, George Meany, insisted that Majority Leader Lyndon Johnson remove "that SOB" from the committee after only one session.[99] Thurmond left for a long-awaited slot on the Armed Services Committee, but he continued to incur the wrath of labor unions in South Carolina. In 1959, the South Carolina Labor Council meeting in

Charleston opened with the cry "Strom Thurmond must go!"[100] Thurmond relished the fight, vowing that union opposition would not deter his campaign against "exploitation of the workers and the public by union bosses, the spending of Southern union dues to promote racial mixing and other socialistic programs."[101]

Curbing unions was imperative in industrial recruitment efforts, which took off in South Carolina in the 1950s. The Wisconsin industrialist Herb Kohler built a $12 million ceramics factory in the state in 1956 in the midst of a nearly decade-long strike against his company by members of the United Auto Workers. In 1958, Spartanburg alone welcomed six new factories. The following year Gerber built a $3 million baby food plant near the city, and local officials showed their support by repealing blue laws that barred work on Sundays.[102] As senator, Thurmond coordinated his efforts with the new state development board. In his first year alone, he wrote letters and placed phone calls to executives at General Electric, Sylvania, and ACF Electronics, urging them to consider South Carolina for their new plants.[103]

He worked closely in these matters with Charles Daniel, whose construction company was listed in 1964 as the seventh-largest contractor in the country, two spots behind Bechtel of San Francisco and one ahead of Brown & Root of Houston.[104] The year before, the Society of Industrial Realtors named Daniel "Industrialist of the Year" in a gala event at the Waldorf Astoria. Thurmond sat next to Daniel at the head table, and former vice president Richard Nixon handed Daniel his bronze statuette.[105]

Thurmond's work with Daniel is a good example of his close relationship with powerful southern businessmen who not only recruited outside industries but also, in the name of preserving the South's unique "business climate," waged war against organized labor. In 1961, after the National Labor Relations Board (NLRB) sided with the Plumbers and Pipe Fitters Union of the AFL-CIO in their petition to hold union elections at Daniel Construction, Daniel immediately contacted Thurmond's office.[106] In a memo addressed to congressional leaders as well as the full delegations of states in which Daniel Construction had offices, Thurmond called the NLRB decision "outrageous," concluding, "The government has . . . in effect joined forces with the union in an effort to shove the union down the throat of the company."[107]

In the early 1960s, the Daniel Construction case was one of several cited by business advocates as evidence of a new, hostile attitude toward business taken by the NLRB.[108] Thurmond and southern business boosters read a string of decisions in the South favorable to labor as a concerted attack on the South's industrial development program.[109] Another recent decision in South Carolina involved a Ware Shoals plant that had moved from Pennsylvania. The NLRB ordered the plant to fire two hundred workers and replace them with union workers from Pennsylvania, and it held the company responsible for the workers' relocation costs. The Ware Shoals decision, Thurmond railed, was "payment for political contributions and IOU's held by Walter Reuther and other ADA socialists."[110] He believed that a coordinated effort was afoot to unionize the South and deter northern industries from relocating.[111]

The NLRB quickly emerged as one of Thurmond's liberal villains. In January 1962, his office contributed to an uncredited article in *Human Events* titled "The New Frontier Throttles Dixie Industry" that discussed NLRB decisions that affected South Carolina industries, including the Daniel Construction judgment. The spread contained a sidebar with a picture of Thurmond and an extended quotation from one of his recent speeches denouncing the NLRB. Thurmond made sure an offprint was mailed to Daniel.[112]

Thurmond's attack on the NLRB dovetailed with another case involving a powerful South Carolina industrialist, Roger Milliken, the Groton- and Yale-educated scion of one of the nation's richest textile families and a man of whom Thurmond was particularly solicitous. The case would become one of the most protracted labor disputes in U.S. history. In 1956, Deering Milliken closed a cotton mill that it owned in Darlington, South Carolina, after employees there voted to unionize, and the Textile Workers Union of America (TWUA) filed charges of unfair labor practices. In 1962 the NLRB sided with the union, ordering Deering Milliken to award back pay to the five hundred Darlington employees who had lost their jobs. At the time it was the largest sum ever ordered by the board.[113]

Milliken denounced the decision as a "damaging blow of unprecedented proportions to the economic liberties of American businessmen" and appealed it all the way to the Supreme Court.[114] A sign of his political connections, part of his case was argued by Senator Sam Ervin of North Carolina, one of the Senate's most respected constitutional authorities and, along with Thurmond, one of its staunchest foes of organized labor.[115] In 1965 the Supreme Court upheld the NLRB's back-pay order. Milliken and the union continued to argue in the courts over the amount the company owed until 1980, twenty-four years after the initial incident, when Milliken finally settled for a $5 million payment.[116]

The nexus between Thurmond and powerful conservative business leaders such as Daniel and Milliken is an example of an emerging coalition of pro-business Republicans and States' Rights Democrats who worked together to preserve the South's "business climate," which included proximity to markets and raw materials but primarily cheap, plentiful labor, an anti-union climate, and state and local officials willing to defend business interests as their own.[117] This was Thurmond's politics of development, an imperative for him of no less importance than the politics of Jim Crow. But in fact he never had to choose between the two.

Despite prognostications that segregation would drive away northern businessmen wary of racial conflict, few if any northern businessmen had moral qualms about resettling businesses in the segregated South. Some southern boosters did pursue racial moderation and token integration as part of a business-friendly public relations campaign; the Atlanta mayor William Hartsfield's famous phrase describing his city as "too busy to hate" is the most memorable example. It was primarily in major urban areas like Atlanta, Houston, Nashville, and Charlotte—with interests in tourism, professional sports teams, and innovative high-tech white-collar industries—that such racially moderate business leadership came to the fore. Most southern industrial boosters, however, never found that their support of segregation hampered their politics of development.[118]

Strom Thurmond certainly did not. The politics of massive resistance provided him with an essential line of attack against organized labor. The best example was an incident in 1960 when he insinuated himself into a high-profile dispute over a local Virginia union's support for a segregated private school. The previous year, Thurmond had given a speech in Front Royal, Virginia, praising the local white community for its stand against court-ordered integrated schooling.[119] In Front Royal, Local 371 of the TWUA had been instrumental in establishing a private segregated school, offering its union hall to serve as makeshift classrooms and spearheading a voluntary fund-raising drive that raised roughly $1,600 per week.[120] When Local 371 voted to commit $8,000 from its treasury to purchase bonds for the construction of new private school buildings, officials at the TWUA, which was on record in support of *Brown*, froze the local union's assets.[121]

Thurmond denounced the TWUA's actions, using them as an example of the insufficiency of a labor reform bill that Congress had passed the previous year. That legislation, the result of extensive investigations into connections between labor and organized crime, created federal penalties for union officials who misused union funds or prevented union members from exercising legal rights. Thurmond urged Congress to "remove the weapon of economic control over a Local by the bosses of the International union."[122]

The Front Royal case was important for Thurmond because it provided a justification for his accelerated assault on labor unions. It allowed him to claim, as he did to a constituent in 1959, that his "heart lies not with the big bosses but with the working man."[123] Throughout the 1950s, labor union struggles over civil rights and corruption charges would open new lines of attack.

Thurmond had not always been so confident in his fight against unions. The mill vote remained influential in South Carolina politics (Thurmond had felt its power in his 1950 defeat), and his advisers, Walter Brown chief among them, warned him not to get too cozy with business interests.[124] As late as 1957, Thurmond's aide Harry Dent, who was emerging as his primary political sounding board, still counseled him not to "appear strictly anti-labor," advice Thurmond seems to have followed with his vote in favor of a minimum-wage hike in his first session of Congress.[125] By 1960, however, he had changed course, denouncing minimum-wage advances as government meddling in the affairs of private business.[126]

The prerogatives of private business and the segregated white South were paramount in a scalding denunciation Thurmond issued of the 1960 Democratic Party platform. He called the document a "blueprint for a welfare state," a "road map for economic collapse and unconditional surrender to the forces of socialism," and a "chart for amalgamation of the races."[127] After the Democrats nominated the Massachusetts senator John Kennedy for the presidency and Kennedy reasserted his support for the party's civil rights plank, Thurmond announced that he would not endorse the Democratic ticket. Hints of his GOP leanings could be seen in a speech he gave in the closing weeks of the campaign. He called the election "a choice of whether to have a labor government or a government of free enterprise."[128]

In 1960, Thurmond won reelection to the Senate unopposed. Afterward, despite repeated requests from reporters, he refused to disclose his vote for president.[129] Pennsylvania's senator Joseph Clark for one had had enough. He urged action against both Thurmond and Virginia's Harry Byrd for not supporting the Democratic ticket. Byrd should be removed as chairman of the Senate Finance Committee, Clark argued, and Thurmond should be run out of the party. In a feisty response that he released to the press, Thurmond invited Clark's challenge. South Carolina Democrats had warned party leaders that attempts to discipline Thurmond would only backfire. When reporters asked Harry Dent if Thurmond would turn Republican before he came up for reelection in 1966, Dent dismissed the question with a laugh, all the while leaving the matter entirely unsettled. "A man would be foolish," he said, "to decide now what he's going to do six years from now."[130]

6

OUTSIDE AGITATORS
(1960–1963)

The early 1960s marked a turning point in the southern civil rights movement. What had remained largely a legal battle played out in courtrooms and legislative chambers moved to the streets. Student sit-ins began in 1960, the Freedom Rides followed the next year, and other direct action protests came after that. That the vast majority of these protesters were native southerners did not matter. Whites explained the agitation as the work of "outside agitators," the bogeymen used to explain why relations between the races had soured.

Power brokers in the Jim Crow Democratic Party recognized another kind of outside threat. By the early 1960s, the Republican Party's Operation Dixie threatened to upend southern politics. Since the Red Shirt campaign, Republicans had been a phantom presence in South Carolina. The state did not even have a secret ballot until 1950. Until then, if citizens wanted to vote Republican, they had to walk into the polling place and request the Republican ballot, exposing themselves to all manner of calumny.

As was true with civil rights protesters, not all of these new southern Republicans were outsiders. Most in fact were native southerners. But in the tightly controlled world of the South Carolina Democratic Party, which in the twentieth century had been the only one that had mattered, they were dangerous and unwelcome. Walter Brown understood the hazard plainly. "These new found Republican Boy Scouts need to be told what the score is," he wrote to Thurmond in September

1961. Republicans were drawing conservative white voters—Strom Thurmond's most ardent supporters—out of the Democratic Party primary election, thus easing the election of "liberals and the scalawags."[1]

The implications of these agitators' activities were not for southern politics alone. Operation Dixie was a key element in the national conservative effort to wrest control of the Republican Party away from the moderate and liberal "modern Republicans," the ones who had so easily accommodated themselves to Roosevelt's New Deal. Where were the voters who would enable the GOP to overcome its decades-long status as the minority party in American politics? Barry Goldwater and conservative Republicans saw them in the West and in the South. "Hunting where the ducks are" was the way Goldwater put it in a speech to southern Republicans in Atlanta in November 1961.

Moderate and liberal Republicans dismissed such efforts as shortsighted and morally suspect. They urged the party to embrace its civil rights heritage and leave to the Democrats the problem of what to do with the racist southern reactionaries. Why take on their baggage? The issue, as one liberal Republican magazine put it, was whether Republicans should "trade Lincoln for Strom Thurmond."[2]

Isolated and superannuated though they seemed to many opinion makers, Strom Thurmond Americans—that misshapen collection of Dixiecrats and John Birchers, conservative businessmen and Kennedy haters—were no marginal group in American politics in the early 1960s. They were at the center of a fight that would soon transform the Republican Party—and, by extension, national politics.

The most significant financial figure in Barry Goldwater's 1964 presidential campaign was also the moneyman behind Republican Party growth in South Carolina. A report from the 1964 Republican National Convention in San Francisco called Roger Milliken "the single most influential delegate."[3] Democrats back home dubbed him the GOP's "Daddy Warbucks."[4] Milliken's passions were for modern industrial management, tough-minded business practices, and conservative politics. He meant to indelibly mark each.

In the fall of 1959, Milliken and the Republican state chairman, Gregory D. Shorey, invited Barry Goldwater to Greenville, South Carolina, to speak at a dinner and appear on a statewide television program.[5] Earlier that summer Milliken had already written to Clarence Manion, dean of the Notre Dame Law School and host of the national conservative radio program *The Manion Forum*, with the idea of kick-starting a Goldwater presidential drive in 1960 by arranging for the South Carolina delegation to go to the convention committed to Goldwater.[6] South Carolina's member of the Republican National Committee, W. W. Wannamaker, elaborated on the plan at a meeting of Goldwater backers that Manion chaired at the Union League Club in Chicago in January 1960. The only concern for Wannamaker, the lone southerner in attendance, was having the movement begin in the South. He worried that it might tie Goldwater too closely to regional reaction. None of the others in attendance shared the concern. The South Carolina GOP convention would dovetail with the publication in March 1960 of a ghostwritten book that would outline Goldwater's position on a range of domestic and foreign issues and, ideally, pressure Richard Nixon, the presumptive Republican nominee, into taking conservative Republicans seriously.[7]

Four hundred delegates, two dozen of whom were African American, heard Goldwater speak in Columbia. It was the largest South Carolina Republican convention in history.[8] Goldwater said that the South had been in his heart ever since his high school days at Staunton Military Academy in Virginia, and he touted the Republican Party as the "only place a conservative can go." Praising southerners for their "steadfast devotion to what they believe" led him to digress into a moment of calculated bipartisanship: "I know this isn't customary for a Republican and particularly for me as chairman of the committee—but I just wish to God we could find some more Strom Thurmonds in this country."[9]

After Goldwater's keynote, Roger Milliken took the floor and moved that South Carolina go to the convention pledged to Barry Goldwater. Delegates responded with "rebel yells of agreement." A parade of county delegations ensued behind Confederate and U.S. flags.[10] Milliken called a delighted Clarence Manion the next day with a play-by-play account.[11]

In July, Goldwater went to the national convention in Chicago with two states lined up, South Carolina and his home state of Arizona. The La Salle Hotel, headquarters for the South Carolina delegation, was

ground zero for the fervid band of conservatives who tried to nominate Goldwater. Fueling the campaign were reports of the "Compact of
Fifth Avenue"—Goldwater called it the "Munich of the Republican
Party"—Richard Nixon's fourteen-point agreement with the New York
governor, Nelson Rockefeller, the leader of the liberal Republicans. For
conservatives the document included numerous heresies on domestic
and foreign issues, but for the southerners foremost among them was
point 9, which assured "aggressive action" on civil rights and voiced
support for sit-in demonstrators.[12]

It was an impassioned campaign, but in the end Goldwater counted
the votes and sided with his professional political advisers. The night
before the nominating vote, he went to the Arizona and South Carolina delegations to tell them not to place his name in nomination. But
by that point he had become a cause, not merely a candidate. When he
met the South Carolinians, Roger Milliken stood up and addressed
Goldwater in the third person: "We were instructed by our state convention to vote this delegation for Senator Goldwater and that's what
we intend to do." The next day Goldwater withdrew his name. He implored conservatives to fall in line behind Richard Nixon while still
continuing the fight to take back the Republican Party. But he did not
finish before supporters celebrated his nomination in the most heart-
felt demonstration of the convention. It was a mixed bag of old-line
Midwestern supporters of Robert Taft, college-aged devotees who faked
credentials to slip past security guards, and Cold War hawks like Phyllis Schlafly, who on the spur of the moment led the Illinois delegation
into the Goldwater parade. Yet prominent among them all were the
Southern Republicans. As they marched around the hall in Chicago,
strains of "Dixie" could be heard over the din.[13]

In early March, Clarence Manion reported to Barry Goldwater with
excitement about the imminent release of Goldwater's book *The Conscience of a Conservative*. It would be a "sensation," he predicted. Manion
was sure that "the Civil Rights disturbance will increase its popularity
throughout the Southland."[14] He was right; the book became a phenomenon. The initial print run was only fifty thousand copies. By June
the book had debuted on *Time*'s bestseller list at number ten; by election

time there were half a million copies in print.[15] The 127-page hardback became the political bible for a rising generation of conservative activists. Ghostwritten by Brent Bozell, the brother-in-law of William F. Buckley Jr., and divided into brief, easily digestible chapters—"The Welfare State," "The Soviet Menace," "Taxes and Spending"—the book explained in straightforward terms the central issues in the conservative revolt.

The third chapter, titled "States' Rights," and the fourth, "And Civil Rights," spoke directly to white southerners. William Workman, the South Carolina syndicated columnist and longtime Thurmond loyalist, published a review of the book the same day that Goldwater was in South Carolina to keynote the 1960 Republican state convention. The "clear and unmistakable terms" in which Goldwater discussed the thorny matter of school segregation thrilled Workman. He quoted favorite passages at length, such as "Despite the recent holding of the Supreme Court, I am firmly convinced—not only that integrated schools are not required—but that the Constitution does not permit any interference whatsoever by the federal government in the field of education."[16]

The book's release coincided with an unprecedented string of direct action protests by African Americans. It began on February 1 in Greensboro, North Carolina, where four students from North Carolina A&T, a historically African American college, were the first to "sit in" at the lunch counter at a Woolworth's department store. The Greensboro students inspired copycat protests in Nashville and Virginia that spread even to the Deep South. Thirty-five black students in Montgomery took seats in the snack shop in the county courthouse. Later, a thousand students from Alabama State College marched quietly to the state capitol and protested segregation by saying the Lord's Prayer and singing the national anthem. In Tuskegee, Alabama, four hundred students marched through the downtown streets. In March, demonstrations were held in Orangeburg, South Carolina; Miami, St. Petersburg, and Tampa, Florida; and Houston, Texas. Most demonstrations remained peaceful, but not all. Thirty whites and blacks were arrested in racial fracases in Portsmouth, Virginia, and High Point, North Carolina. In Columbia, some fifty African Americans armed with bricks and clubs battered cars parked at a white drive-in restaurant.[17] The direct action protest and violence strained race relations to a near breaking point.

The furor over the sit-ins dovetailed with equally dramatic show-downs in Washington. On February 15, the Senate began discussion of civil rights proposals that would last until April 8, the longest legislative deliberation since the Smoot-Hawley tariff debate of 1929–1930.[18] In late February the Capitol became the site of a legislative siege. In hopes of wearing down southern opposition, a majority of the Senate voted in favor of around-the-clock sessions. The sergeant at arms borrowed several dozen cots from the army, moving them into the old Supreme Court chamber and empty committee rooms. Photographers competed to capture senators in escalating states of undress.[19]

Throughout the 1960 filibuster Thurmond acted the loyal Southern Caucus member. Perhaps he was wary of taking on southern Democratic leadership when he would have to run in a South Carolina Democratic Party primary only a few months later. He no doubt understood that a united Southern Caucus could easily foil the round-the-clock regimen of civil rights supporters. Quorum calls were the choice tactic of delay; southerners utilized fifty over a nine-day stretch. The preferred time was the long early morning hours when the Senate chamber emptied of all but a handful of members.[20]

In his speeches, Thurmond relied heavily on William Workman's book *The Case for the South*, a compendium of segregationist arguments that hit all the high points of regional apologia. Yet Workman was a significant figure for Thurmond not merely as a source of segregationist argument. He preceded Thurmond in joining the Goldwater Republican Party, and in 1962 challenged Olin Johnston for a U.S. Senate seat in what would be the most significant statewide Republican campaign in South Carolina since Reconstruction.[21]

A group of Columbia Republicans including J. Drake Edens, who would chair Workman's campaign and eventually become the state party chairman, recruited Workman to run against Johnston.[22] South Carolina Republicans had been emboldened by the election in 1961 of Charles E. Boineau Jr. to the South Carolina House of Representatives, the first Republican elected in the state since 1901. Yet the party still lacked candidates with significant name recognition to run statewide.[23] In Bill Workman, they had an articulate conservative candidate who

was so well-known to South Carolinians that the byline of his syndicated column was simply his initials, WDW.[24]

Workman intended to take advantage of the Goldwater boom
spreading across the South. In March 1962, Goldwater was back in
South Carolina to address the Republican state convention. The turnout for this meeting dwarfed the 1960 gathering. Over twenty-five
hundred people showed up with about seven hundred delegates and
alternates from thirty-four of the state's forty-eight counties. It also
differed from 1960 in that there were no African American delegates
among them. "I think it's time you sent somebody up there [to Wash-
ington] to help Strom Thurmond represent conservatives," Goldwater
told the convention goers.[25]

Workman lost the race, but he managed to win 42 percent of the
vote, a historic achievement for the modern South Carolina GOP.
Years later Harry Dent would downplay the role of the Workman
campaign in spurring Thurmond's party switch two years later.[26] Yet
notes that Workman took on a long-distance telephone conversation
with Thurmond and Dent the month following his campaign suggest
a different story. The three men discussed the "Democratic-Republican-
Independent situation" in South Carolina in light of a law under consideration by the state assembly that would require registration by
party. They worried that if the law passed, "many will not register as
Democrats and will forsake the Democratic primary." Workman
wrote, "That will leave Strom out on limb, for he fears he cannot win
nomination if only trashy Democrats vote."[27]

From comments Workman made during the campaign, who the
"trashy Democrats" were is not hard to discern. They were white Democrats who trafficked in what Workman called the "controlled vote," or
what white southerners derisively referred to as the "bloc vote."[28] Trashy
Democrats were also black Democrats, and in this Thurmond and
Workman revealed racist notions about black political participation
that stretched back to the very moment of African American enfran-
chisement. Many white southerners never accepted the legitimacy of the
Fifteenth Amendment; it was imposed by unscrupulous Republicans,
they believed, as a way of exploiting ignorant freedmen whose vote was
for sale to help prop up illegitimate Republican regimes in the postwar
South. The image of the ignorant African American whose vote was

for sale was a common trope of turn-of-the-century southern disenfranchisement campaigns, and it persisted well into the twentieth century, in both the North and the South. As late as 1948, the NAACP's
Henry Lee Moon decried the tendency, even among white liberals, "to
isolate and stigmatize the vote of the Negro as a corrupt and venal factor in American politics."[29]

Thurmond had been calculating the impact of the new Republican
organizations in the state for several years. No Republican candidate
could win a statewide vote, Walter Brown told him, yet the more conservative Democrats the GOP attracted, the easier it was for liberal
Democrats to win party primary races. "Unless someone knocks in the
head this effort of the Republicans to put a state ticket in the field,"
wrote Brown, "then we are going to be put in the position where we
will lose control of the Democratic Party."[30]

It was a moment of enormous volatility in a state that had known
only partisan stasis for the past eighty-six years. An articulate young
Republican—a white man and a native South Carolinian, no less—had
run for the U.S. Senate talking about states' rights and constitutionalism. He had the backing of an energetic and well-heeled party apparatus with aspirations for changing the face of state and national
politics. Given these dynamics—not to mention the Democratic gang
in Washington: liberals, intellectuals, would-be socialists, and bloc-
vote appeasers—the 42 percent of the vote that William Workman
won was more than a "pretty good poll" for Strom Thurmond. It was a
flash frame of future party politics in South Carolina and the nation.

Moderate and liberal Republicans, convinced that the GOP could still
win black votes if the party stood strongly for civil rights, were upset
over the campaigns that GOP candidates had run in several southern
states in 1962, William Workman's in particular. After passage of the
civil rights bill and Eisenhower's stand in Little Rock, the GOP had
done well with the black community in 1958, and Richard Nixon had
worked hard for black votes in his 1960 presidential campaign. For
these Republicans, Barry Goldwater's emergence and his conspicuous
support for states' rights were alarming.[31]

A new Republican magazine, *Advance*, was the most consistent critic of Operation Dixie and of Goldwater's leadership of the Republican Senate Campaign Committee. Dismissing Goldwater's argument about "hunting where the ducks are" as "immoral," the magazine joined the New York senator Jacob Javits in denouncing efforts by conservatives to "outsegregate the segregationists."[32] Both cited Workman's campaign as an example.[33]

Goldwater and his fellow conservatives countered these criticisms by arguing that it was economics, not race, driving party growth in the South. They advanced an image of an economically dynamic, increasingly middle-class South that naturally identified with the small-government conservatism of the Republican Party. It was the image of the region that only a few years later pundits would refer to as the Sunbelt South. "The kind of leadership that's putting the steam into the GOP drive is the leadership of business and professional men," wrote Anthony Harrigan in a profile of South Carolina Republicans in *Human Events*. Harrigan was a good example of such men. A journalist, Charleston native, and executive vice president of the Southern States Industrial Council, he was a leading regional spokesman for conservative free enterprise politics.[34] Goldwater himself traced Republican gains back through the previous three presidential elections, where Eisenhower and Nixon had won almost half of all presidential votes in the region. "A new and different kind of conservatism is rising to displace the old, rural traditional—almost hereditary—conservatism of the Democrats," he wrote. "It is primarily an economic conservatism stemming from the growth in business activity, the increase in per capita income and the rising confidence of the South in its own ability to expand industrially and commercially." He denounced as "absurd on its face" charges that Republicans had gained based on appeals to "extreme segregationists."[35]

Goldwater made the same argument in an article in *The Saturday Evening Post* that was ghostwritten by Karl Hess, one of his favorite speechwriters. Hess came to conservative politics through his work in public relations with the Champion Paper and Fibre Company, and many of the southern party activists building the GOP in Dixie had similar backgrounds in advertising. Their prior experience was essential. The argument that Goldwater and other conservatives made about the nonracial economic origins of the southern Republican Party had the ring of the adman about it. They were not reporting facts so much as shaping an image.

That is not to say that examples of the southern Republican New Breed could not be found. In South Carolina, the poster child of modern business-oriented southern Republicanism was Gregory D. Shorey, a Massachusetts native who moved to Greenville, South Carolina, in 1950 to start Style-Crafters Inc., a water-sports equipment company. Shorey led efforts for Dwight Eisenhower in South Carolina in 1952 and 1956 and was state party chairman from 1958 to 1961. But as important as Shorey, Milliken, and other conservative businessmen were in organizing the state party, connecting it with national GOP politics, and, not least of all, bankrolling party operations, there simply were not enough of them in South Carolina in the early 1960s to build a broad-based political party. To win elections, they would have to get the votes of disaffected Democrats.

The white whale for South Carolina's New Breed Republicans was Strom Thurmond. Once Thurmond switched parties, there would be tensions between him and the men who had built the party from the ground up, yet he was the unofficial leader of the dissident southern Democrats that the southern Republican Party builders needed so badly. If they were ever going to translate their fund-raising skills and organizational prowess into successful campaigns, Shorey and the Republicans had to win those voters. Thurmond could deliver them.

Revealing in this regard was a speech that Shorey made introducing Thurmond in November 1963. The occasion was the dedication of Shorey's new Style-Crafters plant in Greenville, where Thurmond delivered the keynote address. In his fulsome introduction, Shorey described Thurmond as "one of the greatest statesmen of our time." Referring to his presidential run, Shorey said, "Many of us had prayerfully hoped that he might have made it in 1948. If this happy event had occurred this country would be measurably better off today, and we would have safeguarded many of the freedoms and individual liberties being taken from us by executive order today."[36] This was political talk of the most obvious sort: Shorey was still a resident of Massachusetts in 1948 and a consultant for the Massachusetts State Republican Committee. But in 1963, he was eager to genuflect at the Dixiecrat altar. He had to. Where else would he find the votes that he was hoping would transform not only the South Carolina GOP but the national party as well?

Barry Goldwater and national conservatives were no different from Shorey and the South Carolina Republicans. Both groups needed Strom Thurmond Americans. If Goldwaterites were going to succeed in taking over the GOP from the liberal Republicans, they would have to have conservative white southerners who already believed most of what conservative Republicans believed anyway. The public relations consultants could fashion the Sunbelt image to argue that it was not segregationists driving Republican Party growth in the region, yet Goldwater knew how important opposition to civil rights was to GOP fortunes. He had approved the sections on states' rights and civil rights in *Conscience*, carefully calibrating his position in order to win disaffected southerners.

Conservative Republicans had no patience with liberal Republican hand-wringing over the issue of segregation. As a Goldwater aide put it in a memo to his boss, *Advance*'s concern about southern racism was "one of the reasons the South remains solidly Democrat."[37] Voting rights, for some conservatives, were a different concern; Goldwater himself was always steadfast in supporting black voting rights. But integration in schools? For the conservative opinion maker Raymond Moley, the issue seemed trivial when compared with runaway federal spending.[38] Goldwater's chapters on civil rights in *Conscience* suggested something similar.

Goldwater did have old ties to the NAACP, and southern Democrats were eager to exploit them. He addressed the situation directly in a letter to Workman, explaining that he had been a member of the NAACP "back in 1948 or 1950" to "help stop segregation in the high schools in my hometown." But he said, "I have not been a member since that time and in the interim my most bitter political enemies have been the NAACP." In an aside that would have warmed the heart of every southern segregationist, Goldwater said that the NAACP was "not primarily concerned with the situation involving the Negro, but are beholden to every socialistic cause in America."[39]

The decision by Goldwater and other conservative Republicans to embrace Strom Thurmond, or to recruit segregationist apologists like Bill Workman, or to hunt any of the other ducks who could help them take back the Republican Party from the Rockefellers, Javits, and other liberal Republicans was not a difficult one. Conservative Republican businessmen who pushed Goldwater within the GOP had opposed fair employment laws for as long as white southerners had. Goldwater and other conservatives in every region—North, South, West—shared with a white southerner like Thurmond a grave skepticism about the lengths that civil rights forces were willing to go to ensure equal rights.

In August 1961, for example, Goldwater sent Thurmond a copy of civil rights legislation that had been passed by the legislature of the Virgin Islands, a U.S. protectorate. "If this kind of legislation spreads any further, the present Civil Rights legislation will seem to be a Godsend," Goldwater wrote.[40] He had underlined sections of the bill that he found particularly egregious, including provisions prohibiting discrimination in public accommodations and private clubs and establishing periodic inspections by a commissioner of public safety—provisions that in slightly different form would eventually be incorporated into the 1964 Civil Rights Act. "I agree with you one hundred percent," Thurmond responded. "Isn't this preposterous?"[41]

On the evening of June 11, 1963, President Kennedy addressed the nation on prime-time television on the subject of civil rights. Earlier that day George Wallace had stood in the schoolhouse door in Tuscaloosa, Alabama, attempting to block two African American students from entering the state university. That night in Jackson, Mississippi, the NAACP field secretary Medgar Evers was shot and killed outside his home after returning from a late-night organizing meeting. The month before, national and international attention had been focused on Birmingham, Alabama, where the potbellied and pugnacious police chief, Eugene "Bull" Connor, the embodiment of the Gothic forces of southern resistance, turned police dogs and high-powered fire hoses on nonviolent demonstrators. President Kennedy captured the feelings of a great number of Americans when he called the struggle for civil rights in the South a "moral crisis."[42]

Galling to Thurmond was the response by his fellow southern Democrats. "In a Southern Senators meeting the other day, I again proved to be the Devil's Advocate," he reported to a constituent in mid-June.

Thurmond had recommended that southerners block the president's entire legislative agenda until concessions were made on civil rights. "Unfortunately, this didn't get too far at that meeting," he reported. "I think we can win if we pull out all the stops."[43] He pressed the point to his home-state audience—*The State* ran an article on June 20 about Thurmond's proposed "sit-down"—reviving the image that he had cultivated during the 1957 filibuster of the lone warrior struggling on amid tired old men who had given up the fight.[44]

Perhaps it was this sense of isolation that fueled Thurmond's disputatious performance during Commerce Committee hearings on the civil rights bill in the summer of 1963. The only southern member on the committee, Thurmond played the role of the lonely opposition with equal parts swagger, showmanship, and high dudgeon. "I want to say that I do not think your bill is going to pass the Congress," he told Attorney General Robert Kennedy, leading off two hours of questioning on the first day. At one point, he presented Kennedy with an annotated pocket-sized version of the Constitution. "It says what everyone should know," Thurmond explained. "It is written in such an interesting way that anyone can understand it"—even the attorney general, he implied.[45] Some of Thurmond's colleagues read the exchange as an example of Strom the simpleton—"Bobby didn't know whether to laugh or cry," said a fellow senator. Another reporter recalled Thurmond's "humorless" expression but credited him for proper concern about Kennedy's superficial knowledge of the Constitution.[46] In truth, this was Thurmond's arch version of political theater. Before him was the thirty-seven-year-old attorney general, the president's brash little brother, defending legislation that Thurmond believed would distort the regulatory powers of Congress beyond recognition.[47]

Thurmond called nineteen witnesses, all of whom opposed the bill. They were southern elected officials and small-business owners, as well as the southern firebrand R. Carter Pittman, a Georgia lawyer who had been making the rounds with a presentation titled "Communist Contribution to Equalitarian Dogma and Race-Mixing Turmoil."[48] There were also northern witnesses who denounced civil rights legislation with the same vehemence as the southerners. William Loeb, the conservative publisher of the Manchester *Union Leader*, testified against the bill, as did Thomas L. Poindexter, co-chairman of the

250,000-member Greater Detroit Homeowners Council. Poindexter's explanation of the consequences that flowed from racial desegregation was indistinguishable from ones Thurmond had been offering for years on the Senate floor. Racial integration, he said, led to "an immediate rise in crime and violence . . . of vice, of prostitution, of gambling and dope" and a "general lowering of the moral standards."[49]

Thurmond's most prominent witness was Governor George Wallace of Alabama. Thurmond questioned Wallace in a pas de deux that covered the alleged Communist associates of Martin Luther King and the inevitability of land reform following the legislation's clear usurpation of property rights. Wallace joined Thurmond for lunch in the Senate dining room afterward, where they made an ostentatious display of their good race relations by chatting up the all-black waitstaff.[50]

In their red-baiting, Thurmond and Wallace had powerful and persuasive enablers, chief among them the FBI director, J. Edgar Hoover. In his final report on the Commerce Committee hearings, Thurmond noted that Robert Kennedy's dismissal of Communist infiltration in the civil rights movement directly contradicted Congressional testimony of Hoover, who in 1958 had informed Congress, "The Negro situation is also being exploited fully and continuously by Communists on a national scale."[51] In January 1962, only weeks after Robert Kennedy had told a British journalist that the U.S. Communist Party "couldn't be more feeble and less of a threat, and besides its membership consists largely of FBI agents," Hoover again warned Congress about Communist infiltration of civil rights organizations. Thurmond was likely among the congressmen and senators for whom Hoover substantiated these claims by confidentially disclosing evidence that a New York lawyer named Stanley Levison, one of Martin Luther King's closest advisers, was also a secret member of the Communist Party, subject to orders from the Kremlin. The FBI began wiretaps on Levison in March 1962, a surveillance that eventually extended to King.[52]

The bureau used Thurmond as a means of leaking embarrassing information about civil rights leaders gleaned from FBI wiretaps. On August 2, 1963, in an effort to discredit the major protest march planned for Washington at the end of the month, Thurmond used information supplied by the bureau to attack Bayard Rustin, an important adviser to King and the organizational force behind the March on Washington.[53] Thurmond placed in the *Congressional Record* a series of articles that he said showed "definite leftwing links among some leaders of the planned August 28 march," including material detailing Rustin's history of radicalism.[54] He followed up days later with more bureau-supplied material.[55]

Thurmond waited for the outrage against the march leaders to set in, but none was forthcoming, at least not beyond the confines of his own Senate mailbox. On August 11, *The Washington Post* ran a flattering profile of Rustin, which Thurmond dismissed as a "whitewash."[56] He was appalled that no mention was made of Rustin's arrest on morals charges. The next day Thurmond, with the help of the FBI, upped the luridness quotient by placing in the *Congressional Record* a copy of the police report of Rustin's arrest for "sex perversion."[57] It was a dirty business for a man who had his own sexual secrets to keep, yet Thurmond used Rustin to smear the religious leaders who backed the March on Washington.[58]

In retrospect, Thurmond and Wallace's red-baiting seems the stuff of desperation, Jim Crow's last-gasp defenders grasping at straws. Yet Thurmond had been trying to situate the segregationist defense within the broader, more legitimate context of national security since 1948, and since that time national and international events had seemingly reinforced this tendency. That foreign elements were coordinating events behind the scenes had been his contention during the Freedom Rides in 1961. Back then he had requested that the Senate Internal Security Subcommittee investigate possible Communist influence in the Congress of Racial Equality, the organization sponsoring the rides, and in August and September gave speeches charging several freedom riders with Communist ties.[59]

These efforts must be viewed in the context of not merely his decades-long fight to defend Jim Crow but also his contemporaneous struggle against what he viewed as the Kennedy administration's underestimation of the Communist threat. Thurmond was convinced that for all of his opponents—civil rights activists, union leaders, northern liberals—socialism was the end goal. And in their midst were more sinister forces still, latent revolutionaries deluded by foreign ideologies. In the early 1960s, one of the most intense periods in America's Cold War struggle, he was beginning to suspect that they might even have infiltrated the State and Defense Departments' bureaucracy. His drive to ferret out the would-be subversives and their supporters thrust him to the forefront of right-wing politics in the United States.

7

MUZZLING AND THE AMERICAN RIGHT
(1958–1963)

Strom Thurmond arrived in his Senate office at 9:00 a.m. on the morning of July 21, 1961, having completed his regular morning routine, fifty-eight push-ups (one for each year he had lived), a glass of prune juice, and a vitamin-packed breakfast. Within minutes an aide brought him a copy of that morning's *Washington Post*.[1] An article described a leaked memo prepared by the Senate Foreign Relations Committee for its chairman, J. William Fulbright, Democrat of Arkansas. It complained that military officers participating in right-wing Cold War seminars could become "important obstacles to public acceptance of the President's program and leadership."[2]

Thurmond immediately phoned Fulbright's office to request a copy of the memo. None was available, he was told. A Fulbright staffer who came over to explain the situation "was promptly chewed into small pieces." Thurmond fired off a letter, addressed "Dear Bill," requesting a copy before he left Washington after lunch. Fulbright provided an equally brusque response. The memo was private correspondence, he said, not a public committee document.[3]

The study in question was one that Fulbright had ordered after a string of anti-Communist meetings in Arkansas in which military officers had shared platforms with far-right extremists.[4] The memo urged the Kennedy administration to revoke a 1958 National Security Council resolution that directed the services to establish Cold War education programs. The seminars, it warned, focused inordinately on "internal

Communist infiltration," and the military leaders who spoke at them gave tacit support to reactionary groups that equated "social legislation with socialism, and the latter with communism." Participating military leaders helped fuel this "radicalism on the right" in ways that might tie the hands of American diplomats in the delicate negotiations required in the nuclear age.[5]

Thurmond called a press conference in which he described the Fulbright memo as "a dastardly attempt to intimidate the commanders of United States armed forces" and "a serious blow to the security of the United States." Rejecting the memo's contention that military leaders were not trained to educate the public, he asserted that the military was "the real bastion of knowledge and understanding of the Communist threat."[6] As for right-wing criticism of domestic social programs, he said bluntly, "Communism is fundamentally socialism . . . Many of the domestic programs advocated and adopted fall clearly within the category of socialism. The truth can and does hurt."[7]

For the next two months, Thurmond almost single-handedly spearheaded a campaign to investigate the origins of the Fulbright memo and the necessity for troop education programs. He charged the Kennedy administration with pursuing a "no-win" policy in the Cold War. After the resolution passed, he spent more than a year crisscrossing the country making speeches, poring over documents, and serving as the conservative watchdog of the hearings.

Thurmond's campaign coincided with a surge in right-wing mobilization starting in the late 1950s with new publications, organizations, and individuals. Most important was the John Birch Society, founded in December 1958 by Robert H. Welch, a wealthy candy manufacturer from Massachusetts who had been active in right-wing politics for years. Welch's outlandish conspiratorial statements, including a reference to President Dwight Eisenhower as "a dedicated, conscious agent of the Communist conspiracy," attracted notoriety, yet he also drew a notable list of supporters, including T. Coleman Andrews, who in 1956 had followed Strom Thurmond as the States' Rights presidential candidate, and Clarence Manion, a member of the governing council, along with three past presidents of the National Association of Manufacturers.[8] One of Welch's biggest financial backers was Roger Milliken, who told a close adviser of Barry Goldwater's that the Birch Society provided an outlet for the "temperate Conservative Southerner," a group that was joining the Birch Society "in droves."[9]

While Thurmond turned down a position on the Birch Society's board, his standard practice with such requests, his speeches and public statements in these years increasingly drew on language and themes common on the anti-Communist far right. "The greatest danger to our country is from within," he argued during an appearance on *The Manion Forum* in January 1958. Anticipating a theme that he would return to, he described the pursuit of "human rights" as "a subtle, sometimes even subliminal" tactic that upon closer inspection revealed "an underlying advancement of collectivism."[10]

In the 1950s the fear of "subliminal" Communist tactics was not merely far-right conspiracy theory. The notion took off from a set of ideas that were relatively mainstream and centered on an artifact of Cold War America: brainwashing. At the end of the Korean War, reports surfaced of American prisoners of war (POWs) having undergone psychological reconditioning by Chinese Communists.[11] The fascination over brainwashing of American POWs during the Korean War—along with books such as George Orwell's *1984* and Richard Condon's *Manchurian Candidate*, which in 1962 was made into a Hollywood film starring Frank Sinatra—contributed to Cold War paranoia about the menacing powers of the Communists and a laxness among affluent postwar Americans. These concerns played a significant role in the 1958 National Security Council directive calling for troop indoctrination programs, the one that the Fulbright memo argued should be abandoned.[12]

American military leaders were mindful of psywar tactics, but right-wing anti-Communists were fixated on them. One figure who fed the obsession was the originator of the term, Edward Hunter, a foreign correspondent, intelligence expert, and author of *Brain-washing in Red China: The Calculated Destruction of Men's Minds* (1951) and *Brainwashing: From Pavlov to Powers* (1960). He had served with the Office of Strategic Services during World War II in a clandestine propaganda warfare office and later worked with a similar agency established within the Central Intelligence Agency. Hunter testified before the House Un-American Activities Committee in 1958 and the Senate Internal Security Subcommittee in 1961. In the latter instance, he alleged that a manifesto issued on December 5, 1960, by eighty-one Communist parties meeting in Moscow had called for a "Red anti-anti-Communist drive." Moscow, he asserted, was out to crush the grassroots anti-Communist campaign in the United States.[13]

Thurmond's campaign for the muzzling hearings drew directly from Hunter's 1961 testimony. "Many of our policy decisions when examined must be attributed to our conditioned reaction to stimuli administered as portions of the Communist attacks of psychological war," Thurmond argued. He outlined what he considered to be fallacious assumptions of American leaders—it was essentially the liberal internationalist agenda that Fulbright and the Kennedy administration supported—and alleged that they were the result of "Communist psychological warfare directed against us."[14] Thurmond and Hunter later appeared together on the Citizens' Council Forum Films program, where Hunter cited the Fulbright memo as an example of how liberal elites were trying to brainwash Americans. Thurmond for his part urged everyone to order a copy of Hunter's "anti-anticommunism" testimony.[15]

Thurmond's conduit to right-wing anti-Communist circles was an aide he hired in late 1957, Fred Buzhardt.[16] A member of the U.S. Army Air Corps during World War II, Buzhardt graduated from West Point in 1946 and was a first lieutenant in the air force in 1950, intent on a career in the military, when a problem with his hearing ended his flying days. He went home and earned a law degree, finishing first in his class at the University of South Carolina Law School, and practiced law for several years in McCormick with his father, a close friend and former law partner of Thurmond's. Stopping by the family law office in McCormick one day, Thurmond casually suggested that Buzhardt come work for him in Washington. Frustrated with small-town life, Buzhardt leapt at the chance.[17]

Buzhardt achieved his greatest fame in the early 1970s when he served as Richard Nixon's lawyer during Watergate, but his introduction to the limelight was during the muzzling hearings, when he was tagged as the "prime mover" behind Thurmond's campaign.[18] In Washington, Buzhardt took advantage of old contacts from West Point who had risen up the ranks in the Pentagon. He was a dogged worker and a voracious reader, and as right-wing anti-Communist literature multiplied in number and variety, he consumed it all. He found articles in publications ranging from *The Dan Smoot Report* to *National Review*, made notes on them, and passed them on for Thurmond's nighttime reading.[19]

Buzhardt, who became Thurmond's most prolific speechwriter, had an accomplice who exacerbated his extremist tendencies. The army colonel Philip Corso, a specialist in military intelligence, worked on the staff of Lieutenant General Arthur Trudeau, one of the generals whose speeches had been censored. Buzhardt met him while gathering research, and the two worked together closely. Corso, who joined Thurmond's staff after retiring from the military in 1963, had been a member of the truce delegation at Panmunjom at the end of the Korean War, where he participated in prisoner exchanges and was one of the first American officials to greet returning American POWs. The experience affected him for the rest of his career. He worked on projects dealing with American POWs as a staff member of the National Security Council in the 1950s. In the late 1990s he testified before the House Committee on National Security to having knowledge of hundreds of American POWs who were abandoned in Korea. Around the same time, he co-authored a book, *The Day After Roswell*, in which he claimed to have participated in a secret military program that recovered alien technology from an extraterrestrial spacecraft that crashed near Roswell, New Mexico, in 1947. He said that the program smuggled the recovered materials to private industries that studied them and came up with technological breakthroughs such as computer chips and fiber optics.[20]

Certainly the speeches that Thurmond's advisers prepared for him could venture into the absurd. *The Washington Post* reprinted an excerpt from one, calling it "the longest breath ever drawn in the Senate." Thurmond's office recorded the statement this way:

> Climaxing his talk, Thurmond . . . leveled a scathing blast at the world Communist movement, declaring in one breath it was "a power-seeking, God-denying, man-and-material-worshiping, amoral force operating from bases of territories it dominates, by conspiratorial tactics of subversion, infiltration, propaganda, assassination, genocide, espionage, political and economic blackmail, all under the cover of

nuclear holocaust, through an apparatus composed of agents, tools, opportunists and dupes of all ethnic origins and nationalities, bent on the unswerving goal of world domination and subjection, and the recreation of man himself into the common mold of an obedient slave to the minority for which communism was designed to appeal—the minority which it has ever since captivated, and to the minority—may it ever grow smaller—which may in the future be so blind spiritually and so engrossed materially as to be stricken by the soul-destroying disease promulgated and spread by Marx and his successors."[21]

Intense and taciturn, Fred Buzhardt was the counterweight to the affable Harry Dent, who ran Thurmond's political shop. He was the hard-line ideologue; Dent was the pragmatic politico.[22] It would seem, however, that Jean Thurmond, though twenty-three years younger than her husband, was the real leveling agent in Thurmond's life—to whatever degree he was level in these years. She, however, would not be on hand for Thurmond's anti-muzzling campaign. In the summer of 1959, after a series of blackouts and seizures, Jean was diagnosed with a brain tumor. Doctors performed surgery in September and again in December, but they could not save her. She died on January 6, 1960. She was thirty-three years old.[23]

Decades later Thurmond still kept a picture of his first wife in his desk drawer. Aides noticed how in quiet moments he would pull it out and look at it.[24] Thurmond changed after her death. He had always had workaholic tendencies, but now his work became an obsession. Discussing his muzzling campaign, a friend of Thurmond's wondered if Jean had lived, "whether or not he would have continued this one-man crusade—which is about what it was."[25]

The election of John F. Kennedy in November 1960 had raised new concerns on the right. The last time a Democratic president was in office, the United States had "lost" China, General MacArthur had been unceremoniously fired, and the country had started down a slippery slope of appeasement in Korea. Hard-liners also recalled Communist infiltration of the U.S. State Department exposed in the Alger Hiss trial and through the tireless campaigns of Joseph McCarthy, who, though generally discredited, remained a hero on the right.

Republicans attacked Kennedy from the start on national security issues. They accused him of imposing a "dictaphone type of 'gag rule'" on military leaders. This was the charge of Barry Goldwater, who criticized the Kennedy administration's decision to delete sharp anti-Communist statements in a speech by Admiral Arleigh Burke, chief of naval operations. The ban came during delicate negotiations between the Kennedy administration and the Soviets over the return of two American pilots who had been imprisoned by the Soviets for seven months.[26]

The Burke incident raised the issue of muzzling, but the real controversy came over the case of General Edwin Walker, commander of the Twenty-Fourth Infantry Division in West Germany. *The Overseas Weekly*, a newspaper for American GIs abroad, reported in April 1961 that soldiers under Walker's command were being forced to read John Birch Society literature. The army investigated, and in June the commander in chief of the army in Europe officially "admonished" Walker for indoctrinating his troops with partisan anti-Communist political material. Walker denied any direct connection with the Birch Society, but the information for his "Pro-Blue" troop education program was drawn from the conspiratorial literature that fed the radical Right.[27]

For some Americans, the furor over Walker's case and the close association of military leaders with right-wing groups raised the specter of a right-wing military coup in the United States. Contemporaneous struggles in France created an eerie analogy. There, right-wing leaders upset with President Charles de Gaulle's policies in Algeria attempted to overthrow the French leader. A number of journalists and former government officials pondered whether the French situation could occur in the States.[28] A mock news report in *The New Republic* sketched out what such a coup might look like. After President Kennedy and his family took refuge in the Mexican embassy, General Walker named his new cabinet. Strom Thurmond was defense secretary. Douglas MacArthur was secretary of state and Harry Byrd secretary of the Treasury. Barry Goldwater was secretary of health, education, and welfare.[29]

Another incident that stoked right-wing sentiment was a short documentary film, *Operation Abolition*, produced by the House Un-American Activities Committee. In May 1960, HUAC held hearings in San Francisco to investigate alleged un-American activities among schoolteachers and union organizers in California. Civil libertarians in the Bay Area, many of them university students and college professors, had been outraged over HUAC's decision to turn over investigative materials to local school boards. The film showed footage of protesters chanting outside committee meeting doors and being forcibly pulled away by police officers down long marble steps. The pretext was, the film made clear, conspiratorial: covert Communist agents had stirred up naive students into attacking the one government agency dedicated to exposing the Communist threat. Interspersed were committee members and congressmen who marveled at the brazenness of subversives in their midst.[30]

HUAC printed two thousand copies of the film. By mid-1961, some fifteen million people were estimated to have seen it. Liberals were outraged: the film was nothing more than tax-sponsored right-wing propaganda, they argued. Conservatives defended it with equal fervor.[31]

Thurmond was in San Francisco at the time of the HUAC hearings and saw firsthand the demonstrations at city hall. He was "sickened" by "the spectacle," he told a constituent.[32] Thurmond protested a Defense Department policy banning the film as required training material for military personnel. To another constituent he confided that the Defense Department seemed "to be under heavy pressure from the left wing, and, as you know, the left wing seems to have the upper hand in this country these days."[33]

The Walker case, the *Operation Abolition* controversy, and the Fulbright memo—which had not yet been made public—all factored into a directive issued by the defense secretary Robert McNamara in July 1961 that restricted the right of military personnel to participate in right-wing seminars.[34] The leak of the Fulbright memo days later set off alarm bells across the American Right.

In his campaign to hold hearings, Thurmond squared off once again with Richard Russell, chairman of the Senate Armed Services Committee. Russell's office was flooded with some eighteen thousand belligerent letters, telegrams, and postcards urging prompt inquiry into Thurmond's charges of military muzzling.[35] A remarkable number posed the same question: "ADA or USA—which are you working for?" A Russell aide discovered that the inspiration was a Birch Society newsletter. It was disorienting for Russell, one of the Senate's respected conservatives, to experience such skepticism from the Right.[36]

Russell had been in the middle of a national security firestorm before. A decade earlier he chaired a joint Armed Services and Foreign Relations Committee investigation into President Truman's dismissal of General Douglas MacArthur. Truman's decision to remove MacArthur during the height of Korean hostilities was one of the most controversial presidential orders in twentieth-century American politics. For millions of Americans, MacArthur returned home a hero, and many expected and hoped that he would run against Truman for the presidency in 1952. Republicans immediately called for a full-scale congressional investigation. During the hearings, Russell quietly deflated MacArthur's balloon, revealing the dangerous ends to which MacArthur's military decisions might have led had President Truman not stood firm. By the end of the hearings, even MacArthur's strongest supporters were forced to admit that the general's moment had passed.[37]

Russell had a similar effect on the muzzling hearings. Having been burned once by Thurmond's grandstanding over the 1957 civil rights bill, he was not about to give him free rein with an issue as explosive as military muzzling. Rather than naming a special select committee that Thurmond might have headed, Russell assigned the study to the Preparedness Investigating Subcommittee, chaired by the Mississippi senator John Stennis. Russell added Thurmond to the panel, but Stennis was in control.[38]

In other contexts, these three southern segregationists might be lumped together unthinkingly. Neither Russell nor Stennis was less racist than Thurmond. The difference was in their relationship to the national Democratic power structure. Russell and Stennis were Senate power brokers, whereas Thurmond's 1948 run had marked him as a maverick. The clearest path to the power that Thurmond craved was through helping mobilize the burgeoning anti-Communist populism on the right. This was not the only reason he was energized over the issue—he was sincerely committed to maintaining the strongest national defense possible—yet his ambition for national influence was an important factor.[39]

Thurmond embraced and was embraced by a set of right-wing actors who disdained Russell and Stennis for their loyalty to the Democratic Party establishment. John Stennis's voting record was hardly less conservative than Thurmond's, but Stennis shared Russell's low-key temperament and reverence for Senate traditions. Stennis had a reputation among his colleagues for diligence and honesty as well as a history of opposing anti-Communist grandstanding in the Senate. He had made a name for himself in 1954 when he became one of the first senators to speak out against Joseph McCarthy. As a junior member, he was named to the committee that investigated charges against the Wisconsin senator.[40]

Right-wingers who had helped Thurmond pressure Russell to hold hearings now trained their sights on Stennis. Hundreds of suspicious constituents wrote to Stennis in the fall of 1961 concerned about rumors that he would "whitewash" his report.[41] This pressure culminated in late December 1961 when the Mississippi Citizens' Council invited Edwin Walker to speak in Jackson. In only the second speech that Walker had given since leaving the military, he addressed a crowd of five thousand in Jackson's City Auditorium—the same place that Thurmond had delivered his first major Dixiecrat address back in 1948.[42] While attacking figures ranging from Dag Hammarskjöld, former secretary-general of the United Nations, to Dwight Eisenhower, Walker implied that Stennis's subcommittee might lack the "courage to do its job in the probe of military muzzling."[43] Walker returned to Mississippi in the fall of 1962 during the crisis over James Meredith's admission to the state university in Oxford. He helped incite students and right-wing agitators who had flocked to the campus into rioting against the federal marshals called in to protect Meredith.[44]

Walker personified the mutually reinforcing quality of segregationist and anti-Communist sentiment on the American Right in the early 1960s. Racism and antiradicalism combined to fuel right-wing passions in this period, just as they had throughout the nineteenth and twentieth centuries. Birch Society members were not merely concerned with communism, nor were Citizens' Council members solely obsessed with segregation. The Citizens' Council Forum Films series had the anti-Communist journalist Edward Hunter on the program more than any other guest.[45] His messages about the subtleties of Communist brainwashing seemed a perfect explanation of why so many Americans were abandoning generations-old racial mores. In parallel fashion, after the Meredith incident at Ole Miss, the Birch Society produced the book *The Invasion of Mississippi*, which showed the alleged "storm trooper" tactics of federal agents who seemed like symbols of a federal leviathan.[46] Thurmond's Senate office was a clearinghouse for these kinds of far-right passions.[47]

Clashes between Stennis and Thurmond over the administration of the hearings stoked right-wing suspicions of a whitewash. When Stennis announced that the hearings, scheduled to begin in the fall of 1961, would be postponed until January, the conservative columnist Holmes Alexander lauded Thurmond and implicitly criticized Stennis in a column that anticipated a "half-hearted" effort. "Investigations, to be effective, must be expensive and must get very rough," Alexander wrote.[48]

Thurmond got rough in the numerous hard-edged speeches he gave around the country in the fall of 1961. Speaking at the Coast Cities Freedom Program in Santa Monica, California, in late November, he charged that the muzzling of American military leaders "was the result of orders which came directly from Moscow."[49] The quotation came in the context of his repeating without attribution Edward Hunter's allegations about an "anti-anti-Communist" campaign coordinated in Moscow. Thurmond made a similar charge several days later in a speech in Little Rock and included the claim that he had learned of a State Department paper arguing "for the turning over of our nuclear weapons to the United Nations." He gave no source for the report. In response to reporters' questions whether he was connecting the Moscow meeting to Defense Department efforts to keep military officers from speaking at right-wing seminars, Thurmond responded, "All I'm trying to do is tell the people the facts. They can draw their own conclusions."[50]

The accusations were so reckless as to undermine other anti-Communist efforts. J. Edgar Hoover sent his aide Cartha "Deke" De-Loach to talk with Thurmond, who explained that the press had misquoted his California speech. DeLoach delicately reminded Thurmond to use "absolute facts" and not "stray from the truth." In a memo to his superior, DeLoach concluded that Thurmond was "most anxious to obtain as much publicity as possible. Our dealings with him will, of course, be on a very cautious basis."[51]

On the morning of January 23, 1962, under the suspended crystal chandeliers of the red-carpeted Senate caucus room, all 150 seats reserved for the opening of the military muzzling hearings filled early. Late arrivals crowded in along the edges of the room. Seated at the front were committee members with the chairman, John Stennis, having "the air of a country judge at a big trial," in the middle. To his right was the "thin, studious, serious" Thurmond.[52] Barry Goldwater, who had petitioned for a spot on the subcommittee but was denied a seat so as not to weight matters too heavily toward the military, sat in on the hearings and was invited to ask questions. Earlier, former president Dwight Eisenhower surprised many people by issuing a strongly worded statement condemning military muzzling. A resentful president Kennedy saw it as a swipe at his foreign policy; Thurmond called it "excellent."[53]

A showdown quickly emerged between Thurmond and the Kennedy administration over the issue of executive privilege. On January 31, Thurmond questioned Willis D. Lawrence, assistant director of security review at the Pentagon, about deletions in a statement by an army lieutenant general the previous year. Thurmond wanted to know the name of the censor who had edited the speech. Lawrence refused to provide it, citing an order from the defense secretary, Robert McNamara, not to identify reviewers in respect to particular speeches. Thurmond asked Chairman Stennis to "require" Lawrence to answer the question. High-ranking military officers had testified that certain deletions in their speeches had led them to wonder about the "motivation" of the reviewers, he said. Without questioning censors about specific deletions, the committee could not do its work. Executive privilege—the principle that private deliberations and communications related to the president's duties were confidential—had not been invoked by the administration, nor, Thurmond argued, would it apply in this instance.[54]

Stennis delayed ruling on Thurmond's request until he had time to study the issue further. Later, a crush of reporters and photographers gathered outside Stennis's office to cover a meeting that he brokered between Thurmond and McNamara, causing the men to retreat to an undisclosed office in another part of the Senate Office Building. A letter McNamara sent to the committee argued that it was unnecessary to link deletions with specific censors. They had erred in several instances, he admitted, but he feared the effect that naming specific wrongdoers would have on morale in his department.[55]

This was not mere posturing by McNamara. For several observers, Thurmond's campaign evoked memories of Joseph McCarthy's crusade against the State Department less than a decade earlier. Back then, the State Department had had difficulty defending specific decisions by mid- and low-level officials. Taking them out of their policy context, McCarthy mischaracterized the actions as part of a larger conspiracy, and in the process defamed innocent government employees.[56] For the Kennedy administration, the decision to protect defense officials from Thurmond's questioning was no small matter. It was essential for the operation of an independent and effective executive branch. That is why President Kennedy evoked executive privilege several days later, confirming McNamara's order to his subordinates not to answer Thurmond's inquiries.[57]

John Stennis issued a carefully worded response respecting the president's decision that drew on the example of his mentor Russell during the MacArthur hearings. In fact, he quoted directly from Russell's statement a decade earlier: "The future freedom and security of our country depend as much upon the maintenance of the delicate system of checks and balances designed by the Founding Fathers as upon our armies, our navies and our fleets of airplanes." Stennis sent a copy of the statement to Russell with a note attached: "You blazed the trail, and I was following it."[58]

Mainstream press accounts portrayed Thurmond's insistence on linking censors to specific deletions as evidence of extremism. A bizarre incident involving two investigators loyal to Thurmond reinforced that image. Reports surfaced that the subcommittee staffers Charles A. Byrne and Ben Kaplan had gone to the Marine Barracks in Washington and quizzed marines on their knowledge of Communist ideology and practice. Without informing either Chairman Stennis or the chief counsel, the two men assembled thirty-two marines in a classroom and, with the cooperation of officers on hand, ordered them to answer a list of loaded questions: "Is the international Communist conspiracy a menace to all free people? Is there a difference between a pacifist organization and a subversive organization? Do you agree with the saying—'From each according to his ability, to each according to his needs'? If not, why not?" *Time* called the quiz "the most monumental fool's errand since Cohn and Schine made history as the 'junketeering gumshoes'"—a reference to disreputable investigators from Joseph McCarthy's staff.[59]

In general, Thurmond lost the game of public opinion, but he managed to score points along the way. The investigation brought to light acts of censoring that even Kennedy administration officials admitted were egregious. The committee staff compiled a book of about 170 examples of deletions in speeches or statements about which Thurmond wanted to question State Department officials. Undersecretary of State George Ball decided to testify himself before the committee at the last minute. He issued a general statement in which he warned against oversimplifying issues, but when Thurmond questioned him on why specific phrases were deleted, Ball, who had not studied them, said that he would have to find out. Thurmond was infuriated.[60]

The administration had already invoked executive privilege and frustrated Thurmond's effort to question individual censors about their logic for specific deletions. Thurmond was trying to determine whether the deletions were the result of individual caprice or an intentional policy. Now the second-highest-ranking official in the State Department was unable to explain deletions in speeches that he had had weeks to study. "Why are you not prepared today?" Thurmond shouted. "You knew you were coming here, and you are withholding from us the censors who did the work. You will not let them testify. You will not let them tell us why they did it."[61] At best, the administration looked as if it was unprepared and not taking the investigation seriously. To the conspiratorially minded, Ball's inability to answer could be seen as evidence of a cover-up.

By springtime, when Thurmond's witnesses were scheduled to appear, the excitement with which the hearings had begun had dissipated. The large corps of press correspondents who had attended the early sessions had dwindled to two press associations and four or five metropolitan newspaper reporters.[62] Few Americans caught one of Thurmond's prize witnesses, Major William E. Mayer, an army psychiatrist involved in a study of U.S. Army prisoners during the Korean War. Mayer's expertise was psychiatry, yet his public presentations were remarkable in how they spun the tale of Korean POW brainwashing into an object lesson for the dissolution of family, church, and community in America.[63]

Aside from Mayer, there was one final Roman candle in Thurmond's anti-muzzling fireworks display. Edwin Walker testified before the committee in April 1962, yet by that time no one, friend or foe, was particularly eager to hear from him. His critics did not want rehashed the circumstances that had led to Walker's admonishment, but Thurmond and other supporters were warier still. Back in September 1961, when Thurmond won the vote to hold the muzzling investigation, Walker seemed like the prize example of a military man unfairly censored by civilian authorities. In the interim, however, he had resigned from the military, given a number of speeches before extremist groups in which he advanced all manner of crazed conspiracies, and announced his candidacy for the governorship of Texas. The accusation that had led the military to admonish him was that he had involved himself in partisan politics. As one journalist pointed out, "By openly seeking office on an extreme-rightist platform [Walker] seems to have documented that charge."[64]

Walker's appearance before the muzzling panel was a debacle. George Lincoln Rockwell, the head of the American Nazi Party, who had called Walker "a great American," was ejected from the hearing room by a Capitol guard. The former general sketched a dark conspiracy operating at the highest levels of government. Walker fumbled over his words, leaping from one unconnected thought to the next. He accused Secretary of State Dean Rusk of being a member of a mysterious "apparatus" that sought to "sell out" the United States. He constantly consulted with his aide Medford Evans, a far-right gadfly and author of the book *The Secret War for the A-Bomb*. At the end of his testimony, Walker spoke to reporters outside the committee room. When one reporter asked him about Rockwell's comment from the day before, Walker punched him in the face. He then flew back for more campaigning in Texas, where he finished last in a six-candidate race.[65]

Thurmond did his best to save face: "While I may not agree with Gen. Walker on all of his statements, he is a great American."[66] William F. Buckley Jr. was more frank. He called Walker "politically ignorant" and said that his testimony "tended to submerge" the muzzling issue.[67]

The muzzling hearings petered out in the summer of 1962 even as events in Cuba underscored Thurmond's suspicions about the Kennedy administration's Cold War complacency. Since the late 1950s, Thurmond had been following Fidel Castro's rise through contacts at the Guantánamo naval base. In January 1962, he warned that the Soviets were stockpiling missiles in Cuba that could strike the United States. He was the first member of Congress to bring the matter to public attention.[68] By September, numerous senators were criticizing Kennedy for his failure to confront the Soviets directly over the military buildup. New York's two Republican senators, Kenneth B. Keating and Jacob Javits, urged the president to take action. John Tower exhorted the president to recognize a Cuban government in exile. Barry Goldwater criticized Kennedy for "a policy of indecision and timidity." Strom Thurmond was the only senator to issue an unequivocal call for invasion. The tensions culminated the next month in the Cuban missile crisis.[69]

The final report from the muzzling hearings was issued in the middle of the crisis. Willard Edwards of the *Chicago Tribune* saw this as another attempt by the administration and Senator Stennis to bury the issue. The report found ineptness and capriciousness in Pentagon censoring of military officers but no evidence of appeasement. The report had the "solid agreement" of all members of the committee save for Thurmond, who issued a 157-page minority report, the indefatigable work of Fred Buzhardt.[70]

While the muzzling hearings initiated no lasting change in American military policy, they established Thurmond's leadership role in burgeoning right-wing anti-Communist circles. In February 1962, he was a guest, along with Barry Goldwater, Robert Welch, Billy James

Hargis, Edwin Walker, and others, on a *CBS Reports* episode titled "Thunder on the Right." The following month he received an award from the Young Americans for Freedom (YAF) at the Conservative Rally for World Liberation from Communism at Madison Square Garden. Thurmond joined, among others, Roger Milliken, John Dos Passos, M. Stanton Evans (a rising star in YAF and the son of Edwin Walker's adviser Medford Evans), Ludwig von Mises, and Richard Weaver at the event, which brought in eighteen thousand conservative activists and received front-page coverage in *The New York Times*.[71]

In January 1963, Thurmond was given a permanent seat on John Stennis's Preparedness Investigating Subcommittee, which he used to continue to attack the Kennedy administration for soft-pedaling the fight against the Soviets. It was as a member of this subcommittee that Thurmond indulged his taste for any and every weapons system that American military and industrial designers could dream up, a passion that he maintained his entire career and one that contributed to his reputation for bringing pork-barrel projects back to his home state.

One of his first loves was the Nike-Zeus antimissile system. In 1958, Congress had added $137 million to the defense budget to begin construction of the Nike-Zeus, but President Eisenhower had refused to spend the money because of doubts about its effectiveness. In 1961, with a new administration in place, Thurmond was the congressional point person in a joint military-industry campaign for the Nike-Zeus. On February 1, *Army* magazine published seven articles lauding the Nike-Zeus, four of them by army commanders on active duty. The issue also contained a full-page advertisement by Western Electric, prime contractor for the Nike-Zeus, and eight of its subcontractors. Thurmond, along with delivering speeches in support of the Nike-Zeus, was on the advisory board of the Association of the U.S. Army, which, though technically not a lobby, promoted the interests of the U.S. Army and its contractors in national security matters.[72]

Just two weeks earlier, the outgoing president, Dwight Eisenhower, had given his Farewell Address, one of the most famous speeches of the Cold War era. He warned of the immense power and influence of the industries that had arisen to arm the struggle against the Soviet Union. It marked the first time in American history that the United States maintained a permanent armaments industry, he noted. Added to that was a defense establishment that employed over three and a half million men and women. Eisenhower counseled Americans to "guard against the acquisition of unwarranted influence, whether sought or unsought, by the military-industrial complex."[73]

In response to the president's rather cryptic remarks, *Congressional Quarterly* conducted an extensive study in early 1961 of what it called the "Military Lobby." A summary of the report cited Thurmond's and others' campaign for the Nike-Zeus as an example of the "confluence of service, contractor, and Congressional pressures" that played into national security decisions. Thurmond and all proponents of the Nike-Zeus based their case on "the national interest," the report observed, yet "it is never clear . . . where 'the national interest' begins and self-interest leaves off."[74]

Thurmond certainly went to remarkable lengths to push the Nike-Zeus. In April 1963, he uncovered a Senate rule not invoked since World War II that allowed two senators to call the entire body into closed session. Thurmond used the four-hour closed meeting to argue for a $196 million appropriation to begin production of the Nike-Zeus. His nemesis in this matter was the same as in the muzzling hearings, Richard Russell, who, according to one report, "made oratorical mincemeat" out of Thurmond. The Senate voted down the missile system 58–16.[75]

Thurmond's Nike-Zeus efforts were of a piece with a campaign later that year to oppose a nuclear test ban treaty that President Kennedy had negotiated with the Soviet Union. He accused Secretary of Defense McNamara, whose testimony Thurmond said had implied that American ballistic technology was equal to or surpassed that of the Soviets, of deliberately trying to deceive senators.[76] Pleading with his colleagues to reject the test ban treaty, Thurmond called its military risks "fearsome" and predicted that it would lead to Soviet nuclear superiority in three to five years.[77]

Thurmond's Dixiecrat campaign and his 1957 filibuster had already marked him as a renegade southerner, but the muzzling hearings and incidents like the Nike-Zeus showdown widened an already existing rift. Stennis and Thurmond's clashes during the hearings showed dramatic differences in style and temperament. The two would work together on plenty of issues to come, but the muzzling hearings confirmed Thurmond's sense that, conservative as they may have been personally, many of his fellow southern Democrats were too willing to placate national party leaders, liberal Democrats whom he saw as dangerous appeasers.

With the muzzling hearings Thurmond realized the influence and national renown to be won on the anti-Communist right. They certainly deepened his political relationship with Barry Goldwater. The two men went further out on a limb attacking the Kennedy administration than any other two senators. More important, this era of right-wing mobilization familiarized Thurmond with the constituency that fed Goldwaterism. The muzzling hearings transformed Thurmond's political profile. He was no longer merely a regional figure defending white southern interests but a serious conservative critic on issues of national security. Thurmond joined in spirit, if not quite yet in party identification, a small but feverish clan that was remaking the Republican Party, one whose influence on national politics was just beginning to be felt.

On November 22, 1963, President John F. Kennedy was shot and killed in Dallas, Texas. The young president's assassination led many to ponder the forces of extremism in American life. What was it about Kennedy that had provoked such viciousness and intemperance? Who were these hatemongers who stirred up such strife, and what other evils did they portend?

Strom Thurmond paid tribute to Kennedy's leadership and abilities in a Senate eulogy, yet was disgusted by the talk of hatemongers. He understood the president's critics to be loyal and good Americans. They were an isolated bunch in 1963, yet Thurmond had a well-developed and worldly set of associations that confirmed him in his political views, a network that extended far beyond his native South. An exchange of letters between Thurmond and the conservative journalists Constantine Brown and his wife, Elizabeth Churchill Brown, is illuminating in this regard.

One of the first American newspapermen to interview Lenin during the Russian Revolution, Constantine Brown had been a bureau chief for the *Chicago Daily News* in Turkey, Paris, and London before becoming foreign affairs editor for the Washington *Evening Star* and writing a nationally syndicated column. His wife, Elizabeth, began as a Washington society columnist but in 1956 authored *The Enemy at His Back*, a housewife's commonsense analysis of Communist appeasement in the 1930s and '40s.[78] By 1960, the Browns had become so disturbed by events in the United States that they moved to Rome, where Constantine penned a memoir, the title of which captured their sense of disillusionment over American and world affairs: *The Coming of the Whirlwind*.[79]

Thurmond, who referred to Constantine Brown as a "great reporter and outstanding American and also one of my best friends," began a regular correspondence with the Browns during the muzzling hearings.[80] His letters ranged broadly across a myriad of international intrigues, including his concern about "the opening to the Left of the Vatican" and an ominous report that Kennedy and Khrushchev would meet in Rome later that summer.[81] He also reported on domestic events. "The 'hate-monger' campaign was beautiful to watch," a sardonic Thurmond wrote of the anti-Right reaction following Kennedy's assassination. "It was as good a Communist propaganda campaign as I have seen . . . I wish our side was as well organized." Thurmond also derided the "Negro revolution"—"they actually call it a 'Revolution,'" he wrote disgustedly—which he said was "designed to destroy our Constitution and form of government."[82]

For Thurmond, the Browns were sophisticated, serious people who saw the world as he did—yet not exactly as he did. The Browns had an Old Guard European gloominess about them, one perhaps rooted in their Catholicism, a sense of the world gone to hell with no recovery in sight. For Thurmond, however, the sunny Baptist, any form of despair was an alien sensibility. If southern segregation, constitutional conservatism, and Western capitalism all seemed like lost causes in 1963, it was all right. Strom Thurmond knew something about lost causes. He had been raised on them in Edgefield County. "We go from one defeat to another," Thurmond admitted to the Browns, "but I can not help feeling where would they have been if we had not held the line."[83]

PART THREE

SUNBELT REPUBLICAN

8

PARTY HOPPING
(1964)

It was a Carolina homecoming of sorts. On September 17, 1964, the 727 carrying the Republican presidential candidate, Barry Goldwater, landed in brilliant sunlight at the Greenville-Spartanburg airport. At the Republican state convention four years earlier, South Carolina had kick-started the Goldwater boom by nominating him for president. Back then Goldwater had urged the state to send more folks like Strom Thurmond to Washington. Now Thurmond himself stood at the bottom of the steps of Goldwater's airplane. On his left lapel was pinned a tiny golden elephant sporting a pair of Goldwater's distinctive horn-rimmed glasses, and on his right was a Goldwater button. The day before, Thurmond had delivered a scalding denunciation of the Democratic Party, announcing his new status as a "Goldwater Republican."[1]

A frenzied crowd of twenty thousand South Carolinians joined in the welcome. Traffic along Interstate 85 backed up for three miles. Marching bands blared patriotic music. Goldwater Girls, dressed in blue skirts, white blouses, and crimson sashes, bounced and waved. By the time Goldwater stepped onto the tarmac, the entire law-enforcement details of two counties could not hold back the boisterous crowd, which broke police lines and engulfed the candidate. Trying to reestablish a protective cordon, embarrassed policemen threw punches and shoved teenagers. Roger Milliken could not get close enough to shake the hand of the man whose candidacy he had helped launch. On the red-carpeted podium, Goldwater and Thurmond held their hands aloft while the crowd screamed itself hoarse. By day's end, forty-five people would require first aid. Thirty-five fainted. Two suffered heart attacks. One child broke out in hives.[2]

The six weeks Thurmond spent campaigning for Goldwater were some of the most thrilling of his career. His dramatic party switch shocked the political world, earning him national media attention. Supporters lauded him as a man of courage and principle. Commentators racked their brains for historical parallels for his precedent-shattering actions. He would go on to help Goldwater win five southern states, and in the process he midwifed modern southern Republicanism. Separated by sixteen-year intervals on either side, Thurmond's work for Goldwater in 1964 connected his 1948 States' Rights run with Ronald Reagan's conservative triumph in 1980.

Or at least this was the folklore that developed later about Thurmond and the southern strategy. The actual experience of 1964 was hardly so triumphant. Thurmond went from one political defeat to the next. He traveled across the country advocating a school prayer amendment that never made it out of committee, called for investigations of liberal church groups that went nowhere, and suffered through more liberal Supreme Court rulings that left him and other conservative Americans aghast. Civil rights advocates broke a southern filibuster for the first time in history, passing the most comprehensive and far-reaching civil rights legislation since Reconstruction. And there was the presidential election itself: Thurmond's candidate lost by the largest margin in American history.

Of course, the legend of Strom Thurmond and the 1964 presidential campaign is not entirely false. Over the next forty-four years, the GOP dominated presidential politics across the region. A Republican presidential candidate would fail to carry South Carolina only once. The Goldwater campaign helped put in place conservative GOP organizations that would become the institutional core of the conservative Republican insurgency. Yet these later successes conceal the challenging political terrain faced at the time by Thurmond and other conservative Americans. As joyful as Goldwater and Thurmond were that day at the Greenville-Spartanburg airport, their political union was fraught with unknowns. Goldwater was risking that his association with the South's foremost segregationist would drive away moderate voters. Thurmond had no way of knowing whether Goldwater's nomination was a lasting change in the GOP or a passing fancy.

Thurmond had switched parties only after years of careful calculation, closely weighing how best to position himself for his reelection campaign in 1966. Yet as a Republican, he was in some ways more politically isolated than he had been as a Democrat. Before, at least, he had had a strong base of South Carolina Democrats who controlled state politics. Now he was relying on personal contacts built up over the years. In the Senate he had a cohort of southern Democrats whose seniority gave them enormous power. As a Republican senator in 1965, his main ally, Goldwater, was not even around anymore. In Republican circles, the talk was about losing the extremist label. It was about recovering the GOP heritage, not letting the party of Lincoln become the party of Thurmond.

In February 1964, Thurmond was back in Southern California for a string of appearances before grassroots conservatives. Earlier the issue had been military muzzling; this time it was school prayer. In 1962 the Supreme Court had declared in *Engel v. Vitale* that the reading of an official prayer in New York state public schools violated the First Amendment. Some Protestants—even Southern Baptists, Thurmond's denomination—had praised the Court's decision as a victory for religious freedom, because it had banned an official prayer established by the state. Yet Thurmond was an early and vocal critic, declaring that it had "shocked the conscience of the American people." He tracked closely the political machinations of the "secularists." In 1963, when the Court issued another prayer ban, this time against the reading of the Bible and the recitation of the Lord's Prayer, Thurmond joined six other senators in a resolution proposing a constitutional amendment to permit the offering of prayer and Bible reading in schools.[3]

In the House, 151 measures proposing to save school prayer were sent to the Judiciary Committee. The first and most important was the amendment sponsored by the New York congressman Frank Becker. In the two years following *Engel*, the campaign to enact a constitutional amendment protecting prayer in schools generated one of the largest congressional letter-writing campaigns in history. Organizations co-ordinated some of the mail, but the bulk of it was individually inspired. In the spring of 1964, the House Judiciary Committee held hearings on the Becker amendment. Thurmond's California trip was designed to build public support for the measure. Though the Judiciary Committee chairman, Emanuel Celler, would effectively defuse the Becker amend-ment, ensuring it a silent death in committee, Thurmond's school prayer campaign out west solidified his contacts among Sunbelt conservatives.[4]

To a group of Orange County activists, Thurmond talked about taking the fight to the secularists, who were a minority, he admitted, yet "minorities seem to be winning all the important fights in Amer-ica."[5] His California hosts ran an organization called Project Prayer. The executive director, Sam Cavnar, was the same man who headed the anti-Communist group Project Alert that had invited Thurmond out before. This time, however, alongside rank-and-file right-wingers Cavnar had lined up a glittering array of Hollywood stars, including Gloria Swanson, John Wayne, and Rhonda Fleming.[6] Thurmond sent follow-up letters to all of his new acquaintances, including an actor turned spokesman for General Electric trying to break into politics whose name a Thurmond aide misspelled as "Ronald Reagin."[7]

Anti–Supreme Court animus had been an abiding passion of Thur-mond's ever since he had arrived in the Senate. It began with the Southern Manifesto. The Red Monday and *Mallory* decisions added more heat, broadening the Court's desecrations beyond the issue of seg-regation and fueling a broader right-wing reaction. But the prayer deci-sions added a new element altogether. In North Carolina, an old highway sign that had been around since the mid-1950s originally read:

IMPEACH EARL WARREN

SAVE AMERICA

It was changed to read:

IMPEACH EARL WARREN

SAVE AMERICA

SAVE PRAYER

Another version, in South Carolina, read:

IMPEACH EARL WARREN

SAVE OUR REPUBLIC

JOIN THE JOHN BIRCH SOCIETY[8]

The Birchers and the Citizens' Councils were still the ones yelling the loudest, yet after the prayer decisions they were joined by right-wing Christian organizations. One was a group called Project America, affiliated with the American Council of Christian Churches, a New Jersey organization headed by the controversial fundamentalist preacher Carl McIntire.[9] Liberal opponents cited McIntire's organization as one of the "right-wing extremist groups trying to cloak political motives in respectability by using religion."[10] It is also a good example of the kinds of Christian patriotic groups that Thurmond championed. He headlined a 1963 conference that McIntire organized called For God and Country, and the Reverend Billy James Hargis of Tulsa, Oklahoma, and his organization Christian Crusade helped Thurmond expand his anti-muzzling campaign.[11]

Thurmond's longest-standing connection with right-wing fundamentalist groups, however, was his decade-old affiliation with Bob Jones University in Greenville, South Carolina. Thurmond became a trustee of Bob Jones in 1951, the year after his loss to Olin Johnston. It was a mutually beneficial relationship for Thurmond and the school's founder, Bob Jones Sr., who had moved the campus to South Carolina from Cleveland, Tennessee, just four years earlier. Thurmond used political contacts to help Jones gain accreditation through the South Carolina Department of Education, and Jones provided Thurmond entrée to a base of archconservative religious voters in the South Carolina up-country, where Thurmond had fared poorly in his race against Johnston.

Fundamentalists such as Jones, Hargis, and McIntire despised secularists for trying to remove God from public life, yet they reserved equal loathing for liberal Christians who invoked the cause of Christ to support what they felt were scandalous, anti-American political efforts. Carl McIntire had established his organization back in 1941 to oppose the influence of the Federal Council of Churches, which in

1950 combined with other ecumenical groups to form the National Council of Churches (NCC), the largest and most influential organization of Protestant religious groups and the voice of liberal Christianity. The NCC was on record in favor of the Supreme Court's school prayer decision, which it saw as essential to respecting the First Amendment's establishment clause. But the organization also advocated a number of other positions repugnant to right-wing Americans, whether it was its support for the Supreme Court's decision in *Brown* or its criticism of anti-Communist groups such as the John Birch Society.

In 1964 it was the NCC's outspoken support for civil rights that precipitated Thurmond's attack on the organization. A year earlier it had established the Commission on Religion and Race, committing a first-year budget of half a million dollars and asserting itself as a full partner in the struggle for civil rights. Thurmond chafed at the high-profile participation of Christian ministers in the March on Washington in August 1963. By early 1964, the NCC was among the more effective lobbying organizations for civil rights legislation.[12]

Thurmond was appalled at what he saw as political lobbying by a tax-exempt church group. In early March he called, unsuccessfully, it would turn out, on the Internal Revenue Service to investigate the organization for possible removal of its tax exemption.[13] Conservative church groups had been urging him to speak out against the NCC, and Thurmond placed in the *Congressional Record* denunciations of the organization's lobbying efforts.[14] The backlash against the NCC grew during the summer, as the organization was closely associated with voter registration drives and "freedom schools" in Mississippi. Attributing the racial agitation in the South to collusion between the NCC and "Negro extremist groups," a shocked Thurmond pointed to the NCC's involvement in a protest in Orangeburg, South Carolina, in which protesters bought tickets to an all-white movie theater and then broke up into interracial couples to enter the theater. "Mixing couples" was "in total defiance of social customs," he said shamelessly.[15]

Thurmond's signature failure in 1964 was on civil rights. On June 10 the Senate voted to close off debate on southern senators' fifty-seven-day filibuster against the civil rights bill. Since the adoption of Senate

Rule 22 in 1917, there had been eleven previous attempts to invoke cloture on civil rights legislation. Proponents had never gotten within eight votes. In 1964, they won with four votes to spare.[16]

The southerners had not been entirely without weapons. Aiding them was the FBI director, J. Edgar Hoover, who was involved in his own covert war against Martin Luther King and the civil rights movement and was eager to assert Communist infiltration of the civil rights movement. The evidence had been thin to nonexistent, but Thurmond and others made the most of it.[17] Another source of help to Thurmond and his fellow southerners was the Coordinating Committee for Fundamental American Freedoms. An anti-civil-rights group established in 1963, by the following year it was the biggest spending lobby on Capitol Hill.[18] Hidden at the time was the source of the committee's largesse: the great bulk of its money came from a wealthy, reclusive New Yorker, Wickliffe Preston Draper, who in 1937 had established the Pioneer Fund to promote research into "the problems of heredity and eugenics in the human race." Another venture involved a return-to-Africa program for black Americans.[19]

Thurmond served as a conduit between the committee and conservative South Carolina businessmen such as Charles Daniel and Roger Milliken, who donated $4,000 and $5,000, respectively.[20] Thurmond told Daniel that the committee was doing excellent work in molding public opinion in "the western and mid-western states—in areas in which we have some opportunity of gaining votes against cloture."[21] The special guest at one of the last meetings of the coordinating committee, Thurmond applauded the organization for "great service in the promotion of conservative government," predicting that the civil rights bill would be repealed or amended as soon as some of its "vicious measures" were enforced.[22]

The coordinating committee's efforts dovetailed with George Wallace's surprisingly successful run in several northern Democratic presidential primaries that spring. Wallace won 33 percent of the primary vote in Wisconsin in early April, nearly 30 percent in Indiana in early May, and 42 percent in Maryland two weeks later.[23] He dropped out of the presidential race before the summer was over, but the coordinating committee made the most of his efforts during the civil rights debate, taking out full-page newspaper advertisements timed with his campaign appearances.[24] With southern senators tracking Wallace's success closely, in late May Thurmond introduced into the *Congressional Record* five articles that discussed the Wallace phenomenon. He read the results as evidence of "a strong undercurrent of opposition to the pending so-called civil rights legislation in . . . States outside of the South."[25]

Despite these efforts, the Senate moved steadily toward a historic confrontation with southern racism. The bill's floor manager, Hubert Humphrey, and the Democratic majority leader, Mike Mansfield, succeeded by killing the southerners with kindness. They held no all-night sessions as they had tried in 1960, which made it easier to keep a quorum handy at all times. Nor did Humphrey try to rush a cloture vote, allowing the overwhelming public support for the bill to take its toll.[26]

Thurmond's final speech against the bill was not the most bitter or racist offered by a southerner, yet it was filled with doomsday predictions about the law's impact, none of which would prove true. He said that its passage would give to the attorney general powers that would turn that office into the "Big Brother" envisioned by George Orwell in *1984*. Provisions allowing the withholding of federal funds would create "a concentration of power of economic coercion unequaled in the history of governments." Forcing business owners to provide service against their will violated the "constitutionally-forbidden imposition of involuntary servitude," and he saw in the bill the seeds of an "authoritarian police state" that would "make a shambles of the delicate balances contained in the Constitution."[27]

Not every one of Thurmond's closing points proved so myopic. President Johnson and other supporters talked about the legislation helping move protest from the streets into courtrooms, yet Thurmond quoted James Farmer, director of the Congress of Racial Equality, saying that direct action protest would still be necessary after the bill's passage.[28] More important, Thurmond attacked provisions in the bill that prohibited it from being used to redress "racial imbalances" in public schools. These, he maintained, were added in order to "muffle Northern protests against having their 'de facto' segregation patterns upset by the forced 'busing' of children across town to correct racial imbalances in schools."[29] Threaded into his argument were tendentious distinctions between southern- and northern-style segregation, yet the charges against the "racial imbalance" language would resurface in the early 1970s, when de facto segregation emerged as a Gordian knot in American politics.[30]

On July 2, in a grand ceremony in the East Room of the White House, President Lyndon Johnson used seventy-two ceremonial pens to sign into law the Civil Rights Act of 1964.[31] "Let us close the springs of racial poison," Johnson told his audience of dignitaries. "Let us pray for wise and understanding hearts. Let us lay aside irrelevant differences and make our nation whole."[32] Strom Thurmond's reaction to the scene was not recorded.

His general indignation, however, could be measured by his performance a few days later during confirmation hearings for the former Florida governor LeRoy Collins to head the Community Relations Service, a federal agency established under the new law to help broker desegregation agreements. Collins had won praise as a moderate southern governor, and he had become more progressive and outspoken after leaving office. Thurmond took as a personal insult a widely covered speech that Collins had given in Columbia, South Carolina, shortly after the Kennedy assassination in which he wondered how long the majority of southerners were going to "allow themselves to be caricatured by these Claghorns."[33]

Thurmond grilled Collins for nearly four hours.[34] How could Collins lead a community reconciliation service when he had given such a divisive speech? he asked. Did Collins consider the signers of the Southern Manifesto to be Claghorns? Thurmond read a number of segregationist statements Collins had made as governor and asked him why he had changed his mind.[35] Thurmond skipped several subsequent committee meetings and called in favors with other members, asking them to stay away too, knowing that the absences would deny the committee a quorum and delay Collins's confirmation.[36]

Thurmond's bitterness toward Collins signaled the indignation that he felt as alleged turncoats and longtime enemies celebrated a historic achievement. It overflowed in all directions, surprising perhaps even Thurmond himself. He was standing outside the Commerce Committee room, an aide looking in and counting heads to avoid a quorum, when the liberal Texas senator Ralph Yarborough, a fellow committee member, walked up. The men were polar opposites politically—Yarborough was one of the few southerners who had voted in favor of the civil rights bill—but they shared a jocular friendship as members of the same military reserves unit in Washington. Yarborough grabbed Thurmond and jokingly tried to pull him in, saying, "Come on in, you and me will make a quorum."[37] Thurmond grabbed him back and proposed a test of strength. If Yarborough could pull him into the room, he would go in, but if Thurmond could keep Yarborough out, then neither would go in.

Perhaps Thurmond's proposition was just harmless kidding with an army buddy. Or perhaps there had been something in Yarborough's manner that irked him. Regardless, Yarborough went along at first. Thurmond's wary aide held the two men's suit jackets, pens, and papers. It was all in fun. They were not really going to fight in the halls of the U.S. Senate, or so Yarborough thought. But then some light shoving started, and before Yarborough knew it, Thurmond had grabbed his leg and pushed him up against the wall. Yarborough used it to slide gently to the ground. He wanted to get up, but Thurmond was so intense, so determined to pin him, that Yarborough didn't want to give him the pleasure. Red-faced and out of breath, they wrestled on the floor. Loose change fell out of their pockets and scattered across the marble hallway.

Thurmond eventually succeeded. Like schoolboys, Thurmond wouldn't release him until Yarborough hollered quits, but Yarborough wouldn't holler quits. Finally, Warren Magnuson, the square, gruff committee chair, burst out of the hearing room barking, "Come on, let's break this up." The two men got up, adjusted their ties, called for their suit jackets, and walked into the committee room. Collins's confirmation passed 16–1.[38]

The debate over civil rights legislation coincided with Barry Goldwater's surprising success in the Republican presidential primaries. Goldwater's primary campaign had an enormous impact in reshaping the Republican Party that Strom Thurmond joined later that year. The Draft Goldwater Committee set its sights on the 1964 nomination. Three South Carolina Republicans—Roger Milliken, Gregory Shorey, and Robert Chapman—were charter members, and Milliken served as the group's first finance chairman.[39]

Before 1964, many southern Republican organizations were still controlled by two groups: African Americans, whose party membership dated back to the nineteenth century, and white urban-based, relatively moderate Eisenhower Republicans, who had joined the party in the 1950s. The South Carolina GOP, influenced by an influx of Sunbelt white-collar professionals, was distinctive in the South in that conservatives became the dominant force in the party earlier than most. In other southern states, however, it was not until the spring of 1964 that conservatives predominated, driving African Americans out of the party and marginalizing the "modern Republicans" of Eisenhower-era vintage.[40]

Throughout the spring and early summer, Goldwater had expressed his reservations about the civil rights bill in Congress. His vote against cloture and in favor of a few amendments offered by southerners won praise from Thurmond.[41] The issue came to a head in mid-June, when Goldwater announced that he would vote against the bill. He was one of only six Republican senators to do so.[42] He had supported civil rights legislation in 1957 and 1960—bills that dealt primarily with voting rights—yet he had long opposed fair employment and open housing legislation. In a speech on the Senate floor, he objected to Title II, which prohibited discrimination in businesses such as hotels and restaurants, and Title VII, which prohibited discrimination in hiring. He said that the implementation of such measures would require a mammoth police force and promote an "informer" psychology in American life.[43]

His case against the 1964 legislation was based on a detailed analysis by the future chief justice William Rehnquist, one of the Arizona Republican Party's constitutional experts. Reinforcing it was a seventy-five-page brief by Professor Robert Bork of Yale University.[44] Two southern Republicans who were in Goldwater's office when he left to vote on the bill later recalled his sense of fatalistic duty: he simply could not bring himself to vote for such a constitutionally flawed bill, no matter the politics involved.[45]

In truth, however, it was impossible to know in June what the political fallout of Goldwater's civil rights vote would be in November. In the spring and early summer of 1964, many people assumed that the backlash vote would play a major role in that fall's election. Goldwater's organization kept close tabs on the impact that George Wallace was having in the Democratic presidential primaries. One Goldwater consultant argued that if Wallace won 150,000 votes in Wisconsin, it would "knock down arguments that the Southern strategy of BG is not viable against Johnson." He recommended a Goldwater spokesman "capitalize on any Wisconsin upset."[46] In Wisconsin, Wallace actually won 266,000 votes, not 150,000, and it was not a spokesman who capitalized on the results but Goldwater himself.[47] "There is something to this term backlash," he told reporters. While northerners and westerners were eager for "the Negro to have all his rights . . . [t]he people feel they should have the right to say who lives near them."[48]

Conservative activists predominated among the GOP delegates who met at the Republican National Convention in San Francisco later that summer. They not only nominated Goldwater but also authored a party platform that further alienated GOP moderates and liberals. Far from sheepish about his civil rights vote, Goldwater implied that many of his colleagues who had voted for the bill did so only to protect themselves against charges of racism.[49] Northern Republicans who had vigorously fought Goldwater's nomination now saw the potential of the backlash vote. Governor James Rhodes of Ohio, for example, withdrew as Ohio's favorite-son candidate, ceding all Buckeye State delegates to Goldwater. Rhodes had come to believe that the white backlash in industrial communities such as Cleveland and Youngstown would be enough to push Goldwater and the other Ohio Republicans to victory in November.[50]

Whatever constitutional concerns might explain Goldwater's vote against civil rights in 1964, the political considerations were huge. No candidate for the presidency could have ignored them. In his speech at the Georgia state convention in May, Goldwater had said that "one of the most important political facts of life" was that the "Republican Party can win in 1964 only if it can win substantial support in the South."[51] If Goldwater had voted for the civil rights bill, he would have tossed away the political advantage to be won from the single most important issue dividing the New Deal coalition. If he could hold off a last-minute challenge from liberals in his own party, and maybe catch a break or two along the way, who could really say what would happen come November?

On July 6, Strom Thurmond announced that he would not attend the Democratic convention later that summer. It was the first one that he had missed since his service in World War II. Thurmond expected a "cut and dried" affair, with Lyndon Johnson and "ultra-liberals" calling all the shots.[52] Republicans were just beginning to gather in San Francisco for their convention, a meeting that Harry Dent watched closely. Dent had been a college student back in 1946 when he volunteered to work as a driver during Thurmond's gubernatorial campaign. By 1964, he had become Thurmond's most trusted adviser, a position he would maintain the rest of Thurmond's life, even after Dent left politics. Dent watched the South Carolina delegation in San Francisco cast the deciding votes that secured the nomination for Goldwater and heard the Arizonan deliver a fiery, uncompromising acceptance speech.[53] For several years, he and Thurmond had been talking about the difficulties of running for reelection in a Democratic primary in 1966. Swooning with Goldwater fever, Dent spotted the chance to turn Thurmond's biggest problem into an opportunity.

Over Labor Day weekend, Thurmond and Dent made the rounds of South Carolina political friends to solicit their advice. The first on the list was Thurmond's old friend Walter Brown. It was a dramatic moment as Thurmond sat down between two of his closest political confidants. One had come out of his States' Rights Democratic past; the other represented the future of Goldwater Republicanism. When presented with the prospect of Thurmond joining the GOP, Brown was unequivocal: it would be a "Herculean mistake."[54] It was morally wrong, he contended, to change parties without resigning and running in the appropriate party primary.[55] Dent countered that such a move was unnecessary since Thurmond had first been elected to the Senate in 1954 in a general campaign, not a party primary. Brown talked to every "true friend of Strom Thurmond" and could not find one who thought he should switch parties.[56]

Thurmond returned to Washington, where he met privately with

Barry Goldwater on Saturday, September 12. They discussed the party switch and how Thurmond might help Goldwater in the South. Washington reporters noted the meeting, along with a sighting of Thurmond aides leaving national Republican Party headquarters the following Monday.[57] Dent had all the press materials ready to mail in anticipation of Thurmond's announcement speech in South Carolina on September 16.[58]

Thurmond's speech used all of the charged right-wing language that Fred Buzhardt had been writing for him since the late 1950s. Opening with a reflection on the proverb "For evil to triumph, it is only necessary that good men do nothing," he followed with twenty consecutive staccato paragraphs, each beginning "The Democratic Party has . . . ," that detailed the party's evils: "abandoned the people"; "invaded the private lives"; "encouraged lawlessness"; "endangered the security"; "repudiated the Constitution," and so forth. At the end of this slippery slope was a "socialistic dictatorship." Three-quarters of the way through the speech, as he announced that he would work through the "Goldwater Republican Party," the television screen flashed "Sen. Strom Thurmond, Republican, S.C."[59]

In his speech and in letters to supporters, Thurmond made clear that his switch was motivated solely by political principle. He was taking a great political risk, he said, fully aware that his reelection chances might "go down into oblivion," yet he could only follow his "heart and conscience."[60] Congratulatory notes from friends and supporters struck the same theme. James Byrnes praised him for doing "what you believe to be right without regard to how it will affect Senator Goldwater and Senator Thurmond."[61] Ronald Reagan, Thurmond's new acquaintance from the Project Prayer trip earlier in the year, invoked a maxim he attributed to Churchill: "Some men change principles for party while others change party for principle . . . There is no doubt which course you followed."[62] And M. G. "Pat" Robertson, the son of Thurmond's Virginia colleague A. Willis Robertson and the owner of a fledgling Christian broadcasting station, lauded Thurmond for his "most courageous decision to put your country above personal or party loyalty."[63]

The party switch was a gamble. There were some South Carolinians, as Walter Brown had worried, who would chafe at the fact that Thurmond had been elected as a Democrat and had not resigned and run for reelection. The greater danger was that as a Republican, Thurmond had separated himself from the network of Democratic officials, from the general assembly down through the gamut of county and local governments. This was the "courthouse crowd" that dominated local politics and had at its disposal a range of ways to influence local voters to remain Democratic.

Yet Thurmond was willing to take a chance with the courthouse crowd, because he had been working personal friendships with local Democratic bosses for thirty years. He continued to do so after he became a Republican, sometimes to the frustration of the South Carolina GOP. In his keynote address at the 1965 Republican state convention, for example, Thurmond warned against "partyitis"—building a political party for its own sake rather than for the cause of good government. South Carolina had been blessed, he said, with good public servants in the courthouses, the general assembly, the executive branch, the judiciary, and Congress. GOP leaders resented this as a deterrent to party growth, but not enough to break with Thurmond publicly.[64]

As risky as the party switch was, it would have been riskier still for Thurmond to have remained a Democrat after 1964. This was not true for all southern Democrats; indeed, only his fellow South Carolinian Albert Watson, a Democratic congressman elected in 1962, followed him into the GOP at this point. But it was true for Thurmond owing to a number of factors specific to his career and to South Carolina politics.

One had to do with his standing in the Senate. "Had I supported Goldwater and remained in the Democratic Party," he explained to a constituent shortly after his switch, "my committee memberships and patronage would have been in jeopardy."[65] There is every reason to think that Thurmond would have been proven right.

Of greater concern, however, was the thought of running for reelection in a Democratic primary in 1966. He, Harry Dent, and Bill Workman had been worrying about it at least since 1962. Back then they fretted about the general assembly passing a law that would prevent Republicans from voting in a Democratic primary.[66] In February 1964, that is just what the legislature did. The bill required primary voters to sign an oath pledging that they had not attended a precinct meeting or state convention or voted in a primary of an opposing party. The GOP chairman, J. Drake Edens, described it as an attempt to "legislate us out of business."[67] It had equally dire consequences for Thurmond. "Thousands of Republican-minded voters are among Thurmond's most ardent supporters," noted a South Carolina political columnist. "Attendance at party precinct meetings and other functions will keep them out of the Democratic primary."[68]

As soon as the law passed, Thurmond and his staff explored the possibility of running by petition in 1966, but they also began contacting his loyalists, instructing them not to attend Republican precinct meetings.[69] It was a troubling situation in the spring of 1964, with Goldwater fever running high, the civil rights debate in full bloom, and thousands of conservative South Carolinians eager to support a presidential candidate who, for the first time in years, seemed to understand their concerns. One Thurmond supporter, Thomas Parker of Greenville, loyally followed Thurmond's instructions and showed up at the Democratic precinct meeting. He even ran for a local office but was easily defeated when his opponent pointed out the Goldwater bumper sticker on his car.[70]

The problem was even worse when Thurmond considered his likely opponent in the 1966 Democratic primary, Governor Donald Russell.[71] Elected in 1962, Russell was in the midst of an exemplary gubernatorial administration, one distinguished for his handling of the economy, education, and, not least of all, race relations. Russell shocked many white South Carolinians by holding an integrated inaugural reception at the Governor's Mansion. Ten days later he presided over the peaceful desegregation of Clemson.[72]

One friend warned Thurmond, "If [Russell] should decide to run and begin his race with the support of the NAACP, unions and Olin henchmen he would have a pretty good start."[73] The most detailed analysis came from the head of the Sumter County Citizens' Council, who figured that a Democratic primary race would draw 325,000 voters, 125,000 of whom would be labor supporters, "national minded Democrats," and blacks, all of whom would vote for Russell. Thurmond would have to poll over 80 percent of the remaining votes to beat him. The good news, the Sumter County man reported, was that Roger Milliken had already given word that Republicans "should do nothing that would jeopardize your reelection."[74]

It had been Russell whom Thurmond was eyeing when he had made such a show of interrogating LeRoy Collins during confirmation hearings for the directorship of the Community Relations Service. Russell had introduced Collins before his controversial speech in Columbia. Thurmond asked Collins if Russell had objected to the speech when Collins showed it to him in advance. Collins began an indirect answer, knowing that Thurmond was trying to use him to corner a potential opponent. "Would you answer the question?" Thurmond interjected.[75] Perhaps the wrestling match with Ralph Yarborough that occurred only days later was not some random incident, but rather Thurmond's attempt, as had been the case with his record filibuster, to prove to white South Carolinians his commitment to fighting integrationists.[76]

Thurmond knew that Donald Russell longed to go to Washington, where he had worked as Jimmy Byrnes's assistant secretary of state. In fact, he was so eager that he ended up sabotaging himself. When Olin Johnston passed away in 1965, Russell engineered a plan where he would resign as governor and have his successor appoint him to Johnston's empty seat. It was the kind of insider deal that voters often punish. In the 1966 Democratic primary, they rejected Russell for another former governor, Ernest "Fritz" Hollings.[77]

Richard Russell (no relation to Donald) saw Thurmond's predicament clearly. Renowned for his detailed knowledge of the political standing of each of his Senate colleagues, Russell discussed Thurmond's party switch over the phone with his old friend Lyndon Johnson the day after Thurmond's announcement.[78] Thurmond was just showing "political sense," he said. Thurmond was a better campaigner than Donald Russell, and while he would be the favorite in a general election race, Thurmond would be at a disadvantage in the Democratic primary. Twenty-five percent of the vote in South Carolina was "Nigra," Russell said, and Thurmond would not get any of those. The labor vote would be strongly against him as well. He estimated that Donald Russell would need just over a quarter of the white vote to beat Thurmond.[79]

Richard Russell knew that Strom Thurmond had gotten out of a Democratic primary race because he had to. South Carolina Republicans knew the same thing. They greeted Thurmond's announcement with "mixed feelings."[80] Republicans who had been working for years to build the party feared that Thurmond would take things over and use it for his own purposes. With a high-profile national politician like Thurmond around, state leaders would by necessity have less influence.

Thurmond immediately ruffled feathers when, mindful of the Democratic courthouse crowd, he urged local Republican candidates to drop out of their races and concentrate solely on the Goldwater vote.[81] He also pushed to have Harry Dent named as the party's executive director.[82] William Workman knew the resentment among the party faithful. He counseled Thurmond not to push Dent too hard and risk losing his initial battle as a Republican. Thurmond eventually backed down, and the party named its own executive director.[83]

Thurmond's switch also created waves in the national party. GOP liberals and African Americans protested his switch from the start. Clifford Case of New Jersey and Kenneth Keating of New York denounced appeals to "white backlash" and warned against becoming a "lily-white" party.[84] The National Negro Republican Assembly, formed in San Francisco because of resentment over the treatment of black delegates and alternates to the GOP National Convention, expressed concern over Goldwater's "open-arms welcome" of Thurmond.[85]

Open-armed it was. After the unforgettable Goldwater rally at the Greenville-Spartanburg airport, Thurmond joined Goldwater for several days of joint campaign appearances across the South. They flew to New Orleans, where Thurmond sat next to his old Dixiecrat crony Leander Perez, the boss of Plaquemines Parish, who had been excommunicated from the Catholic Church because of his opposition to school desegregation.[86] Almost everywhere Goldwater went across the South, the crowds topped those that had turned out for Eisenhower and Nixon. According to one local paper, the Beatles would have had a hard time eliciting the adoration that Goldwater enjoyed in Winston-Salem. In Montgomery, organizers planned to have 250 young girls dressed in long white gowns greet the candidate, but so many volunteers showed up that they ended up with 565. These reactions came despite Goldwater's performance on the stump, which was described as "low-keyed . . . listless . . . sometimes stumbling."[87]

In the week following Thurmond's party switch, Republican headquarters received over a hundred speaking requests for him. Most were from southern Republicans, although they included a plea from the Wyoming senator Milward Simpson, who was convinced that a Thurmond visit could help carry his state for Goldwater. Harry Dent resigned as Thurmond's administrative assistant to work full-time organizing his Goldwater appearances. In late September, Thurmond had a four-day stretch in which he spoke in South Carolina four times on a Friday, flew to Atlanta that evening and then on to California for a full weekend of campaign and fund-raising events. He spent the week in Arkansas, South Carolina, and Georgia. The following week he was in Kentucky, Wyoming, and Oklahoma. Another stretch had him in Mobile for breakfast, South Carolina for lunch, and Pennsylvania for supper, before stopping for the night in Washington.[88]

Thurmond regularly drew crowds that overwhelmed event planners. Organizers expected two thousand at the Center Theater in Norfolk, but over sixty-five hundred people showed up. In Memphis he drew five hundred people to a fund-raising dinner designed for two hundred. When he arrived at the airport in Nashville at one in the morning, two hundred Vanderbilt students were unexpectedly on hand to greet him, shouting, "We want Thurmond." He thanked them with an unscheduled stop on campus the next day that drew fifteen hundred students.[89]

Not every stop proved so hospitable. The head of the San Fernando Valley NAACP chapter had called Thurmond's appearance an "affront to Valley voters" and urged Republicans to denounce him. Yet M. Philip Davis, co-chair along with Ronald Reagan of Citizens for Goldwater-Miller, said his organization was "delighted" Thurmond was coming to California.[90]

In his speeches, Thurmond said that Goldwater would solve the "undeclared war" in Vietnam, returning the country to "peace with honor," and he emphasized Goldwater's vote against the 1964 Civil Rights Act. More explicitly than Goldwater himself, Thurmond stressed "morality" issues, declaring that Goldwater would salvage "the rights of the individual, the rights of the states, and protect law-abiding citizens against riots, looting and assaults in the streets."[91] Republican advertisements in the South drew on these themes of race and crime. "Racial Revolution Rocks America," one read, listing the Johnson administration's civil rights transgressions. It included a picture of a distraught white woman in a party dress and heels, clothes torn, hair a mess, aided by three white policemen. "Victims of negro riot," the caption read. The woman and her boyfriend had been "seized and beaten by a negro mob" while stopped at a traffic light. At the bottom in bold letters: "Barry Goldwater, For States' Rights! For the South!"[92]

By mid-October, Thurmond's breakneck pace had begun to take its toll. Though scheduled to have gallbladder surgery that fall, the sixty-one-year-old put it off until after the election. Reporters noted that Thurmond looked "visibly tired, a little drawn, slightly off his normal physically-fit weight."[93] The pace betrayed not only Thurmond's love for the campaign trail but also his determination to carry South Carolina and much of the South for Goldwater. It was critical to his political future. If Thurmond had switched parties and Lyndon Johnson had still carried the South—or South Carolina, God forbid—moderate and liberal Republicans would have rightly asked what value Thurmond held for the party, and why they should accept him into their ranks at all.

In November 1964, Barry Goldwater went down in a defeat of historic proportions, yet he won comfortable victories in South Carolina and four other southern states. Goldwater likely would have carried them with or without Thurmond's help. It is clear in retrospect that in their alliance, Thurmond got a lot more out of the deal than Goldwater did. Once again, Thurmond had used the excitement and intrigue of a presidential election to quietly reposition himself for his next campaign. By getting credit for helping Goldwater carry five southern states, he was like the ballplayer who homered in his team's blowout loss. He put on a sour face publicly, but privately he must have been relieved that things had worked out as well as they had.

9

LAW AND ORDER
(1965–1968)

On Capitol Hill, where the famous and nearly famous regularly filter through, it was not unusual for celebrities to stop by Strom Thurmond's Senate office. A memorable visitor in the mid-1960s was the psychic Jeane Dixon, one of the best-known soothsayers of the day. Dixon's renown spread after the Kennedy assassination. In 1956, she had predicted that a Democrat would win the 1960 election and die or be assassinated in office. She developed close relationships with numerous luminaries, most notably Nancy and Ronald Reagan. After explaining her prophetic powers to Harry Dent, she obtained a meeting with Thurmond, with whom she experienced "strong vibrations." In early 1965 she predicted that Thurmond would play the key role in nominating and electing the next president, who would be a Republican. Thurmond would subsequently meet with Dixon several times over the next few years.[1]

In 1965, the idea that Thurmond would help elect the next president of the United States was the kind of thing only a psychic would have said. This was the high-water mark of America's postwar liberal consensus. The civil rights movement was in full flower. Lyndon Johnson was in the midst of passing a wave of historic liberal legislation, and the stench of the Goldwater debacle still hung in the air. Thurmond was trying to make a place for himself in a party badly divided between its eastern establishment and its repudiated conservative insurgents.

Yet in the mid-1960s Americans' growing concern over a range of issues roughly subsumed under the category of "law and order"—continued civil rights protests, street crime, urban riots, youthful disrespect for authority, the antiwar movement—created a political environment in which the far-right sentiments of a figure like Strom Thurmond experienced a surprising political resurgence.

The origin point for Thurmond's climb was an address he gave in April 1965 before the board of directors of the Christian Freedom Foundation at the Wellington Hotel in New York. The speech, titled "The Road to Oblivion," outlined his objections to the voting rights legislation then before Congress. It began with a list of constitutional objections to the bill before moving on to a denunciation of the use of civil disobedience by protesters in Selma, Alabama. "Disobedience embraces lawlessness," Thurmond declared, and undermines "the rule of law, itself." It was "an insurrection," he claimed, and for Thurmond this extended to other protests that were sweeping the nation, such as pacifists objecting to U.S. involvement in Vietnam and student activists engaged in "the so-called 'campus revolt.' "[2]

Thurmond's speech did nothing to slow the voting rights bill, which passed a few months later. To many observers, his remarks would have sounded like another futile entry in the interminable list of segregationist speechifying. Yet this one would not remain forgotten.

Three years later, amid rampant violence and social disorder in the summer of 1968, Thurmond's fellow Republican John Tower came across a copy of his speech. Tower—who had filled Lyndon Johnson's Senate seat in a special election in 1961, and in doing so became the first Republican elected to the Senate from Texas since 1870—praised Thurmond's "lucid explanation of the equation between 'disobedience' and 'lawlessness.' " Inserting a copy of the speech into the *Congressional Record*, Tower lauded Thurmond as "prophetic" and lamented that Americans "did not have the wisdom to heed Senator Thurmond's words 3 years ago."[3]

Republican senators gathered in January 1965 to chart a way forward in the aftermath of the devastating election. For many of them, Strom Thurmond was not a prophet—he was the problem. The issue in ques-

tion was the committee appointments and seniority Thurmond would
be granted among his new Republican colleagues. Before his party
switch, Thurmond had negotiated with the Goldwater campaign to
retain both his assignments and his seniority, but now no one from the
Goldwater camp was in a position to grant such requests. Conservatives such as Senator Carl Curtis of Nebraska argued in favor of making good on Goldwater's promises as a way of enticing other converts.
Since the fall, however, a number of liberal Republicans had pledged to
challenge Thurmond's standing in the party. Party leaders struck a
compromise in mid-January in which Thurmond kept his post on
Armed Services, with seniority, but lost his spot on the Commerce
Committee. He was also denied his next two choices of Judiciary and
Labor and Public Welfare, ending up with a position on Banking and
Currency. Jacob Javits, the ranking member on Labor and Public Welfare, blocked the antilabor Thurmond from joining the committee and
gave up a privileged position on the Banking and Currency Committee in favor of a bottom slot on Judiciary, again to fend off Thurmond.[4]

Thurmond's standing in the Senate was emblematic of one of the
GOP's larger problems—how to accommodate the new southerners
who had joined the party during the Goldwater campaign. The debate
was the same one that had emerged after the 1962 midterms, only this
time conservatives could show tangible gains in the South. In 1964 the
South was the only place that Republicans experienced any real success. Alabama sent five Republican congressmen to Washington. Mississippi added one, and the GOP chairman there swore there could
have been more if they had only had more candidates.[5]

Despite conservative gains in the South, in early 1965 it was moderate and liberal Republicans who had the momentum. The high-profile
replacement of Goldwater's close associate Dean Burch as chairman of
the Republican National Committee was an encouraging sign to them.[6]
So was Dwight Eisenhower's widely publicized lamentation over the
GOP's "bad image," an opinion with which almost 60 percent of Republican county chairmen agreed.[7] Charles P. Taft and Henry Cabot
Lodge headlined the new Committee for Republican Progress to try to
push a moderate agenda.[8] "All know that the resistance of certain Republicans in 1964 to the progress of the civil rights movement was
wrong, not only politically, but morally," said Charles Percy of Illinois,

a leading GOP moderate who would win a Senate seat in 1966. "The Republican Party must stand as the party of Lincoln in civil rights; it must never become the party of Thurmond."⁹

This was the conventional wisdom in the spring of 1965 as Congress debated a historic voting rights bill. Once again, civil rights protests in Alabama had captured the nation's attention. The protests dramatized the insufficiencies of voting provisions in the 1964 Civil Rights Act, and thousands of Americans turned out for sympathy marches in cities across the country. In Detroit, the Republican governor, George Romney, a likely contender for the next GOP presidential nomination, led an estimated ten thousand people in a downtown march. In the House, a group of liberal Republicans blamed President Johnson for the violence in Selma and criticized his tardiness in sending voting rights legislation to Congress.¹⁰

The resistance that Thurmond and fellow southerners mustered on the voting rights bill was negligible compared with battles past. Richard Russell spent much of the debate hospitalized at Walter Reed Medical Center with severe pulmonary problems.¹¹ In letters home Thurmond complained that Martin Luther King had "more access to the White House than just about anyone in this Country."¹² Lyndon Johnson had given a nationally televised address in which he invoked the anthem of the civil rights movement. "Their cause must be our cause too," Johnson said of the protesters Thurmond had dismissed as insurrectionists. "Because it's not just Negroes, but really it's all of us who must overcome the crippling legacy of bigotry and injustice. And we—shall—overcome."¹³ In a Senate Judiciary Committee clash between Thurmond's past and present party associates, the former Dixiecrat leader Leander Perez of Louisiana testified that the voting rights bill was a "'hand-in-glove' . . . Communist conspiracy" to establish "Negro rule" in the Deep South. Thurmond's new party leader, Everett Dirksen of Illinois, told Perez that his comment was "about as stupid as anything I ever heard."¹⁴

Thurmond was not as boorish as Perez. His speech at the Wellington Hotel denouncing civil disobedience in Selma represented the modern, updated version of the old segregationist harangue. Yet the link between black protest and civil disorder had not yet taken hold for a significant number of Americans. In late May the Senate invoked cloture on a southern filibuster for the second time in two years. The Voting Rights Act passed later that summer. Thurmond and John Tower were the only Republican senators to vote no.[15]

During the most recent presidential campaign, Barry Goldwater had struggled and largely failed to capitalize on concerns about lawlessness and disorder in America, yet Thurmond's worries predated the Goldwater campaign.[16] The alleged threat posed by violence-prone blacks had been an arrow in Thurmond's political quiver at least since his 1950 Senate campaign, when he baited Olin Johnston with concerns over the "pardon racket." Seven years later, Thurmond charged the Supreme Court with its own version of the pardon racket when it freed confessed rapists such as Andrew Mallory. Not for Thurmond alone, by the early 1960s *Mallory* had become the symbol of liberal, permissive Supreme Court decisions that hamstrung law enforcement in its efforts to control crime in American cities.[17]

Through the mid-1960s, white southern attacks on the lawlessness of civil rights protests were easy to dismiss. Of course Freedom Rides or lunch counter sit-ins violated duly enacted laws of southern legislatures. That was the point. The laws were immoral—how else could disenfranchised southern blacks have their voices heard? The peaceful, dignified protests of well-dressed demonstrators at Selma and across the South represented the only form of democratic speech available to them. In this context, civil disobedience was in the best tradition of American democratic practice.

By the middle of the decade, however, Thurmond and other southerners' conflation of civil disobedience with crime and lawlessness found a more sympathetic hearing. There was no exact moment when this happened, although the second week of August 1965 came close. On August 6, Lyndon Johnson signed the 1965 Voting Rights Act into law. Five days later, rioting broke out in the Watts section of Los Angeles, a largely poor African American neighborhood. Widespread looting and arson continued for six days before police and National Guardsmen were able to restore order. By that time, thirty-four people had been killed.

Thurmond knew the Los Angeles area well. He traveled to Southern

California several times a year, visiting political friends and donors and speaking before right-wing audiences in Orange County and other conservative enclaves. He blamed the riots on Lyndon Johnson and other liberals in Washington who had "placated minority groups and led them to believe that they can do anything and get away with it," citing the Supreme Court, with its liberal decisions that "shackled" law enforcement, as an accomplice.[18]

These were not merely the fulminations of a southern segregationist. City officials and law-enforcement officers in Los Angeles blamed civil rights advocates for the violence. The Los Angeles chief of police, William H. Parker, already a figure of national prominence for his strict stance on crime and communism, dismissed civil rights protesters as instigators of social disorder and called civil disobedience a "short step from . . . mob violence." Asked to explain the origins of the riots, Parker said: "One person threw a rock and then, like monkeys in a zoo, others started throwing rocks." He predicted that by decade's end 45 percent of Los Angeles would be black, adding that if Californians wanted to "live with that without law enforcement, God help you."[19] The following year, the mayor of Los Angeles, Sam Yorty, transformed himself into the "George Wallace of California." He rode white backlash against Watts to a near upset of the liberal California governor, Edmund "Pat" Brown, in the Democratic gubernatorial primary.[20]

It was in the hothouse of law-and-order politics that the political career of Ronald Reagan took root. Reagan had burst onto the national scene in the closing weeks of the Goldwater campaign, when he dazzled Republicans with a nationally televised speech that defended conservative principles more effectively than Goldwater. It was the culmination of a decade of after-dinner talks he had given on the banquet circuit as a spokesman for General Electric. Reagan instantly became a front-runner for the Republican gubernatorial nomination two years later.[21]

"Law and order was a concept that Reagan latched on to instantly," writes Matthew Dallek, "and he did so in a way that seemed reasonable, not extremist. Reagan modified L.A. police chief Parker's arguments, softened the rhetoric, and transformed law and order into a potent political weapon."[22] It was the same rhetoric that Goldwater had used in his campaign and that Strom Thurmond employed in his Wellington Hotel address. Reagan vowed not to tolerate those who broke the law under the guise of civil disobedience, which he said had no place in a democracy.[23] He denounced student protesters at Berkeley and explained Watts in terms that Thurmond could appreciate: African American migrants from the Deep South had moved to Los Angeles and, misled by liberals who had promised to eradicate poverty, expected to see streets "paved with gold."[24]

Strom Thurmond's daughter had been one of them. In 1964, Essie Mae Washington-Williams had moved from Savannah, Georgia, with her children to a neighborhood not far from Watts. She did not expect streets of gold, but she had lived briefly in Los Angeles years before and was surprised upon returning by the extent of neighborhood segregation. The Watts riot shocked her. The poverty of her fellow African Americans, the lack of opportunity, and the hostility of Los Angeles police destroyed any lingering sense she had had of Los Angeles as a racial paradise. After Watts, she determined to finish her schooling and become a teacher. She registered to vote for the first time in her life, as a Democrat, and she joined the NAACP. Her life suggested a very different portrait of the southern black migrant from the image Reagan advanced. Thurmond was as callous as Reagan to the situation of his daughter and other black migrants to urban America, though not completely. Washington-Williams lost her husband around this same time. Several money orders with no letter enclosed arrived in the mail from a Washington address, helping ease her transition to California and widowhood.[25]

Poor blacks and poverty programs were easy marks for Reagan and Thurmond, as were the thousands of college students participating in the growing student revolt. In the spring of 1965, as the United States began a bombing campaign against North Vietnam and while a majority of Americans still expressed support for the war, major antiwar demonstrations broke out on college campuses across the country.[26] When antiwar groups announced plans for a Washington rally where protesters would burn their draft cards, Thurmond was the first senator to introduce a bill to criminalize the action. His South Carolina colleague Mendel Rivers, chairman of the House Armed Services Committee, had shepherded the same measure through his committee a few days before, pledging to crack down on the "agitating bums, hoodlums, gooks, cowards, juvenile delinquents, or plain irresponsible misguided Americans."[27] The law touched off a debate over the rights of free speech relative to Congress's ability to regulate the draft, one that would persist throughout the Vietnam era. In 1965, however, Congress passed the measure without hearings, and President Johnson signed it into law a few weeks later.[28]

With the antiwar movement drawing inspiration from civil rights protests, public opinion on racial issues swung sharply in the wake of the historic victories of the previous two years. Riots broke out in a dozen cities during the summer of 1966. Civil rights protesters were marching through the Deep South again, this time as part of the Meredith March in Mississippi. In a mass meeting in Greenwood, the Student Nonviolent Coordinating Committee chairman, Stokely Carmichael, who was quickly emerging as the face of radical black protest, introduced the term "Black Power," a phrase that spoke to African American frustrations over the diluted and dilatory nature of racial progress.[29] For many whites, however, it confirmed exactly what they had long expected: blacks did not want mere *inclusion*; they wanted to "take over," as Thurmond put it in a letter to a South Carolina supporter.[30] One poll taken in the fall of 1966 indicated that 75 percent of whites felt that racial reforms were moving too fast, compared with 50 percent two years before.[31]

Thurmond hoped that northern whites had seen enough to shift the political scale on civil rights.[32] Neither he nor his fellow southerners could have predicted how easy it would be to defeat civil rights legislation in the fall of 1966. Congressional liberals had won unprecedented victories in breaking southern filibusters the previous two years, yet in 1966 a civil rights bill that contained an open housing measure never made it to the floor for discussion. Civil rights forces could not get within ten votes of breaking a filibuster.[33] No marathon speeches by Thurmond or anyone else were required. Simple quorum calls went unanswered, grinding Senate business to a halt. The debate was so paltry that Thurmond was one of only a few senators who actually managed to get on record with an attack against the bill before the Senate adjourned.[34]

For Thurmond, the failure of the 1966 civil rights bill marked the first legislative vindication of his and other white southerners' long-held thesis about white northern hypocrisy on civil rights.[35]

Riots, crime, continued racial protests, and a burgeoning antiwar movement—all of these quickly and dramatically changed the context in which Republican leadership debated Strom Thurmond and conservative southerners' future role in the GOP. Liberal Republicans still warned about an emerging Dixiecrat wing in the South, yet fewer GOP leaders were listening.[36] When, in March 1966, a *Washington Post* reporter asked the House minority leader, Gerald Ford, whether he would campaign for segregationists such as Thurmond and James Martin, the Republican gubernatorial candidate in Alabama, Ford said straight-faced, "I don't think you can categorize these people as outright segregationists."[37]

Strom Thurmond not a segregationist? He could only have hoped that South Carolinians did not read *The Washington Post*. But he would not have worried much. Folks back home knew that Thurmond was the most outright segregationist that the South had sent to the Senate in a generation. For the Republican establishment to bring Thurmond on board, however, this was the shell game that they would have to play. The masterstroke came during the fall election season. Richard Nixon, in the midst of a multistate tour stumping for GOP candidates and laying the groundwork for his 1968 presidential campaign, was in Columbia for a GOP fund-raiser when a national reporter asked if he was embarrassed to have "ole States' Rights Strom" in his party. "Strom is no racist," Nixon said. "Strom is a man of courage and integrity." Harry Dent would later recall Nixon's "unapologetic, gracious comments" as a signal moment for both Thurmond and the South Carolina GOP.[38] It began Nixon's long courtship of Thurmond, who would remain one of his most loyal supporters. It was one thing for Barry Goldwater, the right-wing darling and would-be extremist, to defend Thurmond's racial politics. When Richard Nixon, the symbol of the GOP establishment, did it, it was another thing entirely.

By the time of the midterm elections, Thurmond had settled into his new party status. In the South Carolina GOP, he was more than merely comfortable; he was the kingpin. Longtime South Carolina Republicans had initially blocked his attempt to name Harry Dent the party's executive director, but that only delayed the inevitable. In September 1965, Dent wrested away the party chairmanship from Arthur Ravenel of Charleston, the leader of the South Carolina moderates. The former Democratic congressman Albert Watson had resigned and been reelected as a Republican. Democrats in South Carolina alleged that the GOP was promising $50,000 of campaign funds, courtesy of Roger Milliken, for any conservative Democrats who would follow Thurmond and Watson's lead.[39] "You're going to see a racist tone we haven't had in a long time in this state," predicted one veteran South Carolina political observer.[40] The GOP state convention in March 1966 took place under a huge Confederate banner. No black delegates were in attendance.[41]

Harry Dent and other southern chairmen frequently denied charges of racial extremism. "This is no lily-white setup," Dent said in response to the April report by liberal Republicans. "There are no whooping, hollering, chest-thumping segregationists in the Republican party here."[42]

Dent was right about the chest thumpers. In 1966 in South Carolina, they called themselves South Carolina Independents, not Republicans. Led by Maurice Bessinger, an outlandish owner of a string of barbecue restaurants in Columbia, they were George Wallace supporters who were gearing up for their man's presidential run in 1968. Republicans themselves walked a narrow line on race issues. What Dent did not admit to reporters was that while chest-thumping segregationists were not *in* the South Carolina GOP in 1966, they were working *alongside* it to reelect Strom Thurmond and defeat moderate South Carolina Democrats who were carefully and quietly conceding to the new politics of race. In contrast to the lily-white GOP convention that took place under a Confederate flag, African Americans played a significant role at the Democratic state convention. Democrats adopted a resolution banning racial discrimination at the polls and a platform calling for a compulsory school attendance law.[43]

Such moderate actions contrasted with not only the South Carolina GOP but also some other southern Democratic organizations that continued to capitalize on segregationist resentment. In Alabama, for example, the Democrat Lurleen Wallace won election as a surrogate for her husband. In Georgia an obscure restaurateur named Lester Maddox, best known for using an ax handle to ward off black customers testing public accommodation laws, won an unlikely race for the Democratic gubernatorial nomination, and eventually the governorship itself. In the mid-1960s, backlash politics was still fluid, not the domain of any one party.

In South Carolina, however, it was the Thurmond-led GOP that capitalized on reactionary politics. The GOP gubernatorial candidate, Joseph Rogers—who adapted George Wallace's campaign motto, "Stand Up for Alabama," for the Palmetto State—attacked the Democratic governor, Robert McNair, for going soft on school desegregation.[44] Thurmond himself called President Johnson a "traitor to the nation as well as to the South."[45] Harry Dent's office distributed 500,000 copies of a newsletter called *Had Enuf? News*, which reprinted articles from South Carolina newspapers with altered headlines highlighting alleged Democratic transgressions. Also included were a series of unflattering photographs of Governor McNair, including one of him smiling and shaking hands with a black man. The Democratic state chairman denounced the paper as "axe-handle politics."[46]

The GOP newsletter was tame compared with the glossy eight-page scandal sheet produced by Maurice Bessinger and the Independents, who in late October endorsed Strom Thurmond and all but one of the major Republican candidates.[47] The Independents' publication brought home law-and-order politics to South Carolina in explicitly racist terms, with headlines such as "Black Power Shatters U.S. Cities—Politicians Elected by Negro Bloc Vote Are Powerless to Stop Violence" and "Will Negro Bloc Vote Control South Carolina?" It included a number of pictures of black rioters, and at the bottom of several pages was the banner:

> Stand Up for South Carolina! Support . . .
> Strom Thurmond—Joe Rogers—Marshall Parker
> They Will Fight to Protect Your Rights and Safety![48]

Thurmond's Democratic Senate opponent, Bradley Morrah, condemned the paper as "utter tommyrot." He called on Thurmond to renounce the support of the Independents and remarked that Roger

Milliken and the well-financed Republicans were "on the same ball team with Maurice Bessinger."[49]

While Democrats accused Republicans of ax-handle politics, Republicans accused Democrats of "racism in reverse."[50] Harry Dent justified publishing the picture of Robert McNair shaking hands with a black man by pointing out that the photograph was a reprint from *The Cheraw Chronicle*, the editor of which, Andrew M. Secrest, was a well-known Democrat and an employee of the Community Relations Service who had helped mediate racial strife in Selma, Alabama, in 1965. "Was he appealing to the Negro vote or what?" Dent said of Secrest.[51] If Republicans were playing the race card, the logic went, it was only because the Democrats had done it first.

On Election Day, Strom Thurmond cruised to victory over Bradley Morrah, and while Republicans fared more poorly than they had hoped, they still did better than they had in nearly a century. Albert Watson won reelection to the House. The Republican gubernatorial candidate, Rogers, lost to Robert McNair, and Ernest Hollings edged Marshall Parker for a U.S. Senate seat by a mere fifteen thousand votes. In both races, black voters represented the Democrats' margin of victory, not surprising given how dismissive Republicans had been of the "bloc vote."[52] In all, though, it was a good beginning for a party that could barely convene a statewide convention a decade earlier. The state assembly races were particularly pleasing for the GOP: six new state senators and twenty-three representatives.[53]

The racist hard-right campaigns of South Carolina Republicans did not reflect all of the GOP efforts across the South. Howard Baker, the son of a seven-term GOP congressman from East Tennessee, a pocket of southern Republicanism since the Civil War, won a Senate seat from the Volunteer State. The son-in-law of Everett Dirksen, Baker became the symbol of southern GOP moderation for the next two decades. Winthrop Rockefeller, Nelson's brother, won the governorship in Arkansas, and in Houston an oil executive with roots in Yankee Republican royalty picked up a House seat. George H. W. Bush, who had lost a Senate race against Ralph Yarborough two years earlier running as a Goldwater Republican, embraced moderation and won.[54]

The race that most excited Thurmond and other South Carolina Republicans, however, was in California, where Ronald Reagan won an upset victory over the two-time Democratic incumbent, Edmund "Pat" Brown. Reagan immediately replaced Barry Goldwater as the leading conservative politician. His favorable ratings among South Carolina college students were even better than Thurmond's.[55] In the days following the election, the GOP state chairman, Harry Dent, pressed Thurmond to help line up Reagan for a Republican event to help pay off a $30,000 party campaign debt.[56]

The dinner, held in September 1967 in the Township Auditorium in Columbia, raised $170,000. Described as the "largest political fundraising event in state history," it was part of a trio of events that political observers read as Reagan testing the waters for the 1968 Republican presidential nomination. Thurmond introduced Reagan, praising him as "one of the leading figures in the world, today," and the crowd gave thunderous applause when Reagan described how he had cut government spending and vetoed seven federal antipoverty programs. Cheers of "Reagan in '68" rose from the crowd of thirty-three hundred, an all-white audience save for a lone black couple at the far end of the auditorium.[57]

For Thurmond it was a personal triumph. It was impossible to imagine him hosting an analogous event—feting a rising star of the national party—had he remained a Democrat. By 1967, Thurmond was like a man liberated from a bad marriage. A world of new opportunities lay before him. There were no more bitter accusations of disloyalty. Best of all, he no longer had to apologize for his friends.

One of the first things Thurmond did as a Republican was repair his ties with Young Americans for Freedom (YAF), the organization of conservative youth founded in 1960 at William F. Buckley Jr.'s family estate. He had been forced to resign from the organization's board of directors in early 1964 after the group sent out a fund-raising appeal he had written along with material promoting Barry Goldwater for president. Democrats in South Carolina had passed on copies to the White House, which was deliberating over the appointment of two federal judges in South Carolina, one of whom was Thurmond's old law partner. Thurmond eventually got his judge, but only after resigning from the YAF board and temporarily falling in line behind Lyndon Johnson.[58]

Now, however, Thurmond became one of YAF's most popular speakers. All politicians court young people, the ground troops for the next campaign, but Thurmond seemed to adore the polite, well-dressed patriotic youth whom he met in countless appearances before YAF chapters across the country. His role as a conservative spokesperson stretched much further. Thurmond used his free franking privileges in the Senate to raise money for Clarence Manion's radio program, gave tributes to Raymond Moley on the Senate floor, sent copies of Whittaker Chambers's *Cold Friday* to friends and colleagues, and worked tirelessly in building the southern Republican Party.[59] The goal as always was to make the southern GOP into the vehicle of regional conservatism. Yet he also found time to raise money for Sam Cavnar, the director of Project Alert and Project Prayer, who ran for a House seat in Southern California in 1968, as well as Max Rafferty, the hard-right educator who defeated the moderate Thomas Kuchel in California's 1968 GOP Senate primary.[60]

In 1967, Thurmond was invited to join a small group of conservative luminaries as stewards of the John P. Gaty Trust, established by the former vice president and general manager of Beech Aircraft in Wichita, Kansas. According to Gaty's will, each trustee would distribute $10,000 to his own charity, with consideration given to causes that would "promote individual liberty and incentive as opposed to socialism and communism." Among the trustees were three of Thurmond's Senate colleagues—Barry Goldwater, John Tower, and Frank Lausche of Ohio—as well as William F. Buckley Jr., Clarence Manion, George Benson of Harding College, and Edgar Eisenhower, Ike's younger sibling and the most rightward of the seven Eisenhower brothers. Goldwater nominated Thurmond as chairman. Recalling the moment years later, Buckley described Thurmond as "senior in rank, politically invincible, and also—it seemed even then—biologically evergreen."[61]

The capstone event in Thurmond's emergence as a national conservative leader was the publication in the summer of 1968 of *The Faith We Have Not Kept*, the only book he "wrote" during his long career (Lee Edwards, an assistant press secretary in the Goldwater campaign and editor of a 1965 exposé of alleged Communist connections to the civil rights movement, was the ghostwriter). Published by Viewpoint Books of San Diego, the 192-page treatise on constitutional government, individual liberty, free enterprise, and the Communist menace was the literary equivalent of a southerner who had taken speech lessons to lose his accent. It was the culmination of a process that had begun exactly twenty years earlier when, much to the chagrin of his Dixiecrat advisers, Thurmond had kicked off his presidential campaign in Houston with a nationally oriented speech about constitutionalism and the threat of statism.

Thurmond had hoped to have his old friend Barry Goldwater write a foreword for the book, but Goldwater, who was running for reelection to the Senate, begged off, citing "minor disagreements."[62] When Thurmond politely inquired what the disagreements were, Goldwater hesitated, making clear Thurmond should not change anything in the book but pointing to his gloss on the *Brown* decision.[63] "While I totally disagreed with the way the *Brown* case was settled," Goldwater explained, "I did agree with its principle but in reading your book you reflect, as I know you honestly believe, a continuing disagreement with it."[64]

Thurmond might have pointed out that in attacking *Brown*, his book did not defend segregation but dealt with constitutional principles that he believed the Court had sacrificed in reaching its conclusion. Or he could have asked whether Goldwater's explanation meant that he himself did not have a "continuing disagreement" with "the way the *Brown* case was settled." In fact, Thurmond could have asked how his book's denunciation of *Brown* differed substantively from the one Goldwater had offered in his own ghostwritten book, *The Conscience of a Conservative*, in which he wrote that he had been unconvinced that *Brown* was the law of the land. "The Constitution, and the laws 'made in pursuance thereof,' are the 'supreme law of the land,'" *Conscience* read. "The Constitution is what its authors intended it to be and said it was—not what the Supreme Court says it is."[65]

Yet Thurmond said none of these things. "I can certainly understand why, during election year, you have to be particularly careful in all your actions," he allowed.[66] Thurmond may not have had to apologize for his Republican friends anymore, but now some of them found themselves having to apologize for him.

By the end of 1967, there were over 500,000 American military personnel in Vietnam, up from 23,000 at the beginning of 1965. As American
involvement in the war increased, so did the antiwar movement. Protests that began on college campuses in 1965 increasingly spread to the
streets. In April 1967 over a hundred thousand people attended a peace
march in New York City where Martin Luther King called for a union
of the civil rights movement and the antiwar movement.

During this period of intense polarization over Vietnam, Thurmond was perhaps the Senate's most recognizable hawk. As a member
of the Armed Services Preparedness Investigating Subcommittee, he
regularly grilled Pentagon and administration officials on war policy.
He was one of the first senators to urge U.S. bombing of North Vietnam, and he declared that a "preemptive nuclear strike" should not be
ruled out as a military option.[67] He also attacked the antiwar protesters
and the reporters who favorably covered them. "Young people have a
right to make jackasses out of themselves if they so choose," he said,
"but I am frankly puzzled by the wide news coverage it commands."[68]

As the dramatic rise in troop levels suggests, however, Lyndon Johnson waged an aggressive war. While he did not follow the advice of
Thurmond or others on the right to mine Haiphong Harbor or use
nuclear weapons against North Vietnam, his troop escalations and
conventional bombing campaign against the North allowed him to
parry criticism from hawks. In an East Room briefing for select congressmen in February 1966, Thurmond challenged Johnson for going
too easy on North Vietnam, an accusation the president easily countered. The annihilation of North Vietnam was not his goal, Johnson
said evenly. He had not set the boundary between North and South
Vietnam, yet there it was. His job was to make sure it remained where
it was, nothing more and nothing less. The point was framed in neon
during an exchange between Thurmond and Secretary of State Dean
Rusk later that year. Using the classic right-wing phrase that he had
helped popularize during the muzzling hearings, Thurmond accused
the administration of pursuing a "no-win" policy in Vietnam. "Senator, we can have a general war any time we want it," Rusk replied heat-

edly. He evoked a scenario of nuclear holocaust before adding, "We are trying to build a little peace in the world."[69]

The theme of Thurmond's attacks was not merely that the United States was pursuing a no-win policy but that it was doing so under the leadership of civilian technocrats in the Defense Department rather than military officials with experience and training in how to fight and win wars. The mutual contempt between Thurmond and Secretary of Defense Robert McNamara had been clear during the muzzling hearings, but with Vietnam the simmering feud reached a boil. Thurmond disdained the secretary and his "whiz kid" advisers and portrayed McNamara as a bean counter who consistently overruled the recommendations of more experienced military leaders.

Like his bromides about civil disobedience and lawlessness, however, by 1968 Thurmond's attacks on the Johnson administration's war tactics no longer seemed so extreme. Thurmond's constant criticism was that the Johnson administration was timid and ineffectual. In late January, a series of events reinforced this image. Early on the morning of January 31, the Vietnamese New Year, North Vietnam led a coordinated attack on U.S. and South Vietnamese forces. The Tet Offensive caught American military planners by surprise. The counteroffensive was, militarily speaking, far more damaging to the North than its original incursion against the United States and South Vietnam. But back home the political damage from Tet was devastating. It contradicted administration claims that the end of fighting was near, and televised news reports reinforced the moral failure of the war.[70]

Thurmond agreed that Vietnam was a quagmire, but he believed that it was one caused by inept leadership. For many Americans, the most egregious example had come the week before when North Korea seized an American spy ship, the USS *Pueblo*, in international waters in the Sea of Japan. Not since 1807, during the Napoleonic Wars, when a British man-of-war captured the USS *Chesapeake*, searched its crew for deserters, and absconded with four crewmen, had the U.S. Navy experienced such humiliation.[71] The Johnson administration subsequently came to believe that the attack was coordinated with the Tet Offensive, an act of collusion between Hanoi and Pyongyang intended to divert American attention and force two South Korean divisions in

Vietnam to return home.[72] Regardless, Thurmond and other hawks in Congress screamed.[73]

On March 31, in the hope of spurring negotiations with North Vietnam, Lyndon Johnson announced a unilateral cessation of bombing save for areas immediately north of the demilitarized zone, where a continuing buildup threatened allied troops. Averell Harriman, his personal representative, was willing to meet anyplace, anytime, for peace talks. Near the end of his remarks, Johnson declared his intention not to let the presidency become mired in partisan concerns during an election year. "Accordingly," he declared, "I shall not seek, and I will not accept, the nomination of my party for another term as your President."[74] Johnson's fall from grace had been astounding.

Vietnam abroad and law and order at home—according to *Time*, these were the issues that preoccupied Americans in election year 1968. Thurmond could not have agreed more.[75]

In the mid-1960s, rock throwing and window smashing in American cities had become a common occurrence, yet the long, hot summer of 1967 was unlike anything that had come before. Rioting and violence broke out in over a hundred cities. The largest and deadliest were in Newark and Detroit; authorities in both cities called out the National Guard. In Newark, twenty-one of the twenty-three residents killed were African American. In Detroit, the death toll was forty-three—thirty-three of whom were African American.[76]

Black rioting fueled the political fire of Thurmond and other conservatives, as did the antics of a handful of high-profile Black Power advocates. For years Thurmond had warned about the nonviolent civil rights movement serving as a Trojan horse for covert Communists and their anti-American agenda. By 1967, he presented himself as the sentinel of Troy watching the Greeks creeping out from their hiding place as he documented the escapades of Stokely Carmichael, the former chairman of the Student Nonviolent Coordinating Committee, and H. Rap Brown, the current chairman.

In August, the twenty-six-year-old Carmichael attended a conference of Latin American revolutionary Communists in Havana, where he spoke of the urban violence in the United States as part of an incipient black revolution. Listing Che Guevara and Mao Tse-tung as his political heroes, he described black soldiers adapting guerrilla warfare tactics from Vietnam for use in American cities and speculated about assassination attempts on various U.S. officials. Outrage back home flowed from practically every mainstream political quarter, yet few people took Carmichael more seriously than Thurmond, who warned that the nation was in "open rebellion" and called for Carmichael's arrest upon his return to the United States, a proposal that received significant support in the House.[77]

Thurmond and other conservatives on the Judiciary Committee made Carmichael and Brown their bêtes noires in the fight against civil rights legislation in early 1968. A key provision of the proposed bill protected civil rights workers and others exercising federally guaranteed rights.[78] Thurmond criticized the legislation for failing to deal with the issue of civil disorder, a problem exacerbated, he said, by the very people whom the bill sought to protect. He and the Judiciary Committee chairman, James Eastland, co-authored a minority report that charged the bill with giving "added protection to roving fomentors of violence, such as Stokely Carmichael and H. Rap Brown."[79]

The debate over the 1968 civil rights bill surprised many people, given how unwilling Congress had been to take up such matters since 1966. Liberals managed to keep the civil rights protections in the bill, and in February the Senate even agreed to include a compromise measure on open housing. The Republican minority leader, Everett Dirksen, was almost single-handedly responsible. In 1968, he supported open housing measures that he had vehemently opposed just two years earlier. The summer riots of 1967 had put "this whole matter in a different frame," he said.[80]

Also influencing the debate was the release in late February of the report of the National Advisory Commission on Civil Disorders, the eleven-member body established by President Johnson to investigate the 1967 summer riots. Commonly known as the Kerner Commission for its chair, Governor Otto Kerner of Illinois, the commission produced a report that provided a wide-ranging investigation of the "explosive mix" of poverty, unemployment, and inadequate housing that created the underlying conditions for urban unrest. The report's signature line evoked the indelible language of the *Plessy*-era South, the age

of Jim Crow racism that the legislative triumphs of the 1960s were supposed to have erased: "Our nation is moving toward two societies, one
black, one white—separate and unequal."[81]

Drawing Thurmond's ire was the Kerner Commission's assessment
that "white racism" was responsible for the conditions of ghetto life.
The report substituted an assertive opinion for the volumes of facts
that the commission had gathered, he said, and in the process had built
up "stereotypes of hatred" and given credence to "the inflammatory
propaganda of militant, organized agitators." The commission was
"fighting fire with gasoline," he concluded.[82] Thurmond's comments
were part of a cacophony of criticism from the Right.[83]

The "white racism" charge had obscured the obvious, proximate
causes of the rioting, Thurmond argued. Radical black activists had
incited insurrections, he said, and the commission's emphasis on underlying issues of discrimination, unemployment, and inadequate housing should not be taken as license for lawless behavior. The individuals
themselves must be held responsible. As the conservative editorialist
James J. Kilpatrick summed up the argument: "When one inquires
why the city is burning, it ought not to be amiss to direct a few questions at the man with the torch in his hand."[84]

In early April, Congress passed the final version of the civil rights
bill by a wide margin. Thurmond blamed the bill's relatively easy passage on the "mass hysteria" in Congress following the assassination of
Martin Luther King on April 4.[85] Rioting broke out in dozens of American cities, including Washington, D.C., where the mayhem came
within blocks of the White House. Thurmond drew from King's assassination a lesson about moral and legal relativism. "We are now wit-
nessing the whirlwind sowed years ago when some preachers and
teachers began telling people that each man could be his own judge in
his own case," he said, before circling back to a familiar attack on the
Warren Court: "This theory of ethics is no different from the new theory pursued by the Supreme Court in holding that today's situations
change the meaning of old laws and of the Constitution."[86]

By the spring of 1968, Thurmond had become an established national spokesman of law-and-order politics. He and Frank Lausche, a
conservative Democrat from Ohio who had been galvanized by rioting
in Cleveland in the summer of 1966, proposed an amendment to the

civil rights bill that levied a $10,000 fine and five years of imprison-
ment for anyone who crossed state lines or used interstate facilities,
such as the mail, telephone, or radio, to incite a riot. In introducing the
measure, Thurmond listed incidents of rioting from the previous year
in Nashville, Houston, Atlanta, and other cities and their instigation
by radical black activists. He tallied the carnage from the previous
year: 117 people killed in incidents in 126 cities; more than two thousand injured; more than sixteen thousand arrested; property damage
in excess of $160 million.[87] "A nation which cannot preserve order,"
Thurmond said, "is surely on the road to destruction."[88]

Some version of an anti-riot law had been circulating in Congress
for a while.[89] For Thurmond it went back to the Freedom Rides, when
he co-sponsored a bill that made it a federal crime to cross state lines to
incite a riot or commit unlawful acts.[90] That proposal had been dead
on arrival. Back then white southerners' complaints about "outside agitators" gained little public sympathy. Outweighing them were reports
of white violence against nonviolent riders in Rock Hill, South Carolina, and Anniston and Birmingham, Alabama. Yet much had changed
in seven years. After a slight modification to the language, the Thurmond-
Lausche amendment passed 82–13.[91]

In the winter and spring of 1968, South Carolinians had had their
own experience with law-and-order politics, one that showed the
starkness of the racial and political divide and suggested some of the
unintended consequences of Thurmond's harangues against protesters. On February 7, South Carolina highway patrol officers, all of whom
were white, had fired into a crowd of black students from South Carolina State College in Orangeburg protesting segregation at a local bowl-
ing alley. Three students—Samuel Hammond, Henry Smith, and Delano
Middleton—were killed, and twenty-eight more were injured, many of
them shot in the back. Few if any of the officers had training in crowd
control.[92] All they would have known about the crowd of angry blacks
protesting before them was what their superiors had told them. No one
in the state's law-enforcement or political leadership, or in the nation's
for that matter, had done more than Strom Thurmond to perpetuate
the fear and loathing of black radicals inciting riots.

Early on the morning of March 8, a bipartisan group of state senators introduced a resolution in the South Carolina General Assembly

calling on the U.S. Congress to support Thurmond "in his fight to secure strong, firm anti-riot legislation."[93] Later that morning, roughly ninety African American students from South Carolina State filed into the senate gallery. They were among several hundred students who had come to protest the killing of the three black student demonstrators.

One of the male students stood up at the gallery's brass rail in front of the senate president's desk and called out to the senate president, who immediately rapped his gavel and tried to silence him. The student continued, reading a list of grievances the protesters had prepared. Senate guards came and grabbed the student by the arms and marched him up the steps toward the rear doors. Another student rose to take his place, shouting, "We've got some grievances here." State Law Enforcement Division (SLED) officers moved in to apprehend the disorderly. One of the SLED officers addressed the group and asked them to leave.

"We are not going, sir!" a student called back.

"I ask you to respond and move," the officer replied.

"Why didn't you ask us that night in Orangeburg before you started shooting?" another student shouted back.[94]

A female student stood up and began reading the petition. Officers shoved through rows of seated students to arrest her. Eventually, the group slowly filed out and joined other students in the statehouse lobby. Later, the protesters marched peacefully outside the statehouse. One of them carried a sign that read, "Orangeburg Massacre—a Police Riot."[95]

10

ANNUS MIRABILIS
(1968)

On June 22, 1968, Strom Thurmond endorsed Richard Nixon to be the next president of the United States. The announcement dumbfounded political observers in South Carolina who expected Thurmond to support George Wallace, whose campaign was drawing comparisons to Thurmond's race twenty years earlier. Unlike 1948, however, Wallace actually had support from outside the South, among working-class whites in northern industrial states. One of the favorite topics early in the campaign season was handicapping the "Wallace effect," gauging which party he would hurt more—Republicans in the South or Democrats in the North.

The danger to the GOP in South Carolina was real. Wallace backers had provided invaluable assistance to Thurmond and other Republicans during the 1966 midterms. Throughout 1967 they expected that the GOP would nominate a moderate or a liberal and that Strom Thurmond would eventually be in Wallace's corner.

Yet Thurmond never seriously considered backing Wallace. In February 1968 he issued a statement denying reports that he supported the Alabaman. He was committed to the GOP, he said, because of its strong stand against centralized government and communism and because of its concern about the lawlessness rampant throughout the country. Thurmond was convinced that unlike in 1948 serious differences existed between the two major parties, on both foreign and domestic issues.[1] Not to be discounted either was the fact that he had managed to carve out a pleasant place for himself in both the national and the state GOP. A Wallace endorsement would jeopardize that hard work.

More than Wallace, the person with whom Thurmond's politics fit most neatly was Ronald Reagan, who was expected to get in the race for the Republican nomination soon. As smitten by the new California governor as anyone, Thurmond likened Reagan's glamour to that of the late John F. Kennedy. Reagan's rise had been so meteoric, however, as to leave Thurmond with doubts. He had held down his job in Sacramento for little more than a year, and Thurmond wondered whether he was truly ready to be leader of the free world. Throughout the nominating process, Thurmond and associates admitted that while their hearts were with Reagan, their heads were with Richard Nixon. The question was why Thurmond went with his head.

Fear of failure seems to have been the most important factor. The "Goldwaterloo" of 1964 still weighed heavily on the GOP's collective consciousness. Thurmond had lots of company among Goldwaterites in his preference of Nixon over Reagan. Goldwater himself supported Nixon, as did the leading conservative "columnist-oracles" of the day: William F. Buckley Jr., John Chamberlain, William S. White, and Russell Kirk.[2] Many conservatives worried that an all-out push for Reagan à la Goldwater in 1964 would only ease the path for a dreaded moderate or liberal nominee, such as Nelson Rockefeller or George Romney.[3]

Like all these conservatives, Thurmond settled for Nixon given the alternatives. Yet Nixon was not without attractive qualities. Thurmond saw him as a figure of extraordinary experience in a moment of genuine crisis in American foreign and domestic affairs. Nixon was not an old man in 1968, yet he had been on the national scene for a long time. It had been Vice President Nixon who had administered the oath of office to Thurmond as an incoming senator back in 1954. Nixon's mastery of world affairs made a particular mark on Thurmond. He believed that Nixon would restore American military superiority around the globe, and he was mindful of how a third-party candidate like Wallace would split conservative votes and make it easier for Democrats to preserve the White House during a critical period in American foreign relations. A Democratic president, Thurmond feared, would let victory slip away in Vietnam, which could lead to other appeasements in Latin America and elsewhere.[4]

It was at a meeting of southern Republicans in Atlanta that Nixon finally convinced Thurmond. Nixon would recall in his memoirs that the first and most important issue that Thurmond wanted to discuss was not a parochial one such as school desegregation or textile policy but national security.[5] Thurmond asked for Nixon's pledge to support the antiballistic missile system that Congress was debating that very month. It has more than a ring of truth: an antimissile defense system had been a hobbyhorse of Thurmond's since his failure with the Nike-Zeus in the early 1960s. Yet the idea of Nixon and Thurmond discussing national security issues, not civil rights, also fit the image that both men needed to cultivate. From the Atlanta meeting onward, Nixon fought accusations that he had sold out to the racist Thurmond. Nixon sensed that this was a sore point for Thurmond as much as it was for him. Where others saw a reactionary southern racist and Bircher extremist, Nixon knew that Thurmond fashioned himself a statesman.

Harry Dent promoted Thurmond as such in a letter urging Nixon to make national security the center of his campaign. A hero of the Normandy invasion, the former national president of the Reserve Officers Association, and, as Dent wrote, the man who "now sits on every subcommittee in the U.S. Senate touching on national security," Thurmond could be of great help to Nixon on the issue. Thurmond knew himself to be a serious person of world affairs.[6] Nixon treated him that way, and in doing so earned his devotion.

Nixon had been courting Thurmond at least since his 1966 trip to Columbia. Working through the former party chieftain J. Drake Edens, the earliest Nixon backer in South Carolina, he had also targeted Harry Dent, who was now working in Columbia as party chairman. The night of Nixon's address in Columbia, word was passed through his entourage that the Dent family had suffered a minor tragedy. In the family's rush to get to the hall, their dog had been run over by a car. The Richard Nixon of Checkers-speech fame knew the sentimental value of a puppy and promptly had one dispatched to the Dent family home.[7]

At the end of his South Carolina visit, Dent drove Nixon to the airport and waited with him for his flight out, which was running late.

The talked turned to the 1968 campaign and how to get around the problem of George Wallace in the South. As he recounted in his memoir, Dent "painted a picture for Nixon." He talked about all that Thurmond had done to help Goldwater in 1964 and all that he could do to help Nixon stem the Wallace tide in 1968. Nixon's late plane, Dent wrote later, was the twist of fate that "launched the 1968 southern strategy."[8]

It made for a neat story, yet none of Dent's picture painting would have been necessary for Nixon. It was the reason why he had come to Columbia in the first place. Less obvious given Dent's down-home, aw-shucks demeanor was the fact that if Nixon or any other GOP candidate wanted Thurmond's help, Dent was determined to make him work for it. In early 1968, Dent joined with his party chairman counterparts in Mississippi and Florida, Clarke Reed and Bill Murfin, to plan a strategy for southern influence over the 1968 nomination process. Over elaborate multicourse meals served up by Reed's wife at their home in Greenville, Mississippi—thus the trio's designation as the Greenville Group—the three men planned how, as Dent put it, to make the big candidates "come a-callin', dressed up in their best bib and tucker."[9]

The Greenville Group initiated the plan to invite the three major GOP candidates—Nixon, Reagan, and Rockefeller—to meet with the southern chairmen in New Orleans in late May. Nixon opted for an Atlanta meeting. It was there, after the southern chairmen had completed their rounds with the big three, that Dent phoned Thurmond to tell him to charter a private plane and fly down to confirm things with Nixon. Thurmond planned to announce the endorsement at a meeting of South Carolina Republicans the next week. When Dent told the Reagan campaign to expect the imminent endorsement, they took the news well. Dent expected that they would soon fall in behind Nixon.

But then, on June 5, the New York senator and Democratic presidential candidate Robert Kennedy was shot at the Ambassador Hotel in Los Angeles. Kennedy had just won a hard-fought victory in the California presidential primary, and his death, coupled with Martin Luther King's assassination two months earlier, horrified the nation. For millions of Americans it seemed as though the country was coming apart. Kennedy's assassination set off a mad scramble for the Democratic presidential nomination, but it also affected the GOP race.

As Dent put it, the Reagan campaign "now felt that as a result of the Kennedy tragedy, Reagan's No. 1 issue, law and order, would catapult him into a much stronger position nationally."[10] Thurmond, however, was not swayed by events, nor would he be by Reagan's last-minute push at the convention in Miami Beach. The day before his announcement, Thurmond sent a telegram to Reagan informing him of his decision to back Nixon.[11]

Regardless of the visits, the gifts, and the ego stroking, none of Nixon's courting would have mattered to Thurmond and Dent had they found him unreasonable on the issue of school desegregation, which had reached a new crisis point by the summer of 1968. The notion that Richard Nixon made a deal with Strom Thurmond on school desegregation in return for his help against George Wallace is one of the enduring narratives of the 1968 presidential campaign. While not literally true, the two men had an understanding—a position of trust—that by itself marked a kind of political maturation for Thurmond. In the 1950s, Thurmond was intent on being a fundamentalist defender of the color line. He abandoned that position with his endorsement of Nixon, and in doing so risked the wrath of the Wallaceites. Yet Thurmond's position on school desegregation during the 1968 campaign is another example of the transition he was going through as he grew into his role as a national figure.

By 1968, there was a new thorn in the side of Thurmond and other segregationists regarding schools, the Department of Health, Education, and Welfare (HEW) guidelines. Fourteen years after *Brown*, the pace of desegregation in the South remained glacial. In a number of Deep South states, less than 10 percent of black schoolchildren were in desegregated schools. In South Carolina the number was 6.4.[12] The 1964 Civil Rights Act had given the federal government new powers to coerce recalcitrant southern districts, including the right to cut off federal funds, yet white southerners quickly developed new methods of resistance.

The guidelines represented HEW's attempt to deal with the latest form of segregationist subterfuge, "freedom of choice" desegregation plans. The proposals were based on an elegantly mystifying reading of *Brown*. All that the Supreme Court had done, defenders argued, was to forbid *segregation*. It had not required *integration*. The formulation was taken directly from appeals court rulings applying *Brown* in various districts across the South. One of the acceptable and most popular means for many districts to meet the requirements of *Brown* was to simply give all students the freedom to choose which school they would attend. It was in theory an eminently reasonable position. Where could discrimination be found in a free choice for all, black and white students alike?

In practice, however, freedom of choice left segregated patterns of schooling virtually unchanged, as every segregationist knew it would. In its guidelines, HEW noted how in southern communities with long histories of segregation and discrimination, the burden of choosing which school to attend was hardly free. It rested squarely on black students and parents, who opened themselves up to harassment and economic retaliation by registering at traditionally "white" schools. Such intimidation kept the actual number of black students in desegregated schools pitifully low. Dillon and Florence counties in South Carolina provided good examples. In August 1966, Thurmond had issued an urgent telegram to the president protesting the initiation of HEW enforcement procedures against those two counties. An official responded with a letter noting that only 8 of 1,264 black students were in desegregated schools in Dillon County; in Florence County there were only 3 out of 1,089 students.[13]

Thurmond ignored such damning statistics and focused on the surface plausibility of freedom of choice. "In my state all the schools have been open to all the children," he pronounced grandly in May 1968. "No school refuses any child of any race, color, or national origin attending such schools."[14] He also joined fellow southerners in Congress in going on the offensive against northern liberal opponents. By adopting freedom-of-choice plans, they insisted, southern schools had gotten rid of de jure segregation, which *Brown* outlawed, in favor of the de facto segregation that existed widely in public schools outside the region. Like a "plague of locusts," Thurmond said, HEW henchmen were pestering southern school officials about the compositions of

TWENTY CENTS   OCTOBER 11, 1948

TIME

THE WEEKLY NEWSMAGAZINE

THE DIXIECRATS' J. STROM THURMOND
Is the issue black and white?

$8 A YEAR   1948 © U.S. PAT. OFF.2   VOL. LII NO. 15

Strom Thurmond's 1948 campaign for president as nominee of the States' Rights Democrats, or "Dixiecrats" (a term he loathed), sealed his image as an icon of the segregated South (*left*). Yet Thurmond's racial politics intersected with other right-wing passions—anticommunism, the fight against organized labor, and religious conservatism—in ways that are critical for understanding post–World War II American politics. *Below*, Thurmond speaks at the Young Americans for Freedom "Rally for World Liberation from Communism" at Madison Square Garden in March 1962. (Above left: Time, Inc.; below: Bettmann/Corbis)

Left: Will Thurmond (holding book) with gubernatorial candidate Ira Jones. (Strom Thurmond Institute)

Right: Cole Blease, a notorious demagogue, defeated Jones in a bitterly contested 1912 election. A candidate debate witnessed by a nine-year-old Strom Thurmond marked the beginning of his political ambition. (Library of Congress)

Left: A picture of Strom Thurmond shortly after he had resumed his teaching career near Edgefield. An earlier career switch that took him out of state had coincided with the birth of his African American daughter and her mother's decision to send the child to Pennsylvania to live with relatives. (Strom Thurmond Institute)

Left: Governor Strom Thurmond and his young wife, Jean, pose for a *Life* photographer, 1947. Thurmond loved to be photographed performing manly acts of physical exertion, a trait that critics considered vain and undignified.

(Getty Images/Ed Clark)

Right: Thurmond at the Southern Governors' Conference in 1948, reading a statement that thrust him to the forefront of the southern revolt. To his right are Robert Figg (front) and Walter Brown, important political advisers early in his career. (Strom Thurmond Institute)

Left: Thurmond shaking hands with Fred Buzhardt. Harry Dent stands between them, looking at the camera. Beginning in the mid-1950s, Dent and Buzhardt emerged as Thurmond's closest political aides.

(Strom Thurmond Institute)

Governor Thurmond, pictured with Billy Graham and Bob Jones Jr. (fourth from left) and a young Bob Jones III during a Graham rally in Columbia in the spring of 1950. (Strom Thurmond Institute)

Above left: South Carolina textile magnate Roger Milliken at the 1964 Republican National Convention. Milliken was one of the most influential funders of conservative and Republican causes in post–World War II America and an important figure in Thurmond's party switch. (Bettmann/Corbis)

Above right: Thurmond during a television appearance, advocating an antimissile defense system, a pet cause of his throughout the 1960s. (Strom Thurmond Institute)

Above: Thurmond (second row, far left), pictured with members of the Southern Caucus during the fight against the 1957 civil rights bill. Thurmond seems to be eyeing Richard Russell, dean of the southerners (seated center, arms crossed), whom he would infuriate with his rogue one-man filibuster. (Bettmann/Corbis)

Left: Thurmond campaigning for Goldwater in 1964. (Strom Thurmond Institute)

Below: Thurmond with William F. Buckley, Jr., Edgar Eisenhower, Dr. George Benson, and Clarence Manion, all trustees of the John P. Gaty Trust in Wichita, Kansas. Thurmond chaired the group of conservative leaders whom Gaty chose to distribute money to various conservative causes. (Strom Thurmond Institute)

Some seven hundred African Americans marched on the South Carolina State House in March 1968 to protest the killings of three students at South Carolina State College in Orangeburg. The Orangeburg killings and subsequent protests coincided with Thurmond's "anti-riot" amendment to the 1968 civil rights bill. (Bettmann/Corbis)

Above left: Thurmond with California governor Ronald Reagan at the Silver Elephant Dinner in Columbia in 1967, one of several events Reagan used to test the waters for a presidential run in 1968. (Strom Thurmond Institute)

Above right: Thurmond with Richard Nixon—who had been courting him for two years and whom Thurmond would endorse later that summer—at a Republican gala in Washington in March 1968. (Strom Thurmond Institute)

Right: Despite Republicans' southern strategy, Thurmond was often frustrated by Nixon's school desegregation policies, as this cartoon suggests. (Clifford Baldowski Collection, University of Georgia Libraries)

SCHOOL DESEGREGATION PLEDGE

STROM THURMOND

SOUTHERN STRATEGY

Baldy

"... OOPSIE!"

Left: An African American girl in Lamar, South Carolina, protected by a South Carolina National Guardsman in March 1970. Violence in Lamar, where whites attacked school buses and black schoolchildren, attracted national news coverage. (Bettmann/Corbis)

This *Charlotte Observer* cartoon captured the skepticism many felt about Thurmond's embrace of racial moderation before his 1972 reelection campaign. (Courtesy of Melinda Marlette)

THURMOND

RE-ELECT 'OL STROM

* FREE * WATER MELON *

"SEE! I'SE BEEN REPRESENTING YOU FOLKS ALL ALONG!"

Thurmond with Senator Jesse Helms (R.-N.C.) (left) and Orrin Hatch (R.-Utah) in Panama in August 1977, part of their campaign to retain American control of the Panama Canal. (Strom Thurmond Institute)

Above left: Thurmond escorting his daughter Nancy Moore Thurmond to her first day of school at the racially integrated A. C. Moore Elementary School in Columbia, August 1977. (Strom Thurmond Institute)

Above right: Essie Mae Washington-Williams at the press conference in Columbia on December 17, 2003, where she announced that Strom Thurmond was her father. (AP Images/Lou Krasky)

MAN, SENATE ARMED SERVICES COMMI
ENT PRO TEMPORE, UNITED STATES SE

THE FATHER OF FIVE CHILDREN:
J. STROM, JR. – JULIANA GERTRUDE –
ESSIE MAE

Above: The scarred stone. (Author photo)

Right: The Strom Thurmond memorial on the statehouse grounds in Columbia. (Author photo)

their classrooms, while northern schools carried on with their de facto patterns of segregation.[15]

The issue came to a head in late May 1968 when the Supreme Court weighed in with a decision vindicating the liberal view that freedom of choice was a segregationist ruse. In *Green v. County School Board of New Kent County*, the Court ruled that freedom-of-choice plans in use in three southern states were unacceptable unless they could be shown to offer real progress toward desegregation.[16] Thurmond immediately introduced two bills that would have reversed *Green*.[17] He cited what he believed to be the proper interpretation of *Brown* from a 1964 ruling on Kansas City schools by the Tenth Circuit Court of Appeals. Among last-ditch southern segregationists, the decision had become choice evidence of the federal bias against rural southern schools.[18] The Tenth Circuit had held that "although the Fourteenth Amendment prohibits segregation, it does not command integration of the races in the public schools and Negro children have no constitutional right to have white children attend school with them."[19]

By 1968, the constitutional rights of black children had become a surprisingly fraught issue, one that created the potential for an array of new alliances among creative and motivated politicians. Richard Nixon fit that description well. A civil rights moderate throughout his career, Nixon had developed a more nuanced position as he geared up for his 1968 run. He understood how loathsome the HEW guidelines were to many white southerners, and he knew that his nomination was tied to his success among southern Republicans. In his swing south during the 1966 midterm elections, Nixon amazed the Dixie GOP's fresh-faced businessmen turned party organizers with his mastery of political doublespeak. To a banquet room of Republicans in Jackson, Mississippi, he implored all political parties to stop using race to win elections and to focus on the "issues of the future."[20] National reporters read it as Nixon bravely taking the high road among racist southerners. Southern Republican masses, however, knew who was guilty of making race an issue in the campaign. It was the "trashy Democrats" that Thurmond and his cohort had been worrying about for years, the conniving politicians who would make their election time appeals to the "bloc vote."

Nixon proved equally sly on the issue of school desegregation. He vigorously endorsed freedom of choice in assigning students to schools with the proviso that the Court had outlined in *Green*—as long as freedom of choice was not a subterfuge for maintaining segregation. The emphasis given this qualifier varied according to his audience. The duplicity for Thurmond was in leaving off the qualifier altogether. Nixon supported freedom of choice, Thurmond emphasized to campaign crowds. That was all he said. And he repeated it over and over.

On June 22, the same day that Thurmond endorsed Nixon for the presidency, newspapers reported that Chief Justice Earl Warren had written to President Johnson declaring his intention to retire from the Supreme Court at the end of the current term. Thurmond was "delighted." Warren, he said, had done "more harm to the American way of life than any other one man holding public office in the history of our country." Lyndon Johnson nominated the associate justice Abe Fortas, whom he had appointed to the Court three years earlier, to become chief justice and named as Fortas's replacement Homer Thornberry, a former Texas congressman whom Johnson had previously placed on the Fifth Circuit.[21]

Opponents immediately charged Johnson with cronyism. Fortas was a longtime political adviser, and Thornberry had taken over the U.S. House of Representatives seat that Johnson had abandoned for the Senate in 1948. During testimony, evidence emerged that as a member of the Court, Fortas had advised Johnson on a range of political matters, leading to concerns about a violation of the separation of powers.

The departure of such a strongly liberal chief justice was bound to attract reaction from conservatives, and the Court's controversial decisions on a range of hot-button issues had taken their toll on the Court's standing among the public. A Gallup poll on the eve of the hearings showed that a majority of Americans rated the Supreme Court's performance as fair to poor.[22] Factor in the drama of a presidential election year and the Fortas nomination quickly turned into a referendum on the Warren Court and its legacy. Thurmond did as much as he could to make it so, and his membership on the Judiciary Committee placed him in an influential position to frustrate the nomination.

The opening scene was Fortas's unprecedented testimony before the Judiciary Committee. No sitting member of the Court had ever submitted to committee questioning. During his testimony, Thurmond and North Carolina's Sam Ervin emerged as Fortas's two chief inquisitors. Ervin handled the intricate interrogation of Warren Court jurisprudence, allowing Thurmond to pursue a more theatrical course of attack.

Thurmond had gained experience with such maneuvers a year earlier during hearings on Thurgood Marshall's appointment to the Supreme Court. Noting Marshall's long career as a civil rights lawyer, Thurmond posed some fifty picayune questions about the history of the Reconstruction Congress that had passed the Thirteenth and Fourteenth Amendments. He chided Marshall when, one after the other, the nominee answered that he did not know or could not remember. At best, the questions were Thurmond's attempt to highlight the fact that the Reconstruction Congress took a limited view of the "equal protection of the law" guarantee.[23] If so, it was an abstruse way of getting at the point. More likely, the litany of questions were Thurmond's attempt to embarrass the first African American nominee to the high court. Several times Thurmond condescendingly interjected to ask if Marshall understood the question asked of him. The total effect was to provide a public record that Thurmond's racist supporters could read as evidence of Marshall's alleged ignorance and incompetence.[24]

Against Fortas, Thurmond knew that the witness could not respond to questions that dealt with issues on which the Court might have to rule in the future. It was an established part of the ritual of Supreme Court nominations: senators invoked their "advise and consent" responsibilities in asking questions about important legal issues of the day, and nominees apologized for not being able to answer, citing the separation of powers. Yet when Fortas offered the standard apology, Thurmond responded with withering reproach. "Every American . . . is going to see that you refused today, that you failed today, to answer questions of vital importance to them," he scolded Fortas, playing to the 60 percent of Americans who disapproved of the Warren Court, "and they are going to get an impression and maybe rightly so, that you are using this as a screen or an excuse not to go into these matters." Grumbling from the gallery forced the chair to gavel the room to order. Everyone present recognized Thurmond's attempt to turn standard procedure into liberal conspiracy. Yet Thurmond was not playing to the room.[25]

He proceeded with a two-and-a-half-hour jeremiad against the Warren Court in interrogatory form. *The Washington Post* compared it to slapping a man who had his hands tied behind his back. Fortas tried to offer artful variations on his standard refusal to comment. Thurmond bulldozed ahead, hardly noticing the responses.[26]

He reached full steam when discussing the Court's decisions on criminal procedure. Thurmond read off a list of questions that his staff had prepared for him. Attached to the script, however, were two photocopied pages from his book *The Faith We Have Not Kept* that provided brief criticisms of the Court's key decisions on criminal procedure. He began by noting his concern about the increasing crime rate and the role he believed the Court had played in this development. The prepared text called for him to then ask a rather lame question about the usefulness of confessions in obtaining convictions before moving directly to *Miranda*, by far the Court's most controversial criminal procedure decision.

Not wanting to lose his momentum, Thurmond abandoned his script—something he almost never did—and ad-libbed his own questions from the list of cases on the photocopied page.[27] He wanted to get back to *Mallory*, the first case listed in his book and one that had galled him for years. That the case had been decided eight years before Fortas joined the Court did not bother Thurmond.[28] Every time he mentioned the rapist's name, his voice rose higher:

Does not that decision, *Mallory*—I want that word to ring in your ears—*Mallory*—the man happened to have been from my State, incidentally—shackle law enforcement? Mallory, a man who raped a woman, admitted his guilt, and the Supreme Court turned him loose on a technicality. And who I was told later went to Philadelphia and committed another crime, and somewhere else another crime, because the courts turned him loose on technicalities.

Is not that type of decision calculated to bring the courts and the law and the administration of justice in disrepute? Is not that type of decision calculated to encourage more people to commit rapes and serious crimes? Can you as a Justice of the Supreme Court condone such a decision as that? I ask you to answer that question.[29]

Fortas was flabbergasted. He turned to James Eastland, thinking that the committee chairman would call Thurmond to order. Eastland had his head down, apparently reading.[30]

Even a chief aide found Thurmond's performance distasteful. "Our strategy in the Fortas hearings has been a disastrous mistake," predicted James Lucier in a memorandum sent later that day. Thurmond had turned Fortas into a "martyr," Lucier wrote.[31] He proceeded to list eight points that Thurmond should have raised instead. Number seven read, "He improperly voted to reverse the conviction of his pornographer friend and client."[32]

This was a charge amplified in testimony by James Clancy, legal counsel for an antipornography group called Citizens for Decent Literature. He called attention to a possible conflict of interest when Fortas ruled on a case in 1966 that involved a client for whom his law firm had written an amicus brief. Yet that was the least of Clancy's contributions to the anti-Fortas campaign.[33]

Clancy discussed a 1967 case, *Schackman v. California*, in which the Supreme Court had offered a one-sentence opinion overturning the lower court's ruling that a pornographic film titled *0–7* was obscene and undeserving of First Amendment protection. Denouncing *Schackman* and dozens of other obscenity decisions of the Court, his organization analyzed Fortas's votes in fifty-two obscenity cases from the previous two Supreme Court terms. In all but three of them, Clancy claimed, Fortas had provided the "deciding" fifth vote reversing the lower courts' finding that the material was obscene.[34]

Thurmond arranged for screenings for colleagues and the press of *0–7*, along with a thirty-minute slide presentation by Citizens for Decent Literature titled *Target Smut*. The exhibition "shocked Washington's hardened press corps," Thurmond told reporters.[35] In truth, most press members had giggled throughout the session and cracked rude jokes. There was no screen in the room, so the film was projected onto the wood-paneled wall, which gave the impression that the scantily clad female figure was molting. Other screenings followed, however, and an estimated twenty senators ended up seeing some portion of what came to be called the "Fortas films."[36] Rumors at the Republican Capitol Hill Club had it that Thurmond was intent on screening *0–7* on the Senate floor, leading some to speculate that "ole Strom had gone bananas at last."[37]

In actuality, Thurmond had stumbled upon an explosive issue. The obscenity cases had caused a deep division in the Court over the nature of the First Amendment free speech protections. In the mid-1960s, the justices regularly viewed dozens of books and films that had been deemed obscene. On one side were Hugo Black and William Douglas, who argued that the material was covered under First Amendment protections. On the other was John Marshall Harlan, who believed that the states could regulate obscene material to protect the health, welfare, and morality of their citizens. Fortas was a moderate, but as the most junior member of the Court, he voted last and cast what Clancy and other critics said was the decisive vote.[38]

Since 1954, Thurmond and his fellow white southerners had been arguing that in *Brown* the Supreme Court had arbitrarily invalidated laws that protected community standards, laws that previous courts had found in compliance with the Constitution. With the obscenity decisions, Thurmond leveled a similar charge. The communities whose standards were being violated, however, were not Jim Crow southern towns but cities and suburbs across the nation. Thurmond sent one of his aides out to buy pornographic magazines at newsstands near the Capitol to dramatize "what is being sold in the city of Washington, and in other cities of this Nation, because the Supreme Court has allowed this to be done," he fumed. "How much longer are the parents, the Christian people, the wholesome people, the right-thinking people, going to put up with this kind of thing?"[39]

The anti-smut campaign took a surprisingly heavy toll on Fortas's prospects. Lucier's memo had recommended it because of the conflict-of-interest angle, not as a moral issue. Yet George Smathers, a Judiciary Committee member and White House confidant, gave a sense of its impact in a telephone conversation with Lyndon Johnson. Because so few Supreme Court obscenity cases included written decisions, Smathers noted, they were almost impossible to defend publicly, making it difficult for senators to come out in favor of the nomination.[40] Judiciary chairman James Eastland reported to the president that with Thurmond determined to block any vote before the August recess, there was nothing he could do to get the nomination out of the committee.[41]

Thurmond was at the July 31 meeting of the Judiciary Committee with material ready to filibuster, but not enough of his colleagues showed up to make a quorum.[42] It was convention season by that time. The Fortas nomination would have to wait.

In early August some 2,666 delegates and alternates descended on glittering and garish Miami Beach for the 1968 Republican National Convention. It was Thurmond's first national convention as a Republican. He was the key figure in saving Richard Nixon's carefully orchestrated nomination from an eleventh-hour attack from the Left and the Right. New York's governor, Nelson Rockefeller, mounted a charge in defense of the eastern wing, whose once bright prospects had dimmed under the tidal wave of law and order. Rockefeller's push depended on a simultaneous attack from the Right. Only if Ronald Reagan could undermine Nixon's southern support, the bedrock of his candidacy, did Rockefeller have a chance at pulling off the upset.[43]

Thurmond was indefatigable in holding the South for Nixon. He gave countless interviews on the convention floor, managed the flow of information to reporters, and batted down rumors of Nixon's imminent collapse. On call twenty-four hours a day, he reassured wavering delegations with speeches and private talks. He held off Reagan's furious last-minute raid on Florida.[44] In the final hours before the vote, Thurmond was on the convention floor with a megaphone, imploring southern delegates not to be fooled into taking Reagan and allowing Rockefeller to slip through.[45] As the nation's best-known scribes packed up for the Democratic convention and the bedlam that awaited them in Chicago, they pronounced Thurmond kingmaker. A frustrated Rockefeller supporter told one reporter in disbelief: "It was that crazy old man who ruined us."[46]

Once Nixon sewed up the nomination, attention turned to his vice-presidential choice. Conservatives who recalled Nixon's "Compact of Fifth Avenue" with Rockefeller at the 1960 convention had relied on Thurmond's assurances that Nixon would not choose a liberal. Thurmond and Dent attended a late-night confab with Nixon and other party leaders to discuss the vice-presidential choice. Twenty-two GOP satraps settled into Nixon's suite at the Hilton Plaza, where Nixon aides passed out cigars and poured drinks from tumblers of whiskey. Goldwater was there. Balancing the southern and western influences were centrists such as Governor Jim Rhodes of Ohio, Senator Jack Miller of Iowa, Congressman Donald Rumsfeld of Illinois, and Lieutenant Governor Robert Finch of California. Also among them was a hated old name from Thurmond's massive resistance days: Herbert Brownell, attorney general under Eisenhower and the author of the government's brief defending *Brown*. It had been a long road from the Southern Manifesto to the Hilton Plaza.[47]

Thurmond and Goldwater pushed Reagan, despite his strongly worded pledge earlier in the week that he would not accept the vice-presidential spot. Every candidate the centrists raised—New York mayor John Lindsay, Illinois senator Charles Percy, Oregon senator Mark Hatfield—the conservatives shot down. Nixon himself ruled out Rockefeller.[48] The deliberations continued until almost five o'clock in the morning. As the meeting broke up and everyone filed out of the room, Thurmond pressed into Nixon's hand a piece of paper with his list of acceptable and unacceptable candidates. "You have nothing to worry about," Nixon assured Thurmond and Dent. "You will be pleased."[49]

The next day Nixon announced Governor Spiro Agnew of Maryland as his vice-presidential choice. Agnew had gotten his start in Maryland politics as the county executive of largely suburban Baltimore County. He won election as governor as a moderate reformer, defeating a race-baiting Democratic opponent. Yet once in office, he had risen to national prominence by tongue-lashing black rioters following the King assassination, along with the moderate civil rights leaders who failed to denounce them. He was a compromise candidate for Nixon, a border-state governor who was acceptable to the South largely on the strength of his law-and-order credentials.

In a convention floor interview with NBC that evening, Edwin Newman asked Thurmond if he thought that Agnew would help the ticket in northern industrial states. Newman knew the answer already: northern Republicans were in revolt at that very moment, denouncing Agnew's nomination as a sop to Strom Thurmond and the southern

Republicans. "It's my judgment that he will help him all over the nation," Thurmond answered, staying on message, "because the number one issue in this campaign is going to be law and order." Newman pointed out that it was the governor's controversial stand on law and order that had sparked the opposition against him. "Who can oppose law and order?" Thurmond asked incredulously. "We can have no civilized society without law and order."[50]

NBC cut back to Chet Huntley and David Brinkley in the broadcast booth above the convention floor. Brinkley, a North Carolina native who had gotten his start in journalism in the 1940s covering southern politics, was familiar with the intonations of southern political-speak. He summarized Thurmond's comments, his dry, just-the-facts mien unable to hide his disdain. "Who can oppose law and order?" Brinkley said, his voice rising in subtle satire, adding that everyone was "free to interpret the true meaning of that phrase however he likes."[51] The true meaning of the phrase, Brinkley implied, was racist. Many others agreed. Tom Wicker of *The New York Times* summarized the GOP's dilemma in succinct biblical form: "And what shall it profit any Republican if he gains Strom Thurmond and loses his political soul?"[52]

Undoubtedly, some Americans watching at home took umbrage at David Brinkley holding his nose after Thurmond's interview. Their vindication came after the Gulf Oil commercial break when Chet Huntley segued into an update on a report on an outbreak of violence in Miami. The day before, as Republicans in the convention center fought over the Agnew nomination, two African Americans had been shot and four wounded during widespread rioting. The subtext was powerful. Who can oppose law and order? Thurmond had asked. The question hung in the air as Huntley reported on the mayhem on nearby city streets.[53]

This snippet of television coverage captured in miniature the bewilderment of modern America's great crisis year. There were still millions of Americans who, like Brinkley, felt queasy over hearing the issue of law and order so baldly put in Strom Thurmond's southern accent. The old Dixiecrat seemed to be ventriloquizing ancient southern fearmongering about lawless black men. Yet the turmoil in American politics and in cities across the country over the past several years cast Thurmond in a strange new light. Amid such frustrations, a significant number of white Americans wound up empathizing with fears and resentments that Thurmond had been channeling for more than two decades.

The climax of the week was Nixon's acceptance speech. At 9:49 p.m., Thurmond was part of a delegation of Republicans who escorted Nixon to the podium. Thurmond led the column on Nixon's left, followed by Congressman Robert Dole of Kansas and, behind him, Governor George Romney. As the group reached the podium, Thurmond stood stiffly while others smiled and waved or posed for pictures with arms around each other. Dole put his arm on Thurmond's shoulder and pulled him back a step, so as not to block sight lines to the candidate. After Nixon's speech, as orange balloons fell from the rafters, close-up shots of Nixon showed Thurmond standing in back, continuing to applaud after others around him had stopped.[54]

"If there is one man who never has to apologize for Strom Thurmond," Harry Dent explained to reporters afterward, "it is Richard Nixon, and he never will."[55]

After the convention, Thurmond resumed his campaign against Abe Fortas. Central to that effort was the politics of smut. He was determined to bring Fortas as well as other witnesses back before the committee for more titillating testimony. The White House was intent on getting the nomination out of committee. Thurmond struck a deal in which he and other opponents agreed not to filibuster a committee vote in exchange for more hearings. Fortas himself declined the committee's invitation for more questioning, but Thurmond was allowed to solicit or if necessary subpoena additional witnesses. Among those invited to testify was Don Shaidell, a sergeant with the Administrative Vice Division of the Los Angeles Police Department, who brought more pornographic movies relating to Supreme Court obscenity decisions. Thurmond revived the "Fortas Film Festival," providing regular screenings for colleagues.[56]

Lyndon Johnson was not ready to give up the fight. After a meeting with the Senate minority and majority leaders, who both admitted that the opposition had hardened and that they did not have the votes to block a filibuster, Johnson called reporters in for a surprise press conference in the Cabinet Room.[57] Dismissing Fortas's opponents as "a little group, a sectional group primarily" who resorted to "parliamentary tricks," he reminded reporters that it was unprecedented for the filibuster to be used to block a vote on a Supreme Court nominee. He also subtly introduced the issue of anti-Semitism as a possible source for the opposition's strength. Fortas was the first Jewish nominee for chief justice, and Johnson drew a historical parallel with the nomination of Louis Brandeis as the first Jewish member of the Court.[58] Fear of being seen as anti-Semitic or in alliance with anti-Semites was one reason Richard Nixon had been so quiet about Fortas's nomination.[59]

The White House and Fortas himself had hoped that support from the New York senator Jacob Javits, the Senate's most visible Jewish member, might rally the Jewish community and swing the momentum back to Fortas. Yet Javits, a strong backer of Nixon, heeded warnings from the Nixon camp about damaging revelations concerning Fortas's finances and offered only lukewarm support.[60] The Michigan senator Robert Griffin had been sitting on unconfirmed rumors about dubious funds Fortas had been paid for teaching a law school course at American University, but had not been able to turn up any information. Where Griffin was reluctant to dig too deep in the muck, Thurmond was all too eager.

Griffin's office had received an anonymous phone call describing a tax-exempt foundation that had been established to pay Fortas's salary for the course. Investigations by *The New York Times* uncovered the fee that Fortas had been paid. Griffin's aides, however, were unable to extract any more information from administration officials at American and turned the information over to Thurmond's staff. One of Thurmond's assistants called Dean B. J. Tennery of the Washington College of Law at American and requested that he appear before the committee. When Tennery declined, Thurmond called Tennery himself and indicated that he knew all about the fund established to pay Fortas's salary. This was a bluff: Thurmond had only heard rumors about the fund. But Tennery had little choice in the matter when Thurmond made it clear that he would be subpoenaed if he chose not to appear before the committee voluntarily. Which would be better for the reputation of American University? Thurmond asked menacingly.[61]

As much as Thurmond's antipornography campaign had shifted

the momentum of Fortas's nomination, it was Tennery's testimony that killed it. Tennery explained the otherwise innocuous circumstances by which Fortas had come to teach at American. Yet the size and source of Fortas's salary were troublesome. To help raise funds, Tennery had turned to Paul Porter, a close friend of Fortas's and a former law partner, who had solicited money from five contributors. Tennery testified that for one nine-week summer seminar that met once a week for two hours with seventeen students, Fortas had been paid $15,000.

"I can't hear," Thurmond interjected. "Can you talk a little louder please?" Over the noontime recess, Thurmond looked up the biographies of the five donors to the seminar fund. Among them were the chairman of Braniff Airways; the vice-chairman of Federated Department Stores; and the vice-chairman of the New York Stock Exchange. All were powerful, high-profile business leaders whom Fortas had known for many years. None of them, Thurmond pointed out, had any previous connection with American University. "Any one of these men could easily become involved in any number of suits which might reach the Supreme Court," Thurmond observed. "They represent a complex of business and financial holdings that could scarcely be extricated from anything touching upon the Nation's economy."[62]

Some of Fortas's most enthusiastic backers were blindsided by the news. Republican moderates who the White House hoped could break the filibuster on the Senate floor melted away. So did Lyndon Johnson's old mentor, Richard Russell, whom Johnson was counting on to help him leave this final mark of his presidency. Russell cited the American University matter as justification for his decision, not merely the size of the fund, but also its source. The White House's last hope was that the Republican minority leader, Everett Dirksen, could hold together enough Republicans to break the conservative coalition's filibuster. For Dirksen, however, the American University revelations were a "secondary issue." It had been the "dirty movies" that had really hurt.[63]

Thurmond sensed that the Fortas fight was historic. The justice's defeat would be "a turning point in modern American history," he had written in his newsletter in July.[64] In retrospect, this was true in a number of ways. Not since 1874, when President Grant withdrew his nomination of Caleb Cushing, had the Senate failed to confirm a president's nominee for chief justice.[65] Even more, the Fortas nomination was the first in a series of bruising battles over Supreme Court appointments in late-twentieth-century America. In the 1970s, Richard Nixon would lose confirmation battles on two nominees to the Court, both of them southerners, both of whom suffered from the ill will generated by Thurmond's campaign against Fortas. The late 1980s and early '90s would see vicious battles over the nominations of Robert Bork and Clarence Thomas.

Most important, however, the feud over Abe Fortas's nomination was an early episode in a series of culture wars that fueled modern conservative political mobilization. Present at their creation was Strom Thurmond. His anti-smut campaign, in conjunction with an organization like Citizens for Decent Literature, anticipated the "family values" politics of later decades.[66] Opposition to feminism and the Equal Rights Amendment, abortion, the gay rights movement, and the defense of school prayer—all of these issues galvanized conservative politics in the 1970s and laid the groundwork for the emergence of the modern religious Right. For these conservative activists, the Supreme Court was one of the chief bogeymen of the "permissive society." Yet the roots of this reaction stretched back into the earlier decade to fights Thurmond helped lead over civil rights, school prayer, law and order, and obscenity.

Throughout the fall campaign, northern Democrats used Thurmond to tar Richard Nixon. Thurmond was a symbol of "distrust," said Senator Edmund Muskie of Maine. Governor Richard J. Hughes of New Jersey accused Nixon of "selling half the presidency" to Thurmond. The Democratic nominee, Hubert Humphrey, said that he would never forget the sight of Thurmond walking Nixon to the podium. "I thought that was a most interesting, revealing scene."[67]

Thurmond was accustomed to attacks from northern Democrats. It was the assault from right-wing Wallace supporters back home that was new for him. Longtime allies called Harry Dent screaming that Thurmond was ruining himself politically. At a George Wallace rally in Columbia in September, there were cries of "Give Thurmond hell, George."[68] By the end of the campaign, Wallace hecklers followed Thurmond around to various events. He reported receiving threatening letters from six states. There was a death threat at the Anderson County fair. Orval Faubus, the segregationist hero of Little Rock, said Thurmond had misplaced his faith in Nixon. Maurice Bessinger accused him of "dividing the white vote," no small irony for the man who had spearheaded the anti-bloc-vote campaign in 1966.[69]

School desegregation was the issue on which Thurmond and the southern GOP needed to make up ground. In September, Nixon gave a television interview broadcast widely across the Carolinas in which he expressed reservations about the federal government cutting off funds to school districts. Afterward, Thurmond released a statement declaring Nixon "squarely in favor of the popular 'freedom-of-choice' plan which is in line with the thinking of South Carolinians."[70] William Workman followed up with an editorial in *The State*. Nixon had created space between himself and the Democrats on how to handle school desegregation, the paper declared. Harry Dent fed information to Workman throughout the fall, passing along choice excerpts from Nixon's statements in Charlotte, North Carolina, as well as a speech on school desegregation that he had given in Anaheim, California.[71] At a South Carolina campaign stop in early October, Nixon did not mention the issue of school desegregation. But Thurmond did in his introduction of Nixon, and GOP volunteers passed out campaign materials emphasizing Nixon's position on schools and textiles.[72] Such material, designed to blunt the Wallace appeal, listed the changes that would flow from Nixon's election. At the top of the list was Nixon's pledge to "stop forced busing of school children and return education to local school boards."[73]

On Election Day, Thurmond traveled furiously across South Carolina, missing lunch and dinner both. He stopped in at the Republican campaign office in Columbia long enough to shake a few hands and grab a bite to eat before leaving around 9:00 p.m. to fly to Nixon headquarters in New York. Not until late in the evening, after critical votes in California and Illinois were counted, did Nixon harvest the 287 electoral votes needed for victory. Thurmond was ushered into Nixon's suite around 4:00 a.m. "You did a fabulous job," Nixon told him. While waiting to see the president-elect, Thurmond had chatted amiably with Jacob Javits, his ideological opposite. The sight of the two longtime Senate rivals celebrating together epitomized the feat that Nixon had managed in reconciling the warring wings of the GOP.[74]

The election had been a feat for Thurmond as well. The tight three-way race obscured the fact that over sixty-one million Americans—only two million short of the number that Lyndon Johnson had amassed four years earlier in his landslide victory—had voted for either Nixon or George Wallace, the two candidates between whom Thurmond had triangulated himself. Nixon carried South Carolina with 38 percent of the vote, compared with 32 percent for Wallace and 30 percent for Humphrey. African Americans voted almost exclusively for Humphrey. Offsetting this vote, however, was the impressive new suburban vote in the state's most dynamic and prosperous counties. White suburbanites in Richland, Spartanburg, and Greenville counties voted in equal proportion for Nixon as blacks had for Humphrey.[75]

Thurmond's endorsement of Nixon represented the new political marriage that he had made with the politics of the Sunbelt. White-collar professionals drawn by the Sunbelt's booming economy had been the margin that allowed Nixon to become the first Republican president in the twentieth century to win Spartanburg County, long a textile-oriented Democratic stronghold.[76] The vote symbolized Spartanburg's and Greenville's metamorphosis from overgrown Carolina mill towns to modern Sunbelt cities.

The Sunbelt devotees had come in droves. The 1960s marked the first time since the 1870s that more people moved into the South than out of it. Per capita income grew 14 percent faster than in any other region. New housing starts in the South were 37 percent higher at the end of the decade than at the beginning, compared with just 7 percent nationally. By 1970, southerners were just as likely to have had some amount of college education as were northerners.[77]

The mix of issues that Nixon engineered in 1968—law and order, freedom of choice, free enterprise politics—was designed to entice these middle-class, college-educated suburbanites, inside the South and out. Yet in South Carolina, their fidelity to the emerging GOP would not be foreordained, not when state-level Republicans were willing to make common cause with racist oddities such as the barbecue baron Maurice Bessinger—or, two years later, when national GOP leaders joined in a polarization politics that threatened to upend law and order in South Carolina's desegregating public schools. Suburbanites would represent a new "volatile center" in southern and national politics, one that Thurmond and his closest advisers tracked closely over the ensuing years.[78]

In the final month of 1968, the personal mirrored the political in a remarkable way for Thurmond, capping off his incredible year. On December 8, the sixty-six-year-old Thurmond confirmed reports that he was soon to marry Nancy Moore of Aiken, a former Miss America contestant who was one-third his age. Moore had been an intern in Thurmond's Senate office for four weeks in 1966 and again for three months the following year. News profiles presented her as a classic Carolina beauty, yet her roots in the southern soil were actually shallow. Her father, Paul, was a chemical engineer who had moved his family to Aiken to work for the Atomic Energy Commission at the Savannah River Site. He had worked for DuPont in Tennessee before that, but he was a native of Montana. The Moores were Sunbelt migrants. Thurmond's endorsement of Nixon had cemented his alliance with the politics of the emerging Sunbelt, and now he was set to marry a child of the Sunbelt. Thus, in a strange way, had his life come to imitate his art.[79]

Harry Dent had been certain that the marriage would destroy Thurmond's political career. He and Fred Buzhardt pleaded with him not to marry Moore. A decade later, former aides would reenact the scene in an after-dinner parody at a reunion of Thurmond staffers.[80] In the legend of Strom, his second marriage became one more political deathblow that he slipped. It was an accomplishment to be placed alongside his Dixiecrat run, the write-in campaign, and the party switch for the Palmetto State's political Houdini.

There was another political angle to his second marriage, one that should not be missed in the final analysis of his decision to back Nixon. Thurmond was in his mid-sixties when he both endorsed Nixon and married Nancy Moore, yet as far as he was concerned, he was not near the end of anything. Nancy would be pregnant the next year with the first of their four children.

With his marriage in 1968, Thurmond was making a long-term bet on the future. His support for Nixon was a similar kind of wager. The safer, easier play would have been to lie low, doing little for either Wallace or Nixon so as to preserve the alliance of Independents and Republicans that had propelled him to easy victory in 1966. It was hardly unprecedented for Thurmond to keep a low profile in a presidential election year. This had been his tactic in 1956 and 1960 both.

But 1968 was different for a lot of reasons. Concerns about national defense, school desegregation, building the South Carolina GOP, leveraging help against George Wallace to gain a voice at the White House—all of those were important. Yet not to be discounted was the fact that in 1968, Thurmond was in love. Recall that Thurmond was a man who displayed his vigor by standing on his head next to his first young wife for a *Life* photographer. His bold campaign for Nixon, with all the talk in the press about his political prowess, was a kind of political feat of strength to dazzle his smart, politically minded young sweetheart.

Moore had always impressed him as such, from their earliest correspondence. They had met back in 1965 at the Grape Festival in York. Moore had designs on going to law school, an uncommon aspiration for South Carolina girls in the 1960s. In a letter to Thurmond in August 1965 she included a paragraph about her concern over Negro voter registration drives. ("It is fine for the Negroes to be encouraged to vote, but I do not feel they know what they are voting for or against."[81]) In another she expressed her excitement about his reelection campaign, signing off with the politician's classic closing: "If there is ever anything I can do for you, please let me know." Her letters showed an ambitious young person of notable self-possession. "The letters, clippings, candy and telephone calls from you will always stand out in my mind!" she wrote. "I just wish I were old enough to vote!"[82]

11

PERILS OF AN INSIDER
(1969–1972)

In the months between Richard Nixon's election and his inauguration, Strom Thurmond and the southern Republicans rode high. Nixon named Harry Dent to a high-level job in the White House, and southerners were "serenely confident" that Nixon would not disappoint them on school desegregation. Yet the heady days of late 1968 would not last long.[1] Nixon's first term would turn out to be the most turbulent four-year period in Thurmond's career.

Only a few weeks into the new administration some South Carolinians were already speculating that Thurmond "got took a little bit" by Nixon. Administration officials had frustrated white southerners in early moves on school desegregation and minority hiring practices in textile firms in North and South Carolina.[2] The most contentious issue, however, was school desegregation. In the first year and a half of Nixon's presidency, it seemed as if each week brought charges from both sides about the president's duplicity. One week he was attacked for selling out to Strom Thurmond. The next brought accounts of southern Republicans up in arms over broken campaign promises.

Harry Dent successfully lobbied to have HEW's secretary, Robert Finch, appear in South Carolina alongside Thurmond in April 1969 to explain Nixon's new approach on schools, yet Finch canceled at the last minute after complaints by civil rights groups.[3] President Nixon himself stopped by South Carolina a few weeks later to visit an ailing Jimmy Byrnes as a goodwill gesture, but the bad press down south continued.[4] School officials in Georgia and South Carolina complained that the plans pushed by Nixon officials were not at all what they had expected. Back in December, Thurmond had publicly encouraged officials to drag their feet in negotiations with HEW and wait for a better deal under Nixon. But according to the South Carolina state superintendent of education, letters from Washington were "nicer but still say the same things."[5]

The back-and-forth reflected both the president's constant political tinkering and the divisions inside his administration. On one side stood HEW's secretary, Finch, one of Nixon's close confidants during the campaign. The former lieutenant governor of California who had first worked as an administrative assistant for then vice president Nixon, Finch was the chief advocate of the moderate and liberal Republicans. Since election night, he had been urging Nixon to move away from what he viewed as an overly cautious, southern-obsessed campaign team.[6]

Counterbalancing Finch was Attorney General John Mitchell, along with the presidential adviser Bryce Harlow and the Goldwater Republican Robert Mardian, HEW's general counsel. More highly motivated than any of these officials on the issue of school desegregation, however, was Harry Dent, the aide in charge of interpreting the South to Nixon and Nixon to the South.[7] Thirty-nine years old when he started his White House job, Dent was as congenial a man as could be found in the Nixon White House. The eventual Watergate cronies shut Dent out of the president's inner circle—H. R. "Bob" Haldeman complained that Dent was "too much of a boy scout"—yet Haldeman's description should not obscure the fact that Harry Dent loved hardball politics, and he played it well.[8] He thrived in the overheated realpolitik of the Nixon White House, and by the summer of 1969 he was an increasingly valued adviser. In July, Nixon moved Dent's office from the Executive Office Building to the West Wing, where he took over as the administration's chief political liaison.[9]

Dent clearly attempted to delay or roll back school desegregation for Republican gain in the South. For example, he argued against a fund cutoff in Tennessee, where a Republican was running for Congress, and asked Robert Finch to restore federal funds to the Washington County school system in Georgia on the recommendation of the state's Republican chairman, who promised Dent that if the situation were worked out, "there will be little financial worry for the Republican Party in Georgia."[10] He pressed Finch to drop proceedings against the school district in Columbia, and spoke to a U.S. district judge in Louisiana in an attempt to have him uphold freedom-of-choice desegregation plans.[11]

Publicly, however, Dent downplayed his influence on civil rights. "There's just a bunch of people over there at HEW who every time they see something coming they don't like, scream it's old Strom Thurmond and Harry Dent," he told one reporter.[12] Dent and Thurmond denied, of course, anything like a southern strategy. Nixon was merely making the South once again a full and equal partner in the nation's affairs, they said, using language officially approved by Nixon.[13] In private, however, Dent continually raised the specter of a Wallace challenge to push Nixon toward more lenient policies in the South. In a December 1969 memo to Robert Mardian, he jokingly passed along a bumper sticker that made things explicit: "H.E.W. Helps Elect Wallace."[14]

By the summer of 1969, Dent and White House conservatives had the upper hand against Finch and the moderates. On July 3, the Justice Department and HEW issued a joint statement outlining new desegregation guidelines. The measures were so vaguely stated—one report called it a "masterpiece of ambivalence"—that both sides found evidence to support their criticisms of Nixon, yet the preponderance of the commentary labeled it a conservative victory.[15] The joint statement became the departure point for a new strategy of shifting the emphasis away from federal fund cutoffs by HEW to court-enforced desegregation plans.[16] This allowed southern Republicans to say that under Nixon, HEW was doing all that could be done to bring the South relief and that the real problem was liberal federal judges.

The Nixon administration took a number of other steps that pleased southern Republicans. In August, Attorney General John Mitchell personally intervened to help win passage of an amendment that blocked HEW from ordering busing, closing schools, or forcing children to attend a school against their parents' wishes. Mitchell frustrated attempts by Finch to put HEW on record as opposing the amendment and held a secret meeting with Republican leaders only hours before the vote to ensure passage. That same month, the Nixon administration requested a delay in federal court proceedings against thirty-three recalcitrant school districts in Mississippi, a move that caused widespread dissent among staff attorneys at the Department of Justice.[17]

Later that fall, in hearings before the Supreme Court, Nixon's assistant attorney general for civil rights, Jerris Leonard, sat side by side with John Satterfield of Mississippi—an old acquaintance of Thurmond's from the Coordinating Committee for Fundamental American Freedoms who was once described as the nation's number one segregationist lawyer—to argue for the delay, earning what *The New York Times* called the "odd couple of the year award."[18] When, in late October, in the landmark case *Alexander v. Holmes County Board of Education*, the Supreme Court denied any further requests for delay coming from either Mississippi or Washington and ordered immediate desegregation in all Mississippi school districts, Thurmond proudly noted that "the Nixon Administration stood with the South in this case."[19] The Mississippi case fit perfectly the conservatives' strategy of keeping the blame for school desegregation off Nixon and on the courts.[20]

For all the problems over schools, there were other reasons for Thurmond to be pleased with Nixon's first-year efforts. The president had been steadfast in another campaign promise he had made, support for an antiballistic missile (ABM) system. Fired by the passions of the Vietnam War, Congress debated the issue during the summer of 1969. Nixon's outspoken support helped ABM backers win a narrow Senate vote in August.[21]

Equally important were developments at the Supreme Court. In May, Abe Fortas resigned from the Court amid charges of financial improprieties, the disclosure of which had been carefully orchestrated by John Mitchell and the Nixon Justice Department.[22] It was invigorating news for Thurmond, who had first raised the allegations of misconduct the previous year.[23]

Despite speculation that the president would need to fill the Court's "Jewish seat," John Mitchell urged Nixon to appoint a southerner to undermine a George Wallace challenge in 1972.[24] A name that quickly bubbled to the surface was Clement F. Haynsworth of Greenville,

South Carolina, a Harvard Law graduate and chief judge of the U.S. Fourth Circuit. Early news stories reported that Thurmond was backing the former South Carolina governor Donald Russell and noted that the staunchly segregationist Thurmond had not been completely happy when Haynsworth had first been nominated to the federal bench in 1957.[25]

Yet Thurmond's apparent ambivalence toward Haynsworth was a ruse.[26] Thurmond sold the fake with a strong speech in the Senate in support of Russell, fooling *The Washington Post* entirely. An editorial sarcastically praised "Senator Thurmond's public service," predicting that the "blunderbuss Senator" had merely assured Russell's defeat.[27] Behind the scenes, Thurmond had informed Nixon of his support for Haynsworth as early as June and had been helping Haynsworth line up endorsements.[28] He also warned southern conservatives not to "come out too strongly in support of Haynsworth for this could cause a lot of static from Liberals."[29]

By the fall it became clear that Haynsworth had been Thurmond's true preference all along. *The Milwaukee Journal* denounced the deception as "a shoddy bit of business." In South Carolina, however, *The State* praised Thurmond's cleverness in shielding Haynsworth from undue scrutiny and revealing liberal attacks on Russell as mere guilt by association. Strom Thurmond was "smiling up at Brer Fox out of the briar patch."[30] Yet the misdirection would be for naught.

On November 21, 1969, the Senate rejected Haynsworth by a 55–45 vote.[31] Haynsworth's critics raised a number of ethics charges against him, none of which were substantive. In the poisonous aftermath of the Fortas hearings, however, every charge was amplified. A *Washington Post* staff writer, noting the "Fortas impact," concluded that "in another time he would have been confirmed, and with relatively little controversy."[32] Of only slightly less importance to Haynsworth's defeat was the effectiveness of opponents in portraying the nomination as a "political payoff" to the South in general and to Thurmond in particular. A popular line in some union halls was to refer to the White House as "Uncle Strom's cabin."[33]

Nixon was determined to nominate a southerner. He next turned to G. Harrold Carswell, a former federal district judge in Florida recently appointed to the Fifth Circuit Court of Appeals. Carswell suffered by comparison to the already rejected Haynsworth in almost every respect. His judicial record was of no particular distinction. Civil rights groups who had tried to attack Haynsworth's racial record without much success found easy pickings with Carswell, who in 1948 had run for the state legislature in Georgia espousing white supremacy and whose fingerprints were on a number of segregationist ploys in his adopted hometown of Tallahassee. Nixon supported Carswell "like a man biting down on a toothache," according to the presidential speechwriter William Safire. The Senate's easy rejection of Carswell only sharpened the pain.[34]

In response, Nixon ordered his speechwriter Pat Buchanan to draft a blistering attack on the Senate. The president personally added denunciations of the Senate's "hypocrisy" and "regional discrimination." Nixon read the speech for television cameras with a palpable display of anger comparable to his "last press conference" in 1962 after losing the California governor's race.[35]

"I have reluctantly concluded—with the Senate as presently constituted—I cannot successfully nominate to the Supreme Court any federal appellate judge from the South who believes as I do in the strict construction of the Constitution," Nixon said. Carswell and Haynsworth had endured assaults on their characters, including false charges of racism, but the "the real issue was their philosophy of strict construction of the Constitution . . . and the fact that they had the misfortune of being born in the South . . . I understand the bitter feelings of millions of Americans who live in the South about the act of regional discrimination that took place in the Senate yesterday."[36]

Strom Thurmond loved it.[37] So did the southern Republican chairmen.[38] Richard Nixon had given passionate voice against the slander Thurmond believed white southerners had suffered for decades. The speech capped a series of events in early 1970 that seemed to vindicate long-held positions of southern segregationists. Senator John Stennis of Mississippi had introduced an amendment to an appropriations bill that called for equal enforcement of civil rights policy between the North and the South. It was the culmination of the Mississippians' months-long crusade to spur increased federal action against segregated de facto schools outside the South, the ultimate goal of which was to provoke a northern reaction against civil rights that would aid white southerners' cause. The Stennis amendment prompted one of the most divisive debates over school desegregation since the *Brown* era began.[39] To Thurmond's delight, Richard Nixon weighed in on the side of the South.[40]

Since 1948, southern victimization at the hands of hypocritical liberals had been one of the most consistent themes of Thurmond's career. He had never heard a president speak with such conviction the very words that southern senators and congressmen themselves had used to describe their region's plight. However rocky the relationship would become between the president and Thurmond—and there would be disappointments to come—Nixon had built up a reservoir of goodwill that never completely ran dry.

Southern Republicans looked to the midterm elections in 1970 with great anticipation. The president's conclusion that the Senate would never approve a southerner to the Court included an important qualifier, "as presently constituted." The White House set out to change that makeup. Harry Dent gathered the southern GOP chairmen in January 1970 to outline the strategy. The group had met regularly during the first year of the administration, to the chagrin of liberals like Leon Panetta at HEW, who had been called in to answer irritable questions more than once.[41] Dent reported that despite a recent series of school desegregation efforts, the group left with "the best feeling they have ever had."[42] Moving desegregation into the courts not only insulated the Nixon administration but also put southern Democratic governors on the hot seat, opening opportunities for Republican candidates.

In South Carolina, Thurmond backed the charismatic and telegenic congressman Albert Watson. By the late 1960s, Watson was a rising star in both South Carolina politics and national conservative circles. A board member of the American Conservative Union and a frequent speaker before Young Americans for Freedom chapters, Watson battled moderate and liberal Republicans on civil rights issues and stridently denounced civil rights demonstrators.[43] Only Thurmond bested him as the most requested speaker among southern Republicans, and some groups even secretly preferred the fiery, handsome young congressman.[44]

Challenging Watson in the GOP primary was the moderate Arthur

Ravenel of Charleston. From Ravenel's perspective, Watson was the candidate of the "polarization forces" in the South Carolina GOP. If nominated, he would "get absolutely no Black vote," Ravenel wrote to Harry Dent in January 1970, "and very little support from the White moderates whose numbers are rapidly increasing."[45]

In 1970, however, it was the "polarization forces" in which Thurmond, Dent, and the Nixon White House were interested. Indeed, major figures on the right were waxing strategic on racists and the future of the GOP. William F. Buckley, Jr., for example, argued that Republicans should not blindly follow the Left's characterization of Wallace voters, with its "overtones of neurotic hatred." "Now it is time, I think, to announce a major psychological discovery," Buckley wrote. "It is that Wallace supporters are people." The Wallace vote, Buckley said, was "a legitimate objective of an American politician."[46]

Kevin Phillips agreed. The campaign strategist and special assistant to Attorney General John Mitchell was the public figure most closely associated with this sentiment. In the fall of 1969 he published *The Emerging Republican Majority*, an exhaustive, mercurial analysis of voting trends from every corner of the nation that argued that the New Deal coalition had run its course. On the rise was a new populist conservatism rooted in the "Sunbelt," a term that Phillips himself coined. The press dubbed the book the blueprint for the southern strategy, but the tome was complex and contradictory enough to contain rival visions of the South's political future, one centered on economic transformation, the other on racist exploitation.

The most striking aspect of Phillips's book was its unflinching analysis of the political advantage to be won from capitalizing on the most sordid impulses of the American electorate. Politics was not that difficult to figure out, Phillips confided to the author Garry Wills during the 1968 campaign. Knowing who hates whom—"that is the secret."[47] As for the black vote, Phillips said that Republicans should stop worrying about it. With counterintuitive relish, he said Republicans should strictly enforce the Voting Rights Act in the South. "The more Negroes who register as Democrats in the South, the sooner the Negrophobe whites will quit the Democrats and become Republicans," he said. "That's where the votes are."[48]

Albert Watson did not need Kevin Phillips to tell him to go after the "Negrophobes." Phillips's book simply provided a grand strategic framework for what Watson, Thurmond, and the South Carolina GOP were going to do anyway.

The Supreme Court's decision in *Holmes v. Alexander*, which had put an end to the doctrine of "all deliberate speed," had reverberated across the South. In South Carolina, two districts under orders from the Fourth Circuit—Greenville and Darlington County—became the flash points of the state's school crisis. On January 19, in an order signed by the recently rejected chief judge, Clement Haynsworth, the Fourth Circuit ordered the two districts to submit new plans for immediate desegregation. On January 25 over three thousand white residents of Greenville and Darlington County marched on the state capitol in Columbia and presented petitions to Governor McNair against the school desegregation orders.[49]

It was in this context that Thurmond threw his weight fully behind Albert Watson. He campaigned harder for Watson than for any other non-presidential candidate in his career. He sought an endorsement from John Wayne, secured campaign contributions from conservative heavyweights such as H. L. Hunt and Henry Salvatori, and made numerous campaign appearances during the general election.[50] He even lent Watson his brightest young staffer, the Harvard-educated Hastings Wyman, to run the campaign.

As a segregationist Democrat turned conservative Republican, Watson was the closest thing Thurmond had to an ideological heir. Yet twice before—in 1966 and 1968—Watson had floated the idea of challenging Fritz Hollings for the Senate, and Thurmond had lent no support. Thurmond backed Watson strongly in 1970 for two reasons, both of which had less to do with Watson than with Thurmond's own political interests.

First, Thurmond needed to mend fences with the Wallace voters he had abandoned in 1968.[51] The outcry over the school situation in Greenville and Darlington had enlarged the bull's-eye on his back. According to Harry Dent, Watson had "more credibility with the Wallace people in South Carolina and across the South than even Thurmond."[52] Thurmond had received dozens of letters from angry South Carolinians, including one that enclosed a copy of a Nixon campaign advertisement from 1968 promising the return of educational policies to local school boards. Scrawled across it was the question "What happened to this?"[53]

Second, Thurmond was interested in Watson's race because he viewed it as a trial run for what he was convinced was going to be his own tough reelection campaign against South Carolina's Democratic governor, Robert McNair, in 1972. Reporters started asking McNair about a possible challenge to Thurmond as early as February 1969. By the fall, Thurmond and McNair had already begun to size each other up as chief rivals.[54]

The senator's concern about McNair was not merely political paranoia. McNair had assumed the governorship in 1965 when his predecessor, Donald Russell, had resigned and been appointed to the Senate post vacated by Olin Johnston. He was reelected in 1966 by an overwhelming margin. McNair had weathered a stormy political climate—the low point of which was the violence in Orangeburg in 1968—yet he enjoyed a national reputation as a talented and progressive southern Democrat. He was a confidant of Lyndon Johnson's and, at the 1968 Democratic National Convention, one of the candidates whom Hubert Humphrey considered closely for the vice-presidential nomination. Humphrey forces told McNair that if the choice had been for a southerner, he would have gotten the nod.[55]

As disruptive as the desegregation crisis was in 1970, McNair's handling of it burnished his already impressive national standing. In late January, with the Supreme Court having spoken clearly in the *Holmes* decision and with no hope of appeals forthcoming from the Justice Department, McNair went on statewide television to deliver a historic address in the state's sixteen-year struggle to preserve segregated schools. "We have run out of courts and we have run out of time," he said. "We must admit to ourselves that we have pretty well run the legal course and the time has come for compliance or defiance. In South Carolina, we have always followed the law. We will continue to do so. We will comply with the court rulings."[56] National political commentators hailed McNair for levelheaded, courageous leadership in a time of crisis.[57]

Thurmond scoffed: "The people of South Carolina do not need to be told to obey the law."[58] Behind the scenes, McNair fumed that Thurmond, Watson, and the Nixon administration were "political animals" willing to "exploit any issue."[59] His public statements were only slightly more measured. When responding to criticism from Thurmond and Watson, who had given a televised statement critical of the governor, McNair said that the school situation was "too important to get drawn into political chicanery and political hypocrisy."[60]

McNair wrote a scathing letter to Thurmond that pinpointed the discrepancy between Thurmond's campaign promises and the Nixon administration's handling of school desegregation in South Carolina. "It has always been my policy to be very frank and sincere and honest with the people of South Carolina," he said, the clear implication being that Thurmond had been none of those things.[61] Thurmond wrote an equally charged response. South Carolinians had to be confident that "their elected officials have exhausted every possible legal recourse, even those which have little prospect for success," he told McNair.[62] In a radio address days later, Thurmond continued the public attack on McNair. "There is no requirement to accept a regressive social action as desirable," he argued.[63]

The national commentary that had heaped praise on McNair irritated Thurmond, who rejected the idea that his was the retrograde position. School desegregation was no different from the failed social experimentation of the Reconstruction era, he argued: "More than one social disaster has been visited upon our region in the false name of 'progress,' and it is only by courage and perseverance that we can hope to work towards a just society with freedom of choice for all."[64]

Early on the morning of Tuesday, March 3, 1970, two hundred white parents gathered outside the public high school in Lamar, a hardscrabble tobacco town of 1,350 in eastern South Carolina. Several dozen men in the crowd carried makeshift weapons—ax handles, billy clubs, chains. About seventy-five to one hundred highway patrolmen guarded the school.

Lamar was among the Darlington County public schools that federal courts had ordered to desegregate in the middle of the 1969–1970 school year. It was also home to the state's most vigorous freedom-of-choice parents' group. Jeryl Best, the owner of the local Mr. B's seafood restaurant and the incendiary chairman of the Darlington parents' group, came forward to address the officers, bullying and cajoling them. When the officers ignored him, Best jumped up on a nearby brick column. He instructed the parents to form a double line and to march quietly, looking the officers in the eye as they passed. But the parents were fed up with peaceful protest. The crowd wanted action. Best sensed it and quickly changed his tone. He turned toward the officers, berating them as "the Gestapo." The parents followed, showering the police with obscenities: "Son-of-a-bitch!" "Yellowbellies!" "Nigger-lovers!" One youthful protester would later regret that highway patrolmen were the target of the crowd's fury. "We ought to be fighting the niggers rather than the Highway Patrol," he said. "At least they pay taxes."[65]

The Darlington County parents' group had been desperately trying to hold together a white boycott of Lamar schools that had been in place since February 18, the date set by the court for Darlington County schools to reopen on an integrated basis. The goal was to close down the schools so that negotiations could continue and Lamar schools could eventually be reopened on a segregated basis. But the tide of integration washed all around Lamar. In Greenville, the other major school district ruled upon by the Fourth Circuit, schools had reopened on an integrated basis without incident. Even in Darlington County, two-thirds of white students were attending integrated schools county-wide. Best ran a boycott that at its height included about two thousand students, yet in the larger statewide context he and his organization were a small, obstreperous group of outliers.[66]

Best had organized a freedom-of-choice rally in Darlington County for Sunday, February 22, to inspire the boycotters. He invited the four major figures in that year's gubernatorial race: Governor McNair, Lieutenant Governor John West, the moderate Republican Arthur Ravenel, and Albert Watson. Only Watson showed up. He gave Best exactly what he wanted, a trumpet call for South Carolina's most embittered segregationists. "I've been called a racist, a bigot and a buzzard, but I intend to tell the people where I stand and tell it like it is," Watson told the crowd of roughly twenty-five hundred. He criticized the other state leaders who failed to show and praised Jeryl Best and others in Lamar "who will stand up and be counted." Watson urged the boycotters to ignore "people who call you racist, bigot and hard core rednecks."[67]

Albert Watson had not ordered the parents to assemble at Lamar High School on the morning of March 3. His speech in Darlington County was some nine days earlier. But the parents gathered that morning knowing that Watson and powerful allies like Strom Thurmond supported them, believed in them, and would rattle the cages on the floor of Congress to represent their cause.

Violence erupted as soon as the school buses arrived. The mob used ax handles to beat on the sides of the first bus that showed up. Police officers forced the crowd back. As two more buses pulled in front of the school, the group pressed forward again. They broke the windows of the two buses and ripped out ignition wires. A man with a chain shattered the windshield of the lead bus. Inside the two buses were roughly forty students, most of them African Americans. The eighteen-year-old student driver of one of the buses, Henry Alford, struggled to hold the door closed. "Most of the kids were girls, and they were scared and crying," Alford said. "The boys made the girls get down on the floor and the boys stood in a circle around them to protect them from the glass."[68]

Police managed to get the children out of the front exit of the first bus. Students fled out of the back emergency exit of the second. Several received cuts and bruises in the process. The last child to exit was knocked down by a brick in the back as he ran toward the school. Seconds after the children were cleared, the crowd overturned the two buses. Some protesters tried to set them on fire, but by this time law enforcement had fired tear gas into the crowd. The mob dispersed, but not before pelting officers with bottles and pieces of iron pipe and cement block.[69]

That evening all three major networks carried reports of the violence in Lamar, with NBC broadcasting an extended clip from Governor McNair's press conference in which he denounced the "unspeakable acts." McNair condemned the rioters but also decried "those who have helped to create the type of dangerous and inflammatory public attitude which makes such an act possible."[70]

Strom Thurmond too denounced the violence. He reiterated his vigorous opposition to "federal rulings on forced school integration" but said only legal avenues should be pursued. As state and federal authorities argued over who was to blame for the violence, Thurmond fingered McNair for failing to enforce law and order, and McNair blamed the Justice Department for having only five marshals on the scene. Enforcing a court order was a federal responsibility, he argued, and he had called Attorney General Mitchell the previous day to warn him of the situation.

Thurmond chafed at McNair's implication that he and other Republicans deserved part of the blame for the violence at Lamar. McNair had failed to realize "an important element of human psychology," he argued. "People are less likely to resort to violence if they have faith that their leaders will stand up for them by using every legal resource provided within our system."[71]

The Washington Post rejected Thurmond's logic in an editorial critical of both him and Vice President Agnew, who had become the new White House "star" of the southern strategy.[72] By this reasoning, the *Post* noted, Ross Barnett and Orval Faubus were two of the South's greatest peacemakers. Referring to Thurmond and Agnew, the *Post* concluded: "These men . . . have been playing with matches in public for some time now, and yet they want us to know immediately and for the record that if there is one thing they deplore it's fire."[73]

The reaction to the Lamar violence—and the 1970 midterm election more generally—were notable instances in which Thurmond's vaunted ability at reading South Carolina's white electorate failed him. Thurmond, Watson, and other Republicans missed a subtle shift that had taken place in South Carolina, one that Hastings Wyman, the Thurmond staffer who ran Watson's campaign, observed years later. "Up until 1970, Southern conservatives like Watson and Thurmond and others all over the South could rant and rave about school integration and fight it and oppose it—and it really hadn't happened," said Wyman, who later left Thurmond's staff and in 1978 founded the *Southern Political Report*, a biweekly nonpartisan newsletter on southern politics. "Suddenly, instead of stopping something from happening, the segregationists, myself included, were in the position of when we ranted and raved against something, it had already happened; it was a fait accompli."[74]

Wyman saw in retrospect what was hard to discern in the midst of the political fray. The federal courts had spoken clearly, and schools had been integrated in Greenville and in numerous other places in South Carolina. The dire prognostications of the segregationist hard-liners notwithstanding, the sky had not fallen. With white parents overturning school buses and knocking down black schoolchildren with bricks to the back, the politics of law and order looked much different than it had only two years earlier. The majority of white South Carolinians—at least the majority who had not yet fled to private schools— wanted their children to be able to attend their local school in peace and with security. In this context, for many white South Carolinians, Strom Thurmond's and Albert Watson's harangues about freedom of choice were just dangerous static.

In the fall of 1970, South Carolinians braced for a blockbuster campaign season. National commentators judged the race a test of Strom Thurmond's political strength.[75] Thurmond scheduled eleven speaking engagements for Watson in October. In a recorded television and radio advertisement, he praised the candidate as a man who would "stand up and fight for the people."[76] Harry Dent revved up White House support for Watson, sending along strategy memos and arranging for Ronald Reagan to write a fund-raising letter.[77] The Watson campaign opted for Spiro Agnew rather than Richard Nixon to visit the state on the candidate's behalf. Nixon was too closely tied to the HEW moderates, they figured. By this time Agnew had earned a spot in Thurmond's pantheon of political greats. When introducing the vice president at a Watson campaign event, Thurmond, who had taken to wearing a Spiro Agnew wristwatch, called him "the greatest man this country has produced since John C. Calhoun and Robert E. Lee."[78]

As a new school year started, the Watson campaign doubled down on the politics of polarization. In September the campaign aired a five-minute television program that opened with Watson asking, "Are we going to be ruled by the bloc? Look what it did in Watts . . . in the nation's capital." Film clips of clashes between police and black rioters followed.[79] Charges of racism came not from Democrats alone. The normally conservative Greenville News wrote, "The Republican campaign has to be regarded as racist to a disturbing degree."[80] The Repub-

lican mayor of Greenville, R. Cooper White Jr., boycotted the opening
of a Watson campaign office in his city after viewing the television
commercial.[81]

A rogue operation carried out only weeks before the election by two
Watson campaign workers—one of them Hastings Wyman's brother-
in-law—showed how low the campaign had sunk. The men were sus-
pected of helping instigate a melee between black and white students at
A. C. Flora High School in Columbia in an effort to get photographs of
violent black students to be used in Watson campaign materials. The
Watson campaign denied that it had anything to do with the student
fight. Yet an investigation by local police led J. P. Strom, chief of the
State Law Enforcement Division, to conclude that at the very least, the
two Watson campaign workers were at the school looking to take photographs for the campaign and that one of the Watson aides had earlier
discussed "photographically staging a racial incident."[82]

Watson was in a meeting with key advisers when news of the student riot broke. A reporter from *The State* called campaign headquarters to ask why two Watson staff members had happened to be at the
scene of the fighting. A Republican official at the meeting remembered
years later how Watson's brother, Claude, walked into the room with
tears streaming down his face. He said, "Albert, if you don't fire those
sons of bitches, I'm quitting the campaign."[83]

Instead, Watson rearranged his campaign schedule to call a press
conference in which he urged an immediate investigation into "spreading violence and disruption in our schools."[84] Democrats attacked him
for exploiting racial issues for political gain. Thurmond leaped to Watson's defense, accusing Democrats of being afraid to discuss important
issues of school discipline "because someone might be embarrassed."[85]
In late October, Harry Dent reported to President Nixon that Watson
was closing the gap on his Democratic opponent, John West, thanks to
his hammering away on what he called the theme of "school discipline."[86]

In the end, however, the results of the 1970 gubernatorial campaign
suggested that race-baiting no longer paid in South Carolina politics.
The Democrat John West was not the most charismatic politician, yet
he projected a sense of decency that carried the day. West ran unexpectedly well in suburban areas thought to be the GOP's stronghold.[87]

His victory was part of a surprising trend across the South, where moderate Democratic governors won statehouse races: Jimmy Carter succeeded in Georgia and Dale Bumpers in Arkansas. Fritz Hollings summed up what became a standard postmortem on Thurmond and the Watson campaign. The politics of the three *p*'s—"passion and prejudice and polarization"—was over.[88]

Strom Thurmond's political stock had never been lower than in the months following Albert Watson's defeat. A report by the conservative Americans for Constitutional Action speculated that Thurmond was "in serious jeopardy of maintaining his Senate seat."[89] One political observer put the odds of his beating Robert McNair the following year as little better than even. Another noted that Thurmond was already "running like the election is going to be held two weeks from now."[90]

Thanks to the Republicans' poor showing in the midterm elections as well as the failure of Haynsworth and Carswell to win Senate approval, at the White House both Thurmond and Harry Dent had lost their shine. Increasingly, President Nixon was turning to the former Democratic Texas governor and new Treasury secretary John Connally when he needed soundings on southern matters. Even in Edgefield the news was grim. A group of black students had filed suit in federal court asking that Strom Thurmond High—the formerly all-white public school that had become 65 percent black—be renamed. The students also wanted to ditch the school's rebel mascot, ban Confederate flags from school functions, and stop the school band from playing "Dixie."[91]

Harry Dent worried that the Watson campaign had left a "racist taint" on Republicans, both in South Carolina and at the White House.[92] In early February, in a memo to Thurmond marked "very personal" and "please destroy after reading," Dent recommended that the senator get some moderate South Carolina Republicans up to Washington for an event and for lunch in the Senate dining room.[93] He passed along a copy of a letter from James Duffy, a leading GOP moderate, who was fed up with racist dominance in the South Carolina party. "There is sentiment that if the only way to end this is for Thurmond's defeat then so be it," Duffy had told Dent.[94]

Though he did not put it in such terms at the time, Dent's efforts represented a repudiation of Kevin Phillips's vision of southern politics. Dent had always been Phillips's chief critic inside the White House, dismissing as "hogwash" an article suggesting that he was following Phillips's advice. He viewed Phillips's book as "a gift of political ammunition for the Democrats," and Dent recruited one of Nixon's young liberal aides to write a rebuttal to Phillips.[95] Harry Dent was not above foot-dragging on school desegregation when there was political advantage to be had, and in the fall of 1970 he had voiced no objections to the toxic tactics of the Watson campaign. Yet Watson's race had shown the futility of Phillips's dark vision of intentionally polarizing the races in order to drive Wallace voters into the GOP.

Dent's modulated line fit well with the Sunbelt suburbanization that had been taking place in the South over the last several decades. Whereas Kevin Phillips thought about southern politics primarily in the old terms of racial polarization, Dent helped Thurmond adopt a subtler approach. He and Thurmond had witnessed the new temper firsthand in the Watson campaign when a promising Republican moderate like the Greenville mayor, Cooper White, had refused to appear with Watson. They saw it in the disgruntled supporters of Arthur Ravenel, who had been denied the opportunity of challenging Watson in a party primary. They saw it too in John West's successful campaign as the candidate of decency. Throughout the suburbs of South Carolina was evidence of middle-class, progress-minded whites eager to put the racism and divisiveness of the olden days behind them.[96]

Republicans would have to moderate their racial message if they were to win these voters. A new generation of moderate Democrats was well positioned to pick them off, and when they did, it was difficult for Republicans to beat southern Democrats in statewide races, a fact that is easy to forget given the dramatic Republican rise in the last part of the twentieth century. Democrats had a monopoly on black voters, and the harder Republicans ran to the right, the more it energized this base. Typically, Democrats needed little more than a third of the white vote to ensure victory (in Thurmond's case, with African Americans constituting more than 25 percent of registered voters in South Carolina, the estimate was that a Democrat with only 35 percent of the white vote would beat him in 1972).[97] These Democratic candidates gave high-minded but measured speeches about racial progress in the

South that flattered the prejudices of suburban voters about how much the South had changed. The Democrats' New Deal heritage also gave them easy entrée to working-class whites. Southern Democrats presented their Republican opponents as tools of the country-club crowd. These were the tactics that the moderate "New South" Democrats swore by in the three decades following the civil rights movement. In South Carolina, there was Fritz Hollings, John West, and Richard Riley; in Georgia, Jimmy Carter and Sam Nunn; in Arkansas, Dale Bumpers, David Pryor, and, in a few years, Bill Clinton. All of these politicians were powers at the state and national level, the seasoned successors of the old Democratic establishment. Most southern Republicans had a very difficult time defeating them.[98]

Strom Thurmond, however, was not like most southern Republicans. Watson's failure had shown not only the danger of racially polarizing politics but also the continued strength of the Democratic network. Thurmond worked hard in the aftermath of Watson's loss to reconnect with Democratic power brokers in South Carolina, much to the chagrin of Republicans who complained that his interest in his own reelection was leading him to undercut the South Carolina GOP.[99] In an attempt to dry up support for Robert McNair, Thurmond and Dent orchestrated a risky maneuver that threatened mutiny in the South Carolina GOP.

At issue were two federal judgeships. Thurmond backed Robert Chapman, a former Republican state chairman, for one of them. For the other, he chose Sol Blatt Jr., a Democrat and the son of the longtime Democratic Speaker of the South Carolina House. State Republicans were outraged. When Harry Dent denied that political considerations played a role in the appointment, a *State* editorial remarked, "Well, maybe some of us were born yesterday."[100] As a member of the infamous Barnwell Ring, Blatt had been the subject of Thurmond's scorn during the 1946 governor's race, yet Thurmond knew that Speaker Blatt's political influence reached into every corner of the state. The consensus was that Thurmond was bidding for Blatt senior's support in 1972.[101]

The calculation was more pointed than that. Thurmond and Dent were concerned less about gaining Blatt senior's endorsement than about forestalling any momentum the powerful Speaker might swing for

McNair. They knew that if Blatt had campaigned hard for anyone, it would have been McNair, who as a young legislator in the South Carolina House had been Blatt's most favored protégé. In addition, Sol Blatt Jr. and Bob McNair were old and dear friends—"like brothers," Blatt junior recalled years later.[102]

At the time, Blatt junior had no indication that Thurmond was considering him for a judgeship. In fact, he had traveled with and made calls on behalf of Welch Morrisette, a Republican friend who was trying to line up endorsements for the job. Harry Dent called Blatt junior in early January 1971 and asked him and his father to come to Aiken the next day for a meeting where Dent told the Blatts that Thurmond was going to recommend Blatt junior for the job. "Where my name came from is quite a mystery," Blatt recalled, "and I never worked to find out."[103] Dent made no mention of either Bob McNair or the 1972 Senate race, yet none was necessary. The political calculus showed up in a memo that Dent wrote to John Mitchell after Blatt junior had won Senate confirmation, thanking the attorney general for help in working out the judgeship "in a way that would take Governor McNair out of the race." The Democrats had "all their eggs in McNair's basket," Dent wrote, "and now the eggs and the basket have seemingly been smashed."[104]

As they worked to isolate McNair, Thurmond and Dent also charted a historic shift in the senator's racial politics. This was a strategic calculation, born at the most politically precarious moment in his career, that started Thurmond on a new, more racially temperate path from which he would not stray. Dent was explicit about it in an interview with Thurmond's hometown newspaper in Aiken: "We've got to get him in a position where he can't be attacked . . . as being a racist."[105] Thurmond and Dent had been scheming for weeks on a splashy way to signal the senator's new approach. They decided that the bold play would be for Thurmond to hire a black staffer. No southern congressman or senator had yet done so. Fritz Hollings had been hoping to be the first, but John West had recently snapped up Jim Clyburn, his preferred choice.[106] Thurmond appointed Thomas Moss, a staff member of the nonpartisan South Carolina Voter Education Project, to help with what he said were the increasing number of requests his office had received from black South Carolinians. He said that Moss "could be especially helpful in meeting my responsibilities to serve all the people."[107] A *Washington Post* headline pronounced "Thurmond's Awakening," and a political cartoon in *The State* depicted a public faint with surprise.[108] The cartoonist at *The Charlotte Observer* was more skeptical. He drew a minstrel Thurmond in blackface, offering "free watermelon," with an indignant group of middle-class blacks looking on.[109]

Moss's appointment coincided with a noticeable shift in the tone of articles and press releases that came out of Thurmond's Senate office. Increasingly absent were the catchphrases of segregationist politics. As late as July 1970, for example, Thurmond's office issued a press release in which he denounced the "bloc vote" that almost upended George Wallace's reelection campaign in Alabama (Albert Watson's campaign would make controversial use of the term only two months later).[110] The next year, however, Thurmond wrote an article for a special issue of *Ebony*, the African American publication, in which he expressed his surprise at discovering that "many of my constituents might view me as strongly opposed to their interests." The incredulity was risible. Yet instead of taking his normal defensive approach when attacked on his racial record—recounting his efforts as governor in funding black higher education or supporting the repeal of the poll tax—he pointed to Thomas Moss's hiring as part of a new effort, and Thurmond celebrated white and black southerners' shared religious heritage and their common "sense of estrangement from the rest of the nation."[111] Beginning in 1971, for the first time in his career, Thurmond used his weekly newsletter to celebrate the accomplishments of black South Carolinians, and his press office reported on issues uniquely relevant to African Americans. The heavyweight boxing champion Joe Frazier, a native of Beaufort, was an example of how "the system works," Thurmond wrote.[112] Thurmond entered into the *Congressional Record* a report by a black doctor from Howard about the unique dangers of hypertension for black Americans.[113] Over the next few years, his office developed a two-page list of "accomplishments in behalf of blacks" that Thurmond eagerly displayed to visitors.[114]

The appointment of Thomas Moss played especially well among the moderate Republicans in South Carolina about whom Dent was particularly concerned. Arthur Ravenel, a good barometer of the moderate suburban vote, wrote to congratulate Thurmond on the move.[115] By the summer of 1971, James Duffy enthusiastically supported Thurmond's reelection among his fellow moderates. "Thurmond must win because he has heard the trumpet and has acted," Duffy wrote. "Who else has a black man on their staff from this state?"[116]

So masterful was the job of repositioning that Thurmond and Dent did that it is easy to forget how precarious Thurmond's situation had been in the wake of the Watson defeat. By early 1972, Thurmond's crisis had passed. A voter opinion survey showed that he had improved his standing against Bob McNair from a dead heat in November 1970 to a strong majority.[117] After McNair decided not to make the race, Democrats actually had a hard time even finding a candidate to challenge him. Eventually, a bright and energetic state senator from Florence, Eugene "Nick" Zeigler, emerged as a viable if not daunting opponent. A Harvard graduate and former navy officer, Zeigler had political skills, yet with a Democratic power broker like Sol Blatt Sr. already nullified, Thurmond and Dent had stacked the deck against him.

It was during the 1972 campaign that Thurmond's status as a distributor of political pork reached legendary proportions. Zeigler highlighted the hypocrisy between Thurmond's oft-invoked small-government principles and his profligate advocacy of federal spending in South Carolina—as would political opponents for the remainder of Thurmond's career. But these attacks never registered more than glancing blows. At the White House, Harry Dent wrote memos to administration and executive branch agencies to speed grants and projects that would help Thurmond politically. This included a letter to HEW on behalf of Victoria DeLee, an African American woman who had applied for federal help with a literacy program. Dent noted that DeLee had recently attended a reception for Thurmond in Charleston and afterward had said glowing things about the senator to the press. It was exactly the kind of quotation Thurmond needed to help soften his racist image. "God bless Victoria DeLee and may the HEW do likewise," Dent wrote.[118]

Another incident in the campaign helped Thurmond. Ironically enough, it involved the long-held rumor that he had a black daughter. On October 11, 1972, the *Edgefield Advertiser*, his hometown newspaper, published a headline declaring that Thurmond had "colored offspring while parading as a devout segregationist." It was the work of one of Thurmond's enemies, the quixotic *Advertiser* editor and publisher W. W. Mims, who blamed him for a federal water project in Edgefield that had not turned out as he had wished. Mims had only put into print the rumor that had circulated for decades.[119]

Far from allowing it to hamper him, Thurmond turned the article on its head. He linked Nick Zeigler to the charge, presenting himself as the victim of a racial smear by an unscrupulous opponent. Despite Zeigler's vehement denial of any connection with Mims's story, Thurmond blasted him for running a "scurrilous" campaign that spread "malicious falsehoods." When asked directly if he thought Zeigler was linked to the charges, Thurmond told reporters to "draw your own conclusions" and suggested talking to the state Democratic chairman, who could "probably give you the whole story."[120]

In the 1972 election, Richard Nixon and Strom Thurmond both scored easy reelection victories. Nixon's triumph would prove short-lived as his administration devolved into scandal and recrimination. Harry Dent left the White House after the elections and returned to Columbia to start a law practice and write a book about the southern strategy. Thurmond soldiered on. Safely repositioned politically, he would have other challengers—notably in his 1978 campaign against a charismatic and well-financed young Democrat—but never again would he be as politically vulnerable as he was in the aftermath of the Watson campaign.

12

A NEW RIGHT AND THE OLD
(1972–1980)

The refashioning of Strom Thurmond's racial politics for the 1972 campaign initiated a more general softening of his public image. His wife, Nancy, gave birth to four children in quick succession in the 1970s. Each birth announcement prompted flattering news stories about the vigorous Thurmond and his attractive young family. The older Thurmond became, the more regularly the press published photographs of him working out or performing some strenuous activity. The image of the humorless segregationist firebrand was slowly giving way to that of the quirky, age-defying senator in jogging shorts. It was also in the 1970s that Thurmond negotiated a new, yet still vital role in national conservative politics.

A variety of new organizations and leaders emerged in the 1970s who stoked what observers described as the politics of the New Right— opposition to busing, affirmative action, abortion, the Equal Rights Amendment, and the gay rights movement. In the wake of the Vietnam War and a financial downturn, many people voiced new concerns about national decline. Conservative politicians and activists talked about restoring the sense of national pride that had been sapped by Vietnam, Watergate, and the tumult of the 1960s and about reclaiming the nation's Christian heritage.[1]

Thurmond is incorrectly held up as an example of merely the Old Right. In fact he was central to the creation of the New. For just one example, it was in Thurmond's hideaway office in the bowels of the

U.S. Capitol that a Wisconsin businessman and Republican activist, J. Frederic "Fritz" Rench, wrote the business plan for what would become the Heritage Foundation. Thurmond's top aide, James Lucier, convinced that conservative senators like Thurmond needed to be armed with information on critical issues of the day, made an initial round of introductions of conservative activists, who in turn pitched corporate representatives. But businessmen wanted a business plan and a budget. So Rench went to work in Thurmond's office, and the activist Paul Weyrich finagled an audience with Joseph Coors, the beer magnate, who was looking to get more involved in conservative politics. Thurmond was among the small group of senators and congressmen gathered by Weyrich to give the big sell. It worked. Lucier became president of Analysis and Research Association Inc., which would eventually be rebranded the Heritage Foundation, one of the seedbeds of the New Right insurgency.[2]

In the 1970s, politics on the right evolved, as would the leaders, yet Thurmond's story is a reminder not to draw too neatly the distinction between the New Right and the Old. The lines of continuity ran back to the 1940s and forward to the 1980s, and Thurmond's career captures them all. The same themes that animated the Old Right continued to drive conservative politics in powerful ways: the vigorous defense of business interests and a reflexive opposition to organized labor; national security concerns and the belief in American exceptionalism abroad; and an antipathy to the politics and culture of liberalism, one in which the image of the aggrieved white God-fearing American, mistreated at the hands of forces both elite and minority, stood center stage.

As important as the 1970s were in mobilizing conservative Americans, such an outcome would have seemed unlikely in the decade's early years as the Watergate scandal unfolded. The arrest of five men in June 1972 for breaking into Democratic headquarters at the Watergate apartment and office complex touched off a cover-up that led all the way to President Nixon himself and threatened to wreck the Republican Party. The gradual exposure of the president's role, along with the existence of an extensive wiretapping program of government officials and reporters, destroyed Nixon's presidency and dominated headlines from the beginning of his second administration until his resignation in August 1974. The impact on the Republican Party was only slightly less devastating, as seen in the 1974 midterm elections, when Democrats picked up forty-three additional seats in a House of Representatives that they already controlled comfortably.[3]

Throughout, Thurmond was one of Nixon's most loyal defenders. Like Nixon himself, Thurmond was convinced that Watergate was fundamentally a partisan witch hunt: Democrats were attacking the president for the same kind of surveillance of political enemies that had been common under the Democratic presidents Kennedy and Johnson.[4] In the mid-1960s, staffers in Thurmond's office had been convinced that the Johnson administration was using the FBI to follow up leads derived from the illegal monitoring of Thurmond's Capitol Hill office.[5] One of those former staffers, Fred Buzhardt, was a key figure in the Watergate defense, serving as Nixon's personal lawyer and poring over hundreds of hours of Oval Office tapes, a job that Nixon entrusted solely to him.

Thurmond welcomed the appointment of the special prosecutor Archibald Cox in May 1973 as a chance for the president to clear his name, yet he quickly soured on the Senate Watergate hearings held that summer.[6] He defended Nixon's dismissal of Cox in October, and later during Judiciary Committee hearings he questioned Cox sharply as to his partisan ties.[7] In November, at a Support the President rally in Oklahoma City, Thurmond drew a standing ovation when he urged an end to the "vendetta" against Nixon.[8] The following February he was a featured speaker at a $100-a-plate luncheon sponsored by the National Citizens Committee for Fairness to the President.[9] When the White House released an edited transcript of some of the White House tapes, Thurmond helped out with the public relations campaign, inserting a White House memo into the *Congressional Record* that alleged to undermine the testimony of the former White House aide John Dean.[10]

Thurmond stuck with Nixon until the end. He was among the forty House and Senate members who shared a tearful moment with Nixon in the Cabinet Room an hour before the president went on television to announce his resignation. Afterward, Thurmond praised the president's "great sacrifice" and recited a long list of Nixon's foreign and domestic accomplishments.[11]

Thurmond's charged, partisan performance during Watergate contrasted with his subdued approach to another issue important to him, school desegregation. His relatively muted manner on the subject reflected the changed national political climate. In the 1970s, desegregation efforts took a surprising and, for Thurmond, favorable turn. The controversy over the Stennis amendment in 1970, in which southerners charged the federal government with unequal enforcement of civil rights, was the first sign of the shifting momentum on the issue. Two years later, the effort to attack de facto school segregation in areas in the North and the West was in crisis. Federal district court rulings in Richmond and Detroit opened the way for the busing of students between cities and surrounding suburbs, stoking vehement antibusing opposition.[12]

In mid-March 1972, George Wallace decisively won the Democratic presidential primary in Florida, a victory aided by his harangues against busing. Less than forty-eight hours later, President Nixon gave a televised national address calling on Congress to impose a "moratorium" on federal courts ordering any new busing to achieve racial balance.[13] Nixon's antibusing bill sailed through the House of Representatives but stalled in the Senate. Liberals blocked passage after southerners insisted on including a "reopener" provision, which would apply the measure to busing already taking place in the South.[14] The reopener clause was critical to southerners such as Thurmond. "If it is proper to stop busing in the future," he declared, "it is proper to stop the unreasonable busing which is going on right now."[15]

Over the course of 1972, as northerners and westerners became worked up over busing, Thurmond became calmer and more measured on the issue. One reason had to do with his reelection campaign: rhetorical bombs against Yankee liberals only fed old images of the unreconstructed segregationist. Even more, Thurmond and other southerners were comforted to know that the outrage they had long felt over desegregation was spreading across the country. They had been predicting it for years. Now the polling data proved them correct. Thurmond's scaled-back rhetoric merged with what became a national consensus on busing.[16]

Thurmond's statements on school desegregation in September and October, just weeks before the 1972 Senate vote, reflected the new normal. "I think it's very simple," he said. "If it improves the quality of education, then busing is good. If it doesn't, then I think it's bad."[17] Busing could be good? The admission, if only in the abstract, marked new ground for Thurmond. Toward those who accused him and other busing opponents of racism, Thurmond managed a never-before-seen magnanimity. The accusations placed "an extra burden" on busing foes, he allowed. He and other opponents had to consider the "feelings of those who, through misunderstanding, may believe that our actions cast doubt on the American commitment to freedom and justice for all."[18]

Graciousness, not grandstanding, was the order of the day now that the reopener provision promised to slip southern schools under the national consensus on de facto segregation. When the HEW secretary, Caspar Weinberger, told reporters that his agency was taking a "conciliatory approach" toward northern and western school desegregation, Thurmond took it as an admission of the charge that he and other southerners had been making against the federal government since the passage of the 1964 Civil Rights Act: unequal enforcement between the North and the South.[19]

Soothing Thurmond and other southerners' long-held grievance was a bipartisan antibusing amendment that Congress passed in 1975. Thurmond co-sponsored a bill to prohibit HEW from assigning teachers or students to schools for reasons of race.[20] The author of the bill was the liberal freshman senator from Delaware, Joseph Biden. Elected at the age of twenty-nine, Biden was hailed as one of the Senate's new generation of liberal Democrats. Yet two-way busing between Wilmington and surrounding suburbs had stoked a grassroots antibusing movement, and Biden had been quick to respond.[21]

The sight of one of the next generation of liberals finding so much common ground with Strom Thurmond was an indication of how far public sentiment had shifted to the right on school desegregation. Years later, reflecting on his early career in the Senate, Biden recalled that the reason he had gotten into politics was "to fight the Strom Thurmonds."[22] The busing battles, however, showed how blurred the lines between right and left had become. By the mid-1970s, a softening of Thurmond's rhetoric—not any change in his position—had left him well within the mainstream on one of the signature issues of the modern civil rights movement.

School busing was only one issue in which the longtime right-wing position held by Thurmond came to seem increasingly reasonable. Since his appointment to the Senate Armed Services Committee in the late 1950s, Thurmond had been complaining about liberals' "no-win" attitude in the Cold War. The demoralization over Vietnam—which ended as a military conflict on January 27, 1973, with the signing of the Paris Peace Accords but remained an open national wound for years—created the conditions in which these old arguments about an undaunted America resonated with many people unsettled by a new era of seeming limits.

In the post-Vietnam era, Americans on the left and in the center discussed the need to scale back American ambitions abroad. Yet Thurmond talked about restoring American fortitude and national will. The struggle to bring home American POWs and to identify those missing in action (MIAs) became for conservatives a vehicle for making their point.[23] Early in his administration, President Nixon had identified closely with the families of POWs as a way of countering antiwar protests, and Thurmond had supported him fully. In May 1973, Nixon assembled a cast of celebrities to commemorate the return of nearly six hundred POWs at a lavish White House dinner. Thurmond was there, but little noticed given the presence of VIPs such as Bob Hope, John Wayne, Jimmy Stewart, and the *Playboy* Playmate Miki Garcia, Miss January 1973.[24]

Long after the guests went home, however, Thurmond continued to press the POW-MIA issue and, in the process, stoke conservative resentments over American failure in Vietnam. In June 1973, for example, he berated Jane Fonda and the former U.S. attorney general Ramsey Clark for wartime visits to Hanoi, where they had testified to the humane treatment of American POWs. He derided the pair, along with the singer Joan Baez and the Nobel Prize winner Dr. George Wald, for destroying American morale and introduced a bill to allow the president to restrict U.S. citizens from traveling to countries where armed forces were deployed.[25] He also charged Vietnamese Communists with deliberate foot-dragging in returning POWs as a way of extorting economic aid from the United States.[26]

Even as American officials succeeded in repatriating what seemed to be the last of the prisoners of war in Vietnam, the search for the missing in action took on greater urgency. POW-MIA organizations that had begun as a collection of wives of missing soldiers evolved into a small but politically potent constituency that continued to criticize American leaders. U.S. officials had betrayed soldiers during the war by not committing fully to Communist defeat, they argued, and now they were abandoning soldiers after the war by failing to account for the missing. Calling it "tragic" and "disheartening" that the U.S. government had failed to account for nearly twenty-four hundred Americans missing in Southeast Asia, Thurmond was one of the POW-MIA groups' greatest champions.[27] In April 1975, he introduced a resolution to enact a Senate select committee to investigate the POW-MIA issue.[28] Later that year he co-sponsored a resolution to reduce U.S. contributions to the United Nations if the organization did not help investigate the situation.[29]

Another battlefront in the unending domestic war over Vietnam was the issue of amnesty for wartime dissenters. Thousands of American men had dodged the draft, and thousands more who were drafted but later deserted were serving jail sentences or had been given dishonorable discharges. By December 1969, there were already fifty-six thousand deserters in the U.S. Army, soldiers that Thurmond denounced as "a disgrace to the uniform and to our nation."[30] The question of how the government should handle these cases roiled American politics in the mid-1970s.

Only months after the Paris Peace Accords, Thurmond mounted a vigorous campaign against amnesty.[31] Before a Washington banquet honoring wounded veterans, he thundered against draftees who had gone off to Canada to avoid the war. In 1977, after President Jimmy Carter established a special review program to hear petitions of dodgers and deserters, Thurmond introduced a bill to deny veterans' benefits to deserters whose discharge had been upgraded under the president's plan.[32]

By the mid-1970s, however, concerns about American prestige and national honor became tied up with the United States' relationship with another small former colonial outpost, Panama. Beginning with Lyndon Johnson and continuing through Jimmy Carter, both Democratic and Republican presidents had attempted to renegotiate the 1903 treaty that gave the United States exclusive control over the Panama Canal and the ten-mile-wide Canal Zone that divided the country. The treaty was a relic of America's imperial ambitions in Latin America at the turn of the century and a stumbling block in relations with not only Panama but other Latin American countries. Efforts toward a new treaty reached critical mass during Gerald Ford's presidency, but it was Jimmy Carter who signed a new one in 1977 and was left with the task of shepherding it through the Senate.[33]

Ever since talk of a new treaty had begun, Thurmond had been the Senate's most outspoken defender of U.S. interests in Panama. The canal was essential to American defense of the Western Hemisphere, he argued, and the U.S. military presence in Panama was a vital check on the spread of communism in Central and South America.[34] In late June 1967, after the Johnson administration concluded treaty negotiations with Panama, 130 members of the House supported a resolution urging rejection of the treaties. Thurmond led the fight in the Senate, where treaty approval would have to take place.[35] He gave seventeen speeches against the treaties in the summer of 1967.[36] At the national convention of Young Americans for Freedom, he called the Panama treaties "the greatest give-away since God gave man the world for his dominion."[37] In March 1974, after Secretary of State Henry Kissinger signed a set of principles with Panama promising an end to U.S. control over the canal, Thurmond introduced a resolution in the Senate calling for "undiluted United States sovereignty over the United States–owned Canal Zone." Thirty-four senators signed on, enough to block ratification of any new treaty.[38]

In right-wing foreign policy circles in the late 1960s and early 1970s, the Panama Canal had been a pet cause, but as public awareness of the canal negotiations grew, the issue played an important role in conservative political mobilization. The American Conservative Union spearheaded a lobbying campaign that spent millions. The best example came in the 1976 Republican presidential primaries, when Ronald Reagan challenged the sitting president, Gerald Ford, for the nomination.[39] Conservative Republicans loathed Ford, yet in the early primaries the Reagan campaign had failed to gain momentum. Reagan salvaged his nomination campaign with an upset in the North Carolina primary in March, a victory fueled by his vigorous opposition to the Panama Canal treaties.

Reagan lit up audiences with his passionate appeals for a muscular America that did not kowtow to weaker, inferior nations. "What kind of foreign policy is it when a little tinhorn dictator in Panama says he is going to start guerrilla warfare against us unless we give him the Panama Canal?" he declared.[40] In Texas, the Democrat turned Republican John Connally credited the canal issue with helping Reagan beat Ford in the Lone Star State primary. One reporter covering the campaign noted how the pattern in North Carolina and Texas was repeated throughout the Sunbelt states of the South and the Southwest.[41]

The Senate debate over the ratification of the treaties negotiated by Jimmy Carter drew a remarkable amount of attention. Lasting from February to April 1978, the proceedings went longer than any treaty deliberations except for the Treaty of Versailles. National Public Radio aired the debate, marking the first time Senate floor activity had been broadcast. The Senate eventually ratified the treaty, yet it proved to be a Pyrrhic victory for Carter. Conservative activists used the media attention to portray treaty supporters as servile and out of touch. The issue helped drive fund-raising campaigns, filling the coffers for conservative battles to come.[42]

It was not only the fallout from the Vietnam War that led some Americans to worry about national decline. In the 1970s the United States also experienced what at the time was the most significant economic downturn since the Great Depression. The 1973 oil crisis was the immediate cause, yet economic stagnation in the 1970s also resulted from a historic end to a quarter century of unparalleled economic expansion, one that began with the military mobilization of World War II and was sustained by decades of Cold War military spending.

Different parts of the country experienced the downturn differently. At a time when declining, deindustrializing areas of the North and the Midwest were particularly hard-hit, many areas of the Sunbelt boomed. The sight of southern and southwestern expansion in an era of economic stagnation set the stage for a national debate over the sources of economic growth in post–World War II America.

It was the "Second War Between the States," according to a special report in *BusinessWeek* in May 1976.[43] Economics and regional planning professors weighed in with quantitative studies, and the *National Journal* produced its own lengthy special report, concluding that "federal tax and spending policies are causing a massive flow of wealth from the Northeast and Midwest to the fast-growing Southern and Western regions of the nation."[44] In February 1976, *The New York Times* ran a series of articles profiling the Sunbelt economic marvel, citing among other examples the success of Strom Thurmond and Mendel Rivers in directing military spending to South Carolina.[45]

An influential book that charted the political and economic impact of the Sunbelt was Kirkpatrick Sale's *Power Shift* (1975).[46] Sale brought an irreverent wit and muckraker's sensibility to the nexus of political and economic conservatism that had converged in what he called the "southern rim." More than anyone else at the time, he placed the story of the South's political resurgence within a broader narrative of post–World War II economic restructuring. As Robert Lekachman observed in *The New York Times*, Richard Nixon's southern strategy was in Sale's estimation "much more than a mere reward for hard-core, reactionary types like Strom Thurmond who in 1968 guaranteed Nixon's nomination by warding off Ronald Reagan. Nixon acted out of a rational assessment of the shifting locale of economic power."[47]

Hard as Thurmond had worked in 1968 to earn Nixon's reward, he had worked equally hard in the postwar decades to shift the center of economic gravity southward. In this second War Between the States, he defended the Sunbelt against charges of federal government favoritism. Economic stagnation in the Rust Belt was a self-inflicted wound, he argued, citing a study by A. C. Flora Jr., an economics professor at Baptist College in Charleston. "These States have all too often adopted policies of heavy taxation and onerous regulation," he said. "Such policies have made it difficult for businessmen, wage earners, consumers, and homeowners to conduct their affairs and remain solvent." The South had made up so much ground in recent years, Thurmond maintained, because it had "tried hard to be responsive to the needs of employers."[48]

Thurmond helped make the defense of Sunbelt economic interests a central part of GOP politics. In 1977, as oil lobbyists worried over the recent retirement of Roman Hruska, the previous senior Republican on Judiciary, Thurmond acted. The committee was scheduled to debate once again legislation to break up oil companies, a move industry interests had fought with what Senator Birch Bayh, a supporter of divestiture, described as "the most sophisticated, elaborate and expensive lobby effort" that he had ever seen.[49] In line to replace Hruska was Charles Mathias of Maryland, who according to Americans for Democratic Action (ADA) voted with liberals 83 percent of the time.[50]

Strom Thurmond's ADA rating, by contrast, was zero. Oil lobbyists pleaded with Thurmond to use his seniority to block Mathias, who in 1976 had cast the decisive committee vote to send a divestiture bill to the Senate floor.[51] Senate rules dictated that a senator could not hold two ranking positions, so Thurmond agreed to give up seniority on his beloved Armed Services Committee in favor of the top spot on Judiciary, thus shutting out Mathias.[52] With Thurmond in place, there would be no divestiture bill on the Senate floor in 1977. The best that liberals could do was an amendment offered by Ted Kennedy to block oil companies from further energy acquisitions in coal or uranium, a measure that conservatives easily defeated.[53]

It was a classic Washington power play, one that showed in miniature how the Sunbelt 1970s intensified the long-term trend of moderate decline and conservative ascendancy within the GOP. Mathias had flirted with a presidential run in 1976 and was considered a leading moderate candidate for the 1980 GOP nomination. An outspoken civil rights advocate, he urged Republicans to expand their efforts in wooing black voters. The image of the GOP naming Thurmond, one of the living symbols of civil rights intransigence, as their top representative on the Judiciary Committee made him shudder.[54] In 1977, however, such concerns took a backseat to those of Sunbelt businessmen, who strongly influenced the Republican agenda.

A profile of the Republican Party written by the journalist William

Schneider during the 1976 convention provided a handy description of the new forces: "Easy Street" Republicans. The traditional division in the GOP had been between the eastern wing, or Wall Street, and the Midwestern wing, Main Street, Schneider wrote. Yet the current party leadership of the Midwesterner Gerald Ford as president and Vice President Nelson Rockefeller of New York symbolized the reconciliation of that historic split. Opposing them now was what Schneider termed the "nouveau riche" from the "suburbs and boomtowns of the 'Sun Belt,'" the movement that began with Barry Goldwater but had come to include many former Democrats such as Ronald Reagan, John Connally, and, Schneider noted, Strom Thurmond.[55]

Defending Sunbelt business interests was only one side of the coin. The other entailed a continued attack on organized labor. In 1978, Thurmond was again part of a conservative filibuster, this time concerning the biggest business-labor showdown of the decade. Designed to speed up union representation elections and stiffen penalties for labor law violations, the 1978 Labor Law Reform Act would have provided the first major revision to national labor law since 1959. The House of Representatives had passed the bill easily in late 1977, but labor groups were gearing up for what the AFL-CIO president, George Meany, described as a "holy war" in the Senate. Business opponents readied themselves, declaring that "freedom" itself was at stake. The *Congressional Quarterly* called the showdown "one of the most intense grass-roots lobbying campaigns in recent history."[56]

It was actually more of an Astroturf campaign. Wealthy political action committees (PACs) on both sides waged the war that was ostensibly fought by working-class Americans and small-business owners. Labor groups had been the first to organize PACs back in the 1940s, yet electoral reform laws in 1974 combined with a Supreme Court ruling led to an explosion in the number of PACs in the 1970s. Corporations organizing PACs increased from only 89 in 1974 to 1,204 by 1980. It was a "revolt of the haves," according to one pundit. Membership in the U.S. Chamber of Commerce quadrupled during the decade.[57] The National Right to Work Committee generated a huge response through a high-priced direct-mail campaign, forcing the AFL-CIO to ramp up its own efforts.[58]

News reports emphasized the part New Right politicians such as

Jesse Helms and Utah's freshman senator, Orrin Hatch, played in leading the fight against the bill.[59] Thurmond, who pledged to "fight this bill
and fight it to the last," was no less involved.[60] No one mistook Thurmond as part of a *new* Right; he had been around far too long for that.
Yet his prominent role in the debate, and his decades-old opposition to
organized labor, beg the question of what was new about conservatives'
antipathy to labor reform in the 1970s.

Thurmond's arguments against the bill reprised part of the debate
from the previous year about the sources of Sunbelt growth. Pointing
to statistics that showed that since 1957 employment and personal income in southern states had jumped at rates two to three times that of
northeastern states, he maintained that in South Carolina these gains
were due to its being "an attractive economic climate to workers and
employers alike." Reviving regional conspiracy theories about northerners pushing southern unionization as a backhand way to kill southern economic development, Thurmond accused the bill's supporters of
wanting to "place lead in the shoes of the Sunbelt and other right-to-
work States."[61] His office had said nearly the same thing in the early
1960s in response to NLRB decisions against southern businessmen.[62]
Thurmond also went on the attack, filling up many hours during the
filibuster discussing reports of labor-management racketeering and
violence, a theme of labor opponents throughout the debate.[63]

Supporters of labor law reform got within two votes of breaking the
filibuster but never succeeded.[64] It was the most significant in a series
of losses for labor during the Carter administration. Labor groups had
argued that the legislation was necessary to crack down on companies
that had knowingly and flagrantly violated federal labor law. The best
example was J. P. Stevens, a giant in the textile industry, which was still
the largest and most influential industry in North and South Carolina.
A federal appeals court called Stevens the "most notorious recidivist in
the field of labor law."[65] The company's stance had stoked a nationwide
boycott in the 1970s.[66]

The debate over the sources of Sunbelt growth, past and future, was
captured in a profile of industrial development in South Carolina.
Democrats and Republicans alike, black leaders and white, all agreed
about the state's commitment to luring outside business. "Politicians
do not make business a whipping boy down here," observed Frederick

Dent, secretary of commerce during the Nixon administration and the president of Mayfair Mills near Spartanburg. Consequently, the state enjoyed the highest level of foreign investment per capita of any state in the nation. Manufacturing had grown at three times the national average over the past three decades. Yet the average South Carolina factory worker made 20 percent less than the national average. Per capita income ranked forty-sixth in the nation.[67]

The article dated the present trend back to James Byrnes's governorship, but it should have traced it to Thurmond's. It was as the Dixiecrat candidate that Thurmond had broken decisively with labor unions. In his last two years as governor his profile as a national presidential candidate had gained him access to boardrooms throughout the North. In the 1950s and '60s, he had become a devoted proponent of "free enterprise" and a tireless foe to labor unions. By the 1970s, his commitment to whatever line was pursued by conservative business interests had become as reflexive as his fealty to white supremacy in earlier decades.

In 1978, the national boycott against J. P. Stevens had no effect on Thurmond. A year earlier, Robert T. Stevens, longtime chairman of J. P. Stevens, hosted a reception for Thurmond at the Wings Club in the Biltmore Hotel in New York, a fund-raising kickoff for Thurmond's reelection campaign.[68] "He'll accept blacks now," an AFL-CIO field representative in South Carolina said of Thurmond in 1978, "but you still don't see Strom shaking hands with union people."[69]

Decades before the term "religious Right" was coined, Thurmond was a darling of Christian fundamentalists deeply involved in conservative political activity—leaders such as Carl McIntire, Billy James Hargis, and Bob Jones Sr., at whose 1968 funeral Thurmond served as a pallbearer.[70] He collaborated with them to promote conservative issues of God and country, whether it was the anti-muzzling crusade, school prayer politics, or his campaign against the "permissive society" inaugurated by the Warren Court.[71] The 1970s, however, represented a new period of ferment in conservative Christian politics.

In South Carolina, religious conservatives for the first time organized themselves to gain control over precinct- and state-level Republican proceedings. A network of fundamentalists at Bob Jones University flooded into Republican precinct meetings in 1976 to try to nominate Ronald Reagan.[72] "The Bob Jones people took over the Greenville County GOP precincts this past week," Harry Dent informed Thurmond in March 1976. A Bob Jones University faculty member had led the assault, and Dent urged Thurmond to "stay in good contact with him and BJ III"—the grandson of the school's founder.[73]

At the national level, new religious leaders emerged who were determined to expand the circle of conservative religious influence in American politics. Thurmond helped Bill Bright, founder of Campus Crusade for Christ, open his Christian embassy in Washington in 1976.[74] Another important leader was Pat Robertson, son of Senator Willis Robertson of Virginia, who bought a failing television station in Portsmouth, Virginia, in 1960 and rebranded it the Christian Broadcasting Network. Even more directly associated with New Right politics was Robertson's fellow Virginian Jerry Falwell, the pastor of Thomas Road Baptist Church in Lynchburg and the founder of Liberty University in 1971. In 1979, Falwell joined with a number of other New Right leaders to establish the Moral Majority. One of the dominant story lines from the 1980 presidential campaign was the essential role that religious conservatives played in helping elect Ronald Reagan.

That conservative Christians would prefer Reagan, a divorced Hollywood actor, over the Sunday-school-teaching Jimmy Carter seemed unlikely, yet Reagan's uncompromising stance on a variety of issues thrilled conservative Christians. At Bob Jones University, Reagan drew sustained applause when, referring to Vietnam, he pledged: "We will never again ask the young men of this country to fight in a war that its government is afraid to let them win."[75] In an appearance at Jerry Falwell's university in Lynchburg, Reagan complained that the nation should not have "expelled God from the classroom" and advocated "voluntary, non-sectarian prayer in our schools."[76]

This last issue, school prayer, was vital for the Christian Right in the late 1970s. Its importance dated to the Supreme Court's school prayer decisions of the early 1960s, yet the issue gained urgency with the political mobilization of conservative Christians. In 1979, Thurmond co-sponsored an amendment with Jesse Helms to deny the Supreme Court jurisdiction over cases relating to voluntary prayer. It was

268★STROM THURMOND'S AMERICA

a tactic straight out of the segregationist playbook. Thurmond had proposed countless amendments to limit Supreme Court jurisdiction over school desegregation in the 1950s and '60s. *NBC Nightly News* noted the debate's roots in a "nineteenth century states' rights doctrine."[77] Yet the amendment received surprising support. An initial measure passed 47–37, though Senate leaders were later able to attach it to another bill that had little chance of passage.[78] Thurmond called the vote "one of the most wholesome actions that had been taken in the Senate since I have been in Congress."[79]

Closely related to school prayer was the defense of private Christian schools from government regulation, an issue that showed, once again, how closely the politics of the New Right were connected with the Old. In the 1960s and '70s, school desegregation, in combination with the school prayer decisions, had led to explosive growth in private schools across the nation, but particularly in the South. Jerry Falwell, for example, had established a Christian school, Lynchburg Christian Academy, in 1967 as an extension of his church's ministry. By the late 1970s, the defense of Christian schools from IRS requirements mandating desegregation would become a vital issue in fueling conservative Christian mobilization. Richard Viguerie claimed that the IRS controversy over church schools "kicked the sleeping dog . . . It was the spark that ignited the religious Right's involvement in real politics."[80]

The church school controversy had a complicated history, one in which Thurmond played a conspicuous role. To their defenders, church schools provided a Christian alternative at a time when the Supreme Court was eviscerating religious devotion in public schools. To their critics, the schools were havens for bitter-end segregationists determined to resist school integration at any cost. In many cases, the schools were founded for a mix of racial and religious reasons, as Thurmond as much as admitted in a 1967 newsletter celebrating the rise of "independent, non-governmental schools" in South Carolina that embrace "simple prayers to God in school" and "regional ideals and values."[81] In 1967, Thurmond did not have to spell out the "regional ideals" under assault.[82]

By 1970, the Nixon administration's policy on the tax-exempt status of new private schools represented a contentious subplot in administration debates over the southern strategy. In January, a federal court issued an injunction barring the IRS from granting tax exemptions to new private schools in Mississippi. Moderate officials in HEW and the Justice Department urged Nixon to get out in front of the issue by instituting a new policy banning exemptions for racially discriminatory schools.[83] Thurmond and other southerners railed against the injunction.[84] In the end, Nixon announced a policy denying tax exemptions in July 1970, but he softened the political fallout by having the IRS delay rulings on fifty private schools until after the 1970 midterm elections.[85]

Nixon's decision to deny tax exemptions to new private schools flabbergasted Thurmond. He was convinced that forces inside the administration were trying to push him to break with the president.[86] But Thurmond underestimated Nixon's trickiness. He was quickly placated when it became clear that southern private schools need not actually desegregate to gain approval by the IRS. All they had to do was adopt a written policy of nondiscrimination.[87]

In 1975, civil rights groups tried to counter the Nixon administration's trickiness. They pressed the IRS to do more to ensure that private schools receiving exemptions were not actually discriminating. This process culminated in 1978 when the Carter administration issued a new set of procedures to determine whether or not private schools qualified for tax-exempt status. The new policy provoked outrage among conservative Christians, who charged Carter with establishing "racial quotas." Some 120,000 letters flooded into the IRS—"more than we've ever received on any other proposal," according to one IRS official.[88] Another 400,000 letters were sent to members of Congress.

Thurmond denounced the new procedures during IRS hearings in December 1978, an event covered by CBS and NBC evening news. He described the measures as strict racial quotas, which, he pointed out, the Supreme Court had outlawed in its recent *Bakke* decision, a case involving a white man, Allan Bakke, who sued the University of California for reverse discrimination in medical school admissions.[89] The church school controversy fit perfectly with an emerging conservative narrative of hardworking, God-fearing white Americans victimized by "reverse racism." In addition to Allan Bakke, there was the case of Brian Weber, a lab analyst at a Louisiana aluminum plant. He sued his union and employer for instituting a job-training program according to guidelines established by the Equal Employment Opportunity Commission that, Weber alleged, discriminated against white workers.[90]

In defending church schools, Thurmond made no reference to his support in the 1950s and '60s of "segregation academies," nor to his vehement fights against the very civil rights laws that had precipitated affirmative action programs. His protest was not about thwarting desegregation, he made a point of establishing: "It is impossible for a reasonable man to argue against that." His objection was that the IRS procedure set up a "complicated affirmative action program complete with percentage quotas of certain approved 'minorities,' discriminatory scholarship programs and hiring policies."[91]

In 1980, the Republican Party platform would contain a pledge to "halt the unconstitutional regulatory vendetta launched by Mr. Carter's IRS Commissioner against independent schools."[92] At his appearance that year at Bob Jones University, which was involved in ongoing litigation against the IRS over the tax-exempt ban, Ronald Reagan denounced the IRS for establishing "racial quotas" that simply reversed the injustices of the Jim Crow South. "You do not alter the evil character of racial quotas simply by changing the color of the beneficiary," he said.[93] Weeks before Reagan's inauguration, a federal appeals court reversed a lower-court decision that had granted Bob Jones tax-exempt status, setting the stage for a showdown in the Supreme Court.[94]

Thurmond remained closely involved in the matter, which in January 1982 erupted into one of the most divisive racial issues of Reagan's presidency. The Reagan administration announced that it would no longer deny tax-exempt status to private schools that practiced racial discrimination, and it notified the Supreme Court that it was restoring tax-exempt status to Bob Jones University, whose appeal was pending before the Court.[95] Reagan officials justified the decision on legal grounds, arguing that it corrected overly broad discretion that the government had claimed to deny tax exemptions. Thurmond, who along with Jesse Helms had met with Reagan officials to urge them to reverse the policy, applauded the decision for ending "a decade of trampling on religious and private civil rights."[96] It was a measure of the administration's obliviousness not only to African American concerns but also to the history of segregated schooling in the South that it was actually blindsided by the uproar that ensued. Critics, aghast that the government was proposing a restoration of tax exemptions to dozens of schools formed explicitly to avoid public school desegregation, charged the administration with supporting "tax-exempt hate."[97]

Only four days after the initial policy reversal, an embarrassed Reagan announced that he was calling for legislation to ban the practice that his administration had just made possible. His supporters on the religious Right felt betrayed, but Reagan officials quickly realized the political danger in being so closely tied to segregationist politics.[98] Yet it is not as though Thurmond or his fellow southerners had led Reagan and other conservatives down some primrose path. Denunciations of "racial quotas" and charges of "reverse racism" had been standard conservative talking points for years, for southerners and non-southerners alike. The church school controversy simply laid bare how shortsighted and self-serving such talk actually was.

For all the continuities between the Old and the New Right in the 1970s, some things were new—critical developments that explain the evolution in both Thurmond's politics and the politics of the Right. They involved not so much ideology or issues as technology and tactics.

Direct-mail political marketing was an important technological innovation. It did not originate in the 1970s, but it became more sophisticated and, thanks to changes in election law, a standard part of American politics by decade's end. In 1974, in the wake of Watergate, Congress enacted new campaign finance laws that limited the amount of individual donations. Direct-mail campaigns, tailored to narrow, specific issues that touched a nerve, became a critical tool for mobilizing massive numbers of small donations. As they tracked the responses, direct-mail marketers refined lists of names that they could count on for donations for particular causes or candidates.

Political operatives on the right and the left utilized direct mail, but no one did more to harness the power of the new technology than the conservative political activist Richard Viguerie. A native of Houston, Viguerie went to work for Young Americans for Freedom in the early 1960s and in 1965 founded the Richard A. Viguerie Company, a direct-mail marketing firm specializing in conservative political causes. He started the business by mining campaign records to find the names and addresses of the 12,500 people who had donated $50 or more to Barry Goldwater's presidential campaign. Viguerie quickly developed a stable of right-wing candidates for whom he raised money.[99]

Direct mail provided Viguerie with an end run around the traditional news media, the liberal bias of which was an article of faith for the Right, Old and New alike. It afforded conservative candidates an independent base of funds, helping them avoid being "neutered" by the more moderate Republican Party. A single mailing was unlikely to return enough donations to break even, but with multiple "prospect" or "acquisition" mailings a direct-mail campaign developed lists of potential donors, who could be added to a "house list" that could generate much higher returns when needed at election time. Contributors were customers, and marketers had to recognize their "lifetime value."[100]

Thurmond employed Viguerie's direct-mail firm to raise money for both his 1972 and his 1978 campaigns. Viguerie's approach represented the future of conservative politics, indeed of politics generally, which would be based on polling, targeted mailing, and increasingly sophisticated use of modern techniques. Thurmond was too indebted to his style of politicking to learn new tricks, and he would not need to before he finally left office. But he was not averse to trying. He gave Viguerie a chance but was simply unimpressed with the results.

Viguerie urged candidates that he represented to become identified with single issues pushed by an array of conservative PACs. Several years before a candidate was up for reelection, his firm would send out mailings from a PAC with a cover letter from the candidate. This was the prospect mailing through which Viguerie built a candidate's house list. In 1977, Viguerie's firm prepared a mailing to go out over Thurmond's signature for a group called Americans Against Union Control of Government, a division of the Public Service Research Council, a conservative PAC. The issue perfectly blended Thurmond's antilabor, pro-military politics. In the cover letter proposed by Viguerie, Thurmond would warn of "a handful of union bosses seizing virtual control over our military forces and even the entire federal bureaucracy." Viguerie urged Thurmond to let his firm send the mailings to conservatives outside South Carolina. It would help develop "a list of people who will respond to Senator Thurmond's signature," explained W. Michael Gretschel, vice president at Viguerie's company. "These names will be held separately as a prime prospect list to be used in our fundraising in Senator Thurmond's reelection campaign." Even though in this first mailing the donations coming in would be for the Public Service Research Council, not for Thurmond's reelection campaign, Viguerie's firm believed the mailing would "greatly facilitate the generation of net income to the reelection fund."[101]

This was an example of what Viguerie would later describe as "supply side" fund-raising. The Old Right, he said, "tended to see the conservative movement as a pie with a fixed size. Adding new organizations and causes meant all the existing groups (run by Old Right leaders) would get a smaller share." New Right leaders talked about growing the pie, Viguerie said, "allowing everyone's slice of the pie to grow along with the overall movement."[102]

Thurmond did not buy it. He told Viguerie to kill the mailing and to make sure that nothing was sent out on behalf of any organization other than his finance committee.[103] Ten days earlier, Thurmond had written to Philip Crane, head of the American Conservative Union, to stop the organization's Panama Canal letter-writing campaign that was using his name. He had authorized one mailing, but fifty-two had gone out. It was "completely inexcusable," Thurmond fumed, and he was now having trouble raising money for his reelection campaign because of the saturation mailing. "I have received numerous letters from people informing of the excessive solicitations they have received from me," he said.[104]

Viguerie talked about supply-side methods, but Thurmond still believed in retail politics. That was his approach in his 1978 reelection campaign. For fund-raising, he relied on Sunbelt corporate interests and conservative networks in New York and Los Angeles, but also on the hundreds of friends and supporters in South Carolina he had amassed over his long career. Thurmond toured around South Carolina, rushing from small town to small town, shaking hands and talking with the people. It was his favorite part of the job.

Thurmond's approach contrasted with that of his southern conservative colleague Jesse Helms, who by decade's end had emerged as one of the most powerful figures in conservative politics. Direct-mail marketing allowed Helms to skip some of the hands-on campaigning, which he did not enjoy nearly as much as Thurmond. Helms marveled at Thurmond's zest for the campaign trail. He recounted the story of Thurmond stumping for him in North Carolina in 1972. After four long events on a sticky summer's day, the exhausted Helms retired to his hotel room only to look out the window and see Thurmond, nineteen years his senior, out for a late-night jog.[105]

Helms and Thurmond were in lockstep on practically every issue in the 1970s, yet they were polar opposites when it came to fund-raising and elections. More than anyone, Helms embraced the techniques of the New Right. Exactly because he hated campaigning and fund-raising, he delegated the tasks to the directors of his own political action committee, the Congressional Club, based in Raleigh with a permanent staff of 40 (150 in an election year) and an annual budget that by 1980 had reached $5 million. The Congressional Club represented the state of the art in aggressive, media-savvy, direct-mail-driven politics. Helms was the honorary chairman, but the organization was run by Tom Ellis, chairman, and the treasurer, Carter Wrenn—"two of the most effective New Right leaders in America," according to Viguerie.[106] Helms's organization raised nearly $7 million for his 1978 reelection campaign, a phenomenal sum that almost doubled the previous record for Senate campaign fund-raising.[107]

The Helms camp channeled this bounty into sophisticated, poll-driven television ads, a great number of them attacks against his opponents. Helms had spent a long time as a television editorialist in North Carolina, and he understood the power of the medium. Like other aspects of conservative politics in the 1970s, New Right political strategy represented a complex mix of the new and the old. The ads were on TV now, instead of radio or in newspapers. Their themes were driven not by savvy campaign operatives but by subcontracted, scientific polling firms. Yet at its heart lay a kind of neo-Bleasism, an impulse to turn political opponents into mortal enemies while appealing to the basest instincts of the voting public. The strategy reached its nadir in the racially charged attack ads that Helms used in his 1990 campaign against Harvey Gantt, the African American former mayor of Charlotte and, incidentally, the man who had integrated Thurmond's alma mater, Clemson, in the early 1960s. One ad showed a white man dressed in a red flannel shirt crumpling up a letter in frustration. The camera focused only on the man's hands, his wedding ring showing, while the narrator explained: "You needed that job. You were the best qualified. But they had to give it to a minority because of a racial quota. Is that really fair? Harvey Gantt says it is."[108]

Strom Thurmond was a living link between the racist demagoguery of the Jim Crow South and the inflammatory tactics of modern conservatives, yet he himself never resorted to the neo-Bleasism of Jesse Helms. Thurmond's Bleasism was of a different vintage. Helms slowly usurped Thurmond's role as the Senate's number one bomb thrower, and Thurmond morphed into an almost nostalgic figure of an older, simpler, more personal kind of politics. The roughest edges he had begun to soften back in 1971. Yet the new Thurmond that emerged in the 1980s—and continued to legislate, win elections, and dole out favors to South Carolina constituents into the twenty-first century—had evolved further still and, in doing so, became a controversial symbol of the vast changes that had overtaken the South and the nation.

★ ★

PART FOUR

MYTHS, MEMORIES, AND LEGACIES

★ ★

13

OL' STROM IN THE MODERN SOUTH
(1978–1990)

The 1980s were a decade of triumph for Strom Thurmond and the modern conservative movement alike. Thurmond became revered, a living legend at home and a senator respected by his colleagues for his pragmatism and leadership.[1] For many people, the strident, humorless Thurmond of old became a distant memory. In an age of blow-dried, media-driven campaigns, Thurmond was lionized for embodying an old-school politics of handshakes and thank-you notes, political favors and barbecues, and earnest inquiries about friends and kin, thereby obscuring, though never erasing, his older racist image.[2]

The Thurmond that emerged in the 1980s actually began in 1978 with his Senate reelection campaign. He earned the sobriquet "Ol' Strom" in part because of the juxtaposition with his forty-year-old opponent, Charles "Pug" Ravenel. News stories pegged the race as a "battle of the generations" with Thurmond playing the role of the "Old Pro in a New South."[3] Pug Ravenel was handsome, young, and idealistic—and the most serious challenger Thurmond had faced in his Senate career.

Despite possessing a venerable South Carolina name, Ravenel had grown up in relatively humble surroundings in Charleston. He won a football scholarship to Harvard, where he became a standout quarterback, and later got a job on Wall Street. Ravenel returned to South Carolina in 1973 and with his energy and ambition became the state's biggest political phenomenon since Strom Thurmond came home from

World War II. Ravenel immediately took on the state's Democratic establishment. He won the 1974 Democratic gubernatorial primary and was all set for the customary drubbing of the Republican nominee before the state supreme court ruled him ineligible for not having fulfilled South Carolina's antiquated residency requirement. He was waiting for another shot at governor when he submitted to the urgings of Jimmy Carter's political team to take on Thurmond in the Senate race.[4]

Though his name recognition was nowhere near Thurmond's, Ravenel had momentum on his side. Republicans were coming off an election in which a southern Democrat had won the White House and southern Republicans had lost 20 percent of their seats in Congress and 30 percent in state legislatures.[5] Thurmond was one of three conservative southern stalwarts up for reelection; Jesse Helms and John Tower were the others. It was 1950 all over again, only the roles were reversed. That year three liberal southerners had run for reelection, their races a barometer for the New Deal in the postwar South; Thurmond had been the only conservative challenger who had failed to break through. The 1978 midterm elections would be a referendum on Sunbelt Republicanism and the conservative insurgency in the GOP.

The Ravenel campaign wanted to portray Thurmond as an out-of-touch racist from the state's sordid past, yet Thurmond kept defying the image. He moved his family back to Columbia more than a year before the election and enrolled his eldest daughter in a racially integrated public school. Nancy gave speeches and made appearances across the state, writing lengthy memos to her husband about contacts that he should shore up. No whim of a South Carolinian was too small for Nancy and Strom to attend to. Strom was to call the director of the Greenville Zoo concerning a Clemson alumni group that wanted to buy a tiger to double as a sideline mascot at football games. A high school student named for Thurmond had sent him a letter a few years earlier but never received a response, an oversight Strom corrected immediately.[6]

Thurmond campaigned with his children in an RV that his kids dubbed "Strom Trek." The four youngsters wore matching customized T-shirts that read, "Vote for My Daddy."[7] The personal campaigning and the ubiquitous photographs of Thurmond with his young family or performing some physical stunt (at his six-year-old son's birthday party at a fire station, the seventy-five-year-old Thurmond slid down the fire pole three times so that photographers could get the right shot) were all designed to counter the fact that Thurmond was more than three decades older than his opponent.

As the race tightened in the spring of 1978, Thurmond's young campaign aide Lee Atwater helped craft attack ads against Ravenel. Atwater, whose rough political tactics would win him infamy as the manager of George Bush's 1988 presidential campaign, had met Thurmond as a child trick-or-treating in Aiken. He became a devotee after working as a Thurmond intern in Washington during college. He poured himself into Republican Party organizing in the 1970s and insinuated himself into Thurmond's 1978 reelection campaign, spinning his role after the fact as Thurmond's campaign manager. Atwater would later recall Thurmond's 1978 campaign as formative in developing his aggressive tactics. The most effective advertisement that year came from a clipping passed along by Atwater's fellow Republican operative Roger Stone. It reported on a Ravenel fund-raiser in New York where the candidate declared he wanted to be the third senator from New York.[8]

The line was damaging enough by itself, yet it was only one weapon in a larger arsenal that Atwater used to attack Ravenel as an elitist liberal outsider. The Thurmond campaign charged that Ravenel got the bulk of his money from outside South Carolina. It was an entirely disingenuous attack; both Thurmond and Ravenel received two-thirds of their campaign funds from outside the state.[9] Thurmond was not unaware of the deceit, as shown by a line edit he made in one of the fund-raising letters that Richard Viguerie sent out. The draft letter had Thurmond telling supporters that unlike Ravenel he did not have any "rich New York friends" who could finance his campaign. Thurmond changed it to "rich liberal friends." His own rich New York friends—Robert T. Stevens among them—had held a fund-raiser for him at the Biltmore Hotel just the previous year.[10]

The matchup looked great on paper, and the polls seemed to tighten in the spring. Thurmond campaigned so hard, as always, that it looked for a time as if he were running scared. But the race was never really close. Thurmond had a foolproof electoral strategy mapped out as early as 1975. His campaign estimated that voter turnout in an off-year election would be 71 percent white and 29 percent black. If Thurmond could combine 10 percent of the black vote—a highly optimistic number—with 72 percent of the white vote, he would win with 55 percent of the total. The key for Thurmond was the same as it had been in 1972 and would remain in every campaign he waged in the post–Voting Rights Act era: not to antagonize black voters, which would drive up black turnout and force him to win an uncomfortably high percentage of the white vote.[11]

The campaign's first survey goal, as outlined in an operations manual, was to find "an issue which has high emotional appeal to blacks and on which you can comfortably capitalize."[12] Thurmond found several. He had already helped Matthew Perry, a prominent South Carolina African American leader, win appointment to the U.S. Court of Military Appeals. Now he backed him for the opening at the U.S. district court in South Carolina. Thurmond co-sponsored a bill to provide free medicines and drugs for the elderly and placed a high-profile call congratulating the former civil rights activist John Lewis after he was appointed director of a federal voter education project.[13] He also took action behind the scenes. Thurmond made it clear that no Republican should run for secretary of state. Jim Clyburn, a rising African American star in South Carolina's Democratic Party, was vying for his party's nomination for that post (he ended up narrowly losing the primary). Thurmond wanted to avoid a hotly contested statewide race in which a white Republican challenged a charismatic black candidate. It might increase black voter turnout, Pug Ravenel's best hope for an upset.[14]

The most significant legislative action Thurmond took was his support for voting rights for the District of Columbia, which Ted Kennedy called "the civil rights issue of 1978."[15] Thurmond had voted against D.C. voting rights twice before, in 1960 and in 1973, yet in July 1978 he endorsed the plan in a letter to two prominent black leaders in South Carolina.[16] Evidence from his campaign files suggests that, once again, Thurmond's motive was to suppress black voter turnout. A top Thurmond staffer had tried to establish contact with Jesse Jackson, a South Carolina native, through an African American–owned public relations firm that worked closely with the Republican National Committee. A few weeks after Thurmond announced his position on the D.C.

vote, a representative from the firm wrote to Thurmond congratulating him. She confirmed that "Jesse Jackson will *not* be going into South Carolina to campaign for Pug Ravenel."[17]

Thurmond's efforts had an impact back home, as measured by the reaction of Isaac Williams, the head of the South Carolina NAACP. "We don't care what the senator did in the '40s and '50s but how he is representing us in 1978," Williams said. If voters "just try to punish a politician for the sins of the past, what does it profit him to improve?"[18] The biblical language was notable. South Carolinians, black and white, were accustomed to narratives of sin and redemption, and the black testimony quoted during the 1978 campaign that exonerated Thurmond of his racist past had a scriptural bent, a variation of the Gospel maxim "Ye shall know them by their fruits" (Matthew 7:16).

A common trope emerged in news reporting about Ol' Strom: the African American constituent, often a female figure, granting the senator absolution for his segregationist sins, the indulgence paid via Thurmond's devoted constituent services. In 1972 it had been the civil rights activist Victoria DeLee, who, after Thurmond helped her secure a federal grant, told reporters that she was "for the man who can get the job done."[19] In 1996, it was the eighty-one-year-old Esther Hunter, who showed up at a campaign stop in Union to thank Thurmond for the condolence letter he sent after her husband passed (Thurmond had had staffers scanning South Carolina obituaries and writing condolence cards for years, a practice begun at Walter Brown's suggestion back in 1955 that by now extended to black constituents). "You can't pay attention to everything you hear," she said. "People say, you know, he didn't like black people. But he knows I'm 100 percent black and he sure did pay me respect."[20] In 1978 it was Darley Cochran, a black woman from Clarendon County. She thanked Thurmond for help getting funds for a park and sewage-treatment facility in her black-majority town. "I'm forgetting about the party," she told reporters who asked how she could support the man who had fled the Democrats in 1964 over civil rights. "I'm for the man that's getting the job done."[21] The direct echo of DeLee almost suggests a script.

Even after Thurmond's death, the trope was echoed in the revelations of his African American daughter, Essie Mae Washington-Williams. She told of how he had helped send her to college and had secretly supported her through her years as a single mother in Los Angeles. One wonders whether Thurmond's strategy for dealing with black voters—keeping them quiet through his constituent services and other favors—was born not from Harry Dent's calculation following the Albert Watson campaign of 1970 but rather from Thurmond's own furtive experience with his African American daughter, who remained quiescent all those years as he regularly provided her with material support.

News articles talked of Thurmond perhaps as much as doubling the percentage of black support that he received in 1972, which reportedly had been 8 percent.[22] What they did not say, however, was that nobody had a precise sense of the percentage of the black vote that Thurmond had actually won in 1972, nor the percentage that he would win in 1978. Reporters simply repeated rough estimates in stories filed by other reporters, creating an echo chamber in which journalists suggested that Thurmond might actually win meaningful double-digit support among blacks. The most accurate study of the 1978 midterm elections, however, would estimate Thurmond's support among black voters at a mere 3 percent.[23]

African Americans' wariness about Ol' Strom persisted. It could hardly have been otherwise with Republicans in South Carolina bragging to reporters about how Thurmond's new approach had "anesthetized" the black vote.[24] Thurmond won endorsement from the caucus of black mayors—all ten of them, a group uniquely dependent on his office's help for their political well-being. Yet the caucus of black state legislators called Thurmond "an embarrassment to South Carolina."[25] The effort and staging undertaken to keep black voters home reflected the fact that Thurmond knew well how weakly they supported his candidacy.

No image from the 1978 campaign resonated more powerfully than the news of Thurmond accompanying his daughter to her first day at a racially integrated public school in Columbia. National commentators hailed the scene as a "sign of the political times," a "richly revealing" symbol that said something "quite wonderful about how much the principles—and the politics—of this nation have changed in less than a third of a century."[26]

The real story was more complicated. In the 1970s, public schools in metropolitan Columbia had settled into a pattern followed by count-less communities across the country, north and south, in which white flight to the suburbs left predominantly black city schools and mostly white suburban ones. In the early 1970s, African Americans in Colum-bia along with a handful of white liberal allies struggled to gain seats on local school boards to address the situation but were blocked by a slate of Republican candidates who preserved the status quo.[27] When Thurmond moved his family back to Columbia in preparation for the 1978 campaign, he knew how it would look had he enrolled his daugh-ter in private school or in one of the white-majority suburban schools. A strategy memo written less than two weeks after his daughter started classes made explicit the political implications. "Heavy emphasis should be placed on your family, i.e., your faith and support of the public school system," it read. "You are going to get the private school vote anyway."[28]

The news coverage of Thurmond's daughter's first day and the ora-tions on what it symbolized for the South's history set the tone both for the 1978 election and for the image of Ol' Strom that predominated for the remainder of his career. Only one news item followed up on the story a year later. In October 1979, a reporter noted in passing that after his successful reelection, Thurmond had moved his family to the Washington area. His daughter was now enrolled in the private Potomac School in northern Virginia.[29]

In 1979, all three Sunbelt conservatives—Thurmond, Helms, and Tower—returned to the Senate, the rightward march of the Republican Party undiminished. The conservative trend over the previous decade and a half culminated the following year with the presidential nomina-tion of Ronald Reagan. Thurmond had endorsed the former Democrat John Connally early in the primaries. It was surprising given his staunch conservatism and his support for Reagan in 1976. Yet Con-nally had gone out of his way to help Thurmond in 1978, when Reagan had been tardy with fund-raising help, and early on, Reagan operatives named the freshman congressman Carroll Campbell as his South Car-olina campaign chairman.[30] Campbell had occasionally indicated an interest in Thurmond's Senate seat when it came up for grabs in 1984.[31]

Perhaps Thurmond spied a scenario for reprising his 1968 heroics. Connally's chances hinged on his performance in South Carolina, the first southern primary. If Big John and Big Strom could win the Palmetto State, it might stop Reagan's momentum, throwing the race wide open, and, in the process, position Thurmond once again as the indispensable man for the GOP standard-bearer.[32]

But it was not to be. Thurmond wrangled a Connally endorsement out of Bob Jones III, and the former governor James Edwards pitched in as well, yet Connally provided weak resistance to Reagan in the South Carolina primary. Connally withdrew from the race the next day. Thurmond endorsed Reagan the day after that.[33]

Ronald Reagan's victory over Jimmy Carter in the general election was a watershed moment in twentieth-century American politics. Reagan brought with him a Republican majority in the Senate, giving control of that body to the GOP for the first time since 1954. A generation of American contrarians, steeped in outsiderness, now found itself in the seat of power. Thurmond joined in the jubilation among conservative Republicans.

The Republican takeover of the Senate meant that Thurmond was in line to become chairman of the Senate Judiciary Committee, the first chairmanship of his twenty-five-year Senate career. He would also be president pro tempore of the Senate, an honorary position held by the longest-ranking member of the majority party, and third in line to succeed the president. Thurmond had an official seal designed for the office of president pro tempore (one had not existed previously), and to reporters he declared himself "the third most powerful man in the world."[34] As one of the most powerful committee chairs in Washington, he, along with Nancy, became a sought-after guest on the Washington social scene, sometimes attending three or four parties an evening.[35]

Even more, it was exhilarating to think of Reagan's victory as a vindication of the states' rights politics that had defined Thurmond's career. Reagan himself had invoked the phrase during at least one southern campaign stop, provoking no small amount of controversy.[36] During the campaign, a younger generation of southern Republicans celebrated Thurmond as a kind of John the Baptist of conservative Republicanism. At an event in Mississippi, Thurmond told a crowd of a thousand Reagan supporters, "We want that federal government to keep their filthy hands off the rights of the states." As he left the platform, the Mississippi congressman Trent Lott, the soon-to-be minority whip in the House of Representatives, told the crowd, "You know, if we had elected this man 30 years ago, we wouldn't be in the mess we are today."[37]

Speaking to reporters the day after the election, Thurmond talked about dusting off measures that he had introduced back in the 1950s. In a session with reporters in his hideaway office just off the Senate floor, he discussed a bill that he planned to introduce to remove "the entire field of education from the jurisdiction of the Supreme Court."[38] Presumably, it would have ended busing and restored school prayer, two pet concerns of social conservatives. No reporter picked up on it at the time, yet legislation to remove education from Supreme Court jurisdiction had actually been one of the first bills that Thurmond had introduced when he came to the Senate back in 1955, a measure that had been drafted by Robert Figg, his old Dixiecrat adviser and a member of the defense team in the *Brown* case.[39]

Thurmond also talked about amending parts of the Voting Rights Act, repeating arguments that he had made in the 1960s about how the bill discriminated against southern states. During the lame-duck session of Congress, he and Jesse Helms pushed a measure that would bar the Justice Department from ordering busing as a remedy for racial imbalances. With Republicans pointing to the election returns as a mandate, the measure narrowly passed before being vetoed by President Carter. President-elect Reagan said that he would sign such busing language into law.[40]

"President Reagan ran on practically the same platform that I ran on in 1948," Thurmond boasted to a reporter for the Jackson, Mississippi, *Clarion-Ledger* a few months after the inauguration. "Less federal intervention, less federal control and less federal spending. I'm very pleasantly surprised. I didn't know if it would come in my lifetime."[41]

It was a remarkable statement, one that required a great deal of selective memory. Thurmond elided the heart of his Dixiecrat stump speeches, the denunciations of a litany of civil rights proposals—the FEPC, anti-poll-tax legislation, antilynching legislation—all of which in one guise or another had become federal law, and all laws that Congress had passed at least two years before Ronald Reagan ever won public office. Yet even in 1948 the Dixiecrat "platform" had been a malleable thing for Thurmond. Here, in retrospect, Thurmond repeated the trick he had pulled in Houston in his speech officially accepting the Dixiecrat nomination, laying aside the script prepared by his South Carolina advisers with its standard segregationist appeals, trying to reshape his regional politics and once again claim the mantle of "States' Rights Americans."

If Thurmond overreached in tying Reagan's win to the singular act of his political career, he was not wholly wrong. He could claim a share in the conservative revolution and more than a few similarities to Reagan's career. Thurmond and Reagan both had grown up as Democrats and had voted for Franklin Roosevelt every chance they could. Thurmond's break with the party came sooner, was sharper than Reagan's, and was rooted in a regional white supremacist politics that was a time and a place apart from Reagan's experience. Yet they underwent a similar conversion to the antilabor, free enterprise politics that was so important to GOP conservatism. For Thurmond, it began in the late 1940s, pitching South Carolina relocation sites to northern executives, and expanded in the 1950s with his budding political friendships with conservative businessmen like Charles Daniel and Roger Milliken. For Reagan, it was his years in the 1950s as a spokesman for General Electric, where he served a virtual "apprenticeship" under the pioneering conservative businessman Lemuel Boulware.[42] By 1964—by which time the smartest of the Dixiecrats had learned the value of talking about "conservative" rather than "states' rights" Americans—the differences between how Reagan and Thurmond viewed the civil rights movement, its shady connections to Communist radicals, or its threat to law and order were ones of degree, not kind.

There was a political alchemy at the heart of Reagan's persona that was key to his remarkable ascent in American politics: he had an uncanny ability to take racially conservative positions that when uttered by Thurmond or any other southerner sounded like warmed-over segregationist subterfuge, yet in Reagan's voice—with his movie star glamour, wit, and charm—sounded like principled conservatism.

Robert Figg, one of Thurmond's oldest political friends, understood it well. He and Walter Brown got together after Reagan's election, when Brown was putting together material for a political memoir that he planned to write. A research assistant recorded the conversation and later typed up a transcript. The old friends and former Dixiecrat advisers rehashed in jocular detail their work on Thurmond's 1946 and 1948 campaigns, the race against Olin Johnston, and several other pieces of South Carolina political lore. When they had exhausted the past, they turned briefly to the present.

"You know," Figg said to Brown, "you one time made the statement that someday, somebody's going to run for president on the platform that this is a white man's country? Well, I never heard of Reagan saying that, but the election turned out that way, didn't it?"

"Yeah," said Brown, "now I'm afraid though that he's going to turn around and kiss ass . . ."

"Oh, no," Figg interrupted; "if he just does business with the ones who support him, he can't do us much harm."[43]

Thurmond's preening in the aftermath of the election created political trouble. It jeopardized an election strategy on which both Reagan and Thurmond relied. As mapped out during his campaign by his chief strategist, John Sears, and his pollster Richard Wirthlin, it was not essential that Reagan win a significant number of black votes so much as he not be perceived as "anti-black." Such an image would have jeopardized his support among moderate Republicans and college-educated suburban swing voters.[44] Thurmond was in a similar position back home, though in South Carolina, with its large black population, the real concern was about offending the black community and having to face a large turnout. The danger was dramatized in a special congressional election in Mississippi in July 1981. Reports of Thurmond and the Reagan administration rolling back the Voting Rights Act had led to a massive black voter turnout that helped elect a Democrat and squelched the recent Republican trend in the state.[45] Equally important was the knowledge that Thurmond's old reactionary image could sap his power and effectiveness as Judiciary chairman. It was why his aides slowly began to rein in their boss in the wake of the election.

At a press conference where Thurmond discussed his opposition to voting rights reauthorization, one of his aides, Dennis Shedd, stood quietly in the back of the room, shaking his head. Shedd saw how easily Thurmond's statements fed the image of the unreconstructed segregationist. When the largely retired Harry Dent read the coverage of Thurmond's remarks, he was equally concerned. "You've got to move," he said, calling up his old boss; "it's time to go with the flow."[46]

The advice must have rankled Thurmond. He had already moved, he might have thought. Thurmond told reporters to look at his recent record. "I'm against discrimination," he said.[47] He had employed black staff for almost a decade and had reached out to black constituents. A line he had developed during his 1978 reelection campaign had become his standard response when asked about his evolution on race: "When I was governor, the law said the races should be separate . . . But now the law is different, customs are different, public opinion has changed and it's an entirely different situation."[48]

The answer actually represented an improvement over earlier efforts. In 1974, Thurmond had told Sally Quinn, a reporter writing a profile of the Thurmonds for the *Washington Post* Style section, "I never was a segregationist. I don't know how I got such a reputation as a segregationist. I think my position was just misunderstood. I guess it was because when I was the governor of South Carolina it was my duty to uphold the law and the law required segregation, so I was just doing my duty. You know there's a Strom Thurmond High School in South Carolina that's 70 per cent black. It was named after me."[49] Quinn was making a name for herself in Washington for her profile writing, particularly her ear for "self-immolating quotes."[50] It is hard to imagine a better example.

Thurmond's obfuscations frustrated even some of those closest to him. They knew that Thurmond had changed with the times, yet there remained an odd disconnect between his present and his past. At one point Dennis Shedd and Thurmond were working on a civil rights matter, and Thurmond gave his familiar defense, explaining that back then he was just following the law. "Well, Senator, did you ever think about *trying* to change the law?" Shedd asked. Thurmond looked at him blankly and quickly changed the subject.[51]

Thurmond would never provide his aides or posterity with any accounting of what he had believed in the past, why he had acted as he

did, and how his beliefs had changed. Nor would he ever apologize—
unlike some of the other segregationist warhorses from the earlier era,
George Wallace most notably. Such introspection was not a part of
Thurmond's nature; he prided himself on being resolute and purposeful. Yet more than anything, Thurmond never apologized because he
never felt any need to, either as a matter of principle or as a matter of
politics. When his advisers had suggested he alter his position in the
early 1970s for political advantage, he had done so immediately. He
would make a similar adjustment early in the Reagan administration.

The issue was the Voting Rights Act, one of the landmarks of
America's Second Reconstruction. Portions were set to expire in 1982.
Debate over reauthorization began a few months into the Reagan presidency.[52] Almost every newspaper article on the subject noted the outspoken position of the new Judiciary chairman. Thurmond believed
that if the legislation was to be extended, it should be done on a *nationwide* basis. His long-standing complaint had been with section 5,
the part requiring mainly southern states to gain approval from the
Justice Department before any changes in voting laws or procedures.[53]
Yet in October 1981, when the House of Representatives overwhelmingly passed a strengthened voting rights bill that permanently reau-
thorized section 5, Thurmond, joined by two other conservative
committee members, sent a letter to the president dispelling reports
that his committee would not give the legislation fair consideration.[54]
"The Voting Rights Act of 1965 has had a most salutary effect in increased voter participation," he wrote.[55] It was a notable statement for
the man who in 1965 described the act as "the most patently unconstitutional piece of legislation approved by the Congress since Reconstruction days."[56]

In a meeting with Republican leadership, the White House made it
clear that it wanted to avoid accusations that the GOP sought to weaken
the Voting Rights Act. A GOP strategist put it more bluntly: the Reagan administration position would be "just strong enough so that we
won't be called racists."[57] A White House memo in early November
suggested that Thurmond had gotten the message. "Senator Thurmond's actual position is probably a good deal more flexible than
his prior public statements may suggest," it read.[58] Throughout the
Judiciary Committee hearings, Thurmond reiterated his view that

section 5 should apply nationally—a move that voting rights supporters said was unfeasible and possibly unconstitutional—yet he also pushed a simpler bailout provision whereby affected jurisdictions could prove that they were not discriminating and be removed from the preclearance requirement. Never did he give any hint of resorting to the old parliamentary tricks from his massive resistance days. In fact, in March he cast a subcommittee vote in favor of continuing section 5 for ten years.[59]

For Reagan, voting rights were just one issue that threatened to damage his image. A memo from his aide Edwin Harper in March 1982 noted the "cumulative effect" of Reagan's position on a variety of issues important to black Americans—budget cuts, tax-exempt private schools, affirmative action, civil rights enforcement, and hiring black staffers. Reagan's actions had created "distrust and bitterness within the minority community," Harper wrote, and contributed to the image that Reagan was "engaged in a systematic effort to roll back civil rights achievements of the past."[60]

The most high-profile mishap occurred in January 1982 as the Judiciary Committee was about to begin hearings on the Voting Rights Act. That was when Reagan overturned the policy banning tax exemptions for racially discriminatory private schools. The ensuing uproar, and the administration's quick backtracking, put Reagan on the defensive on racial matters.

As for Thurmond, his determination not to play the villain was made plain when his home county of Edgefield became the focal point for voting rights abuses. The attention in Edgefield stemmed from a lawsuit in 1980 in which a federal judge whom Thurmond had nominated, Robert Chapman, sided with black plaintiffs who had charged that the Edgefield County Council's at-large voting process diluted black voting strength. Five days after the ruling, however, the Supreme Court issued a decision in a voting rights case in Mobile, Alabama, that caused Judge Chapman to vacate his order. In *Mobile v. Bolden* the Court ruled that it was not enough for plaintiffs to show that a voting plan had a discriminatory effect on elections; they must prove that a voting plan was "conceived or operated as a purposeful device to further racial discrimination."[61] The *Mobile* decision was at the heart of the voting rights debate in 1982. Should Congress endorse the "intent" standard in *Mobile* or return to the "effects" standard that had become an accepted part of the case law before *Mobile*?

In testimony before Thurmond's committee, Laughlin McDonald, director of the Southern Regional Office of the American Civil Liberties Union (ACLU) and a South Carolina native, cited the Edgefield case as an example of the kind of blatant discrimination that would be allowed under the *Mobile* precedent. Edgefield was Thurmond's home county, he noted, and the home of "Pitchfork" Ben Tillman. The county had "a long history of intentional discrimination in voting," McDonald said.[62]

It was easy to imagine an earlier day when Thurmond would have berated an ACLU lawyer who had the audacity to accuse Edgefieldians of wrongdoing, giving him the same hostile treatment meted out to LeRoy Collins, Thurgood Marshall, Abe Fortas, and others. Yet Shedd had prepped him for such moments. "Don't let 'em bait you. Don't let 'em bait you," he continually reminded his boss.[63] Thurmond began by asking McDonald if he lived in Atlanta.

"Yes, I do, Senator."

"I know the McDonald family in South Carolina."

"Yes, sir."

"They originally came from Winnsboro. Some moved to Chester, some to Greenwood, some to Columbia. Hayward McDonald is a State senator down there now."

"Yes, sir. He's my cousin, Your Honor."

"Who was your father?"

"Tom McDonald from Winnsboro."

"Tom is your father?"

"Yes, sir."

"Well, he was a good friend of mine."

"I know he was, Senator."

"We've tried cases together."

"Yes, sir."

"And I had the pleasure of appointing your mother to the State Hospital Board. She is a very lovely woman."

"And nothing has ever pleased her any more in her life, I might add, Senator, than that appointment. She speaks about it often to me."

The hearing room laughed warmly.

"I had just wondered if you were connected with the McDonalds there, because they are all very fine people, and friends of mine."

"Well, I appreciate that, Senator Thurmond."

"I have no questions. Thank you."[64]

Here was Ol' Strom on full display. Everyone expected the angry scold but instead got the sweet grandfather, the throwback politician who could tie together all the loose threads that connected his constituents. "I knew Senator Thurmond was a legend in his own time, but I didn't realize he knew everybody in the South," said Orrin Hatch, subcommittee chairman. Even McDonald was charmed: "I think he just got my vote when I move back to South Carolina."[65]

Thurmond's courteousness became part of his legend. His staff adored him for his quirky, old-fashioned manners. Thurmond would collect complimentary bottles of lotions and shampoos from hotel stays and bring them to his secretaries as "treats" (after a visit to China, he instructed staff to "come get you a Communist soap or some Communist shampoo"). Whereas other senators would race through the hallways with their heads down or talking to staff, Thurmond would wave, shake hands, and smile. He took time to regale the staff and visitors of colleagues with a funny story or odd remembrance. And always he would hand them a key chain, the South Carolina state flag on one side and Thurmond's name and the president pro tempore seal on the other.[66]

"I didn't know the Strom Thurmond from the 1940s," recalled Chris Kelley Cimko, one of Thurmond's press secretaries in the 1990s. "The Strom Thurmond I knew was warm, inspiring, smart, kind, a demanding boss, and the last gentleman I think I've known in my life."[67] People talked about funny and charming Ol' Strom, in part, to balance the other stories that everyone knew but that were impolite to talk about, tales about his segregationist past, the screeds against the *Brown* decision, or ugly remarks about Martin Luther King.

His friendliness was good politics, of course, as was the case with

Laughlin McDonald. It could also serve as a shield against the condescension that he sometimes encountered from certain colleagues, their wives, staff members, or visitors. Thurmond defied those who loathed him as a symbol of a South of unending horror and unmitigated injustice by being the nicest senator on Capitol Hill. In doing so, he breathed life into a rival mythology, one that white southerners had always invoked against their skeptics, that of the southern gentleman, the man of elaborate etiquette who was never rude even to the lowliest, who was particularly benevolent to the lowliest because he was a Christian.

These notions of paternalism Thurmond had inherited from his father, Will, whose obituary in the *Edgefield Advertiser* told of how he would absent himself from discussions with fellow whites to speak to a "colored man . . . inquiring earnestly about his work, expressing words of encouragement and always quietly giving him money to help carry on."[68] Strom received them without reflection or irony, and they shaped the way that he thought about himself and about his privilege and power amid the lowly whom he encountered each day: the African American janitors and elevator operators, the freshly scrubbed summer interns in their new dresses and navy blazers, the everyday Americans in shorts and T-shirts walking in their tour groups, thrilled to be in Washington and catch a glimpse of a living legend like Strom Thurmond.

In the voting rights battle, however, Thurmond would not be able to charm his way out of Edgefield's past. Later during the hearings Tom McCain, the African American head of the Edgefield County Democratic Party and the named plaintiff in the Edgefield voting rights case, testified before the Judiciary Committee of discriminatory practices in Edgefield and the need to strengthen voting rights legislation. McCain received sharp questions from Orrin Hatch about the necessity of altering section 2 language. Thurmond asked no questions.[69]

Instead, he read a statement in which he renounced his connection to Edgefield. "While it is true that I was born in Edgefield, I have not lived there in 35 years," he said. He made the point, he insisted, to clarify the record, not to "cast aspersion in any way on the people who live in Edgefield, of whom I am very proud." He recited the names of Edgefield luminaries, adding, at Shedd's insistence, two African American educators, and then attacked the Democratic congressman who represented Edgefield for not defending the county's honor.[70] He closed by minimizing the importance of the Edgefield voting rights case and excusing himself from the remainder of McCain's questioning. A Judiciary authorization bill needed his attention on the Senate floor.[71]

In May 1982, Senator Robert Dole of Kansas worked out a compromise on the nettlesome section 2 language and proposed a twenty-five-year extension of section 5. The Judiciary Committee adopted it with only Thurmond and three others voting against. Yet Thurmond joined all but one of his Judiciary Committee colleagues in voting to send the bill to the floor for consideration. Jesse Helms tried to use procedural methods to slow committee action, but it was Thurmond, of all people, who vowed to hold night sessions if necessary to get a final vote on the bill.[72]

In the end, Thurmond voted to strengthen the Voting Rights Act and extend section 5 for twenty-five years.[73] His vote reflected the same cold calculus shown by the Reagan administration in supporting the compromise bill. There was simply no political advantage for either of them in playing the heavy.

Thurmond made a similar calculation the following year when he backed a national holiday honoring Martin Luther King. Less than twenty years earlier, of course, Thurmond had called King a "notorious troublemaker and inter-meddler" and urged the FBI to work through his office to "expose" him.[74] During hearings on the proposed national holiday in 1979, Thurmond had invited guests such as the Georgia congressman Larry McDonald, who testified that King was undeserving of a holiday because of his "friendship and collaboration with totalitarian Communists and racists, but even more, his teaching of contempt for law and the legal process."[75] Yet in 1983, as Jesse Helms once again led a filibuster and denounced King as a Marxist, Thurmond quietly voted in favor of the King holiday.[76]

Throughout these years, Thurmond and Helms displayed strikingly different approaches to racial issues. Thurmond came to be seen as a pragmatist who accommodated himself to the new era. Helms was the ideologue who took over Thurmond's old role as the Senate's most embittered outsider. It was easy to forget that back in the 1950s and '60s, Thurmond was every bit as contentious as Helms was in the 1980s.

Whatever differences existed between the two in terms of temperament or ideology, the most significant had to do with the racial demographics of their respective states. The African American population was ten percentage points higher in South Carolina than in North Carolina (32 to 22 percent), and South Carolina blacks were registered to vote at a higher percentage, 61 percent compared with 49 percent.[77] In 1978, Thurmond's campaign estimated that African Americans would make up 29 percent of the electorate, whereas in North Carolina black voters tended to make up only 14 percent.[78] Helms was willing to write off the black vote and focus on unifying the white vote. Thurmond could not afford to be so cavalier, not when a motivated black community could make up as much as a third of the electorate. "Politicians know how to count and they don't want to start a campaign by throwing away 25 to 30 percent of the voters," observed the political scientist Merle Black.[79]

Given the security that the 1982 voting rights extension provided for black voters in the South, Thurmond's more moderate approach to racial issues seemed the wave of the future. Yet reapportionment battles in the 1980s and '90s were often marked by an odd alliance of white Republicans and black Democrats who worked together to concentrate the black population in one district to help ensure the election of a black representative. In the process, surrounding districts became "whiter," more conservative, and more likely to elect Republican candidates. The process created a loophole through which harder-edged conservatives slipped. Helms was unique in that, aided by North Carolina's racial demographics, he survived in statewide races. Yet numerous southern conservative hard-liners would be elected from House districts that had been redrawn in the 1980s and '90s in ways that facilitated the election of ideologically conservative Republicans. In the long run, the biggest losers in the voting rights revolution were not conservative ideologues but moderate white Democrats. These were the candidates who since 1965 had combined black votes with working-class whites to frustrate GOP growth.[80]

During the voting rights debate, officials in the White House had already spied how the 1982 voting rights extension would help Republicans. One memo urged President Reagan to turn the tables on Democrats, arguing that they were the ones who had been guilty of diluting the black vote by carving up heavily black areas into different districts to help elect liberal Democrats in the North and conservative Democrats in the South.[81] Another memo labeled "in strictest confidence" observed how reapportionment efforts in the early 1980s had made "strange bedfellows of Republicans and Blacks." In most every state with a sizable black population, it noted, "the GOP has sought to concentrate Blacks with the effect of increasing both Black and GOP prospects."[82]

By most standards, the Voting Rights Act was a remarkable success. On the eve of its passage there were fewer than 100 black elected officials in the eleven states of the former Confederacy; by January 2000, there were 5,579.[83] Despite this success, the voting rights revolution did not eliminate race as a factor in southern politics; it merely transformed the dynamics. Even as Thurmond himself settled into a moderate position in the new racial order, the "white flight" of Republicans continued unabated. Thurmond had initiated it, but leaders like Helms extended it. As the *Washington Post* reporter Thomas Edsall wrote, by the end of the 1980s there was a common response among some South Carolinians when asked whether or not they were Republican: "I'm white, aren't I?" One survey of voter attitudes in South Carolina estimated white support of the Democratic Party at 15 percent. The GOP held a 61 to 7 percent loyalty advantage among young white voters.[84] Here, at the close of the twentieth century, the Democratic Party in South Carolina looked in size and composition not unlike the Republican organization that had existed at the century's start.

Thurmond's support of voting rights legislation and the King holiday sealed his new reputation as a GOP elder statesman. The racist maverick had become the pragmatic insider. He won plaudits from across the aisle for his handling of the Judiciary Committee. Ted Kennedy called him "effective" and "fair to all sides."[85] The nomination of Sandra Day O'Connor to be the first female justice on the Supreme Court earned Thurmond respect from colleagues and the press. After he defended her against religious conservatives in his own party, one reporter marveled that the reserved, solicitous Judiciary chairman was the same man who had led the inquisition against Abe Fortas just thirteen years earlier.[86]

If there was a bit too much chivalry and chauvinism in Thurmond's performance for some people, well, that too became part of the color-ful legend of Ol' Strom. At the opening of the hearings Thurmond escorted O'Connor down the center aisle like a father giving away the bride. Earlier he had taken heat for commenting on a panel of female witnesses, "These are the prettiest witnesses we have had in a long time. I imagine you are all married. If not, you could be if you wanted to be."[87] His toast for O'Connor at a dinner celebrating her confirmation—"We love you for your beauty, respect you for your intelligence, adore you for your charm, and will come to love you . . . because we can't help it"—was better suited for a 1950s bride than for the newest associate member of the Supreme Court. He had used almost the same musty bons mots to toast Senator Ted Stevens's second wife at a reception for the newlyweds earlier in the year.[88]

Given the mix of plaudits and colorful stories, it was easy to miss how as Judiciary chairman Thurmond continued to pursue a number of long-standing priorities. Early on he reorganized the committee to better concentrate on pro-business and national security interests, two issues central to his conservative politics. Thurmond got rid of the twenty-five-year-old Antitrust and Monopoly Subcommittee, once again giving the back of his hand to the moderate Republican Charles Mathias, who was in line to chair the body. Antitrust had been the home of liberal attacks on big business that Thurmond had helped fight off throughout the 1970s. He folded the group's responsibilities into the full committee.[89]

The end of the Antitrust Subcommittee dovetailed with the Reagan administration's lax enforcement of antitrust law. A wave of giant corporate mergers took place during Reagan's first year in office. In the most spectacular, DuPont outbid Seagram's and Mobil for a $7.5 billion acquisition of Conoco, the ninth-largest oil company.[90] Mobil eventually settled for a takeover of Marathon, a mere $5 billion deal.[91]

The other part of the reorganization involved the revival of the Senate Internal Security Subcommittee, one of the most controversial Cold War institutions. The new subcommittee was actually titled Security and Terrorism, but its responsibilities were the same as the old one—to hunt Communists. Joseph McCarthy had used the old subcommittee for his grandstanding before James Eastland took it over to push right-wing anti-Communist causes, usually ones that cast aspersions on civil rights activists. Thurmond had worked closely with the subcommittee in his drive for the muzzling hearings and later served as a member. One of his aides said—in what the *Los Angeles Times* described as equal parts "sincerity and innocence"—that the new subcommittee would "examine the role of the Soviet government in influencing U.S. policy through the U.S. (news) media—but that's got to be balanced against the First Amendment."[92]

Thurmond also used his new power as Judiciary chair to help long-time political allies, perhaps most blatantly Roger Milliken. In a bitterly contested twelve-year-old antitrust suit, Milliken's research company had been found guilty of price-fixing. Milliken initiated a full-press lobbying campaign to have antitrust laws rewritten and applied retro-actively to his case, thereby reducing his company's $21 million penalty by nearly two-thirds.[93] Thurmond pushed the bill through the Judiciary Committee, backing a modified retroactivity amendment and then pressuring the Business Roundtable and the U.S. Chamber of Commerce to support it.[94] Thurmond managed to get the measure to the Senate floor, only to see it filibustered by senators who refused to allow a vote on what they dubbed the "Price Fixers Relief Act."[95]

A longtime cotton lobbyist in Washington, Macon Edwards, recalls a revealing incident between Milliken and Thurmond that occurred a few years later. Edwards accompanied Milliken to Capitol Hill in 1986, when Thurmond was chairing hearings on the appointment of William Rehnquist to be chief justice of the Supreme Court. Milliken sent a note in to Thurmond to meet him in the hallway, where he explained what he regarded as the sorry deal that the White House had just announced involving textile trade between developing and industrialized nations. Thurmond needed to do something about it. Immediately, he said. Thurmond squirmed for a moment, pointing out that this was, after all, the nomination of the chief justice of the Supreme Court and he was Judiciary chairman. But Milliken insisted, and Thurmond soon interrupted the hearings and did as he had been told.[96]

These accounts of Milliken's influence bookend a process that had begun during Thurmond's governorship. Back then, Milliken was pressuring Governor Thurmond to make it easier for him to do business in South Carolina. Thurmond, despite warnings from Walter Brown not to get too close with mill owners, was intrigued by the prospect of embracing South Carolina's emerging industrial barons. He soon passed fully into Milliken's camp. Over the next thirty-odd years, they worked in tandem to remake the political economy of South Carolina and, in doing so, helped reshape the political economy of the nation along the same antilabor, pro-business lines that had fueled Sunbelt growth. The price-fixing deal never came to pass, yet the fact that Thurmond had so nakedly pursued it, and the fact that he would jump so quickly at Milliken's request, are reminders of the powerful intersections of business and politics that had transformed and sustained Thurmond's political career and fed the modern conservative ascendancy.

14

ALL STROM'S CHILDREN
(1990–2003)

In his final decade or so in office, Strom Thurmond gradually slipped from legend into parody. He continued to wield power as a committee chairman, but his interest and importance in national politics waned. Profile articles still told colorful stories, but more and more that is all they told. Concerns about his age dominated his last race in 1996. His former aides Harry Dent and Mark Goodin tried to talk him out of running, but to no avail.[1] The often-addled ninety-three-year-old struggled on the campaign trail in the closest of any of his ten U.S. Senate primary and general election victories.[2] At a Strom Thurmond Appreciation Day event, he recounted the glories of the Edgefield native William Barret Travis, defender of the Alamo, who stood strong with "3,000 Russians threatening to attack."[3] On election night, his victory speech was lifeless and perfunctory. There were no issues or causes, just a recitation of prepared thank-you messages to campaign aides.[4]

Personal tragedies beset him. He and Nancy Thurmond separated in 1991. Two years later, his older daughter, Nancy Moore, was killed by a drunk driver while crossing a street in Columbia. These misfortunes, combined with his ambition to break the Senate longevity mark, rendered him a rather isolated, pathetic figure in his final years in Washington.[5] Thurmond's longtime aide Duke Short and his wife, Dee, lovingly attended to him, yet he was in and out of the hospital regularly. Republican colleagues worked behind the scenes to remove him from the chairmanship of the Senate Armed Services Committee, a move that he fought for several years before finally relenting at the end of 1998.[6] In 2001, Nancy Thurmond visited the office of South Carolina's Democratic governor, Jim Hodges, and played a videocassette in which Strom, to Hodge's amazement, said that he was resigning from the Senate and wanted Nancy to replace him. Several days later, however, Thurmond announced that he had no intention of stepping down, and neither he nor Nancy would comment on the bizarre episode.[7]

Editorials in two establishment conservative journals, *The Wall Street Journal* and *National Review*, called on Thurmond to retire.[8] His age and frailty had the effect of exaggerating the distinction between him and other conservative leaders. As he shuffled through Senate hallways, or was caught on C-SPAN nodding off in the Senate chamber, it reinforced the image of him as a holdover from a bygone era. He seemed to be of a different species from the fresh-faced ideologically honed Republicans who were leading the modern conservative insurgency. The unwitting among them might even have assumed that he always had been.

Celebrations commemorating Thurmond's long career took place regularly in these years and only worked to further the impression of an anachronistic legacy. In 1997, the South Carolina legislature authorized the construction of a monument to Thurmond on the statehouse grounds in Columbia. He joined the likes of George Washington, Wade Hampton, and Ben Tillman, one of only seven individuals to be so honored and the first to be recognized while still alive.[9]

The monument was approved and constructed in the midst of a protracted and nationally publicized debate over South Carolina's historical memorials. African Americans had long complained about the Confederate battle flag that flew above the capitol building. The practice had begun in 1962 as a show of defiance against civil rights activists and the federal government. In 1996, the Republican governor, David Beasley, who during his campaign two years earlier had advocated keeping the flag, waged an unsuccessful effort to have it removed, which was followed by an NAACP-coordinated boycott of the state. Noted first among the "heavyweights" backing Beasley was Strom Thurmond. The King day celebration in 2000 brought out forty-six thousand marchers, the largest march in the city's history, calling for the removal of the flag. Eventually, the state reached a compromise in which it removed the flag and placed a smaller Confederate banner alongside the Confederate memorial on the capitol grounds. In addition, the state constructed a monument to African American achievements on the east side of the capitol building.[10]

Thurmond's name was always prominent among the list of those supporting removal, yet he actually played a marginal role in the dispute. There were rumors that Thurmond would make a statement about the controversy in December 1999, in his speech at the dedication of his own memorial. The NAACP boycott was set to begin the next month. Yet he did not, and he brushed away reporters who asked him about the controversy.[11] When reminded by Lee Bandy, the dean of South Carolina political reporters, about his earlier support of Beasley's effort to remove the flag, the ninety-seven-year-old Thurmond responded, "I did? Well, if you said I did, I did."[12] In general, the combined effect of the controversy was to further suggest some resolution of historic struggles that were of less and less immediate relevance to most South Carolinians, much less most Americans.

In his last month in office, however, an unlikely controversy over remarks made at Thurmond's hundredth birthday celebration in Washington brought to the fore the closeness and indebtedness to Thurmond's earlier career that modern Republicans were so eager to efface. A cast of Washington notables turned out in December 2002 in the Dirksen Senate Office Building to fete Thurmond in what would double as a kind of going-away party. Bob Dole and the soon-to-be Senate majority leader, Trent Lott, were the featured speakers. Thad Strom, a relative and former staffer, warmed up the crowd with funny stories about his old boss, and Dole followed with a string of one-liners, many of them recycled from Thurmond's ninetieth birthday party or similar tribute events. They had become so common that all the prime jokes had been told many times over. When Lott got up to speak, he realized that Dole had already used his best material. So he ad-libbed, beginning with some jokes about Dole, all the while searching his memory for material he had used on the countless occasions that he had shared a podium with Thurmond. A line that sprang to mind recalled Thurmond's Dixiecrat candidacy, ancient history to everyone in the room, yet the one thread that when pulled unraveled completely the nostalgic view of Ol' Strom: "I want to say this about my state: When Strom

Thurmond ran for president, we voted for him. We're proud of it. And if the rest of the country had followed our lead, we wouldn't have had all these problems over all these years, either."[13]

Back in 1980, when he and Thurmond were stumping for Reagan in Mississippi, the line had passed unnoticed, but in 2002 it sparked a controversy that by the end of the following week would cost Lott his leadership position. The image of the southern Republican leader venerating the segregationist politics of the party's longest-serving senator called to mind the most unseemly aspects of modern conservative history. National conservative leaders lined up to renounce Lott's comment and distance themselves from him and, by implication, Thurmond, including President George W. Bush. "The Administration not only opted not to defend him," Thurmond's close aide Duke Short wrote afterward, "they essentially threw Senator Lott to the wolves." The White House's "timidity" saddened Short and Thurmond both.[14] The GOP simply wanted the issue to go away.

It was an ignominious end to Thurmond's near half century of national public service. He returned to Edgefield, where he lived in a specially appointed suite in the county hospital. Separated from his beloved Senate, Thurmond lasted only six months. He died on June 26, 2003.[15]

For three days his body lay in state in the second-floor lobby of the South Carolina State House in Columbia. Thousands of mourners filed through to view the flag-draped coffin, some standing in line as much as three hours. A bevy of Washington dignitaries—including Vice President Dick Cheney, Secretary of Defense Donald Rumsfeld, and some fifty congressional representatives—attended the funeral at Columbia's First Baptist Church, where twenty-five hundred people had gathered. Among the five eulogies delivered, Joseph Biden's was the most memorable. Biden recounted the story, told numerous times before, of how he had entered the Senate determined to take on Neanderthals like Thurmond only to meet the man and discover that he was nothing like the dogmatic, reactionary figure of popular perception.[16] This was the story that fit the image of Ol' Strom, a story about redemption, a story that made a sharp break between then and now.

After the service in Columbia, family and mourners proceeded to Edgefield. At the county courthouse on the main square, an honor squad including soldiers from the famed Third Infantry Division loaded the t onto a horse-drawn caisson. Hundreds of people crowded the sidewalks, many of them with their hands covering their hearts as the casket passed. Despite the steady drizzle, about twelve hundred people gathered on a nearby hill to watch as the honor guard fired a twenty-one-gun salute, a bugler played taps, and the minister offered a final prayer. Thurmond was laid to rest in a fenced family plot in a back corner of Willowbrook Cemetery.[17]

Six months later, a retired African American schoolteacher from Los Angeles, Essie Mae Washington-Williams, held a much-anticipated press conference in Columbia. "My father's name was James Strom Thurmond," she began her statement, confirming a rumor that she and Thurmond had conspired to keep secret for his entire career. For many African Americans in South Carolina, there was nothing new about this news conference. "I've heard all my life that Strom had an outside child," said the South Carolina state senator Kay Patterson, an African American lawmaker who delivered a eulogy at Thurmond's funeral.[18] Given the rumor's pervasiveness, it was remarkable how little there was about it in the printed record. *Ebony* magazine had sent a reporter to South Carolina State College to check out the gossip back in 1948.[19] There was the delicate reference to the matter in the black press back in 1957. Robert Sherrill had mentioned the rumors in a profile of Thurmond in his 1968 book *Gothic Politics in the Deep South*, and in 1972 the *Edgefield Advertiser* had printed the accusation in headlines stretched to fill the entire front page.[20]

The rumor was nearly confirmed as fact in 1992. A small item published in *Penthouse* magazine led to a number of press inquiries at Thurmond's office, but the real work was done by Marilyn W. Thompson, a *Washington Post* reporter who had talked with sources as much as ten years earlier and who published a lengthy report in August of that year. She had first heard the rumor when she talked with Modjeska Simkins, a pioneer of the South Carolina civil rights movement who had known Thurmond since the 1920s. Thompson also interviewed former students at South Carolina State College, who told of then-governor Thurmond coming to campus to visit a quiet student named Essie Mae Washington. Thompson found a typed note in Thurmond's gubernatorial papers from Washington-Williams thanking him for a loan. She tracked her down in Los Angeles, where she was a successful schoolteacher and a widowed mother of four. Washington-Williams described Thurmond as "a close friend of my family—a wonderful man who's helped a lot of people." She said that he had provided her with some financial aid, "but not a lot."[21]

She told a different story in 2003. In a lengthy interview with Dan Rather of CBS News, Washington-Williams told how her mother, Carrie Butler, took her to meet her father for the first time when she was sixteen years old. She was surprised to find out that he was white—no one had ever told her. Despite Rather's probing, she divulged no significant details about her mother's relationship with Thurmond. She was as protective of her father's legacy after his death as she was when he lived.[22] Thurmond's family put out a brief statement acknowledging Washington-Williams's claim. "We have no reason to believe Ms. Williams was not telling the truth," said J. Strom Thurmond Jr., Thurmond's older son.[23]

Washington-Williams's revelation provoked a flurry of commentary as the national media struggled to fit the story into the nation's evolving narrative on race and reconciliation. Numerous people, many of them African American, took umbrage at her characterization of her mother and Thurmond's sexual encounter as an "affair." "An affair connotes choice," wrote the columnist Mary Mitchell. "And a black girl in that situation—at that time in history—had little choice in the matter."[24] Valinda Littlefield, an African American historian at the University of South Carolina, noted the disproportionate power relations between Thurmond and Butler. "She was basically a child," she said. "He can do with her what he wants." Gilda Cobb-Hunter, a South Carolina state representative, bristled at the idea that Thurmond's relationship was a "love affair," characterizing it as a "matter of power and control, not romance."[25]

Another issue that rankled was Washington-Williams's decision to wait until Thurmond's death to make her announcement. "When it was time to talk, Essie Mae Washington-Williams kept her mouth shut," wrote the African American author and cultural critic Stanley Crouch. "Now she and her family want 'closure.' Well, isn't that nice?"[26] Others compared Washington-Williams's reticence with the outspokenness of the southern civil rights activists of her generation. As one letter writer to *The New York Times* put it, "Where would civil rights be today if Rosa Parks had had the 'decency and fortitude' not to make a fuss?"[27]

Others were more understanding. "It's hard to fault a child for the sins of her parents," wrote the columnist Eric Deggans. He resisted "criticizing a 78-year-old woman for not upending her life and destroying her father's career by going public with such a scandal 30 or 40 years ago."[28] Nadine Cohodas, a biographer of Thurmond, noted the personal and professional danger involved in a black woman publicly confronting a man as powerful and well connected as Thurmond.[29] For Washington-Williams, a private person by nature, to "out" Thurmond involved opening herself up to public confrontation, potential ridicule, and scorn. And after 1964, she would have done so as a widow and mother of four. Washington-Williams's participation in the deception helped secure support for herself and her children; indeed, Thurmond helped put her son through medical school. Given the range of options available to her, her choice was not that surprising.

Balancing the criticisms were commentaries that celebrated the propriety and restraint with which Washington-Williams handled her peculiar history. "Williams has emerged from her long silence with honor and dignity," the Newsday columnist Marie Cocco wrote. "She represents the very best of America."[30] The syndicated columnist Cynthia Tucker, noting the long history of miscegenation and secrecy in the South, concluded, "If there is any real news here it lies in the uncommon dignity with which Mrs. Washington-Williams has conducted herself." Thurmond, she wrote, "bore a daughter much too good for him."[31] For some commentators, Washington-Williams's public performance even cast her hypocritical father in a new, more sympathetic light. To those who would characterize Thurmond's financial support of her as "hush money," the syndicated columnist Kathleen Parker answered, "Say what you will about what might have been . . . had Thurmond been straight up about his interracial relationships. Yet he was no deadbeat. He supported his daughter, sent her to college and was financially reliable throughout her life."[32]

In 2004 the monument to Thurmond at the state capitol was altered to include Washington-Williams's name among the list of Thurmond's children. The idea came from the Democratic state senator Robert Ford, an African American from Charleston County and a former staff member of the Southern Christian Leadership Conference, the civil rights organization founded by Martin Luther King in the late 1950s. Governor Mark Sanford signed the bill into law in June 2004, and the monument was altered the next month.[33]

In May 2005, Washington-Williams traveled to Columbia to see the change firsthand. The state senator John Courson, a longtime Thurmond confidant and chair of the Strom Thurmond Monument Commission, said he had "no problem" with adding Washington-Williams's name: "That lady is a class act."[34] Courson escorted Washington-Williams around the capitol, recounting humorous stories of her father's legendary stamina on the campaign trail. Washington-Williams also saw the African American history monument on the statehouse grounds. An article covering the event noted that Strom Thurmond had been one of the first donors for the construction of the African American memorial, pledging $500.[35]

Thurmond's altered monument, along with the warm reception that Washington-Williams received in South Carolina from Thurmond's family and close associates, became a powerful symbol of how much race relations had changed in the South. Robert Ford believed that the altered monument would "go a long way in terms of race relations in the state."[36] One headline writer captured the triumphant tone of the event: "South Rewrites History in Stone."[37]

It is worth considering in what sense exactly southern history is rewritten in Washington-Williams's story. Thurmond's white family and a longtime loyalist like John Courson could embrace Essie Mae Washington-Williams in part because of how carefully protective she was of her father's reputation. There was no trace of resentment or injury in any of her public statements; she was the picture of the loyal and loving daughter. Robert Ford may have wanted Washington-Williams's name on the monument as an affirmation of African American identity, yet Thurmond's family and friends could consent to it readily because they respected the loyalty and faithfulness that Washington-Williams showed Thurmond. The American South has a long and complicated history of whites honoring African Americans for their fidelity. It is one against which Essie Mae Washington-Williams's story should be read.

In the decades following emancipation, particularly as a new generation of southern blacks with no living memory of slavery came of age, it became common for whites to memorialize the faithful slave. Whether it was "mammy," the gentle, asexual elderly black female figure who tended to the master's children, or "old darky," the black male who was the manly figure of protection for white women and children when the head of the plantation was off fighting in the Civil War, these stereotypical figures became part of the mythology of the Lost Cause. White women's groups, usually chapters of the United Daughters of the Confederacy (UDC), started campaigns in various parts of the South to construct "mammy" monuments. The effort culminated in the early 1920s when the UDC lobbied southern congressmen to introduce a bill for the establishment of a mammy monument on national public grounds in Washington (though introduced, it was never passed).[38]

In the twentieth century, as the historian Micki McElya writes, the myth of the faithful slave has lingered because "so many white Americans have wished to live in a world in which African Americans are not angry over past and present injustices, a world in which white people were and are not complicit, in which the injustices themselves—of slavery, Jim Crow, and ongoing structural racism—seem not to exist at all."[39] The image of the loyal slave has always implied a shared sympathy across the color line, one born of mutual affection and a shared Christian heritage. It was a mythology in which a white southerner of Strom Thurmond's generation was born and reared.

As late as 1970, Thurmond invoked this mythology in defending southern segregation as a humane and realistic way of organizing a multiracial society, one that recognized cultural differences and racial preferences. "Within both groups there have always been sublayers and subtle relationships that reached back into family traditions and established places of residence," read Thurmond's constituent newsletter, almost certainly written by a staffer. He contrasted the organic racial order of the South with the "great industrial cities of the North," where residents were "isolated social units, lacking family ties and traditions." In the South, however, "individualism is supported by a natural interrelation and interdependence." Thurmond argued that the civil rights movement and efforts toward school integration upset the social equilibrium that had been worked out over decades. Advocates of integration were "a wedge splitting society asunder."[40]

This vision of the South as an organic society juxtaposed with the impersonal rootless social order of the urban North was part of a regional mythology that stretched back to the antebellum nineteenth century, when southern apologists defended slavery from the attacks of a burgeoning northern abolitionist movement. At the heart of the mythology was the image of the benevolent master and the loyal slave, of meaningful relationships across the color line, the "natural interrelation and interdependence" of blacks and whites in the South.

It is not difficult to imagine that the Thurmond staffer who wrote these passages had in mind his boss's "friendship" with Essie Mae Washington-Williams, who made annual visits to Thurmond's Washington office in these years.[41] She was always described to staffers as an old family friend from Edgefield—and thus an exemplar of the "sublayers and subtle relationships" that existed in the South. To his ghostwriter who penned these lines, Thurmond's regular visits with this "family friend" must have seemed like the embodiment of this tradition. The myth of the loyal slave, and the cross-racial sympathy it implied, obscured, of course, the fact that the "family tradition" that Thurmond participated in was that of fathering children with African American servants.

More than anything, Washington-Williams's public performance made clear that Thurmond's sins were in the past. Her refusal to admit to any anger or resentment over her father's hypocrisy signaled that those sins were fully accounted for and absolved, both by his financial support for her and her children and by his long service to his constituents. Washington-Williams's story, her version, established a clear break between Thurmond's past and the redeemed present. That is understandable perhaps for anyone who had lived with a lie as long as she had, to want to leave the past in the past. Yet history always teaches of the lines of continuity that bind the past to the present. Others among Thurmond's progeny—not just his literal children, but his political descendants who must be included in any discussion of his legacy in American life and politics—highlight those lines of historical continuity.

The 1980s and '90s were decades when a second generation of southern Republicans emerged on the national scene to become the chief lieutenants in the rightward march of the Republican Party. Many of these southerners were people who, like Thurmond, had forged their conservative antigovernment political ideology in the fires of racial conflict in the civil rights South. There would emerge in the twenty-first century South Carolina Republicans who were more diverse racially. Governor Nikki Haley, the child of Sikh immigrants who was elected in 2010, is one example, as is the U.S. congressman Tim Scott, the first black Republican congressman elected from the Deep South since Reconstruction, who defeated one of Thurmond's sons, Paul, in a crowded Republican primary. Yet the party they inherited was built by first- and second-generation southern conservatives whose politics were notable for being so racially charged.

There are plenty of second-generation southern Republicans to choose from in telling this aspect of Thurmond's legacy. Trent Lott is one. Lott got his start in Washington as an aide to the segregationist Democratic congressman William Colmer in the late 1960s. When Colmer retired, Lott switched parties, received Colmer's endorsement, and won his boss's seat. He rose through the ranks of House leadership, becoming minority whip in the early 1980s. A gifted spokesman for conservative causes, Lott maintained close ties to former Dixiecrats in Mississippi and across the South, as his comments about Thurmond at the 1980 Reagan rally suggest. He was closely involved in the controversy over the Reagan administration and Bob Jones University in the early 1980s, and he made a number of controversial appearances over the years before right-wing southern nationalist groups, including the Council of Conservative Citizens, a group directly descended from the Citizens' Councils of the 1950s and '60s.[42]

Equally representative is Lee Atwater, whom Thurmond helped to land a job in the Reagan White House and who went on to become a key adviser in George Bush's 1988 presidential campaign. Atwater recounted tales of his hardball tactics in South Carolina politics to reporters like fraternity pranks. One he told often was of the 1980 congressional campaign that he managed for the Republican incumbent Floyd Spence against the Democrat Tom Turnipseed, an old Wallaceite who had tried to convince Thurmond not to support Nixon in

1968. Turnipseed had been dismissed from George Wallace's 1968 presidential campaign after several episodes of heavy drinking; later he admitted that years earlier as a teenager he had undergone shock treatments for depression. By the 1980 campaign, he had renounced his segregationist ways and become a populist maverick. He accused Atwater of orchestrating phony telephone polls that falsely informed white suburbanites that Turnipseed was a member of the NAACP. It was the last of a series of jousts between the two that ended with Atwater erupting before reporters: "I'm not going to respond to that guy. What do you expect from someone who was hooked up to jumper cables?"[43]

The most infamous incident of Atwater's career, and one that mimicked racial tactics that Thurmond had used against liberal opponents, was the role he played in orchestrating the attack on the Democratic candidate Michael Dukakis during the 1988 presidential campaign. Atwater put his opposition research team to work in search of evidence to paint Dukakis as an elite, out-of-touch liberal, just as he had attacked Pug Ravenel in Thurmond's 1978 campaign. In fact, Ravenel, who had known Dukakis at Harvard and was among a number of Democratic operatives brought in as a national brain trust, warned Dukakis to be on guard against Atwater, whom he described as "the Babe Ruth of negative politics."[44] The figure that Atwater found, Willie Horton, captured in visceral fashion white anxieties about liberalism run amok. A native of Chesterfield, South Carolina, Horton was serving a life sentence in a Massachusetts state prison for a 1974 murder when he was released on a weekend furlough in 1986 and failed to return. A year later he broke into the Maryland home of Clifford Barnes and his fiancée, Angela Miller. After pistol-whipping Barnes and cutting him across the midsection twenty-two times, he tied him up and then raped Miller twice. Barnes later broke free and called the police. Horton fled, was eventually captured, and was charged with eighteen crimes, including rape and kidnapping.[45]

The furlough program had begun in the early 1970s under a Republican governor, but Dukakis had been a firm supporter throughout his two terms as governor. When the opposition team got back to Atwater with Horton's story, the campaign ran a focus group, and references to Horton and the furlough issue started showing up in Bush's speeches in June 1988. The next month, at a meeting of southern Republicans in

Atlanta, Atwater recalled Horton's story and reveled in the prospect of Dukakis trying to win votes in the South. He pushed speculation that Jesse Jackson would be Dukakis's vice-presidential nominee and then, apropos of nothing, said, "So anyway, maybe he'll put this Willie Horton guy on the ticket after all is said and done."[46] Conservative groups generated attack ads using Horton's story and image, while the Bush campaign remained safely distant. The campaign's fingerprints, however, could be seen all over the issue. A Republican colleague said that Atwater funneled millions of campaign dollars into the Horton television ads.[47]

Before Willie Horton, there was Andrew Mallory. Both were black men born in South Carolina who left the state and committed violent crimes against white women. Both became symbols in national anti-liberal political attacks orchestrated by white South Carolinians. And before Mallory there was Dave Dunham, who had assaulted a white couple near Chester and who in 1950 Thurmond turned into a symbol of Olin Johnston's "pardon racket."[48] Each instance was a plot point on a line that traced back to Thurmond's political baptism, when he witnessed the race-baiting Blease destroy Jones on the stump. Instinctually, Thurmond and these white men knew that by recalling violent black men they could conjure evils and aggravate prejudices and thereby shame their political opponents for their inaction and cowardliness, pushing themselves forward as the defenders of all things honorable and manly.

There is one more among the brood of Thurmond's political children worth noting, for his story shows how the history and the memory of battles fought in Thurmond's era shaped the kinds of political narratives that his progeny would construct. He is Katon Dawson, elected chairman of the South Carolina Republican Party in 2002. The first campaign in which Dawson ever worked was Richard Nixon's in 1968, when Thurmond played the kingmaker. In early 2009, after serving two terms as state chair, Dawson ran for the chairmanship of the Republican National Committee and lost narrowly to Michael Steele of Maryland, who became the first African American national chairman of the GOP. For those who opposed him, Dawson represented a hard-edged, inflammatory southern leadership that had dominated the party for the last two decades or more. That reputation was not helped by news that until recently he had been a member of an all-white coun-try club in his hometown of Columbia.[49]

Another, less publicized incident in Dawson's recent past that made the rounds among bloggers also pointed to the party's worrisome image on racial issues. In November 2003, just a few months after Thurmond's death, Dawson spoke to a group of undergraduates at the University of South Carolina about his election as state party chairman. He recounted the following story about how he came to be interested in politics and how he developed his conservative philosophy:

> I've always been involved in politics. And I guess it goes all the way back to my school career and education. I, in the 1960s, was a product of school segregation, where we took our schools and completely dis-banded them, and made racial equality. Fifty-fifty. And the kids had no choices. They closed Booker T. Washington . . . down here. A pretty good school. Closed it and sent the students to A. C. Flora, across town. And they did it over the summer because the laws had been changed by the politicians. And, the day that school opened, we were on CBS news with the buses turned upside down, and one of them lit on fire. By folks who didn't want to go to school there. Not folks who did.
>
> The end of that story was, I was standing in a bathroom in public school . . . This scar over here [pointing to his forehead] was from a baseball bat. I will tell you it was a pretty harsh environment. Govern-ment reached into my life and grabbed me and shook me at the age of fifteen. I remember how blatant it was that government just thought that they knew better, that government just thought they knew better what to do in my school. And I can't say it was so much racial. I can say that people had a lot of stuff thrust on them because politicians thought they knew better. Whether they did or didn't, I don't know. But from that day on I've always been politically active, and wanted my voice heard. Not always right. And my opinion is not always con-sistent with everyone else's. But I care greatly about the State we live in, and greatly about the idea of freedom.[50]

Dawson invoked the history of the 1970 desegregation of the public schools in Columbia, which had played a critical role in the gubernato-rial campaign that year of Thurmond's protégé Albert Watson. Dawson's memory conflicts with the historical record in several respects. First, A. C. Flora was not fifty-fifty white and black; 28 percent of the student body was African American in 1970.[51] Second, school desegregation in Columbia did not occur because "the laws had been changed by the politicians." Federal courts ordered it in response to mandates laid down by the Supreme Court the previous year, which were part of a string of legal actions that stretched back to the *Brown* decision a decade and a half earlier. Most important, no buses were overturned and set on fire—certainly not by black students, as Dawson implies. He seems to have confused his own experience with the incident that occurred in Lamar, South Carolina, in March 1970, when busing opponents attacked school buses carrying black children.[52] Nine days earlier Albert Watson had given his inflammatory speech before a freedom-of-choice rally attended by over twenty-five hundred people.[53]

Dawson's story also leaves out the role, documented in newspapers and police reports, that the Republican Albert Watson's campaign played in stoking racial strife at his very high school in the weeks leading up to the 1970 election. Campaign workers for Watson had been trying to stage a racial incident at A. C. Flora in order to obtain pictures that they could use in campaign materials. Perhaps the student rioting in which Dawson was assaulted in the bathroom was the very one to which Watson's campaign workers were linked, though it is impossible to say for certain.

In the standard narrative of Ol' Strom, the nostalgic figure of the post-civil-rights decades who adapted to the changing times, Watson's 1970 campaign was the turning point. After that loss, Thurmond realized that the old tactics of racial polarization could backfire, and, sly old pro that he was, he embraced a more moderate politics of race. Whatever pragmatic political considerations emerged after the 1970 election for Thurmond himself, Dawson's story is a reminder of the other lessons that Strom Thurmond's children could and did draw about the critical years of civil rights advancement, lessons not about the new reality in which African Americans were finally allowed a full role in southern political life, but rather ones about "government" violating the rights of individuals, about the foolhardiness of politicians' social engineering, and about the danger such efforts posed to "the idea of freedom."

In 1970 a Republican gubernatorial campaign either directly incited or was implicated in racial violence in Columbia public schools. Yet for Dawson thirty-three years later, conflict at A. C. Flora became a life-changing example of government intrusion, an instance of the federal state reaching into his life, grabbing him, and shaking him. In Dawson's telling, however, the violence had not been committed by the anonymous state. The implication was that it had been a black student who had assaulted him in the bathroom with a baseball bat. Here as late as 2003, after old man Thurmond was dead and in the grave, the leader of South Carolina's Republican Party still trafficked in familiar tropes of black violence, white victimization, and federal complicity, tropes that Strom Thurmond had used to such devastating effect in his own day.

EPILOGUE: THE SCARRED STONE

On the south side of the South Carolina state capitol in Columbia stands a seventeen-foot-tall monument to Strom Thurmond. Dedicated in 1999, the bronze likeness depicts Thurmond in mid-stride. It was based on a photograph taken during his 1948 run for president as the Dixiecrat candidate. The artist, William Behrends, chose the image because it was "a time of transition," before Thurmond was elected to the Senate. His stride is said to represent "his eagerness as he moves on to new challenges."[1]

The statue rests on a marble base, the west side of which lists the names of Thurmond's children. Initially, this included four names, but was altered to add Essie Mae Washington-Williams. There was no room at the beginning of the list to add Washington-Williams's name in her pride of place as the oldest, so it was inscribed at the bottom. The typeface is the same, but because the newer letters have not weathered like the others, Essie Mae's name stands out. The difficult part was changing the heading "father of four." The original letters in "four" were wider than the replacement letters in "five," particularly the middle combination of *ou* compared with *iv*. The stonemason filled in the entire word with a mixture of granite dust and Krazy Glue, which when it sets is actually harder than the stone. The dust must be thoroughly sifted so that only the finest particles are used. Otherwise, the hardened glue mixture is prone to chipping when the replacement letters are carved. The stonemason completed the work in stages, pounding in the mixture with a hammer until the old letters were filled in. He sanded the surface smooth and then carved the new letters.

The *i* and *e* have small chips in them, and the left side of the *v* is slightly crooked. The dull brown granite-and-glue mixture contrasts with the stately gray marble. The discoloring is largely hidden in early morning and late afternoon light, but the blemish is visible from dozens of yards away in the noonday sun.[2]

Changing a monument does not change the past. It is appropriate really that the stone bears what is, in effect, a scar. It is a mark that bears great symbolic weight, the significance of which depends on whose gaze the scar holds.

It could symbolize physical or emotional pain that has been overcome. This perhaps is the meaning for Essie Mae Washington-Williams, and perhaps too for some portion of African Americans who view this altered monument, along with other forms of African American inclusion in the broader civic culture, as the culmination of generations of struggle against a dominant white society. It was not long ago when it would have been impossible for an African American woman to make a successful public claim against a powerful and privileged white man. Washington-Williams did just this in the claim that she made against her father's "white" family. Her inclusion on her father's memorial is distinguished from previous forms of white memorialization of African Americans in the fact that it acknowledges Essie Mae not in idealized terms of loyalty or devotion but in her simple condition, as a daughter.

A scar can also be a mark of shame or weakness. In this sense it is a reminder of Thurmond's own moral failings, in both his public and his private lives. The high-profile acts of racist resistance marred Thurmond's career, just as the scar blemishes the most significant manifestation of his life and legacy. For a man renowned for his courage on the battlefield and in the political arena, it is also an ironic marker of cowardice. It is impossible to separate his grandiose acts of segregationist defense—or his later refusal to acknowledge them, much less apologize for them—from the secret of his black daughter. Perhaps it was politically imprudent for Thurmond to have apologized for past actions, or political suicide to have acknowledged Essie Mae publicly. Yet even for this born politician, the fear went deeper than politics. It would have meant publicly confronting a world of forgetting that had made Thurmond who he was.

In all times and places, a scar connotes violence. It is as a marker of both the literal and the figurative violence that white Americans have carried out against fellow Americans of African descent that the scarred stone seems most profoundly suggestive. In the first half of Thurmond's life, segregation and white supremacy remained open wounds. Over roughly the second half, interventions by an array of Americans—black and white, public officials and private citizens— began the slow process of righting those injustices. Whatever quiet actions he took in his private life, Thurmond spent his public life fighting these efforts, and only in his final decades, after the real work was done, did he silently assent to them. What reasons existed for this change beyond the obviously self-serving ones we cannot say, because Thurmond himself never did.

And so today, on the capitol grounds of the South Carolina State House in Columbia, the image of Strom Thurmond strides confidently forward. The imposing bronze is a reminder of a man of outsized energy and ambition. Yet as it was when he walked the earth, it is now and will remain: he stands on a surface scarred by the legacies of white supremacy, scars caused by conflicts that he exacerbated in his own time, scars that remain with us still.

NOTES

ABBREVIATIONS IN NOTES

AC	*Augusta (Ga.) Chronicle*
BMG	Barry M. Goldwater Collection, Arizona Historical Foundation, Hayden Library, Arizona State University
CED	Charles E. Daniel Collection, Special Collections, Strom Thurmond Institute, Clemson University
CNC	*Charleston News and Courier*
CQA	CQ Electronic Library, *Congressional Quarterly Almanac* Online Edition, http://library.cqpress.com/cqalmanac/index.php
CR	*Congressional Record*
CSM	*Christian Science Monitor*
CT	*Chicago Tribune*
HSD	Harry S. Dent Collection, Special Collections, Strom Thurmond Institute, Clemson University
JCS	John C. Stennis Collection, Congressional and Political Research Center, Mississippi State University
JJK	James J. Kilpatrick Papers, Special Collections, University of Virginia
JST	J. Strom Thurmond Collection, Special Collections, Strom Thurmond Institute, Clemson University
LAT	*Los Angeles Times*
LBJ	Lyndon Baines Johnson Presidential Library, Austin, Texas
NYT	*New York Times*
ODJ	Olin D. Johnston Collection, South Carolina Political Collection, University of South Carolina
RBR	Richard B. Russell Collection, Richard B. Russell Library for Political Research and Studies, University of Georgia
REM	Robert E. McNair Collection, South Carolina Political Collection, University of South Carolina

RMF   Robert M. Figg Collection, South Caroliniana Library, University of
           South Carolina

RWR   Ronald Wilson Reagan Presidential Library, Simi Valley, California

State   *The State* (Columbia, S.C.)

STRP   *Strom Thurmond Reports to the People* newsletter

VTNA   Vanderbilt Television News Archive, Vanderbilt University, http://
           tvnews.vanderbilt.edu/

WDW   William D. Workman Jr. Collection, South Carolina Political Collec-
           tions, University of South Carolina

WJB   Walter J. Brown Collection, Special Collections, Strom Thurmond
           Institute, Clemson University

WP   *Washington Post*

WSJ   *Wall Street Journal*

INTRODUCTION

1. *LAT*, Nov. 19, 29, and 30, 1961.
2. John F. Kennedy, Address of the President at the Dinner Honoring Him by the Democratic Party of California, Hollywood Palladium, Los Angeles, Nov. 18, 1961, box 36, President's Office files, John F. Kennedy Library.
3. Frederick G. Dutton, memo on California, Nov. 11, 1961, box 65, folder Western Trip 11/16–11/18/61, Theodore Sorenson Papers, Kennedy Library.
4. *CT*, Oct. 7, 1961; *NYT*, Oct. 7, 1961; *WP*, Sept. 28, 1961, P. W. Gifford to John Stennis, Nov. 13, 1961, box 65, folder Interview/Major Mayer, Series 4, John C. Stennis Papers, Mississippi State University; *CT*, Dec. 3, 1961, 1; Program, Survival U.S.A., Dec. 3, 1961, MF 45, box 12—reel 022.0001.pdf, 55, BMG.
5. George D. Stevens to John F. Kennedy, Dec. 8, 1961, White House Central Office Files, Name File: Thurmond, Strom, Kennedy Library.
6. *CNC*, Dec. 2, 1961.
7. *LAT*, Feb. 8, 1962, *LAT*, Feb. 11, 1962, *LAT*, Feb. 28, 1962.
8. E. W. Kenworthy, "Fulbright Becomes a National Issue," *NYT Magazine*, Oct. 1, 1961, 21.
9. *WP*, Oct. 5, 1965; "Congress 1965—the Year in Review," *CQA* 1965.
10. *CT*, Oct. 7, 1965; "'Right to Work' Repeal Defeated by Filibuster," *CQA* 1965; and "'Right to Work' Repeal Again Loses in Senate," *CQA* 1966.
11. Marshall Frady, *Billy Graham: A Parable of American Righteousness* (New York: Simon and Schuster, 2006), 241. See Darren Dochuk, *From Bible Belt to Sunbelt: Plain-Folk Religion, Grassroots Politics, and the Rise of Evangelical Conservatism* (New York: Norton, 2011); Steven P. Miller, *Billy Graham and the Rise of the Republican South* (Philadelphia: University of Pennsylvania Press, 2009).
12. Gary Gerstle, "Race and the Myth of the Liberal Consensus," *Journal of American History* 82, no. 2 (Sept. 1995): 579–86; Thomas J. Sugrue, *The Origins of the Urban Crisis: Race and Inequality in Postwar Detroit* (Princeton, N.J.: Princeton

University Press, 2006), and Thomas J. Sugrue, *Sweet Land of Liberty: The Forgotten Civil Rights Movement in the North* (New York: Random House, 2008); Robert O. Self, *American Babylon: Race and the Struggle for Postwar Oakland* (Princeton, N.J.: Princeton University Press, 2003).

13. See George Lewis, "Virginia's Northern Strategy: Southern Segregationists and the Route to National Conservatism," *Journal of Southern History* 72, no. 1 (Feb. 2006): 111–46. For northern opposition to fair employment legislation, see Anthony S. Chen, *The Fifth Freedom: Jobs, Politics, and Civil Rights in the United States, 1941–1972* (Princeton, N.J.: Princeton University Press, 2009).

14. There is even shorthand for the shorthand. In his book *The Conscience of a Liberal*, the *New York Times* columnist Paul Krugman writes, "Considering how much has been written about the changes in American politics over the past generation, how much agonizing there has been about the sources of Democratic decline and Republican ascendancy, it's amazing how much of the whole phenomenon can be summed up in just five words: Southern whites started voting Republican." Krugman, *The Conscience of a Liberal* (New York: Norton, 2007), 178.

15. See, for example, Byron E. Shafer and Richard Johnston, *The End of Southern Exceptionalism: Class, Race, and Partisan Change in the Postwar South* (Cambridge, Mass.: Harvard University Press, 2006).

16. Lisa McGirr, *Suburban Warriors: The Origins of the New American Right* (Princeton, N.J.: Princeton University Press, 2001), 14–15.

17. Recent works on California conservatism that emphasize the importance of racial concerns include Matthew Dallek, *The Right Moment: Ronald Reagan's First Victory and the Decisive Turning Point in American Politics* (New York: Oxford University Press, 2004); Michelle Nickerson, *Mothers of Conservatism: Women and the Postwar Right* (Princeton, N.J.: Princeton University Press, 2010); Daniel HoSang, *Racial Propositions: Ballot Initiatives and the Making of Postwar California* (Berkeley: University of California Press, 2010).

18. Strom Thurmond, "Conservatism in America Today," Aug. 26, 1982, Thurmond, Strom, Biographical file, Senate Historical Office, Washington, D.C.

19. Horace Fleming, interview by author, Aug. 30, 2008.

20. Buckley to Thurmond, Sept. 27, 1956, box 1, folder 13, Interim Series, JST.

21. *National Review*, Aug. 24, 1957.

1. EDGEFIELD, U.S.A. (1902–1932)

1. William Watts Ball, *The State That Forgot: South Carolina's Surrender to Democracy* (Indianapolis: Bobbs-Merrill, 1932), 22.

2. Steven Hahn, *A Nation Under Our Feet: Black Political Struggles in the Rural South from Slavery to the Great Migration* (Cambridge, Mass.: Belknap Press, 2003), 305–307; Stephen Kantrowitz, *Ben Tillman and the Reconstruction of White Supremacy* (Chapel Hill: University of North Carolina Press, 2000), 64–71.

3. Kantrowitz, *Ben Tillman*, 72. For more on Hampton, see Rod Andrews, *Wade Hampton: Confederate Warrior to Southern Redeemer* (Chapel Hill: University of North Carolina Press, 2008).

4. There were forty-two lynchings recorded over the fourteen-year period. See Peter Lau, *Democracy Rising: South Carolina and the Fight for Black Equality Since 1865* (Lexington: University Press of Kentucky, 2006), 16. More generally, see Leon F. Litwack, *Trouble in Mind: Black Southerners in the Age of Jim Crow* (New York: Knopf, 1998).

5. See generally Kantrowitz, *Ben Tillman*; and Francis Butler Simkins, *Pitchfork Ben Tillman: South Carolinian* (1994; Columbia: University of South Carolina Press, 2002).

6. Strom Thurmond, interview by James G. Banks, July 20, 1978, Interview A-0334, Southern Oral History Program Collection, University of North Carolina at Chapel Hill.

7. Jack Bass and Marilyn W. Thompson, *Strom: The Complicated Personal and Political Life of Strom Thurmond* (New York: Public Affairs, 2005), 30.

8. "Advice," June 15, 1923, box 17, folder Personal, John William Thurmond Papers, JST.

9. Bass and Thompson, *Strom*, 30.

10. Simkins, *Pitchfork Ben Tillman*, 531–34.

11. *State*, March 25, 1897; *Edgefield Advertiser*, March 31, 1897.

12. *Edgefield Advertiser*, April 14, 1897.

13. Ibid.

14. *Edgefield Advertiser*, March 31, 1897.

15. Quoted in *State*, April 2, 1897.

16. Quoted in *State*, April 3, 1897.

17. *State*, April 29, 1897.

18. *State*, July 20 and Aug. 4, 1897. For biographies of participants, see Edgefield County Historical Society, *The Story of Edgefield* (Edgefield, S.C.: Edgefield County Historical Society, 2009).

19. *Edgefield Advertiser*, Aug. 11, 1897.

20. *State*, Aug. 6, 1897.

21. *State*, Aug. 28 and 31, 1902.

22. Quoted in Kantrowitz, *Ben Tillman*, 121.

23. *State*, Aug. 8, 1921.

24. David W. Blight, *Race and Reunion: The Civil War in American Memory* (Cambridge, Mass.: Belknap Press, 2001); Bruce E. Baker, *What Reconstruction Meant: Historical Memory in the American South* (Charlottesville: University of Virginia Press, 2007).

25. Melvyn Stokes, *D. W. Griffith's "The Birth of a Nation": A History of "The Most Controversial Motion Picture of All Time"* (New York: Oxford University Press, 2007).

26. *State*, Nov. 21, 24, and 28, 1915, and Feb. 17, 18, and 20, 1916.

27. *State*, Feb. 13, 1916.

28. *State*, Nov. 23, 1915.

29. Edgefield County Historical Society, *Story of Edgefield*, 2; Walter Edgar, *Partisans and Redcoats: The Southern Conflict That Turned the Tide of the American Revolution* (New York: HarperCollins, 2001).

30. Thurmond probably recounted the Blease-Jones story untold times, but I have been able to document four instances in which he told it to reporters or biographers: in a television interview in 1961 ("Washington Conversation," Dec. 10, 1961, box 20, folder Thurmond—Statements By, Special Preparedness Investigating Subcommittee Series, JST); to an oral history interviewer in 1978 (Banks interview); in an interview with Marilyn Thompson in 1980 (Bass and Thompson, *Strom*, 25); and in an interview with Nadine Cohodas in 1989 (Cohodas, *Strom Thurmond and the Politics of Southern Change* [New York: Simon and Schuster, 1993], 31).

31. Untitled photograph, ca. 1912, box 1, Photograph Series, JST.

32. Bass and Thompson, *Strom*, 25.

33. David L. Carlton, *Mill and Town in South Carolina, 1880–1920* (Baton Rouge: Louisiana State University Press, 1982).

34. Simkins, *Pitchfork Ben Tillman*, 485–504; Carlton, *Mill and Town*, 215–72; Bryant Simon, *A Fabric of Defeat: The Politics of South Carolina Millhands, 1910–1948* (Chapel Hill: University of North Carolina Press, 1998), 11–58; Bryant Simon, "The Appeal of Cole Blease of South Carolina: Race, Class, and Sex in the New South," *Journal of Southern History* 62, no. 1 (Feb. 1996): 57–86.

35. Simon, "Appeal of Cole Blease," 62.

36. Carlton, *Mill and Town*, 224–25.

37. Ibid., 215.

38. *State*, June 20, 1912.

39. *State*, June 27, July 24, and Aug. 9, 1912.

40. During the Banks interview, Thurmond described the location of the rally in Edgefield, but it seems that he confused it with another political event because the newspaper record shows no appearances by the 1912 gubernatorial candidates in Edgefield. Information on Thurmond's Saluda office came from the Banks interview.

41. *State*, July 25, 1912.

42. Quoted in Simkins, *Pitchfork Ben Tillman*, 495.

43. *State*, Aug. 24, 1912.

44. "Dixiecrat Convention in Birmingham," July 20, 1948, story no. 066-084, Fox Movietone, ITN Source, www.itnsource.com.

45. Quoted in *AC*, Nov. 8, 1958.

46. Banks interview; Cohodas, *Strom Thurmond*, 18–36.

47. Simkins, *Pitchfork Ben Tillman*, 142, 171–72, 230–32.

48. Wayne Greenhaw, *Elephants in the Cottonfields: Ronald Reagan and the New Republican South* (New York: Macmillan, 1982), 214–34.

49. University of South Carolina, Extension Division, *Discussion of Economic Conditions of South Carolina* (Columbia: University of South Carolina, Extension Division, 1938), 35.
50. *AC*, Feb. 2, 1930.
51. Banks interview.
52. Bass and Thompson, *Strom*, 50–51.
53. Horace Fleming, interview by author, Aug. 30, 2008; James Lucier, interview by author, May 5, 2010.
54. James S. Humphreys, *Francis Butler Simkins: A Life* (Gainesville: University Press of Florida, 2008), 24.
55. Francis Butler Simkins, unpublished manuscript, box 3, Francis Butler Simkins Papers, Longwood University, Farmville, Va. Simkins's slip is on p. 24.
56. Ibid., 22–24.
57. Ibid.
58. Essie Mae Washington-Williams and William Stadiem, *Dear Senator: A Memoir by the Daughter of Strom Thurmond* (New York: Regan Books, 2005), 15, 17–44.
59. *AC*, June 16, 1925.
60. *AC*, Oct. 12, 1925.
61. *AC*, March 21, 1926.
62. *AC*, June 13 and Nov. 18, 1926.
63. *AC*, Aug. 15, 1927.
64. Washington-Williams and Stadiem, *Dear Senator*, 44.

2. BECOMING GOVERNOR THURMOND (1932–1947)

1. Francis Butler Simkins, unpublished manuscript, box 3, Francis Butler Simkins Papers, Longwood University, Farmville, Va. (hereinafter referred to as Simkins, unpublished manuscript), 23–24.
2. *Edgefield Advertiser*, Sept. 2, 1931. For more on the cotton holiday plan in South Carolina, see *WP*, Aug. 30, 1931; *WSJ*, Sept. 24, 1931.
3. J. William Thurmond to Hoover, Sept. 24, 1930, box 15, folder Law Correspondence, John William Thurmond Series, JST.
4. University of South Carolina, Extension Division, *Discussion of Economic Conditions of South Carolina* (Columbia: University of South Carolina, Extension Division, 1938), 74.
5. *AC*, Jan. 29, 1933; Jan. 17, 1935; and Feb. 4, 1936.
6. Personal notes, box 5, folder Personal Notes, State Senate Series, JST.
7. Ibid.
8. "Free Vocational Training with Pay," n.d., box 5, folder Bills, Audits, Reports, and Miscellaneous, State Senate Series, JST.
9. James F. Byrnes to Thurmond, Sept. 27, 1934, box 1, folder State Senate Correspondence, A–G, State Senate Series, JST.
10. *AC*, June 24, 1936.

11. *NYT*, June 26, 1936; *WP*, June 24 and 27, 1936.
12. Charles Wallace Collins, *Whither Solid South? A Study in Politics and Race Relations* (New Orleans: Pelican, 1947), 251–52.
13. *NYT*, June 26 and 27, 1936.
14. Quoted in William E. Leuchtenburg, *The White House Looks South: Franklin D. Roosevelt, Harry S. Truman, Lyndon B. Johnson* (Baton Rouge: Louisiana State University Press, 2005), 98.
15. Ibid., 98–102.
16. *AC*, July 25, 1937.
17. Nadine Cohodas, *Strom Thurmond and the Politics of Southern Change* (New York: Simon and Schuster, 1993), 54.
18. Robert Figg interview by Walter J. Brown and Mark Mitchell, n.d., box 20, folder Figg, Robert M., Interview Transcript, WJB; Cohodas, *Strom Thurmond*, 53.
19. Simkins, unpublished manuscript, 24–25.
20. Jack Bass and Marilyn W. Thompson, *Strom: The Complicated Personal and Political Life of Strom Thurmond* (New York: Public Affairs, 2005), 67. The definitive account of the Logue-Timmerman feud is T. Felder Dorn, *The Guns of Meeting Street* (Columbia: University of South Carolina Press, 2001).
21. Dorn, *Guns of Meeting Street*, 51–59; Bass and Thompson, *Strom*, 59.
22. Dorn, *Guns of Meeting Street*, 115–19; Alberta Morel Lachicotte, *Rebel Senator: Strom Thurmond of South Carolina* (New York: Devin-Adair, 1966), 6–7.
23. Dorn, *Guns of Meeting Street*, 126–28; Bass and Thompson, *Strom*, 66–67.
24. Lachicotte, *Rebel Senator*, 8.
25. Bass and Thompson, *Strom*, 45.
26. Strom Thurmond, interview by James G. Banks, July 20, 1978, Interview A-0334, Southern Oral History Program Collection, University of North Carolina at Chapel Hill.
27. Charles J. Masters, *Glidermen of Neptune: The American D-Day Glider Attack* (Carbondale: Southern Illinois University Press, 1995), 19, 35, 61–80.
28. Report of Civil Affairs Sections, "D-Day and Occupation," box 4, Military Series, JST.
29. Strom Thurmond, interview by Dale Rosengarten, Oct. 11, 1996, Jewish Heritage Collection, College of Charleston.
30. See Series Description, Military Series, JST.
31. Robert J. Norrell, *The House I Live In: Race in the American Century* (New York: Oxford University Press, 2005), 123–25, 130–33.
32. *AC*, Nov. 12, 1945.
33. *NYT*, April 4, 1944.
34. *NYT*, April 15, 1944.
35. Bass and Thompson, *Strom*, 74.
36. *AC*, Nov. 12, 1945.
37. Thurmond to Wilmot Riley, Jan. 5, 1946, box, folder Correspondence R, Subseries C: Campaigns, Gubernatorial Series, JST; *AC*, Jan. 4, 1946.

38. George B. Tindall, *The Emergence of the New South, 1913–1945* (Baton Rouge: Louisiana State University Press, 1967), 254–84.
39. *State*, May 15, 1946.
40. Figg to Thurmond, April 1, 1946, box 13, folder General Correspondence 1946, RMF; Thurmond to Figg, Jan. 5, 1946, box 1, folder General Correspondence 1945, RMF.
41. Figg, interview.
42. *State*, June 12, 1946.
43. Bruce J. Schulman, *From Cotton Belt to Sunbelt: Federal Policy, Economic Development, and the Transformation of the South, 1938–1980* (New York: Oxford University Press, 1991), 124–25.
44. *State*, June 28 and July 4, 5, and 9, 1946; Cohodas, *Strom Thurmond*, 55–56.
45. Cohodas, *Strom Thurmond*, 89.
46. *State*, Aug. 20, 1946.
47. *AC*, Sept. 3, 1946; Walter J. Brown, *James F. Byrnes of South Carolina: A Remembrance* (Macon, Ga.: Mercer University Press, 1992), 363.
48. *AC*, Aug. 24, 1946.
49. Figg, interview.
50. Barbara S. Griffith, *The Crisis of American Labor: Operation Dixie and the Defeat of the CIO* (Philadelphia: Temple University Press, 1988).
51. *State*, Aug. 29, 1946.
52. *State*, Aug. 31, 1946.
53. *State*, Sept. 1, 1946.
54. *State*, Sept. 8, 1946.
55. *State*, Jan. 22, 1947.
56. Brown, *James F. Byrnes*, 364.
57. Brown to Thurmond, n.d., box 52, folder 10, WJB.
58. *State*, Jan. 22, 1947; *AC*, Jan. 22, 1947.
59. Figg, interview, 48.
60. *State*, Jan. 22, 1947.
61. *AC*, Aug. 29 and 30, 1946.
62. *State*, May 4, 1947.
63. *NYT*, Sept. 17, 1947.
64. Schulman, *From Cotton Belt to Sunbelt*, 127.
65. Figg, interview, 49–50.
66. Quoted in Bass and Thompson, *Strom*, 44.
67. *State*, April 8, 1947.
68. *State*, Feb. 7, 1947.
69. *State*, Feb. 4, 1947.
70. Robert A. Lively, "The South and Freight Rates: Political Settlement of an Economic Argument," *Journal of Southern History* 14 (Aug. 1948): 357–84.
71. David M. Potter, "The Historical Development of Eastern-Southern Freight Rate Relationships," *Law and Contemporary Problems* 12 (Summer 1947): 416–48.

72. *State*, Feb. 4, 1947.
73. *NYT*, May 13, 1947.
74. *NYT*, Feb. 18, 1947; *Atlanta Daily World*, Feb. 18, 1947.
75. *NYT*, May 23, 1947.
76. *NYT*, May 11, 1947.
77. Rebecca West, "Opera in Greenville," *New Yorker*, June 14, 1947.
78. *CSM*, April 12, 1947.
79. *NYT*, Feb. 23, 1947; *Atlanta Daily World*, May 3 and July 21, 1946.
80. *NYT*, July 27, 1946.
81. *Norfolk New Journal and Guide*, Aug. 10, 1946; *Atlanta Daily World*, Aug. 22, 1946; *CSM*, July 31, 1946; *Pittsburgh Courier*, April 5, 1947.
82. *NYT*, Dec. 6, 1946.
83. *NYT*, Aug. 4, 1946.
84. *NYT*, July 28, 1946; *Pittsburgh Courier*, Aug. 3, 1946.
85. *State*, Feb. 20, 1947.
86. "Disgrace" quoted in *Norfolk New Journal and Guide*, March 1, 1947; *Pittsburgh Courier*, March 1, 1947.
87. *NYT*, May 11 and 18, 1947.
88. *NYT*, May 13 and 18, 1947.
89. Anonymous letter, Feb. 26, 1947, box 47, folder Willie Earle Lynching, Official Series, "In," Gubernatorial Series, JST.
90. *Norfolk New Journal and Guide*, March 1, 1947.
91. McKaine to Thurmond, March 12, 1947, and Dabbs to Thurmond, Feb. 22, 1947, both in box 47, folder Willie Earle Lynching, Official Series, "In," Gubernatorial Series, JST.
92. Keith M. Finley, *Delaying the Dream: Southern Senators and the Fight Against Civil Rights, 1938–1965* (Baton Rouge: Louisiana State University Press, 2008), 15–55.
93. *State*, May 21, 22, 25, and 29, 1947; *NYT*, May 21, 22, and 23, 1947.
94. *Pittsburgh Courier*, May 3, 1947.
95. Quoted in David Robertson, *Sly and Able: A Political Biography of James F. Byrnes* (New York: Norton, 1994), 480.
96. Carol Anderson, *Eyes off the Prize: The United Nations and the African American Struggle for Human Rights, 1944–1955* (Cambridge, U.K.: Cambridge University Press, 2003), 58–112.
97. *State*, Aug. 9, 1912. Also see Bryant Simon, "The Appeal of Cole Blease of South Carolina: Race, Class, and Sex in the New South," *Journal of Southern History* 62, no. 1 (Feb. 1996): 61.
98. *State*, May 23, 1947; *NYT*, May 23, 1947.
99. *CSM*, July 11, 1947.
100. Ibid.
101. *NYT*, Dec. 24, 1946.
102. "Anti–Poll Tax Bill," *CQA* 1947.

103. *CSM*, April 1, 1948. For more on the national coalition that had emerged to fight the poll tax, see Glenda Elizabeth Gilmore, *Defying Dixie: The Radical Roots of Civil Rights, 1919–1950* (New York: Norton, 2008), 336–45.

104. Richard Kluger, *Simple Justice: The History of Brown v. Board of Education and Black America's Struggle for Equality* (New York: Vintage, 1975), 333–35, 340–45, 347–48.

105. Brown to Thurmond, May 21, 1947, box 6, folder Brown, Walter, Subseries A: Official, Gubernatorial Series, JST.

106. *NYT*, May 18, 1947.

107. Brown to Thurmond, May 21, 1947, JST.

108. Kari A. Frederickson, *The Dixiecrat Revolt and the End of the Solid South, 1932–1968* (Chapel Hill: University of North Carolina Press, 2001), 42–46; Robert A. Garson, *The Democratic Party and the Politics of Sectionalism, 1941–1948* (Baton Rouge: Louisiana State University Press, 1974), 117–18.

109. *NYT*, Feb. 22, 1947; *Pittsburgh Courier*, March 1, 1947.

110. *Elmore v. Rice*, 72 F. Supp. 516; 1947 U.S. Dist. LEXIS 2548, July 12, 1947.

111. Tinsley E. Yarbrough, *A Passion for Justice: J. Waties Waring and Civil Rights* (New York: Oxford University Press, 1987).

112. Cohodas, *Strom Thurmond*, 118; Thurmond to Robert Figg, July 26, 1947, box 12, folder States Rights Correspondence 1947, RMF.

113. Lachicotte, *Rebel Senator*, 12–22.

114. Banks interview.

115. Lachicotte, *Rebel Senator*, 19–20; *Life*, Nov. 17, 1947, 44–46.

116. *AC*, Nov. 18, 1947.

117. *NYT*, Dec. 31, 1947.

3. LOST IN TRANSLATION (1948)

1. *NYT*, Feb. 3, 1948.

2. Walter J. Brown, *James F. Byrnes of South Carolina: A Remembrance* (Macon, Ga.: Mercer University Press, 1992), 355; Robert Figg, interview by Walter J. Brown and Mark Mitchell, n.d., box 20, folder Figg, Robert M., Interview Transcript, WJB.

3. Figg, interview; Nadine Cohodas, *Strom Thurmond and the Politics of Southern Change* (New York: Simon and Schuster, 1993), 132.

4. *NYT*, Feb. 8 and 9, 1948; *CNC*, Feb. 9, 1948.

5. *NYT*, Feb. 8, 1948; *WP*, Feb. 8, 1948; *LAT*, Feb. 8, 1948.

6. *CNC*, Aug. 5, 1956.

7. *CNC*, Feb. 11, 1948.

8. Russell to Thurmond, Feb. 17, 1948, box 146, folder 3230, Gubernatorial Series, JST.

9. *NYT*, Feb. 24, 1948; *Newsweek*, March 4, 1948; William E. Leuchtenburg, *The White House Looks South: Franklin D. Roosevelt, Harry S. Truman, Lyndon B.*

Johnson (Baton Rouge: Louisiana State University Press, 2005), 184–85; Kari A. Frederickson, *The Dixiecrat Revolt and the End of the Solid South, 1932–1968* (Chapel Hill: University of North Carolina Press, 2001), 81.

10. *CNC*, Feb. 25, 1948.
11. *CNC*, March 1, 1948.
12. Thurmond felt that he had a better chance of defeating Johnston than South Carolina's other senator, Burnet Maybank, who, like Thurmond, patterned himself after Jimmy Byrnes and was not as closely identified with the national party as Johnston. Thurmond proposed a deal with William Jennings Bryan Dorn, an ambitious South Carolina congressman with obvious designs on the Senate: Dorn would take Maybank's seat, and Thurmond would fight for Johnston's. The two men shook on it. Dorn felt double-crossed when Thurmond eventually ended up running for Maybank's seat after the senator's untimely death. William Jennings Bryan Dorn and Scott Derks, *Dorn: Of the People, a Political Way of Life* (Columbia, S.C.: Bruccoli Clark Layman; Orangeburg, S.C.: Sandlapper Publishing, 1988), 157–58.
13. Cohodas, *Strom Thurmond*, 179. In interviews with the biographer Nadine Cohodas, Thurmond "repeatedly denied" that the 1950 Senate race was a factor in his presidential run, insisting that "his decision to challenge Johnston didn't come until much later—after he finished his last two years as governor." Yet he announced his candidacy in May 1950, and the primary election was in July, when he still had five months remaining in his term.
14. *Time*, March 1, 1948.
15. *CNC*, Aug. 10, 1948.
16. *WP*, Feb. 19, 1948.
17. *Time*, March 1, 1948; Leuchtenburg, *White House Looks South*, 183–84.
18. *CNC*, March 2, 1948.
19. Ibid.; *NYT*, Feb. 29, 1948.
20. John E. Borsos, "Support for the National Democratic Party in South Carolina During the Dixiecrat Revolt of 1948" (master's thesis, University of South Carolina, 1987), 15–16.
21. "President Truman's Civil Rights Program, Columbia Democratic Party Rally, Columbia, S.C.," March 17, 1948, box 1, folder 6, Speeches, Series B, JST.
22. Thurmond to Figg, March 20, 1948, box 12, folder States Rights Correspondence, RMF; *CNC*, March 23, 1948.
23. *CNC*, March 22, 1948.
24. Brown to Figg, April 19, 1948, box 1, folder General Correspondence 1948, RMF.
25. Figg to Brown, April 25, 1948, and Brown to Figg, April 28, 1948, both in box 1, folder General Correspondence 1948, RMF.
26. *CNC*, April 28, 1948.
27. Raymond Moley, "Radio Address on Civil Rights," March 30, 1948, box 145, folder 3218, Gubernatorial Series, JST.

28. Donald R. Richberg, "Radio Talk on 'Civil Rights,'" March 30, 1948, box 145, folder 3218, Gubernatorial Series, JST.

29. Brown, *James F. Byrnes*, 360.

30. *CNC*, May 11, 1948; *NYT*, Sept. 5, 1948.

31. *Atlanta Constitution*, Sept. 17, 1964.

32. *NYT*, Sept. 5, 1948.

33. "Dear Editor Hall," n.d., box 12, folder States Rights Correspondence 1947, RMF. In 1956, the Princeton historian Eric Goldman asked Thurmond to review several manuscript pages concerning the 1948 election for a history of modern America that he was writing. The only correction that Thurmond made was to cross out a reference to him as the "Dixiecrat" candidate and replace it with "States' Rights." The name itself was still significant for him, though not for Goldman, who stuck with "Dixiecrat" in the final text. Thurmond to Goldman, April 12, 1956, box 71, folder 1, Eric F. Goldman Papers, Library of Congress; see Goldman, *The Crucial Decade: America, 1945–1955* (New York: Knopf, 1956), 92.

34. *NYT*, May 10, 1948.

35. Address of J. Strom Thurmond, governor of South Carolina, before Democratic Party rally, Jackson, Miss., May 10, 1948, box 148, States Rights Papers, vol. 1, Gubernatorial Series, JST.

36. Leuchtenburg, *White House Looks South*, 194–95; Frederickson, *Dixiecrat Revolt*, 130; *NYT*, July 15, 1948.

37. See, for example, Harry S. Truman, *Years of Trial and Hope*, vol. 2 of *Memoirs* (Garden City, N.Y.: Doubleday, 1956), 183; and Dorn and Derks, *Dorn*, 92.

38. *CNC*, July 15, 1948.

39. Ibid.; *CSM*, July 15, 1948.

40. Frederickson, *Dixiecrat Revolt*, 130–31; Robert A. Garson, *The Democratic Party and the Politics of Sectionalism, 1941–1948* (Baton Rouge: Louisiana State University Press, 1974), 279–80.

41. *NYT*, July 15, 1948.

42. Thurmond, telegram, n.d., box 52, folder 8, WJB; *CNC*, July 16, 1948.

43. Cohodas, *Strom Thurmond*, 177; Frederickson, *Dixiecrat Revolt*, 138; *NYT*, July 17, 1948.

44. Cohodas, *Strom Thurmond*, 175.

45. *WP*, July 8, 1948; Cohodas, *Strom Thurmond*, 175; Brown, *James F. Byrnes*, 369; Bill Minor, interview by author, Aug. 28, 2009.

46. Ann Mathison McLaurin, "The Role of the Dixiecrats in the 1948 Election" (Ph.D. diss., University of Oklahoma, 1972), 178.

47. *CNC*, July 18, 1948.

48. Brown, *James F. Byrnes*, 368–69; Cohodas, *Strom Thurmond*, 180.

49. *NYT*, July 19, 1948.

50. Frederickson, *Dixiecrat Revolt*, 134; Minor interview.

51. Leuchtenburg, *White House Looks South*, 196.

52. Frederickson, *Dixiecrat Revolt*, 137.

53. J. Barton Starr, "Birmingham and the 'Dixiecrat' Convention of 1948," *Alabama Historical Quarterly* 32, nos. 1 and 2 (1970): 31.

54. "Dixiecrat Convention in Birmingham," July 20, 1948, story no. 066-084, Fox Movietone, ITN Source, www.itnsource.com.

55. For examples, see *WP*, March 17, 1978; *Time*, Oct. 16, 1978, and Aug. 14, 1989; *WP*, Nov. 19, 1989; *NYT*, June 27, 2003.

56. *WP*, July 18, 1948; *CT*, July 18, 1948; Cohodas, *Strom Thurmond*, 177; Frederickson, *Dixiecrat Revolt*, 140.

57. The classic articulation of this elite white southern viewpoint can be found in William Alexander Percy's memoir, *Lanterns on the Levee: Recollections of a Planter's Son* (New York: Knopf, 1945).

58. For insight into how southern white men might have talked in private company, see Melton A. McLaurin, *Separate Pasts: Growing Up White in the Segregated South* (Athens: University of Georgia Press, 1987); or, for a different class perspective, consider Walker Percy's fictionalized scene of Birmingham country clubbers in *The Last Gentleman* (New York: Farrar, Straus and Giroux, 1966), 147–51.

59. *CNC*, July 20, 1948.

60. *Pittsburgh Courier*, July 31, 1948.

61. *NYT*, July 20, 1948.

62. *NYT*, July 19, 1948.

63. *CSM*, July 21, 1948.

64. *WP*, July 21, 1948.

65. *WP*, July 25, 1948.

66. *Louisville Courier-Journal*, Oct. 16, 1948.

67. *Pittsburgh Courier*, July 31, 1948.

68. *CNC*, Sept. 11, 1948.

69. *CNC*, Sept. 23, 1948.

70. *CNC*, Oct. 3, 1948.

71. Strom Thurmond, statement at a press conference in Washington, D.C., Sept. 30, 1948, box 13, folder States Rights Democrats 1948, RMF.

72. Cohodas, *Strom Thurmond*, 186.

73. *CNC*, Oct. 3, 1948; *WP*, Oct. 3, 1948.

74. *CNC*, Aug. 23, 1948.

75. *CNC*, Oct. 7, 1948.

76. *NYT*, Oct. 7, 1948.

77. Brown, *James F. Byrnes*, 370–71.

78. Speech draft attached to C. C. Wyche to Brown, Aug. 20, 1948, box 56, folder 1, WJB.

79. Ibid.

80. Strom Thurmond, "Accepting the States' Rights Democratic Nomination as President of the United States at Houston, Texas," Aug. 11, 1948, box 148, States Rights Papers, vol. 1, Gubernatorial Series, JST.

81. *CT*, Aug. 12, 1948.

82. Thurmond, "Accepting the States' Rights Democratic Nomination as President of the United States at Houston, Texas."

83. Figg, interview.

84. There was grand talk in the week following the Birmingham meeting about getting Thurmond's name on the ballot in all forty-eight states, but party leaders quickly revised this goal once they realized the difficulties involved. *CNC*, July 25, 1948; *CT*, Aug. 9, 1948.

85. Brown, *James F. Byrnes*, 370.

86. Jeff Woods, *Black Struggle, Red Scare: Segregation and Anti-communism in the South, 1948-1968* (Baton Rouge: Louisiana State University Press, 2004), 14-34.

87. *NYT*, Aug. 4, 1948.

88. Thurmond, "Accepting the States' Rights Democratic Nomination as President of the United States at Houston, Texas."

89. *CNC*, Oct. 5, 1948.

90. Ibid.; see also *CNC*, Oct. 17, 1948.

91. Figg, interview.

92. Robert A. Brent, "The Tidelands," *Social Science Bulletin*, Dec. 1952, 51-54.

93. *NYT*, July 25, 1948.

94. *WP*, Feb. 24, 1948.

95. *NYT*, July 12, 1948.

96. *NYT*, July 25, 1948.

97. *CNC*, July 25, 1948.

98. Frederickson, *Dixiecrat Revolt*, 169, 270.

99. McLaurin, "Role of the Dixiecrats," 84; *CNC*, Sept. 21, 1948.

100. Frederickson, *Dixiecrat Revolt*, 168-69.

101. Alexander Heard, *A Two-Party South?* (Chapel Hill: University of North Carolina Press, 1952), 159.

102. Thomas Sancton, "White Supremacy—Crisis or Plot?," *Nation*, July 24, 1948, 97.

103. Frederickson, *Dixiecrat Revolt*, 153-54, 168; Glen Jeansonne, *Leander Perez: Boss of the Delta* (Baton Rouge: Louisiana State University Press, 1977), 164-69.

104. *CNC*, Sept. 2, 1948.

105. Claude Pepper, speech at Montgomery, Ala., Oct. 7, 1948, box 13, folder Democratic Party (1 of 8), ODJ.

106. *CNC*, July 18, 1948.

107. *CNC*, Nov. 1, 1948.

108. *Newsweek*, Oct. 25, 1948, 32-34.

109. *CSM*, Oct. 6, 1948.

110. *CSM*, Oct. 8, 1948.

111. *CNC*, Oct. 1, 1948.

112. *CNC*, Nov. 2, 1948.

113. *CNC*, Nov. 3, 1948.

114. *AC*, Nov. 3, 1948.

115. Remarks of Senator Strom Thurmond, n.d., Strom Thurmond Biographical file, Senate Historical Office, Washington, D.C.; Figg, interview.

116. Frederickson, *Dixiecrat Revolt*, 184.

117. V. O. Key, *Southern Politics in State and Nation* (New York: Knopf, 1949), 342.

118. Ibid., 329–44; Heard, *Two-Party South?*, 251–78; Garson, *Democratic Party*, 312.

119. Alonzo L. Hamby, *Man of the People: A Life of Harry S. Truman* (New York: Oxford University Press, 1995), 490.

120. Thurmond to Goldman, April 12, 1956, box 71, folder 1, Eric F. Goldman Papers, Library of Congress.

121. Remarks of Senator Strom Thurmond, n.d., Strom Thurmond Biographical file, Senate Historical Office.

122. Truman, *Years of Trial and Hope*, 183. Truman even included an apocryphal exchange with a reporter. "President Truman is only following the platform that Roosevelt advocated," the reporter pointed out. "I agree," Thurmond replied, "but Truman really *means* it." Also see Dorn and Derks, *Dorn*, 92.

123. Horace Fleming, interview by author, Aug. 30, 2008. For another example of Thurmond correcting reporters about the 1948 convention, see *CNC*, July 24, 1956.

124. Strom Thurmond, "How It Feels to Run for President and Lose," *Family Weekly*, Sept. 5, 1976.

125. Strom Thurmond, "Conservatism in America Today," Aug. 26, 1982, Strom Thurmond Biographical file, Senate Historical Office.

4. PLUCK AND LUCK (1949–1954)

1. *CNC*, Oct. 10 and 16, 1948.

2. Graves to Thurmond, Dec. 27, 1948, box 52, folder 8, WJB.

3. Brown to Thurmond, Jan. 4, 1949, box 52, folder 9, WJB; Brown to Thurmond, June 27, 1949, box 13, folder States Rights Correspondence, RMF; Brown to George McNabb, Sept. 12, 1949, box 52, folder 9, WJB; Walter J. Brown, *James F. Byrnes of South Carolina: A Remembrance* (Macon, Ga.: Mercer University Press, 1992), 363. Brown was particularly concerned about one of the more reactionary leaders, Charles Wallace Collins. For an assessment of Collins's influence, see Joseph E. Lowndes, *From the New Deal to the New Right: Race and the Southern Origins of Modern Conservatism* (New Haven, Conn.: Yale University Press, 2008), 11–44.

4. Thurmond and his advisers were the South Carolina equivalent of the white elites in Virginia described by J. Douglas Smith who placated segments of the black community as a way of preserving white supremacy in the closing decades of Jim Crow. See Smith, *Managing White Supremacy: Race, Politics, and Citizenship in Jim Crow Virginia* (Chapel Hill: University of North Carolina Press, 2001).

5. Brown to Thurmond, Jan. 4, 1949, box 52, folder 9, WJB.

6. Thurmond to Brown, April 1, 1950, box 56, folder 4, WJB.

7. Kari A. Frederickson, *The Dixiecrat Revolt and the End of the Solid South, 1932–1968* (Chapel Hill: University of North Carolina Press, 2001), 202.

8. David Robertson, *Sly and Able: A Political Biography of James F. Byrnes* (New York: Norton, 1994).

9. *WP*, June 19, 1949.

10. Newspaper plate, Truman to Byrnes, June 21, 1949, box 15, folder 22, Series 7, James F. Byrnes Collection, Special Collections, Clemson University.

11. Quoted in Robertson, *Sly and Able*, 498.

12. Strom Thurmond, "O'er the Ramparts We Watched," Aug. 13, 1949, box 2, folder 12, Speeches, Series B, JST.

13. Strom Thurmond, "Course of Human Freedom," Oct. 21, 1949, box 2, folder 13, Speeches, Series B, JST.

14. Brown, *James F. Byrnes*, 382.

15. *NYT*, Nov. 22, 1949.

16. *NYT*, Nov. 23, 1949.

17. *State*, May 24, 1950.

18. Walter Brown, memorandum on the 1950 campaign, n.d., box 56, folder 6, WJB.

19. Brown, *James F. Byrnes*, 384.

20. *Charleston Evening Post*, May 4, 1950.

21. Robert Figg, interview by Walter J. Brown and Mark Mitchell, n.d., box 20, folder Figg, Robert M., Interview Transcript, WJB.

22. *Atlanta Journal*, May 11, 1950.

23. *State*, June 27, 1950; *AC*, June 27, 1950; William Jennings Bryan Dorn and Scott Derks, *Dorn: Of the People, a Political Way of Life* (Columbia, S.C.: Bruccoli Clark Layman; Orangeburg, S.C.: Sandlapper Publishing, 1988), 117.

24. *State*, June 1, 1950.

25. Brown, *James F. Byrnes*, 384.

26. *State*, May 24, 1950.

27. *State*, June 3, 1950.

28. Brown to TC, May 25, 1950, box 56, folder 6, WJB.

29. *State*, May 24, June 9 (quotation), and June 23, 1950.

30. *State*, May 24, 1950.

31. Frederickson, *Dixiecrat Revolt*, 205.

32. "What Defeated Frank Graham in North Carolina? The Same Disgraceful Political Blunder That Will Defeat Strom Thurmond," n.d., box 112, folder Johnston Campaigns, 1950, Thurmond, J. Strom, ODJ.

33. *Anderson Independent*, June 12, 1949.

34. *State*, June 27, 1950.

35. *State*, May 3 and 4, 1950; Thurmond quoted on May 4.

36. *State*, May 23, 1950.

37. Frederickson, *Dixiecrat Revolt*, 203.

38. *State*, June 25, 1950; untitled political advertisement, ca. 1950, box 13, folder States Rights Topical (Thurmond for Senate), RMF.

39. Frederickson, *Dixiecrat Revolt*, 208; Brown to Ernest Craig, June 8, 1950, box 56, folder 4, WJB.

40. Frederickson, *Dixiecrat Revolt*, 208–15.

41. Modjeska Simkins, "To All True Believers in the Fight for True Freedom and True Democracy," July 8, 1950, box 111, folder Campaigns, 1950 (2 of 4), ODJ; Frederickson, *Dixiecrat Revolt*, 214–15.

42. Telegram to Robert Figg, July 8, 1950, box 13, folder States Rights Topical (Thurmond for Senate), RMF.

43. *Charleston Evening Post*, July 8, 1950.

44. *NYT*, July 12 and 13, 1950; Nadine Cohodas, *Strom Thurmond and the Politics of Southern Change* (New York: Simon and Schuster, 1993), 215.

45. Robert Figg to Palmer Bradley, July 12, 1950, box 13, folder States Rights Topical (Thurmond for Senate), RMF; *State*, July 12, 1950; Frederickson, *Dixiecrat Revolt*, 215.

46. Numan V. Bartley and Hugh D. Graham, *Southern Elections: County and Precinct Data, 1950–1972* (Baton Rouge: Louisiana State University Press, 1978), 385, 387.

47. Brown to Thurmond, July 18, 1950, box 165, folder 3456, Gubernatorial Series, JST.

48. Brown, *James F. Byrnes*, 387.

49. McNabb to Figg, July 18, 1950, box 13, folder States Rights Topical (Thurmond for Senate), RMF.

50. Samuel Lubell, *The Future of American Politics* (New York: Harper, 1952), 106–30.

51. William G. Carleton, "The Southern Politicians—1900 and 1950," *Journal of Politics* 13, no. 2 (May 1951): 220–21.

52. Frank Chodorov, "To Give States' Rights Vitality," *Human Events* 7, no. 5 (1950): 1–4.

53. Quoted in C. R. Canup and W. D. Workman Jr., *Charles E. Daniel: His Philosophy and Legacy* (Columbia, S.C.: R. L. Bryan, 1981), 150.

54. Kim Phillips-Fein, *Invisible Hands: The Making of the Conservative Movement from the New Deal to Reagan* (New York: Norton, 2009), 10–13.

55. Daniel to Thurmond, Feb. 8, 1950, box 12, folder States Rights Correspondence 1950, RMF.

56. Brown to Thurmond, Feb. 13, 1950, box 12, folder States Rights Correspondence 1950, RMF.

57. Quoted in Mary Beth Reed and Barbara Smith Strack, *The Savannah River Site at Fifty* (Washington, D.C.: Dept. of Energy; Stone Mountain, Ga.: New South Associates, 2002), 57. For more on the Savannah River Site's impact on the local area, see Kari Frederickson, "The Cold War at the Grassroots: Militarization and Modernization in South Carolina," in *The Myth of Southern Exceptionalism*, ed. Matthew D. Lassiter and Joseph Crespino (New York: Oxford University Press, 2009), 190–209.

58. Reed and Strack, *Savannah River*, 184.

59. For more on postwar southern industrial recruitment, see Tami J. Friedman,

"Exploiting the North-South Differential: Corporate Power, Southern Politics, and the Decline of Organized Labor After World War II," *Journal of American History* 95, no. 2 (2008): 323–48; and James C. Cobb, *The Selling of the South: The Southern Crusade for Industrial Development, 1936–1990* (Urbana: University of Illinois Press, 1993).

60. Cohodas, *Strom Thurmond*, 236.

61. Walter S. Steele to Thurmond, June 7, 1954, box 18, folder General Correspondence: R, Personal Series, JST; *AC*, May 4, 1952, and April 30, 1953.

62. Thurmond to R. M. Byrd, May 11, 1954, box 5, folder General Correspondence: B, Personal Series, JST.

63. *AC*, June 23, 1954.

64. See, for example, Thurmond, letter to the editor, *National Bulletin*, June 21, 1954, box 5, folder General Correspondence: B, Personal Series, JST.

65. Thurmond to Mrs. Charles W. Sanders, June 3, 1954, box 21, folder General Correspondence: S, Personal Series, JST; also see Thurmond to G. Marshall Moore, July 19, 1954, box 16, folder General Correspondence: M, Personal Series, JST.

66. Dorn and Derks, *Dorn*, 159.

67. *CSM*, Sept. 29, 1954.

68. *AC*, Sept. 2, 1954; *NYT*, Sept. 12, 1954.

69. *CSM*, Sept. 29, 1954.

70. Brown, *James F. Byrnes*, 404–405.

71. *NYT*, Oct. 10, 1954.

72. Ibid.

73. *NYT*, Sept. 5, 1954.

74. Brown, *James F. Byrnes*, 406.

75. *WP*, Sept. 10, 1954.

76. *NYT*, Sept. 7, 1954; Brown, *James F. Byrnes*, 407–408.

77. Brown to Byrnes, Oct. 8, 1954, box 1, folder 5, Series 7, Byrnes Collection.

78. Brown, *James F. Byrnes*, 406–407.

79. *NYT*, Oct. 24, 1954.

80. *NYT*, Sept. 10, 1954; *WP*, Oct. 12, 1954.

81. *AC*, Oct. 8, 1954.

82. *Time*, Nov. 15, 1948.

83. Dorn and Derks, *Dorn*, 160.

84. Brown, *James F. Byrnes*, 412–13.

85. *NYT*, Nov. 7, 1954; *Saturday Evening Post*, Oct. 8, 1955.

86. *NYT*, Nov. 3, 1954.

5. MASSIVE RESISTANCES (1955–1960)

1. *WP*, Jan. 4, 1955; *NYT*, Jan. 5, 1955; Donald A. Ritchie, U.S. Senate Historical Office, ed., *Minutes of the Senate Democratic Conference, 1903–1964* (Washing-

ton, D.C.: GPO, 1998), 498; Thurmond quoted in Nadine Cohodas, *Strom Thurmond and the Politics of Southern Change* (New York: Simon and Schuster, 1993), 273.

2. *LAT*, March 1, 1955.

3. *CT*, March 8, 1964; *Washington Star*, Aug. 1, 1965.

4. *WP*, June 21, 1955.

5. Roy E. Floyd to Johnson, Dec. 14, 1954, folder LBJA Congressional File: Thurmond, Strom, LBJ.

6. Horace Fleming, interview by author, Aug. 30, 2008; Strom Thurmond, interview by Michael Gillette, May 7, 1979, Oral History Collection, LBJ; *Florence Morning News*, June 25, 1955; *CT*, March 8, 1964.

7. *AC*, March 4, 1956.

8. Strom Thurmond, S. 10106, Feb. 9, 1955, box 15, folder Legislation, Subject Correspondence 1957, JST; Figg to Thurmond, Feb. 24, 1955, box 8, folder Figg, Robert, Subject Correspondence 1955, JST.

9. Strom Thurmond, "The U.S. Supreme Court's Decision on Segregation in the Public Schools Will Destroy the Constitution," July 15, 1955, box 4, folder 48, Speeches, Series B, JST; *Myrtle Beach News*, July 21, 1955; *CNC*, Dec. 15, 1955; Strom Thurmond, "The U.S. Supreme Court's Decision to Rule South Carolina's Segregation Law as Unconstitutional," Meeting of States' Rights League in Sumter, S.C., Aug. 4, 1955, box 4, folder 49, Speeches, Series B, JST.

10. *NYT*, Dec. 30, 1955.

11. *NYT*, Feb. 26, 1956.

12. *WSJ*, Feb. 16, 1956; Felix Morley, "The State of the Nation," *Nation's Business*, March 1956, 21–22.

13. *National Review*, Feb. 29, 1956, 5–6.

14. *WP*, Jan. 11, 1956; *NYT*, Nov. 27, 1955, and Jan. 22, 1956.

15. *CR*, Senate, March 12, 1956, 4459–60.

16. Keith M. Finley suggests three different versions of the manifesto's origins: one with Thurmond as the driving influence, another with Georgia's Walter George, and a final one centered on Harry Byrd. See Finley, *Delaying the Dream: Southern Senators and the Fight Against Civil Rights, 1938–1965* (Baton Rouge: Louisiana State University Press, 2008), 142–46. For the fullest account, see John Kyle Day, "The Southern Manifesto: Making Opposition to the Civil Rights Movement" (Ph.D. diss., University of Missouri—Columbia, 2006), 313–35.

17. *Time*, March 26, 1956. No other account was as dismissive of Thurmond's role as *Time*, though several others also reported that fellow southerners toned down Thurmond's initial draft. See *NYT*, March 12, 1956; *New York Herald Tribune*, March 13, 1956.

18. *CNC*, March 28, 1956.

19. Day, "Southern Manifesto," 404.

20. Kyle Longley, *Senator Albert Gore, Sr.: Tennessee Maverick* (Baton Rouge: Louisiana State University Press, 2004), 124.

21. Thurmond to Eastland, Feb. 18, 1956, File Series 1, Subseries 18, folder 10-10, James O. Eastland Papers, Special Collections, University of Mississippi.

22. Thurmond continued to assert his central role in drafting the manifesto years afterward. "I felt particularly flattered that so many of the thoughts contained in my two drafts were embodied in the final document," he wrote to Richard Russell in 1968 (Thurmond to Russell, May 15, 1968, box 17, folder Southern Manifesto, Administrative Assistant Series, JST). In 1979, in an oral history interview, Thurmond corrected a researcher who implied that his colleagues toned down his original draft. Gillette, interview with Thurmond.

23. *CNC*, March 28, 1956.

24. Untitled, ca. 1956, box 17, folder Southern Manifesto, Administrative Assistant Series, JST. Whether or not to include the term "interposition" was one of the drafting committee's thorniest problems. See John Stennis to Richard Russell, Feb. 24, 1956, Series 29, box 5, folder 5, JCS.

25. *CR*, Senate, March 12, 1956, 4462.

26. *Greenville News*, March 13, 1956.

27. Don Oberdorfer, "Ex-Democrat, Ex-Dixiecrat, Today's 'Nixiecrat,'" *NYT Magazine*, Oct. 6, 1968.

28. Strom Thurmond, "Judicial Domination," June 18, 1956, box 4, folder 54, Speeches, Series B, JST.

29. Jonathan M. Schoenwald, *A Time for Choosing: The Rise of Modern American Conservatism* (New York: Oxford University Press, 2001), 35–40.

30. Ibid., 45–48. Examples include Rosalie M. Gordon, *Nine Men Against America: The Supreme Court and Its Attack on American Liberties* (New York: Devin-Adair, 1958); W. Cleon Skousen, *The Naked Communist* (Salt Lake City: Ensign, 1958); and J. Edgar Hoover, *Masters of Deceit: The Story of Communism in America and How to Fight It* (New York: Holt, 1958).

31. *State*, June 27, 1957; *WP*, June 27, 1957.

32. *Greenville News*, July 8, 1957; *NYT*, July 8 and 9, 1957.

33. Untitled, STRP, July 1, 1957, box 5, folder 69, Speeches, Series B, JST.

34. *Time*, July 24, 1972.

35. *State*, June 28, 1957.

36. *Greenville News*, Feb. 2, 1958.

37. *Greenville News*, Sept. 8, 1959; *NYT*, Sept. 8, 1959.

38. "Longer Sessions, More Trouble," STRP, Sept. 14, 1959, box 8, folder 89, Speeches, Series B, JST.

39. *NYT*, Sept. 30, 1958.

40. Strom Thurmond, "The School Crisis and Constitutional Government," Oct. 3, 1958, box 7, folder 82, Speeches, Series B, JST.

41. Strom Thurmond, "The U.S. Supreme Court and Socialism," Oct. 4, 1958, box 7, folder 76, Speeches, Series B, JST.

42. Strom Thurmond, "The South Declares War on the Supreme Court's Unconstitutional Usurpation and Unlawful Arrogation of Power," Nov. 7, 1958, box 7, folder 79, Speeches, Series B, JST; *AC*, Nov. 8, 1958.

43. *WP*, Oct. 13, 1958.

44. *NYT*, Oct. 6 and 13, 1958.

45. "Congress Approves Civil Rights Act of 1957," *CQA* 1957.

46. "History, Techniques of Senate Filibusters," *CQA* 1957.

47. Robert Mann, *The Walls of Jericho: Lyndon Johnson, Hubert Humphrey, Richard Russell, and the Struggle for Civil Rights* (New York: Harcourt Brace, 1996), 77.

48. Gilbert C. Fite, *Richard B. Russell, Jr.: Senator from Georgia* (Chapel Hill: University of North Carolina Press, 1991).

49. C. Vann Woodward, "The Great Civil Rights Debate," *Commentary*, Oct. 1957, 285, 290; *NYT*, Sept. 1, 1957.

50. The history of Lyndon Johnson's role in passing the 1957 Civil Rights Act has been well documented. See Robert A. Caro, *Master of the Senate*, vol. 3 of *The Years of Lyndon Johnson* (New York: Knopf, 2002); Robert Dallek, *Lone Star Rising: Lyndon Johnson and His Times, 1908–1960* (New York: Oxford University Press, 1991); and Mann, *Walls of Jericho*.

51. Untitled, STRP, Aug. 12, 1957, box 5, folder 69, Speeches, Series B, JST.

52. Thurmond to Walter Brown, Aug. 5, 1957, box 13, folder Legislation: Civil Rights, Folder 6, Aug. 5–14, 1957, Subject Correspondence 1957, JST.

53. *WP*, Aug. 21, 1957; *NYT*, Aug. 24 and 27, 1957.

54. "Congress Approves Civil Rights Act of 1957."

55. Memo, n.d., box 420, folder Reedy: Memos—Aug. 1957, George Reedy Files, LBJ; *CR*, Senate, Aug. 29, 1957, 16477.

56. Strom Thurmond, "In Opposition to the Compromise on the Civil Rights Bill," Aug. 23, 1957, box 5, folder 71, Speeches, Series B, JST.

57. The same memo is in both Russell's and Johnson's papers. See memo, ca. 1957, box 89, folder 1, Series 10—Civil Rights, RBR; and memo, n.d., box 420, folder Reedy: Memos—Aug. 1957, Reedy Files.

58. *Time*, Sept. 9, 1957.

59. *WP*, Sept. 13, 1957; *NYT*, Aug. 31, 1957.

60. Statement by Senator Strom Thurmond, Aug. 30, 1957, box 5, folder 71, Speeches, Series B, JST; *WP*, Sept. 13, 1957.

61. *CNC*, Aug. 27, 1957.

62. *NYT*, Aug. 28, 1957.

63. For examples, see box 5, folder Legislation: Civil Rights Speech—Telegrams, Subject Correspondence 1957, JST.

64. Statement by Senator Strom Thurmond, Aug. 30, 1957.

65. *NYT*, Aug. 29, 1957.

66. *WP*, Aug. 30, 1957; *NYT*, Aug. 30, 1957; *CR*, Senate, Aug. 29, 1957, 16442 (Knowland quotation).

67. *CR*, Senate, Aug. 29, 1957, 16456.

68. *NYT*, Sept. 9, 1957.
69. George Reedy, interview by Michael L. Gillette, pt. 3, June 7, 1975, LBJ.
70. *Time*, Sept. 9, 1957; also see box 58, folder Civil Rights, Gen. August, ODJ, and box 122, folder 6, Series 6, Political, RBR.
71. *NYT*, Aug. 30, 1957; *CR*, Senate, Aug. 29, 1957, 16476.
72. *CR*, Senate, Aug. 30, 1957, 16660–62; *NYT*, Aug. 31, 1957; *WP*, Sept. 10, 1957.
73. Robert Figg, interview by Walter J. Brown and Mark Mitchell, n.d., box 20, folder Figg, Robert M., Interview Transcript, WJB.
74. Cohodas, *Strom Thurmond*, 213.
75. Thurmond said that the caucus had lost its cohesiveness in recent years due to infrequent meetings; see *CNC*, Jan. 22, 1956. Gillette, interview with Thurmond.
76. See, for example, Harry S. Dent to Mr. and Mrs. Amos C. Johnson Jr., Feb. 17, 1960, box 4, folder Civil Rights 3 (Race Relations), JST.
77. Gillette, interview with Thurmond.
78. *WP*, Aug. 30, 1957; Cohodas, *Strom Thurmond*, 294.
79. *Chicago Defender*, Sept. 14, 1957.
80. Bertie Bowman, *Step by Step: A Memoir of Hope, Friendship, Perseverance, and Living the American Dream* (New York: Ballantine Books, 2008), 100.
81. See Misc. Dusenbury, ca. 1955, box 7, folder Dusenbury, Subject Correspondence 1955, JST.
82. Lee to Thurmond, Aug. 29, 1957, box 14, folder Legislation: Civil Rights Speech—South Carolina Correspondence, Subject Correspondence 1957, JST. For more on the politics of Thurmond's masculinity, see Kari Frederickson, "'As a Man, I Am Interested in States' Rights': Gender, Race, and the Family in the Dixiecrat Party, 1948–1950," in *Jumpin' Jim Crow: Southern Politics from Civil War to Civil Rights*, ed. Jane Dailey, Glenda Elizabeth Gilmore, and Bryant Simon (Princeton, N.J.: Princeton University Press, 2000), 260–74.
83. Thurmond to Carter Burgess, Sept. 18, 1956; Walter Brown to Thurmond, Sept. 26, 1956; Thurmond to William F. Buckley, Oct. 3, 1956; Mrs. W. R. Thigpen to John U. Barr, Oct. 15, 1956, all in box 1, folder B, Interim Series, JST.
84. *Anderson Independent*, May 16, 1957, and Aug. 29, 1958, in box 160, folder Clippings, Persons, Thurmond, Strom, General, ODJ.
85. Quoted in Howard H. Quint, *Profile in Black and White: A Frank Portrait of South Carolina* (Washington, D.C.: Public Affairs Press, 1958), 158.
86. Brown to Thurmond, Aug. 3 and 6, 1957, box 53, folder 1, WJB.
87. *CT*, Aug. 30, 1957.
88. *NYT*, July 7 and 27, 1956; *LAT*, Aug. 12, 1956; *NYT*, Dec. 3, 1994.
89. Brown to Thurmond, Jan. 15, 1957, box 53, folder 1, WJB; quotation from untitled news manuscript, n.d., in same folder.
90. *WP*, Aug. 30, 1957.
91. *Chicago Defender*, Sept. 14, 1957.

92. *Baltimore Afro-American*, Aug. 21 and 28, 1948.

93. *State*, Sept. 11, 1955.

94. *Anderson Independent*, May 16, 1957.

95. See Elizabeth A. Fones-Wolf, *Selling Free Enterprise: The Business Assault on Labor and Liberalism, 1945–1960* (Urbana: University of Illinois Press, 1994).

96. *LAT*, March 1, 1955.

97. James C. Cobb, *The Selling of the South: The Southern Crusade for Industrial Development, 1936–1990* (Urbana: University of Illinois Press, 1993), 101–102; Bruce J. Schulman, *From Cotton Belt to Sunbelt: Federal Policy, Economic Development, and the Transformation of the South, 1938–1980* (New York: Oxford University Press, 1991), 81.

98. "Stewart E. McClure: Chief Clerk, Senate Committee on Labor, Education, and Public Welfare (1949–1973)," Oral History Interviews, Senate Historical Office, Washington, D.C.

99. Gillette, interview with Thurmond.

100. *CNC*, March 27, 1959.

101. *Greenville News*, April 4, 1959.

102. Rick Perlstein, *Before the Storm: Barry Goldwater and the Unmaking of the American Consensus* (New York: Hill and Wang, 2001), 47–48.

103. Thurmond to Roy W. Johnson, June 30, 1955; Thurmond to S. W. Gable, Jan. 20, 1955; Gable to Thurmond, Feb. 11, 1955; Thurmond to Charles E. Daniel Jr., Feb. 19, 1955; Thurmond to J. A. Crosby Jr., March 16, 1955; all in box 11, folder Industries for South Carolina, Subject Correspondence 1955, JST.

104. *CSM*, Aug. 19, 1964.

105. Thurmond to Daniel, Nov. 15, 1963, box 59, folder Thurmond, Senator Strom— 1963–64, CED; *CR*, Senate, Nov. 14, 1963, 21913.

106. Daniel to Fred Buzhardt, Oct. 10, 12, and 23, 1961, box 59, folder Thurmond, Strom, 1961, CED.

107. Buck Mickel to Fred Buzhardt, Sept. 25, 1961; Daniel to Buzhardt, Sept. 26, 1961; and Thurmond to B. Everett Jordan, Oct. 18, 1961; all in box 14, folder Labor 7, Subject Correspondence 1961, JST. For a list of congressmen to whom Thurmond sent the memo, see box 14, folder Labor 7, Subject Correspondence 1962, JST. For a copy of the Daniel Construction brief to the NLRB, see box 134, folder Labor—National Labor Relations Board: Daniel Construction Company (Case), 1963, Legislative Assistant Series, JST.

108. *WSJ*, Nov. 28, 1961.

109. *State*, Oct. 7, 1961.

110. Thurmond to J. R. Shackelford, Oct. 17, 1961, box 14, folder Labor 7, Subject Correspondence 1961, JST.

111. Harry S. Dent to Dean Livingston, Dec. 29, 1961, box 12, folder Labor, Subject Correspondence 1961, JST.

112. "The New Frontier Throttles Dixie Industry," *Human Events* 19, no. 2 (1962): 29–31; Thurmond to Daniel, Jan. 8, 1962, box 12, folder Labor, Subject Correspondence 1961, JST.

113. Bill Arthur, "The Darlington Mills Case: Or 17 Years Before the Courts," *New South* (Summer 1973), 40–47. Labor historians have cited the Darlington case as a source of union demoralization in the South in the 1950s. In 1958, for example, the union abandoned a campaign at the Cannon chain of mills in North Carolina. TWUA had sufficient support in five branches to conduct NLRB representation elections but withdrew fearing a repeat of the Darlington Mills case. Because it could not organize the entire chain, TWUA officials anticipated that an election victory would cause the chains to be closed and their production transferred to another plant. F. Ray Marshall, *Labor in the South* (Cambridge, Mass.: Harvard University Press, 1967), 278. Even before the Darlington case, the Millikens had a history of union defiance. The army seized the Deering Milliken plant in Gaffney after the company ignored a War Labor Board directive to bargain with the TWUA. When the government turned the mill back over, the company again refused to deal with the union, leading to a twenty-two-month strike that Milliken eventually broke. Deering Milliken also controlled the Dallas Manufacturing Company in Huntsville, Alabama, which it liquidated after fights with the union there (ibid., 276–77). Also see Timothy Minchin, *Fighting Against the Odds: A History of Southern Labor Since World War II* (Gainesville: University Press of Florida, 2005), 68; and, generally, Dana Frank, *Buy American: The Untold Story of Economic Nationalism* (Boston: Beacon Press, 1999).

114. *WSJ*, Oct. 19, 1962; *NYT*, Oct. 19, 1962.

115. *NYT*, Dec. 9, 1964; Karl E. Campbell, *Senator Sam Ervin, Last of the Founding Fathers* (Chapel Hill: University of North Carolina Press, 2007), 178–79.

116. *WSJ*, Dec. 4, 1980.

117. Tami J. Friedman, "Exploiting the North-South Differential: Corporate Power, Southern Politics, and the Decline of Organized Labor After World War II," *Journal of American History* 95, no. 2 (2008): 325.

118. A 1964 *Wall Street Journal* article noted that while race problems were cited for blunting industrial development in Little Rock and Birmingham, "southern businessmen contend the South as a whole has been little affected." *WSJ*, July 21, 1964. For an excellent discussion of the subject, see James C. Cobb, *The Brown Decision, Jim Crow, and Southern Identity* (Athens: University of Georgia Press, 2005), 7–30.

119. Strom Thurmond, "States' Rights Versus Federal Usurpation of Power, Dedication of Confederate Museum, Front Royal, Virginia," June 28, 1959, box 8, folder 86, Speeches, Series B, JST.

120. *WP*, Oct. 3, 1958; Alan Draper, *Conflict of Interests: Organized Labor and the Civil Rights Movement in the South, 1954–1968* (Ithaca, N.Y.: ILR Press, 1994), 45–46.

121. *WP*, May 16, 1960.

122. Strom Thurmond, "Front Royal Union Faces Ouster Vote," May 17, 1960, box 9, folder 105, Speeches, Series B, JST; and "Labor Reform and Threats," Aug. 24, 1959, box 8, folder 89, Speeches, Series B, JST.

123. Thurmond to J. M. Mock, April 28, 1959, box 10, folder Labor 3, Subject Correspondence 1959, JST.

124. Brown to Thurmond, n.d., box 3, folder Brown, Walter, Subject Correspondence 1955, JST.

125. Dent to Thurmond, Nov. 14, 1957, box 134, folder Labor, Legislative Assistant Series, JST; Thurmond to J. A. Graham, Jan. 22, 1957, box 21, folder Legislation: Labor, folder 1, Subject Correspondence 1957, JST.

126. Thurmond to Eugene Calvert, Aug. 24, 1960, box 15, folder Labor 5-1, folder 3, Subject Correspondence 1960, JST; Fred Buzhardt to Alex McCullough, April 8, 1961, box 12, folder Labor 5, Subject Correspondence 1961, JST.

127. *AC*, July 24, 1960.

128. *State*, Oct. 19, 1960.

129. *State*, Nov. 11, 1961, and Sept. 16, 1964.

130. *CNC*, Nov. 16 and 17, 1960; *WP*, Jan. 2, 1961; Thurmond to James O. Eastland, Jan. 2, 1961, File Series 1, Subseries 18, folder 10-10, Eastland Papers.

6. OUTSIDE AGITATORS (1960–1963)

1. Brown to Thurmond, Sept. 29, 1961, box 26, folder Political Affairs 2-2 (1962 Senate Election), Subject Correspondence 1961, JST.

2. "Ideology and the Party Split—Myth and Reality," *Advance*, March 1962, 23–26.

3. *CNC*, July 15, 1964.

4. William Jennings Bryan Dorn and Scott Derks, *Dorn: Of the People, a Political Way of Life* (Columbia, S.C.: Bruccoli Clark Layman; Orangeburg, S.C.: Sandlapper Publishing, 1988), 169.

5. F. Clifton White, *Suite 3505: The Story of the Draft Goldwater Movement*, with William J. Gill (New Rochelle, N.Y.: Arlington House, 1967), 19–20.

6. Manion to Goldwater, July 21, 1959, box 1, folder Victor Publishing Company, "The Conscience of a Conservative" (1 of 4), Subseries Writings, Series 1, Personal, BMG.

7. Abstract of minutes taken at Goldwater meeting, Jan. 23, 1960, box 1, folder Victor Publishing Company, "The Conscience of a Conservative" (2 of 4), Subseries Writings, Series 1, Personal, BMG.

8. *NYT*, March 27, 1960.

9. *Charlotte Observer*, March 27, 1960.

10. *Anderson Independent*, March 27, 1960; *WP*, April 6, 1960.

11. Manion to Goldwater, March 31, 1960, box 1, folder Victor Publishing Company, "The Conscience of a Conservative" (2 of 4), Subseries Writings, Series 1, Personal, BMG.

12. Rick Perlstein, *Before the Storm: Barry Goldwater and the Unmaking of the American Consensus* (New York: Hill and Wang, 2001), 85–87.

13. Ibid., 92–93.

14. Manion to Goldwater, March 9, 1960, box 1, folder Victor Publishing Company, "The Conscience of a Conservative" (2 of 4), Subseries Writings, Series 1, Personal, BMG.

15. Perlstein, *Before the Storm*, 62–63.

16. William Workman, "Senator Goldwater on States Rights," *Greenville News*, box 1, folder Victor Publishing Company, "The Conscience of a Conservative" (2 of 4), Subseries Writings, Series 1, Personal, BMG.

17. *NYT*, Feb. 21 and 28 and March 6, 1960.

18. "Major Issues in the 1960 Civil Rights Debate," *CQA* 1960.

19. *NYT*, Feb. 28, 1960; *Time*, March 14, 1960.

20. "Major Issues in the 1960 Civil Rights Debate."

21. William Workman, *The Case for the South* (New York: Devin-Adair, 1960); *Greenville News*, March 6, 1960; "Thurmond Gives Each Member of the U.S. Senate a Copy of W. D. Workman's Book, *The Case for the South*," March 5, 1960, box 9, folder 100, Speeches, Series B, JST; *NYT*, Nov. 11, 1962.

22. William Workman Jr., interview by Jack Bass, Feb. 5, 1974, Interview A-0281, Southern Oral History Program Collection, University of North Carolina at Chapel Hill.

23. When asked about the prospect of running a statewide campaign, Boineau told Republican leaders that the party had only "a bunch of dedicated little old ladies in tennis shoes, and me, that didn't know what the hell we were doing." Charles E. Boineau, interview by Wilma M. Woods, April 6, 12, 14, and 18, 1995, South Carolina Political Collections Oral History Project, University of South Carolina.

24. Russell Merritt, "The Senatorial Election of 1962 and the Rise of Two-Party Politics in South Carolina," *South Carolina Historical Magazine* 98, no. 3 (July 1997): 284.

25. *CNC*, March 18, 1962; *NYT*, March 18, 1962; Anthony Harrigan, "South Carolina Going Republican?," *Human Events* 19, no. 19 (1962): 343–44.

26. Nadine Cohodas, *Strom Thurmond and the Politics of Southern Change* (New York: Simon and Schuster, 1993), 358; Merritt, "Senatorial Election of 1962," 289.

27. Long-distance conversation with Dent and Thurmond, Dec. 17, 1962, box 39, folder Persons, Thurmond, J. Strom (1 of 4), WDW.

28. Text of speech by W. D. Workman Jr., Sept. 11, 1962, box 5, folder Johnston v. Workman, Speeches, Television, WDW.

29. Henry Lee Moon, *Balance of Power: The Negro Vote* (Garden City, N.Y.: Doubleday, 1948), 40.

30. Brown to Thurmond, Sept. 29, 1961, box 26, folder Political Affairs 2-2 (1962 Senate Election), Subject Correspondence 1961, JST.

31. "Ideology and the Party Split—Myth and Reality," 23–26.

32. "The Charge up Capitol Hill," *Advance*, March 1962, 4–6, 29–30.
33. *WP*, Nov. 21, 1962; *NYT*, Nov. 26, 1962; "Washington Report," CBS News, Dec. 2, 1962, box 5, folder Johnston v. Workman, Critiques and Evaluations of Election Results, WDW.
34. Harrigan, "South Carolina Going Republican?" For more on the Southern States Industrial Council, see Katherine Rye Jewell, "As Dead as Dixie: The Southern States Industrial Council and the End of the New South, 1933–1954" (Ph.D. diss., Boston University, 2010).
35. Barry Goldwater, "The GOP Invades the South," box 2, folder The GOP Invades the South, Subseries Writings, Series 1, Personal, BMG.
36. Gregory Shorey, "Introduction of Strom Thurmond at the Dedication of the Style-Crafters, Inc. Plant in Greenville, South Carolina," Nov. 18, 1963, box 6, folder Audio-Visual Material, Gregory D. Shorey Papers, South Carolina Political Collections, University of South Carolina.
37. Stephen Shadegg to Goldwater, Nov. 27, 1962, box S–Y, folder Shadegg, Sub-Series Correspondence, Series 1, Personal, BMG.
38. Raymond Moley, *The Republican Opportunity* (New York: Duell, Sloan and Pearce, 1962), 236.
39. Goldwater to Workman, May 3, 1962, box 5, folder Johnston v. Workman, General (4 of 4), WDW.
40. Goldwater to Thurmond, Aug. 2, 1961, box 3, folder Civil Rights 1, Subject Correspondence 1961, JST.
41. Thurmond to Goldwater, Aug. 7, 1961, box 3, folder Civil Rights 1, Subject Correspondence 1961, JST.
42. *WP*, June 12, 1963.
43. Thurmond to W. B. Godwin, June 14, 1963, box 5, folder Civil Rights 3, folder 4, Subject Correspondence 1963, JST.
44. *State*, June 20, 1963.
45. Senate Committee on Commerce, 88th Cong., *Civil Rights—Public Accommodations*, p. 1 (Washington, D.C.: GPO, 1963), 84.
46. *CT*, March 8, 1964.
47. Samuel and Robin Stilwell, interview by author, Feb. 20, 2008.
48. *State*, July 27, 1963.
49. Senate Committee on Commerce, 88th Cong., *Civil Rights—Public Accommodations*, p. 2 (Washington, D.C.: GPO, 1963), 1084; for more on Poindexter and the Homeowners' Rights Ordinance, see Thomas J. Sugrue, *The Origins of the Urban Crisis: Race and Inequality in Postwar Detroit* (Princeton, N.J.: Princeton University Press, 2006), 209–29.
50. Samuel and Robin Stilwell, interview. The account of Wallace and Thurmond interacting with the African American Senate dining room staff comes from Robin Stilwell, who worked in Thurmond's office and accompanied the men that day. Stilwell recalled how the black waiters "loved Senator Thurmond" and

how Wallace and the staff "were friendly, laughing, and talking—I mean, it was nothing like the image that you would have of him." The skepticism about the genuineness of such interactions is my own.

51. Senate Committee on Commerce, 88th Cong., *Civil Rights—Public Accommodations*, p. 1, 68.
52. Taylor Branch, *Parting the Waters: America in the King Years, 1954–63* (New York: Simon and Schuster, 1988), 564, 569.
53. Strom Thurmond, statement on the Senate floor, Aug. 2, 1963, box 11, folder 129, Speeches, Series B, JST.
54. John D'Emilio, *Lost Prophet: The Life and Times of Bayard Rustin* (New York: Free Press, 2003), 346.
55. Strom Thurmond, "Statement on the Question of Communist Connections and Influence in the Current Negro Demonstrations," Aug. 23, 1963, box 11, folder 129, Speeches, Series B, JST; D'Emilio, *Lost Prophet*, 346–50.
56. *WP*, Aug. 11 and 14, 1963.
57. *CT*, Aug. 15, 1963.
58. *LAT*, Aug. 19, 1963.
59. *State*, May 24 and 25 and June 10, 1961; Strom Thurmond, "Communists and Freedom Riders," Aug. 8, 1961, box 10, folder 115, Speeches, Series B, JST; *State*, Sept. 27, 1961.

7. MUZZLING AND THE AMERICAN RIGHT (1958–1963)

1. Alberta Morel Lachicotte, *Rebel Senator: Strom Thurmond of South Carolina* (New York: Devin-Adair, 1966), 162–63.
2. *WP*, July 21, 1961.
3. Thurmond to Fulbright, July 21, 1961, and Fulbright to Thurmond, July 21, 1961, box 39, folder Un-American Activities 1-5, folder 1, Subject Correspondence 1961 Series, JST; Lachicotte, *Rebel Senator*, 162–63.
4. J. William Fulbright, recorded interview by Pat Holt, July 8, 1964, John F. Kennedy Library Oral History Program.
5. *CR*, Senate, Aug. 2, 1961, 14395–97.
6. *NYT*, July 22, 1961. Also see Thurmond to Fulbright, July 21, 1961, and Fulbright to Thurmond, July 21, 1961, JST.
7. *CT*, July 22, 1961.
8. Jonathan M. Schoenwald, *A Time for Choosing: The Rise of Modern American Conservatism* (New York: Oxford University Press, 2001), 62; Rick Perlstein, *Before the Storm: Barry Goldwater and the Unmaking of the American Consensus* (New York: Hill and Wang, 2001), 110.
9. Milliken's impression recorded by Stephen Shadegg to Goldwater, Feb. 16, 1962, box S-Y, folder Shadegg, Stephen, Subseries Correspondence, Series 1, Personal, BMG.
10. Strom Thurmond, "The Challenge Facing the American People," *Manion Forum* radio program, Jan. 20, 1958, box 7, folder 76, Speeches, Series B, JST;

Strom Thurmond, "Radio Address, Manion Forum of the Air," Dec. 14, 1958, box 8, folder 76, Speeches, Series B, JST.

11. Robert J. Lifton, *Thought Reform and the Psychology of Totalism: A Study of "Brainwashing" in China* (New York: Norton, 1961); Susan L. Carruthers, *Cold War Captives: Imprisonment, Escape, and Brainwashing* (Berkeley: University of California Press, 2009); Louis Menand, "Brainwashed: Where the 'Manchurian Candidate' Came From," *New Yorker*, Sept. 15, 2003, 88–91.

12. One indication can be seen in a statement filed with the investigating subcommittee by Major General John B. Medaris, who supported the continuation of anti-Communist indoctrination programs for American soldiers. "When one considers that most Americans grow up with little formal explanation of communism," Medaris said, "the success of brainwashing in the Korean war becomes more understandable if no less shocking." *NYT*, March 11, 1962.

13. *WP*, Aug. 27, 1961; House Committee on Un-American Activities, *Communist Psychological Warfare (Brainwashing): Consultation with Edward Hunter, Author and Foreign Correspondent*, March 13, 1958 (Washington, D.C.: GPO, 1958); Senate Committee on the Judiciary, *The New Drive Against the Anti-Communist Program*, July 11, 1961 (Washington, D.C.: GPO, 1961).

14. *CR*, Senate, Aug. 25, 1961, 17101–102; *CT*, Aug. 27, 1961.

15. Citizens' Council Forum Films, reel no. 0089, Mississippi Department of Archives and History, Jackson.

16. Strom Thurmond, news release on staff appointment, Nov. 23, 1957, box 5, folder 66, Speeches, Series B, JST.

17. *NYT*, June 29, 1973; Joe Buzhardt, interview by author, April 29, 2009.

18. *WP*, Feb. 10, 1962.

19. See *Dan Smoot Report*, June 18, 1962, box 22, folder J. William Fulbright, 5, Aug. 1961–1965, Special Preparedness Investigating Subcommittee Series, JST; and *National Review Bulletin*, Aug. 21, 1962, box 1, folder Civil Military Relations, 1950–1951; 1961–1962, Special Preparedness Investigative Subcommittee Series, JST.

20. Philip Corso, *The Day After Roswell: A Former Pentagon Official Reveals the U.S. Government's UFO Cover-Up* (New York: Pocket Books, 1997); House Committee on National Security, *Accounting for POW/MIA's from the Korean War and the Vietnam War*, Sept. 17, 1996 (Washington, D.C.: GPO, 1997), 8–10.

21. *WP*, March 18, 1962.

22. Nadine Cohodas, *Strom Thurmond and the Politics of Southern Change* (New York: Simon and Schuster, 1993), 274.

23. Lachicotte, *Rebel Senator*, 142–56.

24. Dennis Shedd and Mark Goodin, interview by author, May 10, 2011.

25. Quoted in Lachicotte, *Rebel Senator*, 169.

26. *LAT*, Jan. 31, 1961; *CT*, Feb. 1, 1961.

27. Schoenwald, *Time for Choosing*, 100–101, 105–107.

28. *NYT*, Jan. 23, 1962; *Commercial Appeal*, Jan. 28, 1962; Fletcher Knebel and Charles W. Bailey II, "Military Control: Can It Happen Here?," *Look*, Sept. 11, 1962, 18–21.

29. *New Republic*, Dec. 25, 1961, 11–13.

30. Schoenwald, *Time for Choosing*, 55–56.

31. See, for example, National Council of Churches of Christ in the United States of America, *Operation Abolition: Some Facts and Some Comments* (New York: Dept. of Religious Liberty, National Council of Churches, 1961); and Christian Anti-communism Crusade, "Factions and Fiction Concerning the Film 'Operation Abolition,'" May 10, 1961, box 45, folder Operation Abolition, 3-5, Dec. 1960–April 1962, Special Preparedness Investigating Subcommittee Series, JST.

32. Thurmond to C. J. Maddox, March 14, 1961, box 25, folder Walker Related, 18–1, Special Preparedness Investigating Subcommittee Series, JST.

33. Thurmond to William H. Beattie, May 15, 1961, box 36, folder Un-American Activities 1 (Communism), folder 2, Subject Correspondence 1961, JST.

34. *NYT*, June 18, 1961.

35. *LAT*, Oct. 5, 1961.

36. For examples of the letters Russell received, see box 130, folders 7 and 8, Series 9—Legislative, RBR. For the link between the letters and the John Birch Society, see Richard W. Edmonds to Russell, Dec. 3, 1961, box 130, folder 7, Series 9—Legislative, RBR. Also see MGW to BABS, Nov. 7, 1961, box 130, folder 8, Series 4—Legislative, RBR.

37. Robert A. Caro, *Master of the Senate*, vol. 3 of *The Years of Lyndon Johnson* (New York: Knopf, 2002), 370–82.

38. *NYT*, Sept. 22, 1961; *Evening Star*, Sept. 8, 1961.

39. Robert Caro has punctured the myth of Russell's racial moderation; see *Master of the Senate*, 164–202, particularly 184–89.

40. *NYT*, April 24, 1995.

41. For examples of the letters sent to Stennis (on which Thurmond was often copied), see box 41, folder Un-American Activities 1-5 (Fulbright Note Muzzling the Military), folders 14–15, Subject Correspondence 1961, JST.

42. Edwin A. Walker, "There Is No Substitute for Victory!" *Citizen*, Jan. 1962, 8–25.

43. *Times-Picayune*, Dec. 30, 1961, (Mississippi edition).

44. Charles W. Eagles, *The Price of Defiance: James Meredith and the Integration of Ole Miss* (Chapel Hill: University of North Carolina Press, 2009), 331.

45. See Citizens' Council Forum Films Finding Aid, Mississippi Department of Archives and History.

46. Earl Lively Jr., *The Invasion of Mississippi* (Belmont, Mass.: American Opinion, 1963).

47. Good examples include Thurmond to Dan Smoot, Aug. 23, 1961, box 40, folder Un-American Activities 1-5 (Fulbright Note Muzzling the Military), folder 7, Billy James Hargis to Thurmond, Aug. 31, 1961, box 40, folder Un-American

Activities 1-5, folder 9; and Phoebe Courtney to Thurmond, Oct. 2, 1961, box 41, folder Un-American Activities 1-5, folder 15; all in Subject Correspondence 1961, JST.

48. *LAT*, Nov. 21, 1961.
49. *LAT*, Nov. 30, 1961.
50. *CT*, Dec. 3, 1961.
51. DeLoach to Mr. Mohr, Dec. 5, 1961, Strom Thurmond FBI File.
52. *Time*, Feb. 2, 1962; *CSM*, Jan. 27, 1962; *LAT*, Jan. 26, 1962.
53. *CT*, Jan. 31, 1962; *NYT*, Jan. 24 and 28, 1962; *Time*, Feb. 2, 1962; *LAT*, Jan. 26, 1962.
54. *NYT*, Feb. 1, 1962; *CT*, Feb. 1, 1962.
55. *NYT*, Feb. 1, 2, and 3, 1962; *CT*, Feb. 1, 1962.
56. *WP*, Feb. 9, 1962.
57. *CSM*, Feb. 10, 1962.
58. Statement by Senator John Stennis in ruling on plea of executive privilege, Feb. 8, 1962, and Stennis to Russell, Feb. 15, 1962, box 129, folder Armed Services Special Committee, Subseries D, Series 9, RBR.
59. *Time*, Feb. 16, 1962; "Information Questionnaire," n.d., folder Muzzling Clippings, box 3, Series 43, JCS.
60. George Ball, recorded interview by Larry J. Hackman, Feb. 16, 1968, Kennedy Library Oral History Program; *WP*, Feb. 28, 1962.
61. Senate Special Preparedness Subcommittee of the Committee on Armed Services, *Military Cold War Education and Speech Review Policies*, p. 2 (Washington, D.C.: GPO, 1962), 754.
62. *CT*, March 18, 1962.
63. William E. Mayer, "Brainwashing," n.d., box 49, folder POW (Prisoner of War), 4-11, folder 2, May 1956–Jan. 1964, Special Preparedness Investigating Subcommittee Series, JST.
64. *WP*, Jan. 23 and Feb. 9, 1962; Schoenwald, *Time for Choosing*, 85–86.
65. *WP*, April 6, 1962; *LAT*, April 6 and 8, 1962.
66. *WP*, April 6, 1962.
67. *NYT*, April 7, 1962.
68. Lachicotte, *Rebel Senator*, 196.
69. *NYT*, Sept. 3 and Oct. 2, 1962; *CT*, Sept. 7, 1962.
70. *CT*, Dec. 3, 1962; *CSM*, Oct. 25, 1962 (quotation); *NYT*, Oct. 26, 1962.
71. *WP*, Feb. 15 and 22, 1962; *NYT*, March 8, 1962.
72. "The 'Military Lobby'—Its Impact on Congress, Nation," *CQA* 1963.
73. Dwight D. Eisenhower, "Farewell Radio and Television Address to the American People," Jan. 17, 1961, in *Public Papers of the Presidents of the United States, Dwight D. Eisenhower, 1960–61* (Washington, D.C.: GPO, 1961), 1035–40.
74. " 'Military Lobby'—Its Impact on Congress, Nation."
75. *NYT*, April 12, 1963; *LAT*, April 13, 1963; *WP*, April 17, 1963.

76. *NYT*, Aug. 24, 1963.
77. *CT*, Sept. 12, 1963. See generally, "Nuclear Test Ban Treaty Ratified," *CQA* 1963.
78. Elizabeth Churchill Brown, *The Enemy at His Back* (New York: Bookmailer, 1956).
79. Constantine Brown, *The Coming of the Whirlwind* (Chicago: Regnery, 1964).
80. Thurmond to Ben E. Thrakill Jr., Jan. 7, 1963, box 3, folder Civil Rights, Subject Correspondence 1963, JST.
81. Thurmond to Mrs. Constantine Brown, April 5, 1963, box 3, folder Thurmond, Strom, 1961–1964, Elizabeth Churchill Brown Papers, Hoover Archives, Stanford University.
82. Thurmond to Mrs. Constantine Brown, Dec. 20, 1963, box 3, folder Thurmond, Strom, 1961–1964, Brown Papers.
83. Ibid.

8. PARTY HOPPING (1964)

1. *Charlotte Observer*, March 27, 1960; *Greenville News*, Sept. 18, 1964; *NYT*, Sept. 18, 1964.
2. *State*, Sept. 18, 1964; *Greenville News*, Sept. 18, 1964.
3. *CR*, Senate, June 28, 1962, 12175–79; Strom Thurmond, "Prayer in Public Schools," March 8, 1963, box 11, folder 127, Speeches, Series B, JST; *State*, June 20, 1963; Strom Thurmond, "Prayers and Bible Reading in the Schools," June 19, 1963, box 11, folder 129, Speeches, Series B, JST.
4. Joseph A. Fisher, "The Becker Amendment: A Constitutional Trojan Horse," *Journal of Church and State* 11, no. 3 (1969): 427–55; "Congress Fails to Act on School Prayer Amendments," *CQA* 1964.
5. Strom Thurmond, "God and Government," Orange County Conservative Groups, Los Angeles, Feb. 12, 1964, box 11, folder 131, Speeches, Series B, JST.
6. Strom Thurmond, "Project Prayer," Feb. 26, 1964, box 11, folder 136, Speeches, Series B, JST; *State*, Feb. 24, 1964.
7. Thurmond to Reagin [sic], March 10, 1964, box 21, folder Personal 6 (folder 1), Subject Correspondence 1964, JST.
8. Paul Blanshard, *Religion and the Schools: The Great Controversy* (Boston: Beacon Press, 1963), 53.
9. House Committee on the Judiciary, *School Prayers*, pt. 2 (Washington, D.C.: GPO, 1964), 1310.
10. Quoted in "Congress Fails to Act on School Prayer Amendments."
11. Darren Dochuk, *From Bible Belt to Sunbelt: Plain-Folk Religion, Grassroots Politics, and the Rise of Evangelical Conservatism* (New York: Norton, 2011), 241; Hargis to Thurmond, Aug. 31, 1961, box 40, folder Un-American Activities 1-5, folder 9, Subject Correspondence 1961, JST. For more on the politics of school prayer, see Benjamin Eric Sasse, "The Anti-Madalyn Majority: Secular Left, Religious Right, and the Rise of Reagan's America" (Ph.D. diss., Yale University, 2004).

12. James F. Findlay, "Religion and Politics in the Sixties: The Churches and the Civil Rights Act of 1964," *Journal of American History* 77, no. 1 (1990): 80.
13. *CR*, Senate, March 2, 1964, 4126; Strom Thurmond, "An Appeal That a Study of Churches and Civil Rights Be Printed in the Congressional Record," March 12, 1964, box 11, folder 136, Speeches, Series B, JST; *CT*, March 13, 1964.
14. Edgar C. Bundy to Thurmond, Feb. 27, 1964, box 3, folder Civil Rights 1 (Civil Rights Legislation), Subject Correspondence 1964, JST; *CR*, Senate, June 8, 1964, 12967-68.
15. *State*, July 9, 1964.
16. "Senate Votes Cloture on Civil Rights Bill, 71-29," *CQA* 1964.
17. *CR*, Senate, April 27, 1964, 9184; May 6, 1964, 1018-86; and May 7, 10338-339; Taylor Branch, *Pillar of Fire: America in the King Years, 1963-65* (New York: Simon and Schuster, 1998), 293-94; *NYT*, April 22, 1964.
18. *WP*, Aug. 19, 1965.
19. Joseph Crespino, *In Search of Another Country: Mississippi and the Conservative Counterrevolution* (Princeton, N.J.: Princeton University Press, 2007), 91-100.
20. Thurmond to John Synon, May 7, 1964, SCRID no. 6-70-0-1-21-1-1; John Satterfield to Milliken, Jan. 27, 1964, SCRID nos. 6-70-0-41-1-1-1 to 6-70-0-41-2-1-1; Satterfield to Daniel, Jan. 24, 1964, SCRID nos. 6-70-0-43-1-1-1 to 6-70-0-43-2-1-1; all in Mississippi State Sovereignty Commission Records, Mississippi Department of Archives and History, Jackson. For donation amounts, see untitled, n.d., SCRID no. 6-70-0-94-2-1-1, Mississippi State Sovereignty Commission Records, Mississippi Department of Archives and History.
21. Thurmond to Daniel, Oct. 15, 1963, box 59, folder Thurmond, Senator Strom— 1963-64, CED.
22. Erle Johnston, memo to file, June 22, 1964, SCRID nos. 6-70-0-185-1-1-1 to 6-70-0-185-2-1-1, Mississippi State Sovereignty Commission Records, Mississippi Department of Archives and History.
23. *CR*, Senate, May 27, 1964, 12146.
24. Crespino, *In Search of Another Country*, 95.
25. *CR*, Senate, May 27, 1964, 12146.
26. "Senate Defeats Filibuster, Passes Civil Rights Act, 73-27," *CQA* 1964.
27. Strom Thurmond, "In Opposition to the Civil Rights Bill," June 18, 1964, box 11, folder 136, Speeches, Series B, JST.
28. Ibid.
29. Strom Thurmond, "Watering Down of the Civil Rights Bill," May 26, 1964, box 11, folder 135, Speeches, Series B, JST.
30. For a fuller discussion of the politics surrounding the Title IV language, see Joseph Crespino, "The Best Defense Is a Good Offense: The Stennis Amendment and the Fracturing of Liberal School Desegregation Policy, 1964-1972," *Journal of Policy History* 18, no. 3 (2006): 304-25.
31. Branch, *Pillar of Fire*, 387-88.
32. *NYT*, July 3, 1964.

33. LeRoy Collins, interview by Joe B. Frantz, Nov. 15, 1972, Oral History Collections, LBJ.

34. *State*, July 9, 1964.

35. Senate Committee on Commerce, *Nomination of LeRoy Collins*, July 7, 1964 (Washington, D.C.: GPO, 1964), 48.

36. Donald Ritchie, "Oral History with Charles Sargent Caldwell," March 19, 1996, Oral History Interviews, Senate Historical Office, Washington, D.C.

37. Samuel and Robin Stilwell, interview by author, Feb. 20, 2008.

38. Dan Rapoport (former UPI reporter), interview by author, Feb. 24, 2010; *State*, July 10, 1964; *WP*, July 10, 1964. Marilyn Thompson interviewed Ralph Yarborough in 1982; see Jack Bass and Marilyn W. Thompson, *Strom: The Complicated Personal and Political Life of Strom Thurmond* (New York: Public Affairs, 2005), 187-88. Also see Nadine Cohodas, *Strom Thurmond and the Politics of Southern Change* (New York: Simon and Schuster, 1993), 354-55.

39. F. Clifton White, *Suite 3505: The Story of the Draft Goldwater Movement*, with William J. Gill (New Rochelle, N.Y.: Arlington House, 1967), 48, 61-62, 304.

40. Louisiana and Georgia provided good examples of how Goldwater's campaign alienated moderate southern Republicans. See "Special Report," March 20, 1964, box G-M, folder 1964 Presidential Campaign, Louisiana (notebook), Subseries 13: Speeches, Series 2, 1964 Presidential Campaign, BMG; *Atlanta Journal-Constitution*, May 3, 1964; *Washington Star*, May 3, 1964.

41. *State*, June 16, 1964.

42. Timothy N. Thurber, "Goldwaterism Triumphant? Race and the Republican Party, 1965-1968," *Journal of the Historical Society* 7, no. 3 (Sept. 2007): 350.

43. *NYT*, June 19, 1964.

44. Rick Perlstein, *Before the Storm: Barry Goldwater and the Unmaking of the American Consensus* (New York: Hill and Wang, 2001), 363.

45. John Genier, interview by Jack Bass and Walter De Vries, July 17, 1974, Interview A-0009, Southern Oral History Program Collection University of North Carolina at Chapel Hill.

46. Fred H. Taylor, "Special Report," April 4, 1964, box A, folder 1964 Presidential Campaign, Alabama (notebook), Subseries 13: Speeches, Series 2, 1964 Presidential Campaign, BMG. Also see, in same folder, Fred H. Taylor, "Special Report," March 7, 1964.

47. Dan T. Carter, *Politics of Rage: George Wallace, the Origins of the New Conservatism, and the Transformation of American Politics* (New York: Simon and Schuster, 1995), 208.

48. *NYT*, May 2, 1964.

49. White, *Suite 3505*, 386-90.

50. *State*, July 16, 1964.

51. Barry Goldwater, keynote speech, Georgia State Republican Convention, May 2, 1964, box 17, folder 1964 Presidential Campaign Speeches, Keynote Speech,

Georgia Republican State Convention, Subseries 13: Speeches, Series 2, 1964 Presidential Campaign, BMG.

52. *State*, July 7, 1964.

53. *State*, July 16 and 17, 1964.

54. Brown to Thurmond, telegram, Sept. 14, 1964, box 53, folder 7, WJB.

55. *State*, Sept. 18, 1964.

56. See note attached to Brown to Thurmond, telegram, Sept. 14, 1964, WJB.

57. *State*, Sept. 16, 1964.

58. Cohodas, *Strom Thurmond*, 359.

59. *State*, Sept. 17, 1964.

60. Ibid. For an example of this sentiment in his personal letters, see Thurmond to William Loeb, Sept. 21, 1964, box 24, folder Political Affairs (8) (Party Switch) Sept. 16–Dec. 2, 1964, Subject Correspondence 1964, JST.

61. Byrnes to Thurmond, Sept. 16, 1964, box 24, folder Political Affairs (8) (Party Switch) Sept. 16–Dec. 2, 1964, Subject Correspondence 1964, JST.

62. Reagan to Thurmond, Sept. 18, 1964, box 24, folder Political Affairs (8) (Party Switch) Sept. 16–Dec. 2, 1964, Subject Correspondence 1964, JST.

63. Robertson to Thurmond, Sept. 17, 1964, box 24, folder Political Affairs (8) (Party Switch) Sept. 16–Dec. 2, 1964, Subject Correspondence 1964, JST.

64. *NYT*, March 28, 1965.

65. Thurmond to Ernest C. Fackler, Nov. 19, 1964, box 24, folder Political Affairs (8) (Party Switch) Sept. 16–Dec. 2, 1964, Subject Correspondence 1964, JST.

66. Long-distance conversation with Dent and Thurmond, Dec. 17, 1962, box 39, folder Persons, Thurmond, J. Strom (1 of 4), WDW.

67. *State*, Feb. 11, 16, 19, and 20, 1964; *AC*, March 10, 1964.

68. *State*, Nov. 29, 1964.

69. *State*, Sept. 16, 1964; Thurmond to Dorothy M. Anderson, Feb. 19, 1964, box 23, folder Political Affairs 2 (Elections), Subject Correspondence 1964, JST.

70. Parker to Thurmond, Feb. 24, 1964, box 21, folder Personal 7 (folder 1), Subject Correspondence 1964, JST.

71. See J. Arthur Boykin to Thurmond, March 30, 1964, and Bruce Littlejohn to Thurmond, May 6, 1961, among several others in box 21, folder Personal 7 (folder 1), Subject Correspondence 1964, JST. Also see Eugene E. Stone to Thurmond, Feb. 1, 1964, box 23, folder Political Affairs 2 (Elections), Subject Correspondence 1964, JST.

72. *State*, Jan. 17, 1964; *WP*, Jan. 27, 1963; *LAT*, Feb. 11, 1963.

73. B. W. Crouch Jr. to Thurmond, March 2, 1964, box 21, folder Personal 7 (folder 1), Subject Correspondence 1964, JST.

74. S. L. Gentry to Thurmond, Feb. 28, 1963, box 10, folder 1966 Campaign, Executive Assistant Series, JST.

75. Senate Committee on Commerce, *Nomination of LeRoy Collins*, 39–40.

76. *CNC*, July 8, 1964.

358★NOTES TO PAGES 181–187

77. *WP*, June 15, 1966.

78. George Reedy, interview by Michael L. Gillette, pt. 3, June 7, 1975, LBJ.

79. Telephone conversation with Richard Russell, Sept. 18, 1964, WH6409.11 PNO 15, Telephone Conversations, LBJ.

80. Charles E. Boineau, interview by Wilma M. Woods, April 6, 12, 14, and 18, 1995; and Daniel I. Ross Jr., interview by Herbert J. Hartsook, Oct. 4, 2001; both in South Carolina Political Collections Oral History Project, University of South Carolina.

81. Thurmond to Micah Jenkins, Sept. 24, 1964, box 24, folder Political Affairs (8) (Party Switch), Subject Correspondence 1964, JST. Also see James E. Duffy, "In G.O.P. We Trust," unpublished manuscript, folders 171–75, James E. Duffy Papers, Special Collections, Strom Thurmond Institute, Clemson University, 180 (hereinafter cited as Duffy, unpublished manuscript).

82. J. Drake Edens to Thurmond, Nov. 12, 1964, box 39, folder Persons, Thurmond, Strom (3 of 4), WDW.

83. Duffy, unpublished manuscript, 215.

84. *State*, Sept. 21, 1964; *NYT*, Oct. 29, 1964.

85. *CT*, Sept. 21, 1964.

86. *NYT*, Sept. 18, 1964.

87. All press reports in Dick Thompson, "The Goldwater Tour of the South," n.d., box 5, folder Goldwater for President Committee, Thompson Files (Southern States) (3 of 3), Subseries 2: General, Series 2, 1964 Presidential Campaign, BMG.

88. *State*, Sept. 22 and 25 and Oct. 18, 1964.

89. *CNC*, Oct. 11, 1964.

90. *LAT*, Sept. 24 and 25, 1964.

91. Strom Thurmond, "Elect Barry Goldwater President of the United States," Oct. 24, 1964, box 11, folder 131, Speeches, Series B, JST.

92. "A Choice for the South," n.d., Oversize, Campaigns Series, JST.

93. *State*, Oct. 18, 1964.

9. LAW AND ORDER (1965–1968)

1. Harry S. Dent, *The Prodigal South Returns to Power* (New York: Wiley, 1978), 93–94; Thurmond to Ronald Reagan, Jan. 18, 1967, box 33, folder Political Affairs 3-1-1, Subject Correspondence 1967, JST.

2. *CR*, Senate, June 18, 1968, 17640–43; *CT*, July 19, 1965.

3. *CR*, Senate, June 18, 1968, 17640–43; *CT*, July 19, 1965.

4. *LAT*, Jan. 14, 1965; *NYT*, Jan. 15, 1965.

5. Joseph Crespino, *In Search of Another Country: Mississippi and the Conservative Counterrevolution* (Princeton, N.J.: Princeton University Press, 2007), 105.

6. *NYT*, Jan. 13, 1965.

7. George H. Gallup, *The Gallup Poll: Public Opinion, 1935–1971* (New York: Random House, 1972), 3: 1919.

8. *LAT*, Feb. 25, 1965.

9. *CSM*, April 1, 1965.

10. *NYT*, March 10, 1965.

11. Keith M. Finley, *Delaying the Dream: Southern Senators and the Fight Against Civil Rights, 1938–1965* (Baton Rouge: Louisiana State University Press, 2008), 281.

12. Thurmond to Allowee Price, Feb. 26, 1965, box 2, folder Civil Rights 3, folder 1, Subject Correspondence 1965, JST.

13. *NYT*, March 16, 1965.

14. "Provisions of Voting Rights Act of 1965 (PL 89-110)," *CQA* 1965.

15. "Voting Rights Act of 1965," *CQA*, 1965, 1042, 1063.

16. Michael W. Flamm, *Law and Order: Street Crime, Civil Unrest, and the Crisis of Liberalism in the 1960s* (New York: Columbia University Press, 2005), 31–32, 36–45; Rick Perlstein, *Before the Storm: Barry Goldwater and the Unmaking of the American Consensus* (New York: Hill and Wang, 2001), 494–96.

17. See, for example, efforts by conservatives to amend interrogation rules established by Mallory in District of Columbia crime legislation in "D.C. Crime Bill," *CQA* 1965.

18. *WP*, Aug. 16, 1965.

19. Matthew Dallek, *The Right Moment: Ronald Reagan's First Victory and the Decisive Turning Point in American Politics* (New York: Oxford University Press, 2004), 142–43.

20. Ibid., 150–72.

21. Lou Cannon, *Governor Reagan: His Rise to Power* (New York: Public Affairs, 2003), 115–26.

22. Dallek, *Right Moment*, 188.

23. Flamm, *Law and Order*, 71.

24. Reagan quoted in Dallek, *Right Moment*, 187.

25. Essie Mae Washington-Williams and William Stadiem, *Dear Senator: A Memoir by the Daughter of Strom Thurmond* (New York: Regan Books, 2005), 183–87.

26. Gallup, *Gallup Poll, 1935–1971*, 3: 1925.

27. *CT*, Aug. 7, 1965; *CR*, Senate, Aug. 10, 1965, 19746.

28. *WP*, Aug. 23 and Sept. 1, 1965.

29. Peniel E. Joseph, *Waiting 'Til the Midnight Hour: A Narrative History of Black Power in America* (New York: Henry Holt, 2006), 141–42.

30. Thurmond to Ambrose Hampton, April 12, 1965, box 39, folder Persons, Thurmond, J. Strom (3 of 4), WDW.

31. "1966 Civil Rights Act Dies in Senate," *CQA* 1966.

32. *CR*, Senate, May 3, 1966, 9521.

33. "1966 Civil Rights Act Dies in Senate."

34. *CT*, Sept. 13, 1966.

35. Strom Thurmond, "The South's Role in the Civil Rights Movement," Aug. 25, 1966, box 12, folder 150, Speeches, Series B, JST.

36. *NYT*, April 13, 1966; *WP*, March 22, 1966.

37. *WP*, March 28, 1966.

38. Dent, *Prodigal South Returns to Power*, 77.

39. *WP*, Sept. 23, 1965, and May 1, 1966; Duffy, unpublished manuscript, folders 171–75, 253; *NYT*, June 16, 1965.

40. *LAT*, Sept. 27, 1965.

41. *WP*, May 1, 1966.

42. *NYT*, April 13, 1966.

43. *Chicago Defender*, April 2, 1966.

44. *State*, Sept. 30, 1966; *WP*, Oct. 23, 1966.

45. *NYT*, Oct. 8 and Nov. 6, 1966.

46. *State*, Oct. 25, 1966.

47. *State*, Oct. 24 and Nov. 4, 1966.

48. *State*, Nov. 4, 1966; "Black Power Shatters U.S. Cities," n.d., box 16, folder 1966 Campaign, Publicity—Campaign Material, Campaigns Series, JST.

49. *State*, Nov. 2, 1966; *NYT*, Nov. 3, 1966.

50. *State*, Nov. 5, 1966.

51. *State*, Oct. 26, 1966.

52. *NYT*, Nov. 27, 1966.

53. *CSM*, Nov. 15, 1966.

54. Tom Wicker, *George Herbert Walker Bush* (New York: Penguin, 2004), 18–19.

55. Harry Dent to Reagan, Nov. 21, 1966, box 14, folder 1966 Campaign, General, Campaigns Series, JST.

56. Dent to Thurmond, Nov. 16, 1966, and Thurmond to Reagan, Nov. 28, 1966, box 33, folder Political Affairs 3-1-1, Subject Correspondence 1967, JST.

57. *LAT*, Sept. 30, 1967; *NYT*, Sept. 30, 1967.

58. Harry Dent to Walter Jenkins, Dec. 27, 1963; William A. Geoghegan to Kenneth O'Donnell, Jan. 10, 1964, both in box 119, folder PL 6-3 Republican Party, White House Central Files, LBJ.

59. *LAT*, Feb. 2, 1966; Strom Thurmond, "Tribute to Professor Raymond Moley," July 13, 1967, box 13, folder 169, Speeches, Series B, JST; William Workman to Thurmond, Jan. 14, 1965, box 39, folder Persons, Thurmond, J. Strom (3 of 4), WDW; *CT*, Feb. 27, 1967.

60. Thurmond to George Murphy, June 25, 1968, box 26, folder Political Affairs; Thurmond to Harry F. Weyher, June 28, 1968, box 26, folder Political Affairs 1 (Campaigns); and Thurmond to Friends of Rafferty, Feb. 7, 1968, box 23, folder Personal 1 (Finance), all in Subject Correspondence 1968, JST.

61. William F. Buckley Jr., "My Secret Right-Wing Conspiracy," *New Yorker*, Oct. 21, 1996, 120–29.

62. Goldwater to Thurmond, April 18, 1968, box Alpha Files T–W, folder Thurmond, Strom, Subseries Alpha Files, Series 1, Personal, BMG.

63. Thurmond to Goldwater, April 24, 1968, box Alpha Files T–W, folder Thurmond, Strom, Subseries Alpha Files, Series 1, Personal, BMG.

64. Goldwater to Thurmond, April 29, 1968, box Alpha Files T–W, folder Thurmond, Strom, Subseries Alpha Files, Series 1, Personal, BMG.

65. Barry Goldwater, *The Conscience of a Conservative* (New York: Hillman, 1960), 37.

66. Thurmond to Goldwater, April 24, 1968, BMG.

67. *NYT*, Jan. 7, 1965; *WP*, March 4, 1965.

68. Strom Thurmond, "The Press Coverage of the So-Called Peace Demonstrators," May 10, 1967, box 13, folder 168, Speeches, Series B, JST.

69. *WP*, March 14, 1966; *NYT*, Aug. 31, 1966.

70. Robert Dallek, *Flawed Giant: Lyndon Johnson and His Times, 1961–1973* (New York: Oxford University Press, 1998), 502–13.

71. *Time*, Feb. 2, 1968.

72. Dallek, *Flawed Giant*, 514.

73. *NYT*, Jan. 24, 1968; Mike Manatos to Thurmond, Jan. 24, 1968, box 122, folder Thurmond, Strom, WHCF Name File, LBJ; Strom Thurmond, "The North Korean Seizure of the USS *Pueblo*," Feb. 4, 1968, box 14, folder 176, Speeches, Series B, JST.

74. Dallek, *Flawed Giant*, 513, 529.

75. *State*, Feb. 19, 1968; *Time*, Jan. 26, 1968.

76. Flamm, *Law and Order*, 87, 92.

77. *CR*, Senate, Aug. 2, 1967, 21062–63; Strom Thurmond, "Calling for Apprehension of Stokely Carmichael upon His Return to the U.S.," Aug. 2, 1967, box 13, folder 169, Speeches, Series B, 1947–83, JST; *CT*, Aug. 5, 1967.

78. "Congress Enacts Open Housing Legislation," *CQA* 1968.

79. *State*, Jan. 11, 23, and 25, 1968.

80. "Congress Enacts Open Housing Legislation."

81. Dallek, *Flawed Giant*, 415–16, 515–17; "Report by Commission on Civil Disorders Puts Blame on 'White Racism' for Riots," *CQA* 1968.

82. Strom Thurmond, "The Nation's Civil Disorders," March 10, 1968, box 14, folder 176, Speeches, Series B, JST.

83. Strom Thurmond, "Statement on Senate Floor Regarding Columns and Editorials on the Report by the President's Commission on Civil Disorders," March 13, 1968, box 14, folder 180, Speeches, Subseries B, 1947–1983, JST; *State*, Feb. 16, 1968.

84. Kirkpatrick quoted in Thurmond, "Statement on Senate Floor Regarding Columns and Editorials on the Report by the President's Commission on Civil Disorders."

85. *State*, April 11, 1968.

86. Strom Thurmond, "The Slaying of Martin Luther King and the Rioting Which Has Spread to 110 Cities," April 14, 1968, box 14, folder 176, Speeches, Series B, JST.

87. *CR*, Senate, March 5, 1968, 5203.

88. Strom Thurmond, "Statement on Senate Floor in Regard to the Antiriot Amendment to the Civil Rights Bill," March 5, 1968, box 14, folder 180, Speeches, Subseries B: Originals, JST.
89. "1966 Civil Rights Act Dies in Senate."
90. *State*, May 25, 1961.
91. "Congress Enacts Open Housing Legislation"; for "Rap Brown law," see Francis M. Wilhoit, *The Politics of Massive Resistance* (New York: George Braziller, 1973), 211.
92. Jack Bass and Jack Nelson, *The Orangeburg Massacre* (Macon, Ga.: Mercer University Press, 1984).
93. *State*, March 8, 1968.
94. Ibid.
95. *LAT*, March 8, 1968.

10. ANNUS MIRABILIS (1968)

1. *State*, Feb. 11, 1968.
2. Jules Witcover, *Resurrection of Richard Nixon* (New York: Putnam, 1970), 339.
3. *State*, Jan. 14, 1968.
4. *State*, Oct. 13, 1968.
5. *The Memoirs of Richard Nixon* (New York: Grosset and Dunlap, 1978), 304–305.
6. Dent to Nixon, Feb. 23, 1967, box 32, folder Political Affairs 3-1, folder 1, Subject Correspondence 1967, JST.
7. Witcover, *Resurrection of Richard Nixon*, 310.
8. Harry S. Dent, *The Prodigal South Returns to Power* (New York: Wiley, 1978), 76–77; Rick Perlstein, *Nixonland: The Rise of a President and the Fracturing of America* (New York: Scribner, 2008), 89.
9. Dent, *Prodigal South Returns to Power*, 80.
10. Ibid., 83.
11. Thurmond to Reagan, June 21, 1968, box 26, folder Political Affairs 2-1-1, Subject Correspondence 1968, JST.
12. *CSM*, May 29, 1968.
13. Derrick A. Bell Jr. to Thurmond, Aug. 18, 1966, box 12, folder FA 2, White House Central Files, LBJ.
14. *State*, May 11, 1968.
15. Strom Thurmond, "The School System of the South," March 23, 1967, box 13, folder 167, Speeches, Series B, JST.
16. *Green v. County School Board of New Kent County*, 391 U.S. 430 (1968).
17. *CSM*, May 29, 1968.
18. *Augusta Courier*, March 15, 1965.
19. *CR*, Senate, May 29, 1968, 15606–607.
20. Perlstein, *Nixonland*, 88.
21. *NYT*, June 22, 1968; *State*, June 22, 1968 (quotation); Laura Kalman, *Abe Fortas: A Biography* (New Haven, Conn.: Yale University Press, 1990), 327–28.

22. George H. Gallup, *The Gallup Poll: Public Opinion, 1935–1971* (New York: Random House, 1972), 3: 2147.

23. *WP*, Sept. 4, 1967.

24. Senate Committee on the Judiciary, *Nomination of Thurgood Marshall* (Washington, D.C.: GPO, 1967); for Thurmond's questioning, see pp. 161–76.

25. Senate Committee on the Judiciary, *Nominations of Abe Fortas and Homer Thornberry* (Washington, D.C.: GPO, 1968), 183 (hereinafter cited as Fortas hearings).

26. *State*, July 19, 1968; *WP*, July 19, 1968.

27. *State*, July 21, 1968.

28. In an obvious slap at Thurmond, a division of the American Bar Association later admonished senators for interrogating Fortas "as to the rationale or motivation of particular judicial decisions, whether or not the nominee participated therein." *WP*, Aug. 8, 1968.

29. Fortas hearings, 191.

30. Kalman, *Fortas*, 340. Fortas could not answer Thurmond in the hearing room but responded obliquely a few weeks later, in a speech before the American College of Trial Lawyers. Warning about the "professed friends of law and order," he reminded his audience that "to set aside the conviction of a man who has been tried in violation of the Constitution is not to set it aside on a mere technicality . . . Constitutional rights are not technicalities." Echoing Thurmond's attack in the committee room, he added, "This is the phrase that should ring in the nation's ear." *NYT*, Aug. 4, 1968; *CT*, Aug. 4, 1968.

31. Lucier to Thurmond, memo, July 19, 1968, box 45, folder Fortas Speech/Statement Drafts, folder 1, Legislative Assistant Series, JST; James P. Lucier, interview by author, May 5, 2010.

32. Lucier to Thurmond, memo, July 19, 1968.

33. Fortas hearings, 296.

34. Bruce Allen Murphy, *Fortas: The Rise and Ruin of a Supreme Court Justice* (New York: Morrow, 1988), 443–44. Fortas's defenders disputed the claim of Clancy and later Thurmond that Fortas had issued the "deciding" vote, noting that all justices had one equal vote. A South Carolina reporter working in *The State*'s Washington bureau explained that Supreme Court justices vote in order of seniority, and since Fortas was the Court's newest member, he voted last and thus "decided" cases that were split 4–4. *State*, Sept. 7, 1968.

35. *State*, July 23, 1968.

36. Murphy, *Fortas*, 448.

37. John Corry, "Strom's Dirty Movies," *Harper's Magazine*, Dec. 1968, 30–40.

38. Murphy, *Fortas*, 457–62.

39. Fortas hearings, 359.

40. Telephone conversation with George Smathers, July 25, 1968, WH 6807.02 PNO 8, Telephone Conversations, LBJ.

41. Mike Manatos to Johnson, memo, July 29, 1968, box 170, folder LE 5, White House Central Files, LBJ.

42. *State*, Aug. 1, 1968.
43. Theodore H. White, *The Making of the President, 1968* (New York: Atheneum, 1969), 236–38.
44. *State*, Aug. 10, 1968.
45. Lewis Chester, Godfrey Hodgson, and Bruce Page, *An American Melodrama: The Presidential Campaign of 1968* (London: Deutsch, 1969), 468, 474.
46. *WP*, Aug. 11, 1968; *State*, Aug. 10, 1968.
47. Chester, Hodgson, and Page, *American Melodrama*, 486–87.
48. Ibid., 486–88.
49. *State*, Aug. 10, 1968.
50. "Republican Convention," Aug. 8, 1968, record no. 818848, VTNA.
51. Ibid.
52. *NYT*, Aug. 11 and 12, 1968.
53. "Republican Convention," Aug. 8, 1968, record no. 818848, VTNA.
54. "Republican Convention," Aug. 8, 1968, record no. 819136, VTNA.
55. *State*, Aug. 13, 1968.
56. *WP*, Sept. 12 and 13, 1968.
57. *State*, Sept. 6, 1968.
58. *NYT*, Sept. 7, 1968; *WP*, Sept. 7, 1968.
59. Murphy, *Fortas*, 472–76.
60. Ibid.
61. Ibid., 451–52, 478, 497.
62. Fortas hearings, 1289, 1306; *State*, Sept. 14, 1968.
63. Murphy, *Fortas*, 503–13.
64. "How Can They Refuse?" *STRP*, July 22, 1968, box 32, folder 100-11A-2729, Speeches, Series A, JST.
65. "Attempt to Stop Fortas Debate Fails by 14-Vote Margin," *CQA* 1968.
66. For a broader analysis of the Fortas nomination and the politics of the New Right, see Whitney Strub, *Perversion for Profit: The Politics of Pornography and the Rise of the New Right* (New York: Columbia University Press, 2011), 80–145.
67. *State*, Oct. 11 and 24, 1968; *WP*, Aug. 12, 1968.
68. *State*, Sept. 15 (quotation) and Oct. 13, 1968.
69. *State*, Oct. 1 ("white vote" quotation), 8, 11, and 29, 1968; "Help Change Strom Thurmond's Mind!," Sept. 15, 1968, box 39, folder Persons, Wallace, George, General, 1969–1975, WDW; *State*, Nov. 5, 1968.
70. *State*, Sept. 17, 1968.
71. *State*, Sept. 20, 1968; Dent to Workman, Oct. 9, 1968, box 38, folder Persons, Nixon, Richard M., Campaigns, 1968, WDW.
72. *State*, Oct. 5, 1968.
73. Campaign flyer, ca. 1968, republished in Matthew D. Lassiter, *The Silent Majority: Suburban Politics in the Sunbelt South* (Princeton, N.J.: Princeton University Press, 2006), 235.
74. *State*, Nov. 6, 7, and 10, 1968.

75. *State*, Nov. 6, 1968.
76. Ibid.
77. *NYT*, Oct. 19, 1970.
78. Lassiter, *Silent Majority*, 121–221.
79. State, Dec. 8, 1968; Wayne Robbins, interview by author, March 2, 2010.
80. Dent to Samuel Stilwell, Nov. 13, 1979, box 30, folder 616, HSD.
81. Moore to Thurmond, Aug. 13, 1965, box 19, folder Personal 7, Subject Correspondence 1965, JST.
82. Moore to Thurmond, Sept. 17, 1965, box 19, folder Personal 7, Subject Correspondence 1965, JST.

11. PERILS OF AN INSIDER (1969–1972)

1. *State*, Dec. 28, 1968.
2. Richard Wilson, "Interpretive Report," March 9, 1969, box 38, folder Persons, Nixon, Richard M., Race Relations, 1969–1970, WDW; *State*, Jan. 30 and Feb. 9, 1969; *NYT*, Jan. 30, 1969.
3. *State*, April 26, 1969.
4. *Washington Star*, May 12, 1969.
5. *State*, May 25, June 15, and July 12, 1969.
6. *State*, Nov. 10, 1968.
7. *State*, April 26 and March 2, 1969.
8. Quoted in Rick Perlstein, *Before the Storm: Barry Goldwater and the Unmaking of the American Consensus* (New York: Hill and Wang, 2001), 636.
9. *Time*, July 11, 1969; *State*, May 9, 1969.
10. Dent to Bob Mardian, memo, Feb. 13, 1969, box 1, folder White House Communications, Robert C. Mardian Papers, Hoover Archives, Stanford University; G. Paul Jones Jr. to Dent, memo, May 19, 1969, box 3, folder 82, HSD.
11. *WP*, March 15, 1970.
12. *State*, July 11, 1969.
13. Dent to Nixon, memo, Dec. 11, 1969, box 2, folder 45, HSD; Thurmond quoted in *State*, Dec. 29, 1969.
14. Dent to Mardian, memo, Dec. 9, 1969, box 1, folder White House Communications, Mardian Papers.
15. *State*, June 29 and July 4, 5, and 6, 1969; quotation in *State*, Sept. 10, 1969.
16. *State*, July 13, 1969.
17. *State*, Aug. 6 and 8, 1969; *NYT*, Aug. 21, 1969.
18. Joseph Crespino, *In Search of Another Country: Mississippi and the Conservative Counterrevolution* (Princeton, N.J.: Princeton University Press, 2007), 183–84; *State*, Oct. 22, 1969.
19. Strom Thurmond, "Supreme Court Decision Concerning Desegregation in Mississippi Schools," Oct. 29, 1969, box 15, folder 186, Speeches, Subseries B: Originals, JST.
20. Dent to John Ehrlichman, memo, Nov. 13, 1969, box 1, folder 20, HSD.

21. Perlstein, *Nixonland*, 390; *State*, May 13, July 11, and Aug. 7, 1969.
22. Laura Kalman, *Abe Fortas: A Biography* (New Haven, Conn.: Yale University Press, 1990), 367–70.
23. *State*, May 4, 6, 7, and 16, 1969.
24. *State*, Sept. 7, 1969.
25. *State*, Aug. 3 and 19, 1969.
26. In his 2008 memoir, Fritz Hollings wrote, "The White House recognized that Thurmond had political baggage and that his involvement would complicate its efforts to promote a Judge from South Carolina to the Supreme Court. It appeared that they got the message to him to be circumspect, lie low, and essentially confine himself in the Senate to written comments other than a few perfunctory remarks. I would handle the nomination." Hollings, *Making Government Work* (Columbia: University of South Carolina Press, 2008), 144.
27. *WP*, July 22, 1969; for criticism of the *Post* editorial, see *State*, July 26, 1969.
28. Bruce H. Kalk, *The Origins of the Southern Strategy: Two-Party Competition in South Carolina, 1950–1972* (Lanham, Md.: Lexington Books, 2001), 94.
29. Quoted ibid.
30. *State*, Sept. 28, 1969 (*Milwaukee Journal* quoted therein).
31. *State*, Nov. 22, 1969.
32. *WP*, Nov. 16, 1969, and April 9, 1979.
33. *State*, Nov. 9 and Dec. 6, 1969.
34. Kalk, *Origins of the Southern Strategy*, 118–19; William Safire, *Before the Fall: An Inside View of the Pre-Watergate White House* (New York: Doubleday, 1975), 267–68.
35. Safire, ibid.; Stanley I. Kutler, *Wars of Watergate: The Last Crisis of Richard Nixon* (New York: Knopf, 1990), 148.
36. Richard Nixon, "Statement About Nominations to the Supreme Court," April 9, 1970, in *Public Papers of the Presidents of the United States, Richard Nixon, 1970* (Washington, D.C.: GPO, 1971), 345–47.
37. Strom Thurmond, "Radio, Television Tape Regarding the Defeat of Carswell," April 10, 1970, box 16, folder 202, Speeches, Series B, JST.
38. Dent to Nixon, memo, April 21, 1970, box 7, folder 210, HSD.
39. For more on the Stennis amendment controversy, see Crespino, *In Search of Another Country*, 173–204.
40. Strom Thurmond, "Encouraged by President Nixon's Statement on School Desegregation," Feb. 13, 1970, box 16, folder 197, Speeches, Series B, JST.
41. Leon E. Panetta and Peter Gall, *Bring Us Together: The Nixon Team and the Civil Rights Retreat* (Philadelphia: Lippincott, 1971), 92.
42. Dent to Bob Haldeman, Jan. 13, 1970, box 7, folder 210, HSD.
43. *State*, March 10, April 11, and June 13, 1968.
44. *State*, Sept. 26, 1968, and March 16, 1969.
45. Ravenel to Dent, Jan. 13, 1970, box 6, folder 207, HSD.
46. *CNC*, March 1, 1970.

47. Garry Wills, *Nixon Agonistes: The Crisis of the Self-Made Man* (Boston: Houghton Mifflin, 1970), 256.

48. *NYT*, May 17, 1970.

49. *State*, Jan. 20 and 26, 1970; *CNC*, Jan. 26, 1970.

50. See box 23, folders Political Affairs 1 (Campaigns) and Political Affairs 1-1 (Campaign Contributions), Subject Correspondence 1970, JST.

51. *State*, May 3, 1970.

52. Dent to Nixon, June 4, 1971, box 11, folder 321, HSD.

53. For examples of such letters, see box 2, folder Civil Rights 2, Subject Correspondence 1970, JST.

54. *State*, Feb. 18 and Sept. 18, 1969.

55. *State*, Aug. 31, 1968.

56. Quoted in Philip G. Grose, *South Carolina at the Brink: Robert McNair and the Politics of Civil Rights* (Columbia: University of South Carolina Press, 2006), 277.

57. Commentary by Howard K. Smith, ABC News, Jan. 29, 1970, box 31, folder Civil Rights, Desegregation, Public Schools, Greenville/Darlington, 1970, REM. Also see *NYT*, Jan. 28, 1970; *LAT*, Feb. 1, 1970; *Houston Chronicle*, Feb. 1, 1970; *State*, Feb. 1, 1970; *Pensacola Journal*, Feb. 2, 1970.

58. Strom Thurmond, "Support for Congressman Albert Watson on the Current School Crisis," Jan. 30, 1970, box 16, folder 197, Speeches Series, Original Subseries B, 1947–1983, JST.

59. See McNair's handwritten note on Wayne Seal to McNair, memo, April 3, 1970, box 31, folder Civil Rights, Desegregation, Public Schools, General 1970, REM.

60. *Atlanta Constitution*, Jan. 28, 1970.

61. McNair to Thurmond, Jan. 28, 1970, box 31, folder Civil Rights, Desegregation, Public Schools, Greenville/Darlington, 1970, REM.

62. Thurmond to McNair, Jan. 30, 1970, folder Civil Rights, Desegregation, Public Schools, Greenville/Darlington, 1970, REM.

63. Strom Thurmond, "The School Crisis," Feb. 8, 1970, box 16, folder 202, Speeches, Series B, JST.

64. Ibid.

65. *State*, March 4, 1970; *CNC*, March 4, 1970; "An Account of the Incident at Lamar Schools, Tuesday Morning," March 3, 1970, box 28, folder Education, School Desegregation, Lamar, S.C., WDW.

66. *State*, Feb. 18 and 20 and March 3, 1970.

67. *State*, Feb. 23, 1970.

68. *Time*, March 16, 1970.

69. *State*, March 4, 1970; *CNC*, March 4, 1970.

70. "Lamar/Racist Violence," March 3, 1970, record no. 208972; "Desegregation/Lamar/Rilling," March 3, 1970, record no. 9743; and "Lamar/Racial Trouble," March 3, 1970, record no. 450459, VTNA; *CNC*, March 4, 1970.

71. Strom Thurmond, untitled, March 5, 1970, box 6, folder 207, HSD.

72. *WP*, Nov. 7, 1970.
73. *WP*, March 9, 1970.
74. Hastings Wyman, interview by author, May 7, 2009.
75. *WP*, Oct. 30, 1970; *LAT*, Oct. 11, 1970.
76. *State*, Oct. 1 and 3, 1970.
77. Dent to Watson, memo, April 27, 1970, and Dent to Dan Carrison, memo, Aug. 20, 1970, both in box 6, folder 207, HSD.
78. *LAT*, March 22 and Oct. 27, 1970.
79. *NYT*, Oct. 4, 1970.
80. Quoted ibid.
81. *State*, Sept. 19, 1970.
82. R. E. Stone, "Offense Report," Oct. 14, 1970, box 31, folder Civil Rights, Desegregation, Public Schools, A. C. Flora Incident, REM; *State*, Oct. 16, 17, and 22, 1970. J. P. Strom agreed with the report filed by E. L. McGowan, Forest Acres Police Commissioner; see *State*, Oct. 29, 1970.
83. Daniel I. Ross Jr., interview by Herbert J. Hartsook, Oct. 4, 2001, South Carolina Political Collections Oral History Project, University of South Carolina.
84. *State*, Oct. 16, 1970.
85. *State*, Oct. 18, 1970.
86. Dent to Nixon, memo, Oct. 22, 1970, box 5, folder 181, HSD.
87. *AC*, Nov. 4, 1970.
88. *State*, Nov. 15, 1970.
89. *WP*, Jan. 30, 1971.
90. *WP*, May 16, 1971; *Atlanta Constitution*, Jan. 24, 1971.
91. *Atlanta Daily World*, Dec. 4, 1970.
92. Dent to Nixon, memo, Jan. 21, 1971, box 10, folder 306, HSD.
93. Dent to Thurmond, memo, Feb. 4, 1971, box 10, folder 306, HSD.
94. Duffy to Dent, Jan. 30, 1971, box 10, folder 306, HSD.
95. *State*, Oct. 2, 1969.
96. For a broader survey of this phenomenon beyond South Carolina, see Matthew D. Lassiter, *The Silent Majority: Suburban Politics in the Sunbelt South* (Princeton, N.J.: Princeton University Press, 2006), 251-75.
97. *WP*, May 16, 1971.
98. Lassiter, *Silent Majority*, 251-75.
99. James Duffy to Harry Dent, March 26, 1972, box 15, folder 411, HSD.
100. *State*, May 27, 1971; for more on Blatt's political influence in Barnwell County, see Jack Bass and Marilyn W. Thompson, *Strom: The Complicated Personal and Political Life of Strom Thurmond* (New York: Public Affairs, 2005), 273.
101. *NYT*, May 30, 1971.
102. Solomon Blatt Jr., interview by author, June 15, 2009.
103. Ibid.
104. Dent to Sue Morrison, July 28, 1971, box 10, folder 307, HSD.
105. Quoted in *WP*, May 16, 1971.

106. *State*, Feb. 1, 1971.
107. "Appointment of Thomas Moss of Orangeburg," press release, Feb. 15, 1971, box 45, folder 100-11A-3794, Speeches Series, Subseries A, JST; *WP*, Feb. 16, 1971.
108. *WP*, Feb. 15, 1971; *State*, Feb. 27, 1971.
109. Untitled, box 2, Political Cartoon Series, JST.
110. Strom Thurmond, "In My Judgement," June 10, 1970, box 16, folder 203, Speeches, Series B, JST.
111. "White Voices of the South," *Ebony*, Aug. 1971, 166–67.
112. "The System Works," *STRP*, Nov. 22, 1971, box 45, folder 100-11A-3817, Speeches, Series A, JST.
113. Strom Thurmond, "Medical Report on Hypertension as It Affects Black Americans," May 31, 1972, box 53, folder 100-11A-4322, Speeches, Series A, JST.
114. *Time*, Sept. 27, 1976.
115. Ravenel to Thurmond, March 1, 1971, box 10, folder 306, HSD.
116. Dent to Thurmond, memo, June 15, 1971, box 10, folder 307, HSD.
117. "Voter Opinion Survey: South Carolina, Jan. 28–Feb. 7, 1972," box 29, folder Polls, folder 1, 1972 Campaign, Campaigns Series, JST.
118. Dent to Richard S. Brannon, Feb. 22, 1972, box 11, folder 355, HSD. Also see Dent, to Bill Gifford, memo, Aug. 3, 1971, box 10, folder 305, HSD.
119. Jon Buchan, "Fighting the Good Fight in Edgefield County," *Osceola*, Jan. 18, 1974.
120. Eugene N. Zeigler Jr., *When Conscience and Power Meet: A Memoir* (Columbia: University of South Carolina Press, 2008), 264–65.

12. A NEW RIGHT AND THE OLD (1972–1980)

1. Alan Pell Crawford, *Thunder on the Right: The "New Right" and the Politics of Resentment* (New York: Pantheon, 1980); William C. Berman, *America's Right Turn: From Nixon to Bush* (Baltimore: Johns Hopkins University Press, 1994); Laura Kalman, *Right Star Rising: A New Politics, 1974–1980* (New York: Norton, 2010); Donald T. Critchlow, *The Conservative Ascendancy: How the GOP Right Made Political History* (Cambridge, Mass.: Harvard University Press, 2007), 104–83.
2. Lee Edwards, *The Power of Ideas: The Heritage Foundation at 25 Years* (Ottawa, Ill.: Jameson Books, 1997), 6–11.
3. "1974 Elections: A Major Sweep for the Democrats," *CQA* 1974.
4. For evidence that this was Nixon's view, see Bob Woodward and Carl Bernstein, *The Final Days* (New York: Simon and Schuster, 1976), 51–53.
5. Cartha DeLoach to Mr. Mohr, Nov. 3, 1964, Strom Thurmond FBI File.
6. Nadine Cohodas, *Strom Thurmond and the Politics of Southern Change* (New York: Simon and Schuster, 1993), 432.
7. Senate Committee on the Judiciary, 93rd Cong., 1st sess., *Special Prosecutor*, pt. 1 (Washington, D.C.: GPO, 1973), 41–45.
8. *LAT*, Nov. 5, 1973.

9. *NYT*, Feb. 23, 1974.

10. *LAT*, May 14, 1974; *CR*, Senate, May 2, 1974, 12921–24.

11. *LAT*, Aug. 10, 1974; "Statement by Senator Strom Thurmond (R-SC) Concerning the Resignation of President Richard Nixon," Aug. 8, 1974, box 59, folder 100-11A-04709, Speeches, Series A, JST.

12. "Congressional Anti-busing Sentiment Mounts in 1972," *CQA* 1972.

13. Dan T. Carter, *Politics of Rage: George Wallace, the Origins of the New Conservatism, and the Transformation of American Politics* (New York: Simon and Schuster, 1995), 425–26.

14. "President's Two Anti-busing Measures Shelved," *CQA* 1972.

15. *WP*, March 18, 1972.

16. "What Is Quality Education?" *STRP*, April 3, 1972, box 51, folder 100-11A-4196, subseries A, JST.

17. *WP*, Sept. 23, 1972.

18. Strom Thurmond, "Anti-busing Legislation," Oct. 6, 1972, box 54, folder 100-11A-4381, Speeches, Series A, JST.

19. Strom Thurmond, "Federal Policies on Desegregation in the North and South," Sept. 10, 1974, box 61, folder 11-11A-4879, Speeches, Series A, JST.

20. Strom Thurmond, "Biden Amendment to Labor-HEW Appropriations Bill, Which Would Prohibit Any Funds in This Bill to Be Used for Assigning Teachers or Students to Schools for Reasons of Race," Sept. 17, 1975, box 65, folder 100-11A-5086, Speeches, Series A, JST.

21. Brett Gadsden, *Between North and South: Delaware, Desegregation, and the Myth of American Sectionalism* (Philadelphia: University of Pennsylvania Press, 2012).

22. Quoted in Julian E. Zelizer, *On Capitol Hill: The Struggle to Reform Congress and Its Consequences, 1948–2000* (New York: Cambridge University Press, 2004), 135.

23. For more on the POW-MIA controversy and its implications for conservative politics, see Michael J. Allen, *Until the Last Man Comes Home: POWs, MIAs, and the Unending Vietnam War* (Chapel Hill: University of North Carolina Press, 2009).

24. *WP*, May 25, 1973.

25. "Hostile Travel," *STRP*, June 11, 1973, box 55, folder 100-11A-4450, Speeches, Series A, JST.

26. "Still Missing," *STRP*, July 9, 1973, box 55, folder 100-11A-4450, Speeches, Series A, JST.

27. Strom Thurmond, "Missing in Action in Southeast Asia," June 20, 1974, box 60, folder 100-11A-4833, Speeches, Series A, JST; Strom Thurmond, "'Missing' Accountability," Nov. 25, 1974, box 59, folder 100-11A-4697, Speeches, Series A, JST.

28. Strom Thurmond, "To Introduce Resolution to Establish Senate Select Committee to Investigate Prisoner of War/Missing-in-Action Problem," April 24, 1975, box 64, folder 100-11A-5017, Speeches, Series A, JST.

29. Strom Thurmond, "Amendment to S. 1517 Reducing America's Contribution to United Nations if They Refuse to Aid America in Obtaining Complete Accounting of Dead and Missing in Southeast Asia," Sept. 8, 1975, box 65, folder 100-11A-5079, Speeches, Series A, JST.
30. Strom Thurmond, "Deserters from Our Army," box 15, folder 193, Speeches, Series B, JST.
31. Strom Thurmond, "The Case Against Amnesty," box 55, folder 100-11A-4450, Speeches, Series A, JST.
32. *WP*, March 30, 1974; *LAT*, April 30, 1977.
33. Natasha Zaretsky, "Restraint or Retreat? The Debate over the Panama Canal Treaties and U.S. Nationalism After Vietnam," *Diplomatic History* 35, no. 3 (2011): 535–62.
34. *State*, Jan. 18, 1964.
35. "Panama Canal," *CQA* 1967.
36. Untitled news release, Aug. 15, 1967, box 78, folder 44, Donald M. Dozer Papers, Hoover Archives, Stanford University.
37. Strom Thurmond, address before Young Americans for Freedom National Convention, Sept. 2, 1967, box 78, folder 44, Dozer Papers.
38. Strom Thurmond, "Senate Resolution in Support of Continued Undiluted U.S. Sovereignty over the Canal Zone," March 29, 1974, box 60, folder 100-11A-4775, Speeches, Series A, JST; Adam Clymer, *Drawing the Line at the Big Ditch: The Panama Canal Treaties and the Rise of the Right* (Lawrence: University Press of Kansas, 2008), 9.
39. Crawford, *Thunder on the Right*, 8.
40. William A. Link, *Righteous Warrior: Jesse Helms and the Rise of Modern Conservatism* (New York: St. Martin's Press, 2008), 150–57; Reagan quoted in Clymer, *Drawing the Line*, 30.
41. *NYT*, May 16, 1976.
42. Clymer, *Drawing the Line*, 105, 197.
43. *BusinessWeek*, May 17, 1976, 92–114.
44. Carol L. Jusenius and Larry C. Ledebur, "The Northern Tier and the Sunbelt: Conflict or Cooperation?," *Challenge*, March–April 1977, 44–49; "Federal Spending: The North's Loss Is the Sunbelt's Gain," *National Journal*, June 26, 1976, 878–91.
45. *NYT*, Feb. 9, 1976.
46. Kirkpatrick Sale, *Power Shift: The Rise of the Southern Rim and Its Challenge to the Eastern Establishment* (New York: Vintage, 1975).
47. *NYT*, Nov. 30, 1975.
48. *CR*, Senate, March 4, 1977, 6362.
49. "Vertical Divestiture," *CQA* 1976.
50. *WP*, Nov. 20, 1976.
51. *WSJ*, June 16, 1976; *NYT*, Feb. 11, 1977.
52. *WP*, Jan. 21, 1977; *NYT*, Feb. 11, 1977.
53. *CR*, Senate, Sept. 8, 1977, 28219; *LAT*, Sept. 9, 1977.

54. *WP*, Jan. 21, 1977; *NYT*, Feb. 11, 1977.

55. *LAT*, June 20, 1976.

56. *WP*, May 28, 1978; "Filibuster Kills Labor Law 'Reform' Bill," *CQA* 1978.

57. Clymer, *Drawing the Line*, 131; Nancy MacLean, *Freedom Is Not Enough: The Opening of the American Workplace* (Cambridge, Mass.: Harvard University Press, 2006), 239. For more on business and conservative politics in the 1970s, see Benjamin Cooper Waterhouse, "A Lobby for Capital: Organized Business and the Pursuit of Pro-Market Politics, 1967–1986" (Ph.D. diss., Harvard University, 2009).

58. *WP*, May 28, 1978.

59. *WSJ*, March 29, 1978.

60. *WP*, May 17, 1978.

61. *CR*, Senate, May 16, 1978, 13832, and May 25, 1978, 15524.

62. Harry Dent told a South Carolina newspaperman that the NLRB was "determined to unionize the South not just as a pay off to the unions but also to stop industry from going South." See Dent to Dean Livingston, Dec. 29, 1961, box 12, folder Labor, Subject Correspondence 1961, JST.

63. *CR*, Senate, June 9, 1978, 17019–22; June 14, 1978, 17552–56; and June 19, 1978, 18069–74.

64. *NYT*, June 15, 1978; *WSJ*, June 23, 1978.

65. *WP*, Sept. 1, 1977.

66. Timothy J. Minchin, *"Don't Sleep with Stevens!" The J. P. Stevens Campaign and the Struggle to Organize the South, 1963–1980* (Gainesville: University Press of Florida, 2005).

67. *WP*, April 30, 1978.

68. See letters in box 46, folder New York City Reception at Wings Club, 1978 Campaign, Campaigns Series, JST.

69. Quoted in *WP*, April 30, 1978.

70. *State*, Feb. 15, 1968.

71. Jones to Thurmond, Aug. 10, 1953, box 26, folder Subject Correspondence: Bob Jones University, Personal Series, JST; Thurmond to Hargis, Aug. 28, 1961, box 39, folder Un-American Activities (folder 8), Subject Correspondence 1961, JST; Strom Thurmond, excerpts from address to 20th Century Reformation Hour Freedom Rally, June 13, 1969, box 15, folder 185, Speeches, Series B, JST; Strom Thurmond, "Discussing Some of the Urgent Problems That Face the Nation," June 12, 1970, box 15, folder 195, Speeches, Series B, JST.

72. James L. Guth, "South Carolina: The Christian Right Wins One," *PS: Political Science and Politics* 28 (March 1995): 8–11.

73. Dent to Thurmond, March 8, 1976, box 30, folder 615, HSD.

74. *WP*, Feb. 27, 1976.

75. Donald M. Rothberg, "Reagan Says He'll Debate Rivals in South Carolina," Associated Press, Jan. 30, 1980.

76. *NYT*, Oct. 5, 1980.

77. "Senate/Prayer in Schools," April 9, 1979, record no. 504119, VTNA.

78. *NYT*, April 6 and 10, 1979.

79. *CR*, Senate, April 9, 1979, 7639.

80. Viguerie quoted in Joseph Crespino, "Civil Rights and the Religious Right," in *Rightward Bound: Making America Conservative in the 1970s*, ed. Bruce J. Schulman and Julian E. Zelizer, (Cambridge, Mass.: Harvard University Press, 2008), 91.

81. Strom Thurmond, "Meeting an Educational Crisis," June 4, 1967, box 27, folder Education, Private Schools, 1959–1970, WDW.

82. Elliott Wannamaker to Roy R. Pearson, Nov. 18, 1966, box 27, folder Education, Private Schools, 1959–1970, WDW.

83. *WSJ*, Jan. 14, 1970.

84. Strom Thurmond, "Enjoining the IRS from Granting Tax Exemptions," Jan. 14, 1970, box 16, folder 197, Speeches, Series B, JST.

85. Harry Dent to Ed Morgan, memo, Sept. 18, 1970, box 4, folder 139, HSD.

86. Harry Dent to Nixon, memo, July 21, 1970, box 7, folder 210, HSD.

87. Strom Thurmond, "IRS Assuring That Private Schools Awaiting Approval of Tax Exempt Status," July 15, 1970, box 16, folder 198, Speeches, Series B, JST; Strom Thurmond, "Presidential Advisors," July 26, 1970, box 16, folder 204, Speeches, Series B, JST.

88. Crespino, "Civil Rights and the Religious Right," 98–105, quotation on p. 100.

89. "IRS/Private School Discrimination Controversy," Dec. 5, 1978, record no. 256234, and "Discrimination/IRS and Private Schools," Dec. 5, 1978, record no. 497302, VTNA.

90. MacLean, *Freedom Is Not Enough*, 249–56.

91. Strom Thurmond, statement before the Internal Revenue Service, Dec. 5, 1978, box 76, folder 100-11A-5794, Speeches, Series A, JST; *WP*, Dec. 6, 1978.

92. "1980 Republican Platform Text," *CQA* 1980.

93. Crespino, "Civil Rights and the Religious Right," 104.

94. *WP*, Jan. 1, 1981.

95. *NYT*, Jan. 9, 1982.

96. Summary of meeting with IRS commissioner Roscoe Egger Jr., Dec. 18, 1981, box 109, folder Tax Exemptions: Private Schools—Bob Jones University, folder 2, Legislative Assistant Series, JST; *NYT*, Jan. 10, 1982.

97. *NYT*, Jan. 12, 1982.

98. *NYT*, Jan. 13, 1982; Aaron Haberman, "Into the Wilderness: Ronald Reagan, Bob Jones University, and the Political Education of the Christian Right," *Historian* 67 (Summer 2005): 234–53.

99. Richard A. Viguerie, *The New Right: We're Ready to Lead* (Falls Church, Va.: Viguerie Company, 1980), 19–34.

100. Richard Viguerie and David Franke, *America's Right Turn: How Conservatives Used New and Alternative Media to Take Power* (Chicago: Bonus Books, 2004), 114, 120–25.

101. Gretschel to Tony Campbell, Sept. 28, 1977, box 52, folder Viguerie Company, 1978 Campaign, Campaigns Series, JST.

102. Viguerie and Franke, *America's Right Turn*, 127.

103. Thurmond to Viguerie, Nov. 14, 1977, box 52, folder Viguerie Company, 1978 Campaign, Campaigns Series, JST.

104. Thurmond to Crane, Nov. 4, 1977, box 44, folder Direct Mail, 1978 Campaign, Campaigns Series, JST. Thurmond and Viguerie clashed again when Viguerie's company failed to meet fund-raising targets (Viguerie to Alison Dalton, May 10, 1978, box 44, folder Direct Mail; and Viguerie to Thurmond, June 21, 1978, box 52, folder Viguerie Company; both in 1978 Campaign, Campaigns Series, JST). Thurmond's frustration with Viguerie stretched back to the 1972 race, though the exact nature of his grievance is unclear. It might have been the percentage of the returns that Viguerie's firm kept. In 1978, the Viguerie corporation settled a lawsuit with the New York state attorney general for keeping an "unconscionable" portion—as much as 75 percent—of the money it raised for three charities. Viguerie settled the case by agreeing to take no more than 35 percent in any future deals with New York charities (*WSJ*, Oct. 6, 1978).

105. Jesse Helms, *Here's Where I Stand* (New York: Random House, 2005), 54–55.

106. Viguerie, *New Right*, 108; Link, *Righteous Warrior*, 145–46.

107. *WP*, Oct. 31, 1978.

108. Link, *Righteous Warrior*, 376–79.

13. OL' STROM IN THE MODERN SOUTH (1978–1990)

1. *WSJ*, Oct. 2, 1978.

2. *WP*, Aug. 13, 1978.

3. *WP*, Oct. 23 and 25, 1978.

4. *WP*, July 26, 1977; Feb. 28 and Oct. 23 and 25, 1978.

5. *WP*, Nov. 20, 1977.

6. Nancy Thurmond, to Strom Thurmond, Nov. 10, 1977, box 44, folder Campaign Notes to Senator from Mrs. Thurmond, 1978 Campaign, Campaigns Series, JST. There are roughly twenty such memos or letters from Nancy to Strom in this folder.

7. *WP*, July 17, 1978.

8. John J. Brady, *Bad Boy: The Life and Politics of Lee Atwater* (Reading, Mass.: Addison-Wesley, 1997), 70.

9. *LAT*, Nov. 19, 1978.

10. Ann Stone to Tony Campbell, memo, Feb. 9, 1978, box 52, folder Viguerie Company, 1978 Campaign, Campaigns Series, JST.

11. William Reynolds Williams, "Campaign Operations Manual 1978," April 24, 1975, box 44, folder Campaign Operations Manual 1978, 1978 Campaign, Campaigns Series, JST.

12. Ibid.

13. *NYT*, Oct. 23, 1977.

14. *NYT*, April 4, 1978; *WP*, Aug. 13, 1978.
15. *CSM*, Aug. 21, 1978.
16. *WP*, July 20 and Aug. 27, 1978.
17. Phyllis Berry to Thurmond, Aug. 8, 1978, box 44, folder Black Voters 1978, 1978 Campaign, Campaigns Series, JST.
18. *WP*, March 17, 1978.
19. *WP*, Feb. 27, 1972.
20. *NYT*, Oct. 24, 1996.
21. *WP*, Oct. 23, 1978.
22. *NYT*, Oct. 23, 1977; *WP*, March 17, 1978; *Atlanta Daily World*, March 8, 1979.
23. Joint Center for Political Studies, *Election '78: Implications for Black America* (Washington, D.C.: Joint Center for Political Studies, 1979), 23.
24. *WP*, Oct. 23, 1978.
25. Nadine Cohodas, *Strom Thurmond and the Politics of Southern Change* (New York: Simon and Schuster, 1993), 449, 451.
26. *CSM*, Sept. 2, 1977; *WP*, Aug. 29, 1977.
27. John Egerton, *The Americanization of Dixie: The Southernization of America* (New York: Harper's Magazine Press, 1974), 157–64.
28. Dennis Whitfield to Thurmond, memo, Sept. 9, 1977, box 51, folder Strategy and Tactics, 1978 Campaign, Campaigns Series, JST.
29. *WP*, Oct. 28, 1979.
30. *LAT*, Oct. 4, 1978.
31. *WP*, Dec. 31, 1979; Dennis Shedd and Mark Goodin, interview by author, May 10, 2011.
32. *NYT*, Dec. 28, 1979.
33. *WP*, March 8, 9, and 11, 1980; *NYT*, March 8, 1980.
34. Horace Fleming, interview by author, Aug. 30, 2008; Jack Bass and Marilyn W. Thompson, *Strom: The Complicated Personal and Political Life of Strom Thurmond* (New York: Public Affairs, 2005), 290.
35. *NYT*, Feb. 9, 1982.
36. *WP*, Aug. 11, 1980; *NYT*, Sept. 27, 1980; Joseph Crespino, *In Search of Another Country: Mississippi and the Conservative Counterrevolution* (Princeton, N.J.: Princeton University Press, 2007), 1–3.
37. *Clarion-Ledger*, Nov. 3, 1980.
38. *CSM*, Nov. 18, 1980.
39. Strom Thurmond, S. 10106, Feb. 9, 1955, box 15, folder Legislation, Subject Correspondence 1957, JST; Figg to Thurmond, Feb. 24, 1955, box 8, folder Figg, Robert, Subject Correspondence 1955, JST.
40. *WP*, Nov. 14, 1980; "Anti-busing Rider Draws Veto of Justice Bill," *CQA* 1980.
41. *Clarion-Ledger*, April 25, 1981.
42. Thomas W. Evans, *The Education of Ronald Reagan: The General Electric Years and the Untold Story of His Conversion to Conservatism* (New York: Columbia University Press, 2006).

43. Robert Figg interview by Walter J. Brown and Mark Mitchell, n.d., box 20, folder Figg, Robert M., Interview Transcript, WJB. Though the document is undated, it is clear from events discussed that the conversation took place sometime in late 1981 or early 1982.

44. *Baron Report*, May 25, 1981.

45. *NYT*, July 9, 1981.

46. Cohodas, *Strom Thurmond*, 455–58.

47. *CSM*, Nov. 18, 1980.

48. *WP*, Oct. 23, 1978.

49. *WP*, May 12, 1974.

50. Evgenia Peretz, "Something About Sally," *Vanity Fair*, July 2010.

51. Shedd and Goodin, interview.

52. *NYT*, April 8, 1981.

53. Thurmond to Ed Meese, June 2, 1981, box OA5102, folder Voting Rights Act (4), Ed Meese Files; Thurmond to Reagan, July 10, 1981, box 1, folder Voting Rights, Subject File HU015; Thurmond to James A. Baker III, July 28, 1981, box OA5102, folder Voting Rights Material (3), Ed Meese Files; Thurmond to Reagan, Aug. 5, 1981, box 1, folder Voting Rights, Subject File, HU015; Thurmond to Lee Atwater, Sept. 21, 1981, box OA8269, folder South Carolina: Strom Thurmond (6), Lee Atwater Files; all in RWR.

54. "Voting Rights Act Extended, Strengthened," *CQA* 1982.

55. Thurmond, Orrin Hatch, and Charles Grassley to Reagan, Oct. 22, 1981, box 2, folder Voting Rights, Subject File, HU015, RWR.

56. *CT*, Aug. 7, 1965.

57. *Baron Report*, May 25, 1981.

58. Talking Points on Voting Rights Act for Meeting with Senators Baker, Thurmond, and Hatch, Nov. 3, 1981, box OA9460, folder Voting Rights Bill, Ed Meese Files, RWR.

59. "Voting Rights Act Extended, Strengthened."

60. Harper to Reagan, memo, March 5, 1982, box 2, folder Voting Rights Act, Subject File, HU015, RWR.

61. *City of Mobile v. Bolden*, 446 U.S. 55 (1980); *CR*, Senate, June 17, 1982, 14125.

62. *Voting Rights Act: Hearings Before the Subcommittee on the Constitution of the Committee on the Judiciary*, U.S. Senate, 97th Cong. 2nd sess. (Washington, D.C.: GPO, 1982), 370.

63. Cohodas, *Strom Thurmond*, 469.

64. *Voting Rights Act: Hearings*, 420–21; Laughlin McDonald, interview by author, Feb. 4, 2011.

65. *Voting Rights Act: Hearings*, 420–21.

66. R. J. Duke Short, *The Centennial Senator: True Stories of Strom Thurmond from the People Who Knew Him Best* (Columbia: University of South Carolina Press, 2008), 296–97, 301; "Senator Thurmond 100th Birthday Party," Dec. 5, 2002, C-SPAN Video Library.

67. Short, *Centennial Senator*, 17.
68. *Edgefield Advertiser*, July 4, 1934.
69. *Voting Rights Act*: Hearings, 1132–35.
70. Shedd and Goodin, interview.
71. Ibid.
72. *WP*, May 4, 1982.
73. "Voting Rights Act Extended, Strengthened."
74. *CT*, Sept. 12, 1965; Cartha DeLoach to Mr. Mohr, memo, Sept. 15, 1965, in *Martin Luther King, Jr., FBI File* ed. David Garrow (Frederick, Md.: University Publications of America, 1984), microform, 0381–82.
75. *Atlanta Daily World*, June 24, 1979.
76. *CSM*, Oct. 5, 1983; *LAT*, Oct. 20, 1983.
77. Kenneth H. Thompson, *The Voting Rights Act and Black Electoral Participation* (Washington, D.C.: Joint Center for Political Studies, 1982), 5, 14.
78. Williams, "Campaign Operations Manual 1978"; *WP*, Nov. 18, 1984.
79. *NYT*, Nov. 5, 1990.
80. For an overview on minority redistricting, see Charles S. Bullock III, *Redistricting: The Most Political Activity in America* (Lanham, Md.: Rowan and Littlefield, 2010), 49–86.
81. Richard S. Beal to Edwin Harper and Melvin Bradley, March 18, 1982, box 2, folder Voting Rights Act, Subject File, HU015, RWR.
82. Richard S. Beal to Edwin L. Harper, April 22, 1982, box 2, folder Voting Rights Act, Subject File, HU015, RWR.
83. Laughlin McDonald, "Redistricting and Voting Rights Issues, 1992–2001: A Legal Analysis," in *Voting Rights and Minority Representation: Redistricting, 1992–2002*, ed. David A. Bositis (Washington, D.C.: Joint Center for Political and Economic Studies, 2006), 17.
84. *WP*, Sept. 3, 1990.
85. *LAT*, April 25, 1982.
86. *NYT*, Sept. 16, 1981.
87. Cohodas, *Strom Thurmond*, 460–62.
88. *WP*, Jan. 28 and Sept. 22, 1981.
89. *WP*, Nov. 27 and Dec. 6, 1980.
90. *CSM*, Sept. 25, 1981.
91. *CSM*, Nov. 10, 1981.
92. *LAT*, Feb. 9, 1981.
93. *WP*, March 9, 1982.
94. *WSJ*, April 1, 1982; *WP*, April 2, 1982.
95. *WSJ*, Dec. 3, 1982.
96. Macon Edwards, interview by author, April 21, 2009; *NYT*, Aug. 2, 1986.

14. ALL STROM'S CHILDREN (1990–2003)

1. *WSJ*, Nov. 9, 1998; Dennis Shedd and Mark Goodin, interview by author, May 10, 2011.
2. *Charlotte Observer*, Nov. 7, 1996.
3. *NYT*, Oct. 24, 1996.
4. Earl Black and Merle Black, *The Rise of Southern Republicans* (Cambridge, Mass.: Harvard University Press, 2002), 1–2.
5. *Charleston Post and Courier*, May 25, 1997.
6. *NYT*, May 26, 1997; *AC*, Dec. 5, 1997.
7. *Time*, March 5, 2001.
8. *WSJ*, Nov. 9, 1998; *National Review*, Nov. 23, 1998.
9. *Bulletin's Frontrunner*, April 1, 1997.
10. *Washington Times*, Nov. 30, 1996; *NYT*, Nov. 28, 1996, Jan. 18 and May 12, 2000.
11. *AC*, Dec. 5, 1999.
12. *Charlotte Observer*, Dec. 5, 1999.
13. *WP*, Dec. 7, 2002; Trent Lott, *Herding Cats: A Life in Politics* (New York: Regan Books, 2005), 246, 254.
14. R. J. Duke Short, *The Centennial Senator: True Stories of Strom Thurmond from the People Who Knew Him Best* (Columbia: University of South Carolina Press, 2008), 413–14.
15. *NYT*, June 27, 2003.
16. *Charleston Post and Courier*, June 30 and July 2, 2003; *AC*, July 1, 2003; *Atlanta Journal-Constitution*, July 2, 2003.
17. *AC*, July 1, 2003; *Charleston Post and Courier*, July 2, 2003.
18. *Charleston Post and Courier*, Dec. 14, 2003.
19. Essie Mae Washington-Williams, interview by Dan Rather, Dec. 17, 2003, pt. 2, CBS News Archives, www.cbsnews.com/stories/2003/12/17/60II/main589107.shtml.
20. Jon Buchan, "Fighting the Good Fight in Edgefield County," *Osceola*, Jan. 18, 1974.
21. *WP*, Aug. 4, 1992.
22. Washington-Williams, interview pt. 1.
23. *NYT*, Dec. 16, 2003.
24. *Chicago Sun-Times*, Dec. 21, 2003.
25. *NYT*, Dec. 21, 2003. For a broader discussion about the politics of rape in the civil-rights-era South, see Danielle McGuire, *At the Dark End of the Street: Black Women, Race, and Resistance—a New History of the Civil Rights Movement from Rosa Parks to the Rise of Black Power* (New York: Knopf, 2010).
26. *New York Daily News*, Dec. 26, 2003.
27. *NYT*, Jan. 3, 2004.
28. *St. Petersburg Times*, Dec. 28, 2003.
29. *NYT*, Dec. 27, 2003.
30. Quoted in *St. Petersburg Times*, Dec. 28, 2003.

31. *Los Angeles Sentinel*, Jan. 1, 2004. For other examples, see Newhouse News Service, Dec. 19, 2003; Albany *Times Union*, Dec. 30, 2003.

32. *Milwaukee Journal Sentinel*, Dec. 20, 2003.

33. Associated Press, March 11 and June 28, 2004.

34. *Charleston Post and Courier*, Jan. 14, 2004.

35. Associated Press, May 20, 2005.

36. *Charleston Post and Courier*, Jan. 15, 2004.

37. *CSM*, Jan. 29, 2008.

38. Micki McElya, *Clinging to Mammy: The Faithful Slave in Twentieth-Century America* (Cambridge, Mass.: Harvard University Press, 2007), 116–59. Also see Kimberly Wallace-Sanders, *Mammy: A Century of Race, Gender, and Southern Memory* (Ann Arbor: University of Michigan Press, 2008).

39. McElya, *Clinging to Mammy*, 3.

40. Strom Thurmond, "What the South Wants, II," July 29, 1970, box 16, folder 204, Speeches, Series B, JST.

41. *WP*, Dec. 23, 2003; Horace Fleming, interview by author, Aug. 30, 2008.

42. *WP*, Dec. 16, 1998.

43. John J. Brady, *Bad Boy: The Life and Politics of Lee Atwater* (Reading, Mass.: Addison-Wesley, 1997), 82–84, 105; *WP*, April 6, 1991.

44. Brady, *Bad Boy*, 177.

45. Ibid., 171–73.

46. Ibid., 182.

47. Ibid., 189–90, 200, 208; *Boogie Man: The Lee Atwater Story* (InterPositive Media, 2008).

48. *State*, June 9, 1950.

49. *WP*, Jan. 6, 2009; *NYT*, Jan. 11, 2009; *Washington Times*, Jan. 29, 2009.

50. "Preston College Seminar with Mr. Katon Dawson," Nov. 17, 2003, http://westforum.sc.edu/OtherInterviews/031117DawsonSCRepChair/PrestonSeminar%20Dawson%20031117%20Text.htm. The link to this Web site works inconsistently. A printed version of the transcript is in the author's possession.

51. *State*, Oct. 16, 1970.

52. *NYT*, March 5, 8, and 10, 1970; *CSM*, March 7, 1970; *WP*, March 7 and 9, 1970; *LAT*, March 7 and 9, 1970; *Time*, March 16, 1970.

53. *State*, March 1, 1970.

EPILOGUE: THE SCARRED STONE

1. Associated Press State and Local Wire, Dec. 30, 1998.

2. Ricky Worth, interview by author, March 21, 2011. Worth is the owner of Bruns Monumental Company in Columbia, South Carolina, which was hired to alter the Thurmond monument.

ACKNOWLEDGMENTS

I have many people to thank for their help with this book, but at the top of the list are the archivists at the Strom Thurmond Institute at Clemson University. The entire staff there, and Alan Burns in particular, have been enormously helpful over the years.

The great bulk of the research for this book has come from archival collections—not only Thurmond's but also those of presidents, senators, congressmen, party officials, aides, journalists, and others. Yet a number of former Thurmond staffers and associates were generous in sharing their time and memories, and in pointing me in helpful research directions. They include Betty Dent, Dennis Shedd, Mark Goodin, Horace Fleming, Phil Kent, Wayne Robbins, Hastings Wyman, and Samuel and Robin Stilwell.

Dr. B. E. Nicholson, a descendant of an old and distinguished Edgefield family, introduced me around Edgefield and provided a fascinating driving tour. My most important contact there was Bettis Rainsford, whose passion for Edgefield's history is surpassed only by his courteousness and generosity.

Nadine Cohodas shared insights from her own research on Thurmond, and Donald Ritchie at the Senate Historical Office pointed me to some wonderful materials. Valerie Bauerlein, formerly of the *The State* in Columbia, guided me through contemporary South Carolina politics, and Kent Germany at the University of South Carolina was a great interlocutor during numerous research trips to Columbia.

The National Endowment for the Humanities supported this work through a summer research stipend. At Emory University, Deans Robin Forman and Michael Elliot allowed me to juggle my teaching schedule in ways that enabled me to finish more quickly than I would have done otherwise. During a year's leave from Emory, Cam Murchison, Dean of Academic Affairs at Columbia Theological Seminary, and Richard Dubose allowed me to use library office space that was a mere five-minute walk from my home. It was the best year of my academic life, one during which I wrote the majority of the manuscript.

This book has benefitted from my participation in a number of academic conferences, seminars, and lectures. For these opportunities to present my work, I am grateful to Jacquelyn Dowd Hall, Robert Mason, John McGreevy, Iwan Morgan, Darren Dochuk, Michelle Nickerson, Elizabeth Shermer, James Sparrow, Clive Webb, Jared Rolle, Bill Link, Bruce Schulman, Brian Balogh, and Brent Cebul.

A number of scholars have provided important feedback at various stages of the process, including Matt Dallek, Darren Dochuk, Elizabeth Shermer, Nancy MacLean, Donald Critchlow, Darren Grem, Kevin Kruse, David Chappell, Nelson Lichtenstein, Tim Thurber, Gerard Alexander, Alan Brinkley, Jennifer Burns, Jason Ward, Stephen Mihm, and James Campbell.

Four scholars—David Payne, Bruce Schulman, Matthew Lassiter, and Patrick Allitt—read the entire manuscript at its biggest, baggiest stage. I am enormously grateful to them and look forward to repaying the favor.

At Emory, colleagues who helped with this project include Jeff Lesser, Yanna Yannakakis, Tom Rogers, James Roark, Jonathan Prude, Gyan Pandey, Ruby Lal, Ben Reiss, Brett Gadsden, and James Van Melton. In addition, a number of graduate and undergraduate students have provided research help, including Lisa Spees, Rory Hart, Grant Mannion, and Colin Reynolds. The help that Asher Smith provided went far beyond what the title "undergraduate research assistant" can convey. He may be hiding his light under the bushel of law school at present, but I suspect it won't be too long before we see his own histories in print.

Geri Thoma has been a wonderful guide and advocate in the unfamiliar world of trade publishing. At Hill and Wang, Dan Gerstle has been incredibly helpful and efficient. Having the opportunity to work with Paul Elie and Sarah Crichton at Farrar, Straus and Giroux has been a pleasure.

No one has done more to help make this book what it is than Thomas LeBien. His professionalism, wisdom, and insight about the whole process, from our vague initial conversations to the final line edits, have been extraordinary.

Carrie and Sam Crespino have not done a single thing to help me finish this book. In fact, they've been nothing but distractions to me—distractions of the most essential and life-giving sort. Caroline Herring, on the other hand, has helped in almost every way imaginable. For this reason—and countless others that only she and I know—I dedicate this book to her, with all my love.

Democratic Party, 83, 86–87, 97, 137–38, 143, 185, 236; African American voters and, 110, 191, 213; break-in at headquarters of, *see* Watergate scandal; business interests' antagonism to, 9–10, 77; conservatives in, 103, 151–52, 161, 204; defections from, 5, 111–12, 126, 132, 133, 165–67, 177–83, 187, 194, 197, 237, 238, 261, 264, 283, 285, 288, 312, 325*n14*; Great Depression programs of, *see* New Deal; machine politics in, 81, 93; moderates and liberals in, 91, 95, 109, 112, 113, 134, 161, 244–49, 257, 297, 298; National Conventions, 37, 46, 57, 68, 78, 119, 177, 219, 239; national leadership of, 101, 151, 161; in presidential elections, 125–26, 148, 207–210, 225, 226, 313; primaries of, 21, 44, 56–58, 92, 101, 104, 128, 132–34, 171, 176, 179–81, 190, 210, 256, 280, 282; reapportionment and, 297–98; segregationists in, 4, 6, 16–17, 127, 312; in Senate, 102, 104, 121, 138–39; South Carolina, 64, 89, 90, 95–96, 99–100, 127, 133–36, 167, 181–82, 195–97, 239, 251, 252, 265, 280, 295–96, 298, 303, 308, 314–15; southerners' bolt from, 61–64, 68–69, 79–80, 83, 93 (*see also* States' Rights Party); states' rights advocates in, 9, 27, 63, 66–67, 72–74, 79, 82, 124, 177; support for Eisenhower in, 118, 121; Thurmond's switch to Republican Party from, 3, 126, 133, 167, 177, 179, 182, 183
Dent, Frederick, 265–66
Dent, Harry, 125, 148, 185, 225, 228, 267, 290, 302, 372*n62*; and judicial appointments, 248–49,; and 1970 midterm elections, 236–38, 244–47; Nixon and, 193, 209–11, 219–20, 222, 226, 230–32, 244, 246; shift in Thurmond's racial politics charted by, 249–52, 284; as South Carolina Republican Party chairman, 194–97; and Thurmond's party switch, 126, 133, 177, 179, 182, 183

desegregation, 7, 140, 173; of schools, *see* school desegregation; *see also* integration
Detroit riot (1967), 202
Dewey, Thomas, 74, 75, 81, 82
Dies, Martin, 76
Dillon County (South Carolina), 212
direct action protests, 131–32, 162, 170
direct-mail campaigns, 264, 271–74
Dirksen, Everett, 114, 188, 196, 203, 224
Dixiecrats, *see* States' Rights Party
Dixon, Frank, 69, 70
Dixon, Jeane, 185
Dixon, Thomas, Jr., 23
Dole, Robert, 222, 296, 304
Dorn, Fred, 40
Dorn, William Jennings Bryan, 333*n12*
Dos Passos, John, 159
Dubose, Captain, 20
Duffy, James, 246, 251
Dukakis, Michael, 313–14
Dunham, Dave, 90, 314
DuPont Corporation, 95, 96, 228, 299

Earle, Willie, 51, 52, 54, 56, 72
Eastland, James, 69, 73, 106, 114, 203, 217–19, 299
Ebony magazine, 250, 306
Economic Stabilization Office, 87
Edens, J. Drake, 132, 180, 209
Edgefield County (South Carolina), 15–33, 41, 43, 162, 246, 302, 311; elections in, 81–82; establishment of, 16; farming in, 34–35; federal relief programs in, 36; literacy program for African Americans in, 29, 55; Thurmond family in, 19–22, 96; Thurmond's childhood and adolescence in, 18, 22–25, 28; Thurmond's death and funeral in, 305–306; violence in, 16–17, 39–40; voting rights abuses in, 292–93, 295–96; white supremacy in, 48
Edgefield Advertiser, 21, 251–52, 295, 306
Edgefield High School, 29, 32, 33

gay rights movement, 225, 253
Gantt, Harvey, 274–75
Garcia, Miki, 258
Gary, Martin, 17, 48
Gaty, John P., Trust, 198
General Electric, 122, 168, 190, 288
George, Walter, 38, 341*n16*
Georgia, 46, 62, 69, 70, 139, 296, 341*n16*;
    Carter as governor of, 246, 248;
    Dixiecrats in, 116; Goldwater
    campaign in, 183, 356*n40*; lynchings
    in, 52; poll tax repealed in, 55;
    Republican Party in, 176, 232;
    Roosevelt in, 38; segregationists in,
    195, 231, 235; Supreme Court of, 111;
    see also Atlanta; Augusta
Gerber baby foods, 122
Germany, Nazi, 46
Gettysburg, Battle of, 63
Goldbugs, 111
Goldman, Eric, 334*n33*
Goldwater, Barry, 9, 132–35, 137, 138,
    144, 149, 158, 193, 197, 220, 231, 264;
    presidential candidacy of, 3, 5, 84,
    128–31, 165–67, 174–80, 182–85, 187,
    189, 190, 196, 208, 210, 272, 356*n40*;
    in Senate, 8, 114, 121, 154, 161, 198, 199
Gonzales, N. G., 21
Goodin, Mark, 302
Gore, Albert, 106, 112
Gothic Politics in the Deep South
    (Sherrill), 306
Graham, Billy, 5, 109
Graham, Frank Porter, 91, 94
Grant, Ulysses S., 19, 63, 224
Graves, John Temple, 63, 78, 85
Great Depression, 9, 34, 40, 50, 261;
    federal programs initiated in,
    see New Deal
Greater Detroit Homeowners Council,
    139–40
*Green v. County School Board of New
    Kent County* (1968), 213–14
Greensboro (North Carolina), 131
Greenville County (South Carolina),
    165–66, 182, 227, 233, 267, 280; school
    desegregation in, 238, 241, 244–45

Greenville Group, 210
Greenville News, 99, 244
Greenwood County (South Carolina), 92
Gretschel, W. Michael, 272–73
Griffin, Robert, 223
Griffith, D. W., 23
Groton School, 123
Guantánamo naval base, 158
Guevara, Che, 203
Gulf Oil, 79, 221

Had Enuf? News, 195
Haldeman, H. R. "Bob," 231
Haley, Nikki, 312
Hall, Wilton E., 118
Hammarskjöld, Dag, 152
Hammond, Samuel, 205
Hampton, Wade, 16, 17, 38, 91, 303
Harding College, 198
Hargis, Billy James, 158–59, 169, 266
Harlow, Bryce, 231
Harper, Edwin, 292
Harrigan, Anthony, 135
Harriman, Averell, 202
Harris, Willie, 20–21
Harrison, Benjamin, 68
Hartsfield, William, 124
Harvard University, 238, 251, 279, 313;
    Law School, 234
Hatch, Orrin, 265, 294, 295
hatemongers, 161, 162
Hatfield, Mark, 220
Haynsworth, Clement F., 233–35,
    238, 246
Health, Education, and Welfare (HEW),
    U.S. Department of, 211–13, 230–32,
    236, 244, 251, 257, 269
Heard, Alexander, 79
Helms, Jesse, 9, 91, 265, 267, 270, 273–75,
    280, 285, 287, 296–98
Hemings, Sally, 11
Hendersonville (North Carolina), 81
Heritage Foundation, 254
Hess, Karl, 135
High Point (North Carolina), 131
Hinton, James N., 57